Children at Play

CHILDREN AT PLAY

Clinical and Developmental Approaches to
Meaning and Representation

Edited By

ARIETTA SLADE
DENNIE PALMER WOLF

New York   Oxford
OXFORD UNIVERSITY PRESS
1994

*To Sam and Daniel, whose love and great spirit
have taught me what play is all about.*
A.S.

*To Lea and Lex, who as adults can still
play their way to understanding.*
D.P.W.

Oxford University Press

Oxford   New York   Toronto
Delhi   Bombay   Calcutta   Madras   Karachi
Kuala Lumpur   Singapore   Hong Kong   Tokyo
Nairobi   Dar es Salaam   Cape Town
Melbourne   Auckland   Madrid

and associated companies in
Berlin   Ibadan

Published by Oxford University Press, Inc.,
200 Madison Avenue, New York, New York 10016
Oxford is a registered trademark of Oxford University Press

Library of Congress Cataloging-in-Publication Data
Children at play:
clinical and developmental approaches to meaning and representation
edited by Arietta Slade, Dennie Palmer Wolf.
p.   cm.   Includes bibliographical references and index.
ISBN 0-19-504414-2
1. Symbolic play.   2. Symbolism (Psychology) in children.
3. Cognition in children.   I. Slade, Arietta.
II. Wolf, Dennie.
[DNLM: 1. Play and Playthings.   2. Symbolism (Psychology)
3. Child Development.   WS 105.5.P5 M691   1994]
BF717.M59   1994   155.4'18—dc20   DNLM/DLC   for Library of Congress   93-606

2 4 6 8 9 7 5 3 1

Printed in the United States of America
on acid-free paper

Preface

One of the most famous "studies" of play is Freud's observation of a toddler:

> Without the intention of making a comprehensive study of these phenomena, I availed myself of an opportunity which offered of elucidating the first game invented by himself of a boy of eighteen months old. . . .
>
> The child was in no respect forward in his intellectual development . . . but he made himself understood by his parents and the maidservant, and had a good reputation for behaving "properly." . . . [A]bove all he never cried when his mother went out and left him for hours together, although the tie to his mother was a very close one: she had not only nourished him herself, but had cared for him and brought him up without any outside help. Occasionally, however, this well-behaved child evinced the troublesome habit of flinging into the corner of the room or under the bed all the little things he could lay his hands on, so that to gather up his toys was often no light task. He accompanied this by an expression of interest and gratification, emitting a loud, long-drawn-out "O-o-o-o-o-oh" which in the judgment of the mother (one that coincided with my own) was not an interjection but meant "go away" [fort]. I saw at last that this was a game, and that the child used all his toys only to play "being gone" [fortsein] with them. One day I made an observation that confirmed my view. The child had a wooden reel with a piece of string wound round it. It never occurred to him, for example, to drag this after him on the floor and so play horse and cart with it, but he kept throwing it with considerable skill, held by the string, over the side of his little draped cot, so that the reel disappeared into it, then said his significant "O-o-o-oh" and drew the reel by the string out of the cot again, greeting its reappearance with a joyful *"Da"* [there]. This was therefore the complete game, disappearance and return, the first act being the only one generally observed by onlookers, and the one untiringly repeated by the child as a game for its own sake, although the greater pleasure unquestionably belonged to the second act. . . . This interpretation was fully established by a further observation. One day when the mother had been out for some hours she was greeted on her return by the information "Baby o-o-o-oh" which at first remained unintelligible. It soon proved that during his long lonely hours he had found a method of bringing about his own disappearance. He had discovered his reflection in the long mirror which nearly reached to the ground and had then crouched down in front of it, so that the reflection was "fort."
>
> Quoted in E. Erikson (1950). *Childhood and Society.* New York: Norton, p. 215.

By attributing this kind of play, and consequently such a powerful imagination, to young children, Freud and those who followed—Anna Freud, Melanie Klein, and others—virtually invented contemporary views of childhood. They taught us that young children constructed the world long before cognitive psychology broke through to constructivism. They also insisted on the intensity of young children's emotional experience, pointing out that toddlers and infants could register not only the immediate, Darwinian emotions of anger and fear but the complex, intensely human affects of loss and betrayal or delight.

Given a view of play that is both deep-seated, and, in many senses, productive, why write another book about children's play? The reason is clearly because the contributors to this volume hold a view of play that has evolved considerably since Freud's original conceptualization. It is a view of play that is profoundly mutual and social.

Like all studies, Freud's observations partake of their time. Freud inherited— from Goethe and others—the nineteenth century's view of imagination as an activity distinct from thought. And this invention, like any other, came furnished with a number of silent corollaries—that imagination is an *internal* force, one that grows and functions in *isolation,* one that integrates and defends the *individual,* and thus often defies the external world. And its intent is to reinvent the world as the soul would have it. It is, therefore, only or chiefly a form of private make-believe. The argument of this volume is just the opposite of Freud's: play, if anything, is about the health of a mutual social system, the development of intersubjectivity, and learning to use the materials of a culture to make meanings that are understandable or, at least, negotiable.

Nowhere are the consequences of Freud's view clearer or more concrete than in the apparently simple details of methodology. Freud's methods for studying play were Victorian, aloof, if not bordering on voyeuristic. He made his notes while standing, half hidden, behind a door and interviewed the mother without—at least to the best of our knowledge—ever crouching down to play with the child, making eye contact, or taking a turn with the reel. The consequences are profound. We never see the child formulating, explaining, or reworking the rules of his play in the face of another. Even more emphatically, we never see the observer at risk, having to improvise his way toward a turn that belongs in, extends, or probes the play.

Since this volume includes the work of many child clinicians, play is not observed but performed. Play is not solitary comfort but an exchange between mother and child, or among children. Frequently the observer—whether mother or clinician—is rarely a witness safely hidden behind a door. She (or he) is an engaged—and thus an endangered—player. She could perform stupid, blunt moves that make children disinterested or wary and reduce the play. Her jokes could fall flat. Her turn could be ignored. With this kind of danger and engagement comes the following insight: issues of mutuality—its authenticity, the rhythm of its turns, its emotional range—become noticeable and alive. The process of jointly making meaning—of forming messages, having them break down, revising them, or turning away—is paramount in play.

Moreover, because these chapters offer accounts of play that stretch beyond the usual accounts of toddlerhood, they hint at quite a different use or endpoint for playing. In essence, many of the authors in this volume either implicitly or explicitly argue that play is not "just" about imagination but about the possibility or the defeat of intimacy. In this light, playing may be a prelude to empathic child rearing, sexuality, friendship, or even to being able to think of work and its end products as offerings or exchanges. Gunther Stent, a molecular biologist, speaks in just this way about his reasons for doing what many of us would imagine to be the extremely lonely and isolating work of scientific research:

GS: Of course it's exciting, but I think the final excitement, the real source of the gratification, is not so much beating nature as being able to tell it. . . . I think the happiness mainly derives from being able then to write a nice paper. Let's say, if I was on a desert island, Robinson Crusoe, I think I wouldn't do science.

INTERVIEWER: Because there would be no one to tell it to?

GS: Exactly. If I was marooned on an island with a lab, I don't think I'd do any experiments.

> Quoted in L. Wolpert & A. Richards (eds.) (1988), *A Passion for Science.*
> Oxford: Oxford University Press, p. 116.

Finally, the chapters in this volume counter the view of play as autistic or simply self-expressive. Instead, the proposal is that in play children learn to negotiate meanings using the opportunities and materials a culture makes available. In Freud's example the string and reel are "bent" to the child's purposes. Nowhere is there mention made that he has undoubtedly seen others reel in and let out strings—on fishing rods, laundry lines, or leashes. The child is playing with the social and cultural materials of his world; he borrows meanings as much as he expresses or invents them. And, because Freud gives us a child alone in his cot or in front of the mirror, we lose sight of how meaning is much more often negotiated than known or experienced and then simply sent out. Consider this six-year-old playing with a set of jungle animals on a table top in her living room:

CHILD: The giraffe won't stay up.

ADULT: All right. Well, you can make them sleeping maybe. *(Picks up a dragon figure.)*

CHILD: What is that? The dragon? Cathy has one of those, but it's broken.

ADULT: OK.

CHILD: I'm having some trouble standing the giraffe.

ADULT: OK. Why don't we have the giraffe sleeping then. Why don't you spread out everything so it's not right in the pond (e.g., *a piece of colored felt they have earlier agreed was to be a pond in the jungle*).

CHILD: I'll put the shrubs here. This needs to stand up. *(She stands up the big, sturdy giraffe and tries to stand the wobbly baby giraffe next to it.)*

CHILD: That is better. *(She adds some shrubs around the smaller giraffe to keep it standing.)*

ADULT: OK?

CHILD: Pretend it was called the messy jungle.

ADULT: OK, the messy. . . so one day in the messy jungle all of the animals lived together.

This child never intended to create a messy jungle. That possibility arose somewhere in the negotiations between intention and physical possibility and between two people jointly building an account of a world where four-legged creatures don't stand. The chapters in this volume point to quite similar processes: we encounter toddlers and their mothers reinventing age-old "leaving games" to capture their personal experiences of separation and then jointly giving those games new emotional contours as their affective experiences shift from panic to patience. We also observe older children and clinicians (or observers) take up familiar cultural icons— squirrel toys, Snow White, or astronauts—and jointly arrive at meanings and uses for them.

Again, what these varied instances suggest is that the negotiated meanings so characteristic of play are not unique either to childhood or to the labile world of toys and jokes. Play is, in its own way, a preface to an ongoing and vital cultural activity of making and remaking meaning. At one time, we could take "The Tempest" as a fable about magic and rationality, but when a theater company sets the shipwreck in the Carribean, its performance insists that where we once saw a fairy tale we now also or instead see a world struggling with the after effects of colonialism and racism. The performance reminds us that Prospero and Caliban are not—in a world where there is still a divided South Africa—simply "civilized" and "primitive" characters.

It is in this spirit of recognizing the enduring importance of mutuality and intimacy, of joint invention and reflection, that we have brought together these chapters on children at play.

Cambridge, Mass.   D.P.W.
Roxbury, Conn.   A.S.
May 1993

Acknowledgments

This book has been a long time in coming, and we would like to thank the contributors to this volume for their patience and generosity through all the waiting. We are fortunate to have had them as colleagues in this endeavor. We would also like to thank Vicky Bijur, who got everything started by helping us find our way to Oxford University Press, and Larry Aber, Wendy Haft, and Valeda Slade for all their help, support, and friendship. Joan Bossert was our editor at Oxford, and we thank her for her enduring enthusiasm and commitment to the project; her good humor and faith in our efforts sustained us through some tough times. Thanks, too, go to Helen Greenberg, our freelance copy editor, and to Allison Sole, Henry Krawitz, and Ellen Fuchs, at the press, for their tremendous help in getting the book through the production process. We are grateful to you all.

Contents

Contributors, xiii

I AFFECT IN SYMBOLIZATION

1. Representational Elaboration and Differentiation: A Clinical-Quantitative Approach to the Clinical Assessment of 2- to 4-Year-Olds, 3
   Stanley I. Greenspan and Alicia F. Lieberman

2. The Relation Between Anxiety and Pretend Play, 33
   Malcolm W. Watson

3. Play, Cure, and Development: A Developmental Perspective on the Psychoanalytic Treatment of Young Children, 48
   W. George Scarlett

4. Constructing Metaphors: The Role of Symbolization in the Treatment of Children, 62
   Jan Drucker

5. Making Meaning and Making Believe: Their Role in the Clinical Process, 81
   Arietta Slade

II RELATIONSHIPS AND SYMBOLIZATION

6. The Leaving Game, or I'll Play You and You Play Me: The Emergence of Dramatic Role Play in 2-Year-Olds, 111
   Elsa First

7. Self–Other Action Play: A Window Into the Representational World of the Infant, 133
   Anni Bergman and Ilene Sackler Lefcourt

8. Play: A Context for Mutual Regulation Within Mother–Child Interaction, 148
   Lorraine McCune, Donna DiPane, Ruth Fireoved, and Mary Fleck

III DIFFERENCES AND DISTORTIONS IN SYMBOLIC FUNCTIONING

9. Windows on Social Worlds: Gender Differences in
   Children's Play Narratives, 169
   Louisa B. Tarullo

10. He's a Nice Alligator: Observations on
    the Affective Organization of Pretense, 188
    Greta G. Fein and Patricia Kinney

11. Symbolic Development in Children with Down Syndrome and in Children
    with Autism: An Organizational, Developmental Psychopathology
    Perspective, 206
    Dante Cicchetti, Marjorie Beeghly, and Bedonna Weiss-Perry

12. Development of Symbolic Play of Deaf Children Aged 1 to 3, 238
    Elsa J. Blum, Barbara C. Fields, Helen Scharfman, and Diana M. Silber

13. Play and Narrative in Inhibited Children: A Longitudinal Case Study, 261
    Lou-Marié Kruger and Dennie Palmer Wolf

14. Symbolic Play in the Interactions of Young Children and Their Mothers with
    a History of Affective Illness: A Longitudinal Study, 286
    Elizabeth C. Tingley

Index, 307

Contributors

MARJORIE BEEGHLY
Harvard Medical School
Child Development Unit
Children's Hospital, Boston, MA

ANNI BERGMAN
Clinical Psychology
The City College and Graduate Center
   of the City University of New York

ELSA J. BLUM
Department of Psychiatry
The New York Hospital-Cornell
   Medical Center
Westchester Division

DANTE CICCHETTI
Mount Hope Family Center
University of Rochester

DONNA DIPANE
Graduate School of Education
Rutgers University

JAN DRUCKER
Department of Psychology
Sarah Lawrence College

GRETA G. FEIN
College of Education
University of Maryland

BARBARA C. FIELDS
New Rochelle, NY

RUTH FIREOVED
Graduate School of Education
Rutgers University

ELSA FIRST
New York University Post-Doctoral
   Program Psychoanalysis and
   Psychotherapy

MARY FLECK
Graduate School of Education
Rutgers University

STANLEY I. GREENSPAN
Department of Psychiatry
George Washington University
   Medical School

PATRICIA KINNEY
U.S. General Services Administration
Office of Child Care and
   Development Programs

LOU-MARIÉ KRUGER
Clinical Psychology
Boston University

ILENE SACKLER LEFCOURT
Sackler Lefcourt Center for Child
   Development
New York, NY

ALICIA F. LIEBERMAN
Department of Psychiatry
University of California San
  Francisco
San Francisco General Hospital

LORRAINE MCCUNE
Graduate School of Education
Rutgers University

W. GEORGE SCARLETT
Eliot Pearson Department of Child
  Study
Tufts University

HELEN SCHARFMAN
Lexington School for the Deaf
Jackson Heights, NY

DIANA SILBER
Lexington School for the Deaf
Jackson Heights, NY

ARIETTA SLADE
Clinical Psychology
The City College and Graduate Center
  of the City University of New York

LOUISA B. TARULLO
Laboratory of Developmental
  Psychology
National Institute of Mental Health

ELIZABETH C. TINGLEY
School of Human Development
The University of Texas at Dallas

MALCOLM W. WATSON
Department of Psychology
Brandeis University

BEDONNA WEISS-PERRY
Institute for the Study of Child
  Development
Robert Wood Johnson Medical
  School
New Brunswick, NJ

DENNIE PALMER WOLF
Graduate School of Education
Harvard University

I

AFFECT IN SYMBOLIZATION

Clinicians and developmentalists alike consider early symbolic play a window to critical aspects of the child's experience and have therefore studied its early development extensively. However, the questions they ask about early make-believe have historically been quite different. Clinical, typically psychoanalytic, approaches to symbolic play emphasize its role in defense and mastery. Like dreams, play provides a "royal road to the unconscious" and, therefore, a means of unraveling the child's unconscious fantasies and impulses. It also provides a mode of coping with and transforming these experiences. Developmental psychology, by contrast, has set aside questions of content and meaning, focusing instead upon the description and delineation of structural development as it is exemplified in the stages of play and in the development of narrative abilities. In this view, play provides a window to the child's level of understanding and to the degree of organization he or she brings to experience. Thus, the question of the child's emotional life has historically been considered apart from the question of cognitive structure. However, as the chapters in part I demonstrate, there is much to be gained from considering these phenomena as integrated and necessarily complementary. Just as the development of cognitive structures may play an important role in the resolution of emotional conflict, so emotional consolidation may provide an impetus to cognitive advances and integration.

1

Representational Elaboration and Differentiation: A Clinical-Quantitative Approach to the Assessment of 2- to 4-Year-Olds

STANLEY I. GREENSPAN
ALICIA F. LIEBERMAN

A major problem in modern psychology has been the absence of a unified conceptual framework encompassing both emotional and cognitive development and the reciprocal influences between these two processes. Research on personality organization, particularly in the areas of assessment and outcome, has been hampered by the resulting inability to evaluate the emotional and cognitive development within a cohesive framework.

The two most comprehensive theories of human development stem from separate attempts to understand each of these two developmental lines. Psychoanalytic developmental psychology delves most deeply into emotional processes, whereas Piaget's cognitive developmental psychology offers an account of the unfolding of cognitive abilities. Both theories appear to probe different and incompatible realms of experience: the *dynamic unconscious* and *rational intelligent thought*. Wolff (1963, 1965) made an attempt to synthesize both theories by using the state of the organism as an explanatory link between them: He postulated that the Freudian system was a valid account of behavior under high drive states and that the Piagetian system accounted for behavior in states of low organismic arousal. But this view depends on a form of dualism involving two parallel systems rather than on a true synthesis of emotional and cognitive developmental processes.

Greenspan (1979) has offered an integration of psychoanalytic and Piagetian developmental psychologies by attempting to elucidate the transformational bridges or functional relationships between emotion and intellect. His developmental structuralist approach (Greenspan, 1979, 1981; Greenspan & Lourie, 1981; Greenspan, Lourie, & Nover, 1979) views development as a multilinear process in which experience is organized according to state-specific psychological structures. These structures are defined in terms of state-specific tasks that involve the psychological processing of emotional as well as cognitive experiences.

The developmental structuralist approach, described more fully later, has yielded promising empirical applications. The Greenspan–Lieberman Observational Scale (GLOS) focuses on the first 18 months of life, and it yields a quantitative profile of mother–infant interaction that shows clear convergences with independent clinical observations of the same mother–infant dyad (Greenspan & Lieberman, 1980). This chapter extends to the second 18 months of life the effort to develop quantitative clinical assessment instruments that are rooted in a unified conceptual framework in which both the emotional and cognitive aspects of experience are simultaneously examined. In the first section, we provide a theoretical account of the emotional and cognitive manifestations of the toddler's representational capacity and its environmental concomitants. Two stages in the toddler's representational development are described: (1) the emergence of the representational capacity, and (2) representational differentiation and consolidation. Illustrations of adaptive and maladaptive patterns in both stages are presented, as are patterns of adaptive and maladaptive parental responses. In the second section, we present an instrument for the assessment of the child's representational capacity and the environmental support for this area of functioning, discussing clinical as well as empirical applications of these assessments.

General Background

The transition from sensorimotor to representational functioning is the major developmental accomplishment occurring between 12 and 36 months of age (Piaget, 1962). The shift is characterized by a process of decentration that involves the child's increasing ability to separate meaning from sensorimotor patterns centered in his or her own body. This enables the child to differentiate between his or her own perceptual, cognitive, and affective points of view and the perspectives of others. In this process, meanings acquire progressively more abstract symbolic representations, which in turn become sequentially integrated into complex representational patterns.

The cognitive manifestations of this transition—from sensorimotor to representational functioning—have been extensively investigated, not only in the context of the child's emerging mental operations but also in the context of the child's social communications through play and language. In two of the first investigations of early symbolic play, Lowe (1975) and Nicolich (1977) described the transition from self-oriented pretend (e.g., pretending to feed oneself) to activity centered on a doll or other toy object to planful and thematic make-believe behavior. Their initial findings concerning the emergence of structured and planned pretend play have since been expanded and elaborated (Bates, Benigni, Bretherton, Camaioni, & Volterra, 1979; Fein, 1981; Fenson & Ramsay, 1980). In addition, other researchers have examined the nature of object substitution, particularly the degree of similarity between the conventional object and its substitute at different ages (Fein, 1975; Fenson, Kagan, Kearsley, & Zelazo, 1976). These elements of pretend play illuminate the cognitive structural characteristics of play activities as well as the changes that occur with age.

In contrast to descriptive and experimental studies, clinical analyses of representational play have focused more on the psychic conflicts expressed through thematic content and on the role of play in the child's mastery of conflict. The work of Waelder (1933), Erikson (1940, 1943), and Peller (1954) is of particular interest because these investigators attempted formulations in which clinical observations of children's play were integrated within the larger psychoanalytic conceptual framework. These authors view play primarily as a tool for alleviating anxiety and for mastering painful experiences and, in this sense, as a reflection of the ego's resiliency. Thus, Waelder (1933, p. 218) writes of play as a vehicle for "assimilating piecemeal an experience which was too large to be assimilated instantly at one swoop." The child may achieve this by changing either the roles she or he played in or the outcome of a real-life episode. In either case, there is a switch from passivity to activity that facilitates the child's mastery of the situation. Peller (1954) expanded Waelder's conception of the role of play to include the mastery of anxiety produced by inter-systemic conflicts, as well as the anxiety produced by external events. Erikson (1940) made extensive observations of play disruption when the anxiety generated by the representation in play of a conflict becomes unbearably acute.

Although the clinical observations and interpretations of children's play have reached high levels of refinement, there apparently has been no attempt to assess systematically the affective developmental features of representational play. Structural analyses have been limited to cognitive features and have not addressed concomitant issues of personality organization such as the level of differentiation attained by the child; clinical studies have been primarily oriented to the study of content. While Peller (1954) came closest to such an integration, her work has not yielded a systematic assessment approach.

In this chapter we will describe an instrument that attempts to capture the meaning of representational behavior by addressing both structural features and affective content. The instrument is based on a developmental structuralist conceptual framework that views development as a multilinear process (Greenspan, 1979). A description of this framework follows.

Early Development: Developmental Structuralist Approach

Our views on the emergence and consolidation of representational capacity were based on a developmental structuralist framework for the classification of adaptive and pathological personality organization in infancy and early childhood (Greenspan, 1979, 1981). The developmental structuralist framework assumes that stage-specific psychological structures underlie both emotional and cognitive experiences. Thus, *both* kinds of experiences are processed by the same set of organizations or structures; these structures change over time and in accord with maturational processes. The degree of adaptability versus pathology in this experiential process may be assessed in terms of three basic parameters: the range and depth of phase-appropriate experiences; the relative stability of experiential organization and its resilience to stress; and the presence of a unique individual style of interaction with the environment. An adaptive pattern consists of the child's ability to integrate and organize a full range of age-appropriate experiences in identifiable personal configurations that are stable and resilient under stress. At each stage, the most adaptive structures bridge the transition to the next stage, and in this sense they promote further development.

In our original developmental structuralist classification of infancy and early childhood (Greenspan, 1979; Greenspan et al., 1979), we proposed a set of four sequential, stage-specific tasks that underlie both cognitive and emotional experiences and unfold during the period of sensorimotor or *practical* intelligence (Piaget, 1972), before the emergence of the representational capacity. These are homeostasis, attachment, somatopsychological differentiation and behavioral organization, and initiative and internalization. Along the lines of this conceptual framework, we subsequently presented an instrument for the quantitative, clinical assessment of infants, based on the identification of individual and dyadic behaviors that serve as observable, measurable manifestations of the abstract issues negotiated at each of the four developmental stages of infancy (GLOS; Greenspan & Lieberman, 1980). According to the developmental structuralist framework, the next developmental stage is the emergence of the representational capacity. In the sections that follow, we will first describe the unfolding of the characteristics and developmental role of this capacity. We will then describe an extension of the GLOS, which can be used clinically to assess children's functioning once they have moved into the representational phase of development.

Representational Stage I: The Emergence of the Representational Capacity

The emergence of the representational capacity involves a qualitative leap in intelligent functioning. Children are no longer limited to somatic and behavioral responses to environmental occurrences; they can now form mental representations, an ability with enormous adaptive value. Out of sight no longer means out of mind, an achievement that involves a new capacity for organized psychological experience. This has far-reaching consequences for interpersonal relationships. For example, mental representations of the mother can be stored and then retrieved in her absence. If there is internal stimulation such as a yearning for the mother's physical presence, the child can use mental representation to organize memories associated with her visual appearance, voice, smell, and touch, thus gaining some satisfaction in her absense. The magnitude of this achievement can be better appreciated if we keep in mind that in an earlier phase the child needed to use imitation to gain a sense of relief; in even earlier phases the child could only cry in protest and distress, or use somatic patterns such as rocking or sucking to gain comfort.

The emerging ability to conserve internal representations of animate and inanimate objects, and the concomitant consolidation of an internal sense of self and non-self, are evidenced in the increased emotional, cognitive, and interpersonal repertoire of the 2-year-old. Behavioral manifestations are the ability to say "no"; the development of personal pronouns; the ability to recall past events (as shown in the child's recounting of a past experience or the search for animate and inanimate objects); the ability to recall emotional experiences and to locate experiences that pertain to the self and the nonself; and the beginning of cognitive insight (e.g., combining internalized schemas); being able to identify the various parts of the self; relating in a less demanding way; and the beginning of cooperation with and concern for others. In the section that follows, a range of the developmental phenomena associated with emergent representation will be presented in light of both adaptive and maladaptive manifestations.

Illustrative Adaptive Modes

At the earliest stage of representational capacity, one criterion in assessing the child's adaptive use of this mode is the range of affective experience that can be represented. Is this range broad or constricted? Can many experiences involving pleasure, exploration, assertiveness, negativism, and anger be represented, or is the representation of experience limited to only a few of these affective domains?

A child who uses representational capacity adaptively is able to use mental representation to process a broad range of experience. A pleasurable interaction with the parent may be represented in the child's play with the doll at a later time. The representation of assertive and exploratory experiences is seen, for example, in the toddler's ability to demand cookies by pointing to the cabinet in which they are kept and by the search for favorite objects when they are not in sight. Angry protest and negative behavior also become organized at the symbolic level as the child uses "no" more frequently and begins to show selectiveness in agreeing or disagreeing with different offers—for example, rejecting the offer of spinach but accepting the offer of ice cream.

A second assessment criterion is the depth and richness with which experience is represented. When a pleasurable experience is represented with smiles, laughter, and animated chatting, for example, the experience is more richly conveyed than if the child shows only a few little smiles in the course of the activity; similarly, if one child cuddles, kisses, and clings to a doll and another child merely holds the doll, we may surmise that the depth and richness of the experience represented are different for these two children. Other experiential domains and their accompanying affects also have depth and richness when representational capacity has developed properly.

The progressive elaboration of the representational capacity is an important way of assessing the range of experience or adaptive functioning. At first, an experience is represented only in its most basic components, whether through language or gesture. As the child's capacity to perceive and represent detail increases, representations become correspondingly more elaborate and more experiences can be represented, either through sequential themes in play or through building more complex spatial arrangements. Language becomes more complex, the activities depicted in pretend play become more detailed and varied, and the youngster spends a lot of time naming, describing, imitating, and elaborating. Here again, it is important to assess the range of experience in which symbolic elaboration occurs: Does it occur across the affective domain of pleasurable, assertive, exploratory, negative, and angry experiences, or does it occur only in one or a few of these domains?

As symbolic elaboration occurs, the toddler also expands the representation of experience from the descriptive to the interactional level. A child may switch from "this is the doll's mouth" to "the doll is talking to me"—that is, from a descriptive to an interactional representation of experience. This shift from the descriptive to the interactive mode happens not only in language and representational play, but also in direct interactions. The toddler who uses personal pronouns and verbs in an action-oriented sense ("Please give me that," "I want you to stay.") is using language instrumentally in interaction. At a broader level, the toddler is using symbolic capacities instrumentally in interaction.

Here again it is important to assess whether the child can use the interactive mode across the various experiential domains—pleasure, exploration, assertiveness, negative behavior, anger. As the child learns to use the symbolic mode across the various domains in its interactive form, exchanges lose their infantile quality and the child begins to emerge as a young person. The interactional dramas that are elaborated, whether in reality or in play, are rich dramas encompassing multiple themes across the different experiential domains.

Under favorable conditions, the gradual elaboration of the representational capacity and the switch to the interactive mode should enable the child to acquire more effective coping mechanisms. When used adaptively, the ability to use symbols to represent experience allows the child to communicate more clearly, to deal more effectively with frustration, to delay gratification more readily, to be more self-reliant, and to master new situations more easily than at earlier phases. An adaptive mastery of representational skills should also lend stability and resilience to these coping mechanisms. Under moderate stress, such as a relatively brief separation from parents, the child may feel angry or afraid and suffer a temporary regression in the capacity to use symbolic representation, but he reverts to the previous level of functioning as soon as he feels secure again. On the other hand, a child who shows a maladaptive use of representational skills may lose the ability to engage at the symbolic level for days after the occurrence of the stress, or may use these skills in a manipulative way because negative affect cannot be tolerated even temporarily.

Another dimension of the representational capacity that should be considered is its specific individual character. Are there distinct, personal patterns that are beginning to emerge? Does the child's expression of pleasure, assertiveness, aggression, or negativism show a personal style that gives a unique "signature" to her behavior? Or is there a random quality, with no sense of uniqueness? In brief, has the child begun to put a personal stamp on her experience, even as she continues to imitate and identify with others? Or does the youngster seem to be more like the adult "as if" personality, who imitates social partners at random? The adaptive child, while encompassing a deep, rich, and stable affective repertoire, will also begin to put a personal signature on her experience.

In this very early period in the development of the symbolic mode, the representation of experience proceeds in piecemeal fashion, with the formation of islands of experience that are symbolically represented but still fragmented, without integration with other islands of represented experience. A child may switch from one topic to a totally unrelated one or function at a symbolic level at one moment, only to revert to a sensorimotor behavioral pattern soon afterward. Experiences that happened separately may be described as if they occurred at the same time. This *primary process thinking* is the norm in the early stages of representational capacity, where symbols are organized into small, cohesive islands that remain unconnected to others by logical or reality-oriented linkages. These connections are formed as the representational capacity continues to develop and to be elaborated.

Illustrative Maladaptive Modes

We may think of the maladaptive organization of early representational capacity as a continuum from most severe to least severe disturbance. At the most severe level, there is a paucity of mental representations. Imagery does not coalesce into organized experiential units. Language may be sparse or may remain at the descriptive level, without expanding to encompass interpersonal relations. Language may also remain fragmented, so that cohesive islands of verbal description do not emerge.

Children at this level of maladaptive functioning often demonstrate disorganized emotional and motor responses; chronic, unrelenting clinging, with complete disruption of exploratory behavior; pervasive and primitive aggressive behavior (biting, scratching, kicking); chronic fearfulness; and either social promiscuity or withdrawal. Thus, the inability to form internal mental representations as a means of stabilizing the behavioral organization and initiative of the prior stage gives rise to severe forms of regressive behavior, including autisticlike behaviors and fragmented, disorganized patterns of interpersonal behavior. The child may speak nonsense syllables, and recognizable words may be used continuously but with little logical relation to each other.

When mental representations are not organized in the service of structuring experience, the gains in behavioral internalization, initiative, and organization made during the preceding developmental stage are often lost, at least to some degree. The attainment of the next level seems to be important in consolidating the earlier gains. If the stage of internal representation is not accomplished, the toddler is at a disadvantage in making efforts to manage developing motor capacities, increased discriminatory sensory capacities, and growing awareness at the concrete impersonal level, without the accompanying capacity to organize the broadening range of human experience.

At less severe levels of disturbance, other maladaptive patterns may be observed. A toddler may attain representational capacity for the inanimate world but may have a very limited capacity to elaborate the representations of experiences with the human environment. Alternatively, a child may develop representational capacity in both the inanimate and human environments but may show severe limitations in certain affective areas. Examples are children who can use symbolic modes to express negativism, dominance, and aggression (e.g., through a vocabulary limited to "no" or "Give me"), but with little range of symbolic expression in the pleasurable or intimate domains; or children whose symbolic capacities are manifested mostly in passive, compliant, overly dependent relationships with others. Another maladaptive trend is illustrated by children who cannot maintain their otherwise richly developed symbolic capacities in the face of even minor stress. An additional and especially subtle maladaptive trend is the absence of a unique signature in the symbolic elaboration of experience, so that the choice of pleasure, intimacy, exploration, anger, or negativism is not accompanied by a recognizably individual style on the part of the child.

In summary, the disorganized patterns at this stage of development may range from severe disorders where no representational capacity has developed in terms of the animate or human experiential world to more subtle, individual differences where certain areas of experience are constricted, where there is a lack of stability in particular experiential organizations, or where the personal signature of uniqueness has either not developed or has developed only in the most limited realms of experience.

The Adaptive Environment

In the broadest sense, the adaptive environment encourages the child's use of the symbolic mode in both descriptive and interactive processes. Parents achieve this not only by using language in interacting with the child, but also by using the symbolic mode, whenever appropriate, as a substitute for concrete physical responses to the child. However, there should always remain a balance between the two, representational and concrete. Until an adaptive balance is reached, this optimally gradual substitution of symbolic for physical forms of interaction should take place in all aspects of the parent–child relationship: the pleasurable domain, the expression of anger and disapproval, the meeting of dependency needs, disciplinary action, and so on. Language and representational play are the most obvious instruments for encouraging the development of the symbolic mode, but more subtle behaviors may also be used. Nonverbal communications such as facial expressions or hand gestures can convey messages that are readily understood and responded to by the child: A 2-year-old may readily retreat from a cookie jar when she notices her mother's disapproving expression; alternatively, the child may continue to pursue her goal while conveying through her own facial expression or body movement that she is aware of the meaning of her action. In any event, a rich sequence of meanings may be exchanged between mother and child in a very short time without recourse to language.

The adaptive environment fosters stability and a capacity to deal with stress by helping the child to reengage at a symbolic level after a disruption. Stage-appropriate developmental regressions have been beautifully documented by Mahler, Pine, and Bergman (1975) in their discussion of the rapprochement stage and by Piaget (1972) in his description of vertical *décalage* in the early phases of the representational capacity. In the adaptive environment, the child finds understanding and support for these regressions, but also encouragement to reengage at a higher level after the disruption has been surmounted. This also applies in the case of developmental regressions triggered by external events such as a separation or an illness.

The adaptive environment also supports the child's individual style, including specific interests and preferences for specific toys and games. It is particularly challenging to support the child's individuality while at the same time striking a proper balance between offering support and security and setting appropriate limits. Yet such a balance is essential for the optimal development of the symbolic mode. A child whose individuality is neither recognized nor respected or a child who finds himself either overprotected and pampered or not challenged by adequate limit setting may find little motivation for engaging with the world at higher levels of representation.

The Maladaptive Environment

In contrast to the adaptive environment, the maladaptive environment fails to support the development of representational capacities. At its most extreme, such an environment undermines the child's emerging capacity to use symbols by discouraging language or representational play or by distracting or misreading the child's symbolic communication.

At a more circumscribed level, the maladaptive environment may encourage only the descriptive level while ignoring the interactional level. Or it may support only some areas of representational elaboration while undermining others. For example, parents with conflicts over aggression may be able to support pleasurable pursuits or dependency needs but may distort or ignore symbolic expressions of anger. Similarly, the child's individual style may be undermined by parents who feel threatened or conflicted by the child's idiosyncratic use of the representational mode in a particular experiential domain. If the parents respond with punishment or withdrawal to the child's emotional style, interactive patterns, or preferences, the child may react to chronic negativism as a means of maintaining a fragile yet stubbornly persistent sense of personal uniqueness; or may give up on interpersonal relations and accept loneliness as the only alternative; or may become promiscuously imitative, chameleonlike, to find approval from others.

Representational Stage II: Differentiation and Consolidation

This period becomes dominant during the third year of life and involves the gradual organization of experiences that were previously represented internally as isolated or fragmented units. In the early development of the representational capacity, the child is capable of only a rudimentary differentiation between self and nonself, fantasy and reality, past, present, and future, and cause and effect: The different symbolic categories intermingle in the child's mind in ways that often make his speech appear disjointed or illogical. This level of functioning is characteristic of primary process thinking and is also described by Piaget (1972) as an illustration of the degree to which experiential units remain unconnected with each other. However, as the child matures, the representational capacity undergoes differentiation and consolidation, and the personality achieves a cohesiveness that is akin to the concept of libidinal object constancy (Mahler et al., 1975). This attainment implies both a delineated system of self-representation and a delineated system of object (other) representations. These differentiated organizations form the foundation for many of the basic ego functions, including reality testing, regulation of impulses, and organization and regulation of thought and affect. As the sense of self becomes increasingly coherent, it reaches a stage of relative stability where, for instance, the sense of self is not undermined by simple, brief separations or by intensely negative feeling states. Concurrently, the isolated islands of affect that existed in the early representational stage (and that were evidenced by the child's quick shifts from one affect to another, i.e., from one island of experience to another) merge with one another to form a more stable emotional pattern, what we commonly call *mood*. Not only do these isolated affects merge to form a mood, but affects also become integrated with thoughts and ideas. Moreover, the differentiation of islands of experience pertaining to self and nonself facilitates the sense of interpersonal causality, responsibility, judgment, and planning for the future—all fundamental to reality testing, impulse control, and the capacity for concentration and formal learning.

Illustrative Adaptive Capacities

In the most global sense, the child's adaptive capacities are evidenced in the differentiation of the real from the unreal and the animate from the inanimate. This differentiation may be expressed verbally, but even more impressive are the nonverbal ways in which the child conveys a reality orientation and a sense of self by carrying out tasks, functioning in interpersonal relationships, and responding differentially to real and pretend events. Series of behaviors are strung together in a way that suggests an organized internal representation of the child's plans: for example, when the child searches for her favorite toy and then hugs her mother before going off to preschool. At this time the child is able to follow implicit rules and regulations in the household more effectively: She does not need to be told repeatedly not to touch a forbidden object. In interpersonal relations, there is also a cognitive awareness of the mood states and tensions of the partner and the needs of the self that permit the negotiation of complex reciprocal exchanges. The adaptive child can sustain this level of functioning even in the face of moderate stresses such as routine illness, anger, or brief separation from the parents.

Adaptiveness is also manifested in the range of experience that comes under the aegis of the new structural capacity. Is the child able to use these complex activities for the pursuit of pleasure, as well as for expressing anger or assertiveness, for acquiring mastery of new cognitive challenges, and for coping with sadness and pain? The most adaptive child can employ the new strategies across the full range of experience; still another index of adaptiveness is the depth and richness of expression associated with the various domains of experience.

In the adaptive child, security and confidence in the reality orientation have developed sufficiently so that regression may occur for brief intervals without endangering the sense of what is real and what is not real. Thus, aggressive and frightening games may be played without obliterating the boundaries between reality and pretense, without rendering the child overly fearful or anxious. In addition, if the child "scares himself," recovery is possible with only a brief period of *reassurance* and support.

Finally, an important aspect of adaptive functioning is the integration of themes and affects across the polarities of human experience. As differentiation and integration increase, there is less polarization of emotional themes; a play sequence will tend to reflect a variety of emotions instead of only one emotional theme. For example, the aggression expressed in a game of "cops and robbers" may give way to glee as goodness triumphs over evil and then to a peaceful mood as the "cops" go home to a good dinner with their families. As the child reaches the final stages of early representational differentiation and the consolidation of these capacities, affective integration across polarities can be observed not only in play but also in the real-life interpersonal exchanges of the child.

Illustrative Maladaptive Capacities

Maladaptive or pathological propensities in toddlers at the most severe levels are consistent with those disorders that are later diagnosed as borderline psychotic personality organizations in adults or in older children. While there may be some capacity for organized internal psychological life, there is little or no differentiation. Where some differentiation exists, it is extremely vulnerable to the vicissitudes of stress, such as separation or strong feeling states. Under such stress, or where differentiation has not occurred at all, there are islands of organized representational activity that exist in isolation from one another. Their personality has no cohesion. In essence, primary process thinking predominates.

At a less severe level basic differentiation may occur, but at a cost that includes major distortion in the flexibility of the personality. Here we see what are later described as severe personality disorders in very negativistic, withdrawn, schizoid, paranoid, or very depressed, apathetic youngsters.

In the youngster who is not moving toward representational differentiation and the establishment of basic ego functions, the shift from fantasy to reality is not taking place. It may also be that under emotional stress, he experiences severe distortions in reality-oriented thinking. In some instances there may be a perpetual lack of organization and regulation of emotions and impulses, as well as chronic patterns of disorganized aggressive or regressive behavior. Distortions in the flexibility of the personality may be hypothesized in cases where there is a worsening of the normal, age-expected negativism; failure to learn to control bodily functions; a tendency to blame others; and severe fears of loss of self, security, love, and bodily injury that lead the child to perceive progressive development as dangerous and to relinquish intimacy, assertion, curiosity, and self-control.

If differentiation occurs but there are compromises in the consolidation of this capacity (the consolidation of object constancy), we may see some milder disorders, such as vulnerability to regression, states of anxiety and depression, and moderate impairments in the flexibility of the personality. In essence, while differentiation of the inside from the outside and of the self from the other does occur, the child cannot tolerate stresses of separation or strong affect states (e.g., there is regression to dependent, clinging patterns in the face of severe separation anxiety). At times, instead of regression, we may see phase-specific symptom formations in terms of certain developmental conflicts, or moderate distortions of flexibility of the personality, such as moderate obsessive-compulsive patterns, hysterical patterns, patterns of impulsive behavior, or patterns of externalization. Often these moderate rigidities in personality or distortions of character serve to keep the growing child from experiencing certain thought and feeling states, such as anger or intimacy. These states, for dynamic reasons, may threaten the stability of the personality's organization— the organization of experience relating to the self, the organization of experience relating to important others in the youngster's life, the differentiation of self and other, and the fundamental sense of security and attachment to the important people (objects) in the youngster's life.

Mild or moderate difficulties at this stage do not usually interfere with further development, which moves into what is often called the *triangular* or *phallic-oedipal* phase of development. Frequently, the final crystallization of these more moderate character distortions and symptoms reflects a condensation of these early experiences with the experiences in the next phase of development (the triangular or oedipal phase).

Adaptive Environment

The adaptive environment that nurtures representational differentiation and consolidation is able to achieve four major goals. First, it is able to help the youngster move toward a reality orientation—that is, toward a differentiation of inner–outer, self–nonself, and means–ends (cause–effect). Second, it is able to help the youngster deal with intense interpersonal experiences and affects, and with such events as separation, so that representational differentiation and representational capacity are not lost during these stressful situations. Third, it provides those interpersonal experiences that help the youngster resolve the developmental tasks of the stage of representational differentiation. Fourth, it prepares the youngster to move on to higher levels of development, where a more differentiated psychic structure and new, expanded relationship patterns are possible.

Differentiation and a reality orientation are enhanced by the adaptive environment's capacity to read correctly and respond to both the cognitive and affective aspects of the symbolic communications of the growing child in an appropriate temporal sequence. Responses of the environment to the symbolic communication must be selective and differentiated if they are to help the youngster differentiate his own internal world. For example, the child may be symbolically communicating his assertiveness and competitiveness by assembling a puzzle and "doing it better than Mommy." In trying to prove himself, he works tensely and somewhat successfully by finding the various parts of the puzzle and placing them correctly. Smiling gleefully, he says, "See, I can do it," and he may even say, "You can't do it." At the cognitive level, his mother may appreciate this communication and respond by entering into the competitive play, saying, "Okay, now I'll try"; by saying supportively, "Gee, that's terrific"; or simply by letting the message register and giving her child the satisfaction of watching him closely and sharing his pleasure. Although her response is different in each instance, she has nevertheless interpreted the event correctly at both emotional and cognitive levels. Not only must the cues be read accurately, there must also be an empathic understanding of the child's communication. In the present example, such an understanding is manifested in the mother's comfortable acceptance of the child's competitive strivings and in her ability to encourage the child's mastery and self-esteem without feeling threatened or antagonistic.

The adaptive environment is capable of great subtlety in reading symbolic communications and in responding appropriately and flexibly at the temporal level. A special point should be made about the appropriate temporal response. In most instances an empathic emotional response, either through a facial expression or a verbal communication to the child, should be made within a reasonable period of time so that the youngster can connect it with her own communication. This does not suggest that learning about delay is unimportant. Instilling a capacity for delay and a tolerance of frustration is vitally important at this stage of development. Sometimes the capacity for delay must be taught through verbal communication such as "Tommy, you must wait." After repeating this several times, one may choose to ignore the constant requests for candy or to engage in play. But the importance of waiting and other issues is best confronted directly and can be explained simply but explicitly to the child. Through this method, the child gets the idea that tolerating delay is often necessary. Occasionally, of course, the strategy of ignoring a child may also be appropriate.

The adaptive environment responds to the child across various representational themes, ranging from pleasure and dependency to assertiveness and curiosity, to aggression and negativism, and the like. It responds to the child's interest in the animate and inanimate worlds, dealing with complex interpersonal communications with a variety of individuals: the parents and other significant adults, siblings and friends, and so on. The various developmentally appropriate themes become elaborated by the child in a variety of contexts, and in each of these contexts the caregiver may respond with a more or less reasonably accurate reading and empathic understanding of the communication, and with flexible and temporally effective responses. In this way, the representational mode employed by the child undergoes its own pattern of differentiation through the continual and repetitive experience of having an impact on the environment.

In its most adaptive form, the environment also tries to be half a step ahead of the child, leading her toward more differentiated capacities. The especially adaptive environment not only reads the child's intention accurately but tries to take it one level beyond the child—but only just beyond. Thus, when the youngster says "I want twenty-three toys by noon tomorrow" and seems to be half teasing, half serious (which is quite expectable at this age), the adaptive parent may decide not to assume that this is a serious demand that would have to be refused, or a teasing request that might be laughed at, and responds with "Where are you going to put them all?" This middle course might help the child to become aware of a subtle behavioral distinction that he has not yet clearly demarcated for himself. Because he lacks this awareness and is therefore unable to signal clearly whether he is teasing or not, the adaptive parent might respond, "Is this a pretend wish or what you really want?" At first the child may be confused by this question, but eventually he may be able to laugh and say, "Just pretend." Later on he may be able to say, "Just pretend, but I do want five presents on my birthday." In the latter case, the child now appreciates the difference between a make-believe request and a real one by making it clear that he would like at least part of the fantasy to come true at an appropriate time—a birthday. This indicates a highly differentiated capacity on the child's part.

The adaptive environment is also able to engage the child in a balanced way. It is not polarized toward fantasy or toward reality alone. When the child temporarily suspends the reality orientation, and the dolls and animals become real and even frightening, the adaptive parent can engage the child as the fear becomes evident. For example, when the child asks the parent to be a wolf and then asks the parent to save her from the wolf, the adaptive parent, moving back and forth in his roles (as protector and as wolf), is able to engage in elaborating this bit of fantasy with the youngster. If the child wishes to play the wolf, the adaptive parent will run in fear, showing the youngster the other side of the drama. At the same time, when the youngster tires of this game and wishes to watch television, the adaptive parent can also change directions to watch television too and may even help the child learn some words or letters from the screen.

When this same child, however, takes the role of the wolf and snaps at a younger sibling, or begins to act even more aggressively toward the baby as if to hurt him, the adaptive parent can bring the child back to reality by saying, "The game is over," explaining that such seemingly playful behavior can hurt the baby. The child thus learns the consequences of complex actions. She begins to make a subtle distinction between acceptable, playful behavior with a parent or sibling and unacceptable play in which she can hurt someone else or even herself. The adaptive parent does not shirk responsibility for making this distinction clear.

Some parents believe that to set limits for the child in his play would interfere with his fantasy life. On the contrary; by making these distinctions clear, by setting and explaining the limitations, the adaptive parent actually provides a greater sense of security for the youngster and permits the child to enjoy a richer, more varied, and deeper fantasy life. He acquires the ability to distinguish clearly between situations in which acting out a fantasy may, in fact, hurt somebody and harmless situations that are purely in the realm of fantasy.

The adaptive environment also helps the child consolidate these capacities for representational differentiation by aiding her to deal with intense internal feelings or interpersonal experiences (e.g., angry arguments, fights, separations, intensely dependent or loving feelings). In other words, even when the child is under the stress of certain internal wishes and affects or frightening experiences of separation, the adaptive environment helps her maintain the capacity for representational differentiation and the representational capacity itself, in spite of the stressful experiences.

How is stability fostered? There are a number of ways. The most important—and a fundamental principle common to all of them—is to provide for the child, and help the child provide for himself, the sense of being able to deal with intense experiences. This *coping* capacity is provided in several ways by the parents. One way is to show the child that the parents are not afraid of engaging him around intense affects. They do not withdraw, become fragmented or disorganized, or excessively aggressive themselves as they tolerate and engage the child in intense interpersonal affects. When the youngster is angry and demanding, they can set firm limits without withdrawing or becoming disorganized or overly aggressive themselves. The child learns in the natural way of give-and-take that his own anger does not frighten the world or cause its disorganization. He learns that such intense feelings are not dangerous as the parents interact with him in a differented way at such times. Thus, the youngster incorporates the quality of their responses. Similarly, when the child has strong feelings about sensual urges or dependency needs, no matter how intense, adaptive parents will remain engaged around this issue, at times setting appropriate limits.

The adaptive environment offers yet another feature that, although not absolutely necessary, is highly desirable. This has to do with helping the child negotiate certain interpersonal dimensions of the developmental phase of representational differentiation and consolidation. During this early period of life, most children are involved primarily in what may be called the *dyadic* relationship patterns. In dyadic relationship patterns, whether with the mother, father, or others, the world is viewed as a two-person system in a one-to-one relationship. This other person can be the fulfiller of needs, the setter of limits, or the partner in a variety of activities. The two-person system, however, does not afford as much flexibility as does the system that will emerge later on as a capacity for three people to interact in a triangular system.

In order to foster the child's capacity to consolidate his representational differentiation and to shift to higher levels of relating (e.g., the three-person system), it is necessary, or at least helpful, for the child to have a significant other available, so that the intensity of wish and affect and of need and its gratification are not directed toward one person alone. When there is a second significant other available (usually the father in the family situation), the youngster can then be angry at the mother, and fantasize that she is angry in turn, but still feel relatively secure because the father is available. This permits the child to tolerate more intense affect states without resorting to distorting mechanisms. Because an ally is available, the child can afford to feel angry or intensely loving and needy without resorting to projection, incorporation, and displacement. The child's tentative experimentation with avoiding the use of these more primitive undifferentiated capacities helps him to give them up. The tentative but successful sortie into the triangular mode permits the child to relinquish emotionally the earlier undifferentiated ways of thinking as he perceives that these more realistic ways are much less dangerous than they might be were the ally (the father) *not* available. This maturation is consistent with the child's growing ability for differentiation.

To summarize, the adaptive environment encourages representational communications and responds empathically as well as cognitively to them. The adaptive environment responds in a flexible and temporally effective manner and across multiple thematic realms. It sets appropriate limits, offering structure and support when the youngster is overwhelmed by intense experiences. The adaptive environment makes available a significant other who, as an ally, helps the child to negotiate the symbiotic elements of this phase of development and to move ahead into triangular relationship patterns.

Maladaptive Environment

The most fundamental flaw in the maladaptive environment is a basic deficit in reading the child's symbolic communications at the cognitive and empathic levels. For example, the mother who projects her own inner experience onto the child and misreads his signals is likely to respond inappropriately in a way that undermines a growing orientation toward reality or a growing capacity for differentiation—for example, the father who responds to his son's intimacy as an attack and then goes off into a discussion of how his son and the house are dirty and need to be cleaned up. Where the child evidences a complex symbolic communication and is responded to inappropriately or not at all, the means (i.e., the child's communications) are not tied to the appropriate ends. Means/ends differentiation along realistic lines does not occur, although it may occur with distorted modes of communication.

The child's capacity for differentiation is also undermined by the overly intrusive, controlling, or withdrawn environment. For example, the girl who is playing a complex symbolic game, perhaps of wolves chasing little girls, may encounter a maternal demand to shift attention from her game to another theme of girls giving a tea party (perhaps because the mother is anxious about the implied aggression in the child's original play theme). If this switching of themes is repeated frequently and too intrusively, the youngster feels an encroaching disruption in her capacity to elaborate her own experiences symbolically. She may stop further development of the symbolic mode or may begin responding aggressively and impulsively in presymbolic modes. The withdrawing mother can have a similar effect on the growing child.

At more subtle levels, while the environment may not undermine general differentiation, it may undermine differentiation in particular ranges of experience. Here the maladaptive environment may be incapable of offering differentiating experiences of pleasure or dependency, assertiveness or curiosity, and aggression or negativism.

The maladaptive environment may be unable to provide in-depth differentiated experience with certain themes in specific areas where there are conflicts either in the parents or in the family unit as a whole. Here again, the maladaptive environment fails to engage the child in a reality-oriented way in pleasurable or assertive or curious pursuits. Or this environment may fail to engage the child in a rich, deep way in one or another of these themes; for example, where there are conflicts involving pleasure or dependency we may see limited tolerance, with a rather abrupt shift of theme when parents or other family members become anxious.

On the other hand, a family can engage realistically in certain themes but cannot facilitate fantasy elaboration. Some parents who may be able to deal with reality and set limits grow anxious about symbolic play that is fanciful and may deal with deep, rich themes involving, for example, make-believe bodily exploration and sensuous bodily pleasure. Such a stance inevitably compromises the richness of their youngster's experiential world.

In contrast to the adaptive environment, the maladaptive environment also fails to respond to the developing uniqueness of the child. Whereas the growing child begins to manifest preferred affective expressions, preferred games, complex symbolic communications, and other activities and modes of expression that distinguish his unique personality, the maladaptive environment has a vested interest in keeping the child's uniqueness diffuse. As the child develops a liking for assertiveness and curiosity, the maladaptive environment does not support such growth by showing interest and by engaging the child in this area, but immediately points out the other aspect of the situation by encouraging the child to be more creative and sensitive instead. For example, if a child shows his creativity and sensitivity by an interest in music and other expressions, the maladaptive environment may immediately require him to shift to another area of endeavor, with the ostensible worry that the child is showing "effeminate" qualities and should engage in more aggressive games to combat such qualities. The adaptive environment, in contrast, not only tolerates these individual differences but helps foster their further differentiation by encouraging the child's preferred modes, while at the same time helping to build flexibility into the child's personality structure if he seems too absorbed in a particular orientation.

In general, where dependence and symbiotic styles are supported and assertiveness and independence undermined, where the child is not taught to handle aggression or other overwhelming affects (e.g., loss, separation), there may be little or no progress beyond early dyadic experiences. Thus, maturation toward more differentiated ways of dealing with the world may not occur, or there may be an arrest at a level where, while some differentiation may occur, it will not be up to the expected level of the child's chronological age.

We have now summarized a number of features of the maladaptive environment. They range from distorted communication patterns wherein the environment does not respond appropriately to the youngster's signals, thereby undermining differentiation; to the environment that does not help the youngster deal with intense experiences through supportive structuring or limit-setting actions; to the environment that does not supply certain developmental tools, such as making an ally available to help the child negotiate the dyadic phase of development.

As we described earlier, such maladaptive environments are often associated with two kinds of impairment. One is a gross deficit in the capacity for differentiation (often associated with adult borderline and psychotic states). In the second type of impairment, at a less severe level, the flexibility of the personality structure is limited. Here certain experiences can be dealt with in a differentiated way, but others exist at a more primitive, undifferentiated level. For example, individuals who use mechanisms of projection, denial, and incorporation to deal with their angry feelings can nevertheless achieve more differentiated patterns concerned with love and intimacy. Other individuals, who can sustain differentiated patterns in impersonal but nonetheless socially active relationships, and are comfortable with assertion and aggression, may function in undifferentiated ways in their intimate and dependent relationships. Often such relationships are feared because, when frustrated in such a dependent relationship, angry feelings become frightening and in an undifferentiated fantasy (i.e., one that is believed) often lead to an abrupt rupture in the relationship. The classic personality disorders at severe to moderate levels may emanate from difficulties associated with undifferentiated modes and secondary compromises in character structure that ironically protect the personality from further lack of differentiation or dedifferentiation (e.g., where intimacy or assertiveness is totally avoided because it leads to disorganization or dedifferentiation).

An Instrument for the Systematic Clinical Assessment of Mental Representation in Early Childhood

The theoretical framework already described served as the basis for an instrument that can be used to assess systematically the mental representations in early childhood. We used the theoretical framework as a guide for the identification of *indicator behaviors*—that is, behaviors that occur spontaneously in children's free play and talk and that exemplify the level of representational organization under consideration. The concept of indicator behaviors implies that these behaviors are observable and measurable manifestations of the abstract constructs hypothesized for each developmental level.

The indicator behaviors were selected for their clinical relevance. In the selection process we attempted *not* to ignore the harder-to-measure issues of affective functioning; for this purpose, we sought measures that would capture the richness of clinical meaning in both a structural and a thematic sense. From the perspective of structural capacity, these measures are intended to reflect the child's representational elaboration and differentiation in terms of range, depth, and flexibility. From the perspective of affective and thematic content, the measures aim to reflect the dramas that the child is involved in. In language, we assess both the structure (the stage) and the content (the drama being played on the stage). Some indicator behaviors assess primarily the structure of representational thought; others assess primarily its thematic content. For example, the capacity for age-appropriate affects—their flexibility and reciprocal nature—tells us more about the stage; the particular affects chosen and their relative dominance over other affects tell us about the drama being played out on the stage.

There is another reason for assessing structure and theme separately. All symbolic behaviors have in common differentiation between the signifiers and the signified. Piaget (1954) argued that language and representational play, both symbolic systems, differ in an important way. In language, the relationship between the signifier and the signified is arbitrary, dictated by social convention and acquired by the child through social relationships and with the surroundings. In representational play, the relationship between signifier and signified is highly personal: A shell can represent a cat for one child and a car for another. According to Piaget, play becomes accommodation—that is, partaking of the social conventions governing play symbols—only in latency, when the child is 8 or 9 years old. Whether this timetable is indeed accurate is open to investigation, but the theoretical argument is compelling. Given this difference, it seems appropriate to undertake a separate assessment of the individual child's progress along these two developmental lines.

The Observational Setting

In choosing a setting for gathering our data, we were guided by the free-associative method developed early in the history of psychoanalysis. As Anna Freud has repeatedly pointed out, the free play of children resembles the free association of adults in the access it provides to the complexities of emotional life. Assessing infants and very young children, however, is different from assessing older children because the latter have an internalized psychic structure, whereas the former function primarily in the context of a dyadic relationship, most often with the mother. In our earlier paper on assessment in the first year of life (Greenspan & Lieberman, 1980), we reasoned that mother–infant free play "may provide us with an access to complex emotional phenomena similar to the free play of childhood and to the free association of adulthood" (p. 273). In the present chapter, we continue to adopt that viewpoint but extend it somewhat. We are now talking of children 2 to 4 years old, who may be capable of independent functioning that may not necessarily emerge in their relationship with their mothers. We must therefore assess their representational capacity not only in the context of the mother–child relationship but also in the context of a play and talk interview with a skilled clinician. Observing the unstructured interaction between mother and child, and then between clinician and child, gives us the best opportunity to observe both the child's structural capacity and the thematic content of the internal dramas he is involved in.

Experience has taught us that structured tasks, while manifestly geared to bringing out certain behavior and affects, generally have the opposite effect. They also obscure the far richer spontaneous communications, whether overt or covert, through gesture or word, activity or inactivity, that all children quickly engage in. At the Clinical Infant Development Program (Greenspan, Wieder, Lieberman, Nover, Lourie, and Robinson, 1987), where the data were collected, interaction took place in a playroom. The instructions to the mother were given by a familiar person— most often by the infant specialist who gave her developmental guidance in child-rearing issues. The instructions to the mother were: "Please play with your child as you would at home." Mother and child were then left alone for 20 minutes. The interaction was videotaped behind a one-way mirror with the mother's knowledge and permission. The videotapes were automatically timed with a date–time generator in order to facilitate coding.

The play session between child and clinician took place either immediately after the mother–child play session or on another day. The clinician was unfamiliar to the child and simply invited the child to participate in exploring the playroom, an activity that included interacting with the interviewer, playing with the toys, sitting silently, or talking. The play session lasted approximately 30 to 45 minutes and was also videotaped behind a one-way mirror.

Measures of Representational Play

The first measure involves quantification of the *incidence of representational play* in the free play episode by stating the percentage of time the child is engaged in this type of activity.

A second measure assesses the *highest structural level attained in representational play* during the whole episode. An ordinal scale is used in which higher scores indicate higher structural levels. The measure derives from the stage-specific behaviors described by Piaget (1972) and was influenced by the assessment of symbolic maturity developed by Nicolich (1977). Piaget defined the levels of play on the basis of the child's actions vis-à-vis objects and other people. Initially objects are treated realistically in the context of their intended purpose. Play becomes progressively more abstract and accrues a larger number of behavioral units, until the play sequence incorporates planned elements that demonstrate clearly that the sequence was represented mentally prior to its enactment.

A third measure assesses *affective themes*. The affective themes displayed measure the child's capacity to experience and symbolically express an age-appropriate range of affects through representational play. A child who represents a narrow range of affective themes is using the symbolic mode less adaptively than a child who uses a broader range.

A fourth measure assesses the *clarity, depth, and richness* with which a theme is conveyed to gain additional understanding of the structural components of representational play. Also assessed is the child's capacity to establish an *integrated balance between polarities of affect.*

The extent to which the *child is able to engage others* in her representational play is an important structural dimension of the child's symbolic ability. A continuum from solitary play to play with an adult character in representational play, and the ability to shift back and forth between reality and pretense are assessed.

The degree of adaptiveness in the child's environment is measured through the *affective role of the mother or adult present.* Here we use three measures developed in our earlier paper on mother–infant assessment (Greenspan & Lieberman, 1980): contingent, anticontingent, and noncontingent responses. *Contingency* refers to the parent's (or other adult's) behavior and is defined as a direct, appropriate response to the child's signals, a response that meets the aims of the child's behavior as evaluated by the observer. An adult who enters into the representational mode being used by the child and uses it to interact with the child engages in contingent responses. An adult who actively intervenes to change the child's use of the symbolic mode, or to change the theme chosen by the child, is using anticontingent behavior. Finally, an adult who does not respond to the child either in symbolic or in presymbolic modes shows noncontingent behavior.

We conceive of these three types of behavior as a continuum of adaptiveness. Contingent responses support representational elaboration and, at the appropriate time, support means–end differentiation. Anticontingent responses are inherently frustrating, but they at least show a direct causal connection to the child's behavior, showing both recognition of the symbolic mode and subsequent differentiation of it. The child is recognized as an agent whose behavior deserves and receives a response, even if it is not the response desired by the child. Noncontingent responses are likely to be the most maladaptive because they involve the adult's ignoring the child, either through gross misreading of the child's message or through avoidance, thereby undermining her self–nonself boundary. The child's signals and communications are simply not taken into account by the adult, and thus deprive the child of a sense of herself as a causal agent in eliciting responses from the adults she tries to address.

Against this notion of a continuum of adaptiveness, it may be argued that normal childrearing involves all three types of responses, and that anticontingent and noncontingent responses are essential instruments in socializing the child. Could a responsible parent fail to respond anticontingently to a toddler's attempt to put a finger in the electric plug by saying "no" and thereby removing the child from the source of danger? A noncontingent response to a toddler's low-grade fussing in the middle of the night might be the most adaptive means of restoring sleep. The answer to these very plausible arguments is quite straightforward. The meaning of the adult's response, and hence its adaptiveness, cannot be separated from the context in which it occurs; a profile involving a balanced pattern will separate adaptive from disturbed functioning. In the free-play context, a certain balance will be seen in the adaptive situation and a lack of balance in the maladaptive situation.

Measures of Language as a Representational Tool

The measures of language parallel the measures of representational play. The first measure assesses whether language is used at a descriptive or an interactional level. At each of these levels, the use of language may vary in degree of elaboration. In general, however, the descriptive levels are reflected in language that involves recognition of an object, whereas the interactional level involves attempts to influence others and the evocation, in a social context, of past events.

Another measure addresses the structure of representational language. This measure is parallel to the measure of level of representational play in the sense that words are considered equivalent to action schema. Does the child use isolated words unconnected with each other? Alternatively, is either a rudimentary or an elaborate theme conveyed through word combinations and the use of diverse types of words?

Another measure assesses the context in which language is used. Is it only used factually, standing by itself as pretend speech, or does it occur in the context of representational play? What is the social character of speech, that is, does the child talk mainly to himself or does he clearly and purposefully address others? Finally, the affective theme conveyed by language—its clarity, depth, and richness—and the balance of polarities between positive and negative affect are measures that parallel those developed to assess representational play.

Empirical Application of the Measures

The first step in our application of the measures was to assess the goodness of fit between our clinical impressions of a child's functioning and the empirical profile that emerged when we systematically analyzed videotapes of free-play behavior in our playroom. We will discuss three such cases. One of the children was clinically considered to function at a normative age level in all areas of development. A second child was functioning well cognitively but showed clinical signs of affective inhibition in play. The third child had marked language delays and disturbances of affect, as reflected by a low threshold for frustration and failures in self-control (e.g., frequent episodes of overexcitement, tantrums, and disorganized motor discharge). Videotapes of these children's behavior were coded by one of us (A.F.L.), who had no knowledge of the children's identity and was not familiar with the case histories of the children or their families.

Case 1: Diana

Diana's mother, Mrs. Sommers, was 4 months pregnant when she joined our program. She had two adolescent children from a previous marriage that had ended in divorce. She was currently living with her boyfriend and her children, and was working long hours in a demanding, highly stressful position with the city government. An intelligent, competent, intensely appealing black woman, Mrs. Sommers had sought and welcomed the present pregnancy, only to find herself rebuked by her boyfriend and children when she joyfully announced it to them. The boyfriend, a chronic alcoholic with an erratic work history, expressed fear about the loss of income should Mrs. Sommers stop working. The adolescent children openly accused their mother of selfishness because, in their view, she was thinking only of her own wishes and had not considered their financial and psychological needs when she decided to have a new baby.

Mrs. Sommers, who had thought of this pregnancy as an expression of her love for and commitment to her boyfriend, was crushed. She started experiencing fatigue and lack of motivation at work and outbursts of rage at home. The family situation deteriorated. The boyfriend started to stay out overnight and come in drunk in the mornings. The children, who had been average students, started skipping school; their grades plummeted. There were angry confrontations daily—between mother and children, mother and boyfriend, boyfriend and children. It was a family at war.

Mrs. Sommers joined our program in the fourth month of her pregnancy, seeking relief for her feeling of guilt for being pregnant, a condition that she felt had triggered the conflicts in her family. She was well motivated and insightful, and was able to delve rather deeply into her intrapsychic conflicts in the course of psychotherapy with her primary clinician. Occasional family sessions helped defuse family tensions. This therapeutic alliance helped Mrs. Sommers and the other family members to protect Diana from their own conflicts. The baby's birth was greeted with primarily positive feelings by the family. Mrs. Sommers, in particular, relished the baby to an extent that, in her words, she had never experienced with her other children. Although she returned to work after the baby's birth, Mrs. Sommers found excellent substitute care for Diana with an elderly neighbor. The family situation improved. There was chronic tension about the alcoholism of the baby's father, but as the primary clinician became a familiar and trusted figure in the home, he began to join in the sessions and soon became an active participant. The work with both parents was useful in helping them to manage their conflicts in ways that were unobtrusive in terms of the children's development.

In this context, Diana's development proceeded uneventfully. From infancy, she was an alert, endearing little girl with luminous eyes and a friendly, ready smile that became more pronounced when she interacted with her mother. She explored readily both her social and physical environments, used her mother as a secure base from which to explore, and successfully achieved affective and cognitive milestones. At the age of 2, her predominant emotional tone was one of security, intense curiosity, and pleasure in exploration. At the same time, she was negotiating issues of autonomy and was capable of both clinginess and negativism, although these affects did not predominate. She sometimes reacted to frustration by slapping her mother or other adults. At times, these behaviors were laughed off by Mrs. Sommers, who enjoyed her daughter's freedom in expressing anger. Mrs. Sommers herself had a quick temper, and yelled at and slapped either her children or her boyfriend, but she felt guilty about these outbursts. Surprisingly, she accepted Diana's outbursts as a normal childhood expression of anger. Part of our therapeutic intervention at this age focused on discussing with Mrs. Sommers ways of helping Diana gradually to express her anger in other than physical ways. This work also helped Mrs. Sommers to find new channels of expression for her own anger (i.e., talking, going for a walk, cleaning the house).

This overall picture is clearly reflected in the empirical profile of Diana's representational play with her mother at 2 years of age. She had a relatively high incidence of representational play (30%), and her play was at a high level for her age. She consistently used two behavioral units linked together to form a recognizable theme.

The dyadic play between Diana and her mother was strikingly harmonious. Diana sought her mother out in ways that brought Mrs. Sommers into the play as a reciprocal partner while preserving her real identity as a mother. Mrs. Sommers, in turn, was responsive to Diana's overtures. She made herself available to Diana but did not attempt to direct or control her daughter's play. In fully 80% of the play intervals, Mrs. Sommers responded contingently to Diana's play signals.

A variety of affective themes were represented. The theme of nurturance was shown in a play sequence where Diana held a baby doll closely, fed her, and then showed the doll's hair ribbon to her mother, who looked at it carefully and helped Diana to fix it better. Pleasure was expressed in joyful pretend play and singing at the toy piano. Curiosity and exploration of the surroundings were depicted in a prolonged play sequence where Diana explored farm animals and opened and closed the doors of the barnyard to see how they worked while pretending to put the animals to sleep. The theme of separation and reunion was acted out in the same play sequence as Diana put a baby cow to sleep and then "woke it up" again. Some negativism was shown when Diana chose to ignore the mother's attempt at playing to imitate the sounds that farm animals make. These affective themes were age-appropriate. They were clear, coherent, and easy to recognize, but they were still rudimentary in the sense that the play did not involve elaboration in a range of affects and themes. There was an emerging balance of polarities of positive versus negative affect, but positive affective themes tended to predominate (nurturance, curiosity, pleasure).

Diana used language in 50% of the play episodes. Language was primarily interactive and occasionally reflected Diana's evocation of past events and objects not present in the room. In general, the level of language was below the level of representation. Diana did not use language to convey affective themes in a deep, coherent, or elaborated manner.

When Diana was 3 years old, a clinical play session took place. Diana's play clearly reflected the excellent social and cognitive development we were observing clinically. The most impressive aspect of her play was the predominance of complex, nonrepetitive play sequences lasting for 2 minutes or more. These sequences showed a variety of age-appropriate affective themes that were highly elaborated and showed a well-modulated integration of positive and negative affects. The doll play, for example, incorporated the themes of self-control and limit setting, assertiveness, negativism, anger, aggression, and reconciliation followed by nurturance and pleasure. An intricate plot involved the doll's wrongdoing, Diana's telling her what to do, scolding her, punishing her with a potentially dangerous train ride, and then rescuing her and hugging her tenderly for a long time while smiling and talking to her. Another representative sequence involved a second train ride in which the themes of possible death, curiosity about and exploration of the surroundings, aggression, and mastery of painful experiences were integrated as Diana built a train with cubes, peopled it with assorted characters, and made it almost crash as she watched in mock horror before making sure that the ride came to a safe end and the welfare of every passenger was attended to. In this sequence, language was fully at the level of representational play. Diana used language in elaborate evocation of events, carrying on free-flowing conversations where topics were elaborated by the incorporation of multiple themes. Language was consistently used to accompany representational play, and as such, it also served to convey the affective themes in a rich, coherent manner.

Case 2: Jelain

Jelain was the third boy born to Mrs. Malcolm, a 27-year-old married black woman. Although the family was financially stable when Jelain was born, Mrs. Malcolm was experiencing some concern about her capacity to raise three children on her husband's income as a house painter. A controlling woman who tried to convey an image of unruffled competence, Mrs. Malcolm considered her unplanned pregnancy with Jelain as a blow to her careful plans to finish raising her children and return to work as a secretary once they started attending school. She was unwilling to terminate the pregnancy for religious reasons, but she was also unable to reconcile herself to having a new child. As a result, Mrs. Malcolm experienced little pleasure in Jelain. Yet she tried hard to play the role of a "good mother," by which she meant a mother who talked to her children, played with them, and taught them. The combination of this conscientious effort to be available to Jelain and her simultaneous anger at his presence resulted in a pattern of mothering that was highly didactic and overly intrusive. Mrs. Malcolm seemed to feel that she was guilty of ignoring Jelain if she allowed him to play by himself, yet it was clear that she felt bored and pressured by her self-imposed task of playing with him. As a result, their exchanges had little spontaneity. Mrs. Malcolm constantly interrupted Jelain's play to draw his attention to herself or to toys that interested her; she also constantly monitored his activities and directed him to play in specific ways when his own play was not clear to her. This regimentation resulted in a very restricted imaginative life for Jelain, although his cognitive performance was solidly at age level.

In the videotaped free-play session with Jelain at 3 years of age, the incidence of representational play was quite low: only 5% of all 15-second intervals. The play sequences were at a low representational level: 85% of the play episodes involved the use of objects in ways that were not concretely realistic, with a single unit of behavior and pretending to perform the activities of others. This play was rather fragmented and lacked symbolic elaboration. Jelain limited himself to brief pretend conversations on the telephone, to giving the toy bottle to a doll or a puppet, and to hugging a toy elephant. The affective themes involved nurturance (as in feeding and hugging) and establishing contact with others (as in speaking on the phone), but these themes lacked richness and symbolic elaboration. There was also no overt expression of negative affect through representational plan, and hence no balance of affective polarities. We attributed this to an affective inhibition due to the mother's controlling behavior (or excessive interest in what he never had or had only too fleetingly).

Strikingly, the mother responded noncontingently in 50% of the 15-second intervals and anticontingently in 30% of them. In the first instance, she interrupted Jelain's ongoing play by initiating new activities with him or by drawing his attention to a new toy and away from the toy he was currently playing with. Her anticontingent responses involved sharp rebukes of the child when he played in novel or unconventional ways. For example, she questioned him sharply when he gently overturned a chair and laid it on its back on the floor. It seemed that this action was the prelude to novel representational play that was never carried out due to the mother's intervention. In spite of the mother's lack of permissiveness in play, Jelain sought her out as a partner. In 60% of the symbolic play sequences, she participated as her real self in the interaction, and in 20% he asked her for help or information. Interestingly, he did not use her as a "refueling station," a common use of the mother's presence at this age.

Jelain's use of language reflected his social orientation. He used language primarily for interaction rather than mere description. The structure of language was such that it gave flexibility to the child's speech through the use of adjectives and adverbs as well as verbs and nouns. However, language was used as an accompaniment to representational play in only 20% of the representational play sequences; the most common context for language was factual, nonpretend, reality-oriented (80%). There was no identifiable affective theme conveyed by language independently of representational play.

The clinical free-play session (with Dr. Reginald Lourie) showed that under optimal conditions Jelain was capable of more highly developed symbolic play than he had shown in play with his mother. During this session, he engaged in representational play in 20% of the 15-second intervals, and the level of the play was higher than before. He was now able to use two behavioral units linked together to form a recognizable theme. There was a dramatic contrast between the affective themes that predominated in the play with the mother. With Dr. Lourie, Jelain could engage in the representational expression of negative affects, and in fact the highest level of play was achieved when he was involved in depicting an elaborate fight between cows that bit each other, hurt each other, and then needed to get painful shots in order to get well. Thus the themes of death, anger, aggression, and mastery of painful experiences were vividly represented in this play; in fact, this was the only play sequence where the theme was clear and coherent, and where it carried the child's affective involvement in a range of elaborated themes. Even in this higher play, however, there was only a primitive balance of positive and negative themes, with a predominance of negative themes. Interestingly, Jelain seemed to rely on a splitting mechanism in the representation of affect, engaging in positive affective themes in the presence of the mother and only feeling safe in expressing negative affect in the permissive presence of the interviewer. This was consistent with our clinical impression of the mother as a restrictive influence on the child's emotional life. Convergent information in this regard is the fact that Jelain's language was more sophisticated with Dr. Lourie than with his mother. With Dr. Lourie also, language was used to accompany representational play, whereas with the mother it was primarily factual and reality-oriented. However, as with the mother, Jelain could not use language with Dr. Lourie to convey affective themes clearly and with depth or to achieve a balance of affective polarities.

Case 3: Robbie

The case of Robbie illustrates a situation of double vulnerability in which both mother and child had difficulties in establishing a reciprocal relationship conducive to the child's developmental progress. Mrs. Linden, the mother, had had a chaotic childhood characterized by abandonment, physical abuse, and psychological rejection. She had a long history of psychiatric disturbances that included pronounced paranoid features, disorganization of thinking under stress, and difficulties with impulse control. Robbie, the baby, appeared to be a constitutionally vulnerable infant. From birth he tended to become easily irritable and was difficult to console. He had tense musculature and many tremors and startles. Gaze aversion was noted as early as the first month of life, and throughout infancy it remained particularly pronounced in interactions with the mother. Although intensive intervention helped Robbie to sustain a relatively adequate level of functioning, his development in the first 2 years was marked by lacunae that seemed to mirror his mother's difficulties. At age 2, for example, Robbie had age-appropriate cognitive performance but was unusually responsive to variations in the environment. He responded with marked disorganization to even moderately stressful events. He was often extremely defiant with the infant room staff, and he had prolonged temper tantrums when he was angry or frustrated. With his mother, in contrast, Robbie seemed to plead for attention and love. He seemed frightened and subdued by Mrs. Linden's outbursts of yelling, which alternated with a chilling emotional withdrawal. Perhaps as a result, Robbie had developed a pattern of leaving the room when there was tension in the interaction between himself and his mother. He did not seem to feel secure enough to show anger in her presence.

Robbie's 2-year free play with his mother was characterized by the complete absence of spontaneous representational play. Robbie seemed mesmerized by his mother's activities, and she, in turn, took over the situation and played as gleefully as if she were a child herself. She made cookies with play dough; greeted Robbie through a puppet, and made the puppet squeal and get away when Robbie tried to touch it; started a telephone conversation with Robbie and told him what to say (he dutifully repeated it); made Robbie "write" his name with a crayon; and showed Robbie pictures in a book. Robbie was pleasantly responsive; yet on three occasions he suddenly left his mother's side without further ado, opened the door, and left the room, as if he needed relief from his mother's one-sided structuring of the situation. Robbie appears in this session as a pretext for the mother's own play. He received the lowest ratings in all the categories of representational play, since at no time was there affective depth and richness or elaboration of themes. Similarly, language use was extremely primitive: Robbie said only a few simple words in the course of the entire sequence.

At 3 years of age, a clinical play session (with Dr. Robert Nover) took place. There was a higher incidence of representational play (25% of the intervals): Robbie's play was at a higher level; he used two behavioral units linked together to form a recognizable theme. He offered raisins to the cows and made them eat; dialed the phone and engaged in conversation; and gave a shot to Dr. Nover and instructed him to say "ouch." One striking sequence involved pretending to take real candy that Robbie found in a desk drawer in the playroom, in spite of Dr. Nover's admonishments not to open the drawer and, later, not to take the candy. Robbie finally abandoned the play stance and actually ate the forbidden candy. The negotiations surrounding this incident were lengthy and complex, and reflected vividly the theme of negativism that was such a salient aspect of Robbie's clinical picture. The other affective themes portrayed were nurturing (feeding the cows, giving Dr. Nover a drink), mastery of painful experiences (playing doctor), and aggression (the cows biting each other). The themes were clear and easy to recognize; they were midrange in terms of depth and richness of elaboration. There was some balance of polarities, but either the positive or the negative one predominated.

Robbie's language had also become more sophisticated. There was speech in 50% of the intervals, and it was evenly divided into factual, reality-oriented speech and speech accompanying representational play. Language was primarily social.

Differences in Performance Between a High-Risk and a Normative Sample

A second step in our application of the measures was to attempt to compare groups of children using the GLOS. A pilot study was conducted to determine whether the measures differentiated between a high-risk and a normative group of preschoolers. The high-risk group came from families with incomes below the poverty level who were enrolled in the Clinical Infant Development Program. The normative group comprised children from middle-class families, none of whom were receiving treatment for developmental problems or difficulties in parent–child interaction. There were four children in each group, two boys and two girls. Two of the children in the high-risk group were black; all the children in the normative sample were white. The age of the children was similar in the two groups. The mean age was 3.6, but the oldest child in the high-risk sample was 4.0 and in the normative sample the oldest was 4.2.

The data used consisted of videotaped free-play sessions. There were some differences in setting between the two groups. For the high-risk group, all the sessions had a clinician as the primary interacter with the child; in two cases, the mother was also present during the entire session, and in a third case she was present for 20 minutes out of the 30-minute session. The normative sample had no clinician present; the mother and child were alone for the entire session.

The tapes were coded by an experienced child therapist (Marian Birch). A subset of the data (two high-risk and two normative) was independently coded by one of the authors (Alicia F. Lieberman). Intercoder agreement was calculated by dividing the number of agreements by the number of agreements plus the number of disagreements. The mean intercoder agreement was .86, ranging from a high of 1.0 for the role of the adult to a low of .60 for clarity, depth, and richness of theme. This latter scale was relatively difficult to score, and it may not reflect a single dimension. In some situations the affective theme of an episode was very clear but not at all rich, and in still other episodes the reverse was the case.

In spite of the small sample, there were clear differences between the high-risk and low-risk groups. The high-risk group spent much less time in representational play (40% vs. 86%). The mean duration of a bout of representational play was 2.1 minutes for the high-risk group and 4.5 minutes for the low-risk group. The level of representational play was lower for the high-risk group (3.5 vs. 4.7 on a 6-point scale). The themes tended not to differ in the two groups, with one exception: There were nine play episodes (distributed among three of the four children) concerned with an attack by an adult in the high-risk group but only two such episodes in the low-risk group (both episodes in the play of the same child). There was also a lower percentage of episodes showing a balance of polarities in the low-risk group than in the high-risk group (29% vs. 56%).

These findings must be considered preliminary, as the two groups differed from each other on a number of critical dimensions, including the history of intervention, the use of a clinician as a play partner in the high-risk group, socioeconomic status, and ethnicity. Certainly, application to a larger sample with more rigorous controls is necessary. Nevertheless, these results are encouraging in their suggestion that this adaptation of the GLOS can be used to detect differences between groups of children in representational activity.

Concluding Remarks

The examination of representational processes and their cognitive, affective, and social elaborations provides clinicians and developmentalists with a crucial view of the modes children have for structuring and organizing their knowledge of the world. We have presented both a theoretical rationale and an outline for a method of assessing representational processes in children from ages 2 to 4; this is an expansion to older age groups of the GLOS. The rationale derives from the developmental structuralist perspective (Greenspan, 1979), which assumes an underlying continuity between affective and cognitive processes, and which provides a cohesive approach to linking psychoanalytic and cognitive perspectives on development. We have applied the GLOS to three clinical cases and have described preliminary results of an effort to apply it empirically in comparing high-risk and normative groups. These efforts make evident the validity of this broad-based approach for clinicians and researchers alike.

REFERENCES

Bates, E., Benigni, L., Bretherton, I., Camaioni, L., & Volterra, V. (1979). *The emergence of symbols: Cognition and communication in infancy.* New York: Academic Press.

Bloom, L. (1973). *One word at a time: The use of single word utterances before syntax.* The Hague: Mouton.

Bowlby, J. (1979). *Attachment and loss.* New York: Basic Books.

Brown, R. (1973). *A first language: The early stages.* Cambridge, MA: Harvard University Press.

Erikson, E. (1940). Studies in interpretation of play: I. Clinical observations of play disruption in young children. *Genetic Psychology Monographs, 22,* 557–671.

Erikson, E. (1943). Clinical studies in childhood play. In R. C. Barker et al. (Eds.), *Child behavior and development* (pp. 411–428). New York: McGraw-Hill.

Fein, G. (1975). A transformational analysis of pretending. *Developmental Psychology, 11,* 291–296.

Fein, G. (1981). Pretend play in childhood: An integrative review. *Child Development, 52,* 1095–1118.

Fenson, L., Kagan, J., Kearsley, R., & Zelazo, P. (1976). The developmental progression of manipulative play in the first two years. *Child Development, 47,* 232–236.

Fenson, L., & Ramsay, D. (1980). Decentration and integration of play in the second year of life. *Child Development, 51,* 171–178.

Flavell, J. H. (1963). *The developmental psychology of Jean Piaget.* Princeton, NJ: Van Nostrand.

Flavell, J., Botkin, P., Fry, C., Wright, J., & Jarvis, P. (1968). The *development of role-taking and communication skills in children.* New York: Wiley.

Gouin-Decarie, T. C. (1965). *Intelligence and affectivity in early childhood: An experimental study of Jean Piaget's object concept and object relations.* New York: International Universities Press.

Greenspan, S. I. (1979). Intelligence and adaptation: An integration of psychoanalytic and Piagetian developmental psychology. *Psychological Issues,* Vol. 12, No. 3/4, Monograph 47/48. New York: International Universities Press.

Greenspan, S. I. (1981). Psychopathology and adaptation in infancy and early childhood: Principles of clinical diagnosis and preventive intervention. *Clinical Infant Reports,* No. 1. New York: International Universities Press.

Greenspan, S. I., and Lieberman, A. F. (1980). Infants, mothers, and their interaction: A quantitative clinical approach to developmental assessment. In S. I. Greenspan & G. H. Pollock (Eds.), *The course of life: Psychoanalytic contributions toward understanding personality development,* Vol. I, *Infancy and early childhood* (pp. 271–312). DHHS Pub. No. (ADM) 80–786. Washington, D.C.: U.S. Government Printing Office.

Greenspan, S. I., & Lourie, R. S. (1981). Developmental structuralist approach to the classification of adaptive and pathologic personality organizations: Infancy and early childhood. *American Journal of Psychiatry, 138* (6), 725–735.

Greenspan, S. I., Lourie, R. S., & Nover, R. A. (1979). A developmental approach to the classification of psychopathology in infancy and early childhood. In J. Noshpitz (Ed.), *The basic handbook of child psychiatry,* Vol. 2 (pp. 157–164). New York: Basic Books.

Greenspan, S. I., Wieder, S., Lieberman, A. F., Nover, R. A., Lourie, R. S., & Robinson, M. (Eds.) (1987). Infants in multirisk families: Case studies in preventive intervention. *Clinical Infant Reports,* No. 3. New York: International Universities Press.

Krauss, R., & Glucksberg, S. (1969). The development of communication: Competence as a function of age. *Child Development, 40,* 255–266.

Lourie, R. S. (1971). The first three years of life. *American Journal of Psychiatry, 127,* 1457–1463.

Lowe, M. (1975). Trends in the development of representational play—An observational study. *Journal of Child Psychology and Psychiatry, 16,* 33–47.

Mahler, M. S., Pine, F., & Bergman, A. (1975). *The psychological birth of the human infant, symbiosis and individuation.* New York: Basic Books.

Nelson, K. (1973). Structure and strategy in learning to talk. *Monographs of the Society for Research in Child Development, 38* (1–2, Serial No. 149).

Nicolich, L. (1977). Beyond sensorimotor intelligence: Measurement of symbolic sensitivity through analysis of pretend play. *Merrill-Palmer Quarterly, 23,* 89–99.

Peller, L. (1954). Libidinal phases, ego development, and play. In *Psycho-analytic study of the child* (Vol. 9., pp. 178–198). New York: International Universities Press.

Piaget, J. (1954). *The construction of reality in the child.* New York: Basic Books.

Piaget, J. (1972). The stages of the intellectual development of the child. In S. I. Harrison & J. F. McDermott (Eds.), *Childhood psychopathology* (pp. 129–137). New York: International Universities Press.

Piaget, J. (1968/1970). *Structuralism,* New York: Basic Books.

Sinclair, H. (1970). The transition from sensorimotor to symbolic activity. *Interchange, 1,* 119–126.

Sroufe, L., Waters, E., & Matas, L. (1977). Attachment as an organizational construct. *Child Development, 48,* 1184–1199.

Stern, D. (1985). *The interpersonal world of the infant: A view from psychoanalysis and developmental psychology.* New York: Basic Books.

Waelder, A. (1933). The psychoanalytic theory of play. *Psychoanalytic Quarterly, 2,* 208–224.

Wolff, P. (1963). Developmental and motivational concepts in Piaget's sensorimotor theory of intelligence. *Journal of the American Academy of Child Psychiatry, 2,* 225–243.

Wolff, P. (1965). Contributions of longitudinal studies to psychoanalytic theories. (Report of a Panel; Recorder: Roy Schafer.) Reported in *Journal of the American Psychoanalytic Association, 13,* 605–618.

2

The Relation Between Anxiety and Pretend Play

MALCOLM W. WATSON

One of the reasons that children's play is so fascinating yet paradoxical is the frequent observation of children enacting some theme that seems to be traumatic or negative for them. Common examples are a child playing out the anxious anticipation of beginning kindergarten or reenacting a recent hospitalization or a frightening movie that the child recently viewed. Why would anyone want to engage voluntarily in an activity that was painful or anxiety-provoking? Of course, we know that adults sometimes relive anxiety-provoking situations, often by talking about them. Indeed, play therapists base their therapy techniques and the interpretations that they make on the assumption that children use play, as adults use talk, to work through anxieties (Axline, 1947; Schaefer & O'Connor, 1983).

However, there is a seeming paradox in the use of play to work through anxieties. It would seem that the most reasonable process would be to find a distraction or stimulus substitution for the conditions causing the negative affect—in other words, to avoid the anxiety-provoking situation rather than to return to it. Yet, the tendency for individuals to return to and repeat or simulate the same negative antecedent conditions suggests that distraction or avoidance may not always be effective. The success of play therapy hinges in large part on the assumption that children benefit from reworking negative experiences in pretense.

A specific question addressed in this chapter is, how do children use play to deal with anxiety? Four naturalistic play episodes, all observed over a few months in the same 4-year-old girl, Nancy, whose parents had just separated, illustrate the kinds of play children can use. In the first episode, Nancy pretended to have a mother doll and a father doll leave a little girl without a babysitter. The girl doll climbed to the roof of the doll house and teetered, about to fall off. A week later, in the second episode, Nancy created a large doll family. As the story progressed, the doll family was scattered all over the world, and the girl doll drove around, without success, trying to pick up the family members and reunite them. In the third episode, Nancy pretended that the mother and father dolls were separated (as in her own family) but that they decided to live together again, and the entire family was happily reunited. The fourth episode is somewhat different. After attending the movie *Pinnochio* and becoming frightened by some of the scenes, Nancy refused to play with her mother using a Pinnochio theme and refused to look at the pictures of Pinnochio in a story book, even after her mother tried to get her involved in the story. These episodes illustrate the multifunctional nature of play, as described in the following section.

The Theoretical Functions of Anxiety-Invoked Play

Although the various functions of play described in contemporary reviews seem somewhat disparate, they can be thought of as falling on a continuum from direct mastery attempts to an avoidance of direct mastery (Ellis, 1973; Rubin, Fein, & Vandenberg, 1983; Singer, 1973). Although not mutually exclusive, there are essentially three alternative play actions on this continuum that are available for a child in dealing with anxiety: to directly repeat an anxiety-provoking situation, to modify the situation or its outcome, or to avoid the situation entirely. Individual reactions to anxiety and interpretation of meaning may lead different children or the same child in different circumstances to choose one alternative over another; however, one type of action usually overlaps another in much of children's play.

In the first episode of play described earlier, Nancy experienced the anxiety-provoking situation of the parents separating and possibly leaving her, which was repeated in her play regarding the child being left in a precarious situation without a babysitter. The child simply acted out the negative situation without really improving on it. Simply put, the story did not have a happy ending. According to Freud (1948), when children are traumatized by a negative event, they have an urge to restore the original, stable condition, and this leads to a compulsion to repeat the event to reduce the arousal associated with it. Elaborating on Freud's ideas, Waelder (1933) more explicitly described the psychoanalytic view of play. According to Waelder, in pretend play, children are attempting to understand and control strong emotions, to repeat negative experiences in order to make them more predictable, and to rehearse and look for solutions to unresolved conflicts.

At least three related processes seem to accomplish these functions. First, play can act as a catharsis to organize unfocused emotions and express them in a harmless way. Second, because an inability to understand an event seems to be a major cause of some fears, an individual may experience a vague, undefined anxiety because she does not comprehend a particular event. By using fantasy characters and plots, a child can create a concrete embodiment of the unfocused fears and can distance herself from these fears as she deals with them (Bettelheim, 1975). Third, by actively controlling the event rather than passively being a victim, the child gains control over the rate and amount of incoming stimuli (Erikson, 1963). By this active control, the child can divide stimuli into smaller portions and can repeatedly retrieve parts of the event until the entire event is assimilated (Piaget, 1962).

In repeating negative experiences in their pretense, children may be desensitizing themselves to the stimuli that caused the negative affect. This process of desensitization seems to work in the same way in which children are desensitized to repeated viewings of media violence such that they become insensitive to real violence (Cline, Croft, & Courrier, 1973). Through repetitions of a "re-presented" event, the person processes information, a little at a time, so that the event becomes more predictable and the negative affect of uncertainty is eliminated.

This desensitization process may actually lead to errors in a person's understanding of reality. A person may not actually be able to predict and control the stimuli but by this process simply deludes himself into thinking that the stimuli are predictable. Nevertheless, if children think they have understood an event and can control it, they can then shift from negative to positive affect (Geer, Davison, & Gatchel, 1970).

An additional anecdote may illustrate this process of desensitization to master emotions. Wickes (1927) told of a young girl who had trouble going from her bedroom to the bathroom in the dark because of her fear of numerous ghosts in the hallway. Only when she pretended to be a ghost herself was she able to overcome her fear by siding with the enemy, so to speak, thus taking charge of the negative aspects of the situation. As a ghost, she could conclude that ghosts were no more to be feared than she herself was to be feared. She thus gained predictability of what would happen to her and convinced herself of the lack of danger. In this example the girl's apparent lack of differentiation of fantasy and reality seems to have led to both the problem (i.e., fear of ghosts) and the solution (i.e., becoming a ghost). This incident brings up another question: If a person can distinguish reality from fantasy and is not deluded into assuming more predictability than actually is present, will she find fantasy to be of much value in resolving conflicts? Perhaps one reason for the decrease in pretend play with increasing age is the decreasing value of play as a desensitization technique because the child knows too much about fantasy and reality. However, before clearly differentiating fantasy and reality, a child may use pretense to sharpen the difference (DiLalla & Watson, 1988).

In the second play episode described earlier, Nancy again played out the theme of a separated family. In this story she pretended to work at getting the family back together again. She repeated a negative situation similar to her real-life situation, but rather than simply repeating it as she had experienced it, she attempted (without success) to modify the outcome. Thus, this episode of play is subtly different from the first episode of play. By being a more active participant in the play, Nancy was able to work on a solution in the play itself. However, at the same time, she was still showing a compulsion to repeat the negative experience.

In another example, a girl, who was frightened by a visit to her pediatrician from whom she had received an injection, persisted over several days in pretending to be a doctor giving shots. In this process, she gradually changed her doctor role from one who hurt patients to one who never gave injections and was friendly. The next time she went to the doctor, she told her mother that the doctor was not going to give her a shot. In this example, the child's modification of the re-presented event in order to create a happier outcome seemed to be effective in reducing her anxiety, although it is unclear whether she had deluded herself into believing that the physician would never give her an injection.

In the third play episode described previously, Nancy simply changed the negative situation to a positive situation: The separated family decided to get together again. A child who views his world as less than ideal or is not entirely satisfied with his own talents may wish to create an alternate world in fantasy (Ellis, 1973). In certain cases, children may want to change negative affect to positive affect but without an accompanying necessity to process new information. Fantasizing special, magical powers may compensate for real-life helplessness; creating imaginary friends may compensate for a lack of companions; and reuniting a separated family may compensate for a sense of loss.

Psychoanalytic theorists (Waelder, 1933) have defined this kind of fantasy as a form of wish fulfillment. As I see it, the major difference between repetition compulsion and wish fulfillment is the degree to which the child repeats the same anxiety-provoking situation unchanged and the degree to which the child modifies the negative situation and replaces the negative outcome with a positive outcome. Some play, as in the previous two examples, seems to begin as a repetition compulsion and evolve into a wish fulfillment. Positive affect is likely experienced as a compensatory replacement for the negative affect rather than simply as a desensitization to the negative experience.

The following example of play illustrates a case of wish fulfillment in which the children also showed some need to process new information and make a novel situation more predictable. When we moved recently and my two sons were having problems making new friends, almost every day for over a month they pretended to be space cadets in the company of their two closest friends whom they had left in their previous neighborhood. They constructed elaborate homes and space ships and carried out well-organized stories, but with each story including a central place for their two past (and now imaginary) friends, who now lived with them in their fantasies. As they became more familiar with their new neighborhood and peers, the fantasies involving their previous friends declined. Their pretend play compensated for a lack of friends, allowing them to experience positive affect in play.

The fourth play episode described earlier involved Nancy avoiding play that reminded her of the anxiety-provoking situation (the movie *Pinnochio*) and substituting completely different play scenarios. As in this example, some theorists (e.g., Erikson, 1940, 1963) speculate that play often functions at the other end of the continuum from those described thus far. Rather than engaging in pretend play to attempt to master new skills and gain control or to re-create more desired scenarios, children may use pretense simply as a way to escape temporarily or avoid an ongoing situation involving challenge, conflicts, problems, or any reminder of the antecedent anxiety.

It seems that an optimal level of anxiety exists for a particular child at a particular time that elicits anxiety-related play, such that too low a level will not elicit pretend play involving repetition compulsion or wish fulfillment and too high a level will elicit only pretend play for escape and avoidance of the anxiety (see chapter 10 by

Fein and Kinney). In summary, play may be a repetition of real life in order to rework and master a conflict head-on, a wish fulfillment in relation to real life in order to compensate for a lack of positive affect, or an escape from the anxiety-provoking situation altogether in order to avoid anxiety that is simply too intense to deal with at that time. As Levin and Wardwell (1971) argued regarding the use of doll play for research, it may be incorrect to assume that the child acts consistently over time or even in the same play episode. Clearly, one kind of play does not exclude other kinds. Play, like so many other human actions, is multidetermined.

The theoretical question now becomes an empirical one: What kinds of play do children use to deal with anxiety? Also, do individual style differences and antecedent conditions, such as anxiety level, determine the kind of play? If only a minority of children use play to work through conflicts, and then only in highly specific situations, should we use play to encourage children in general to repeat emotionally traumatic experiences? Should we expect that children in general will be better off if they can work out problems through play? At what point in a child's dealings with a trauma should we intervene?

Some authors have discussed case studies of play and intervention (Schaefer & O'Connor, 1983); however, they leave unanswered many of the questions just posed. Although case studies have contributed greatly to the content of our theories concerning the relation between anxiety and play (as previously discussed), they have not systematically tested these theories or the conditions under which most children will engage in anxiety-invoked play. The purpose of the rest of this chapter is to review the extant (though limited) experimental research regarding children's anxiety-invoked play to determine if any experimentally derived conclusions can augment and help us systematize our existing clinical knowledge.

Experimental Research on Anxiety-Invoked Play

On the one hand, naturalistic case studies, usually reported by play therapists, have provided us with most of our insights as to what kinds of play children use to deal with anxiety (Axline, 1947; Wickes, 1927). On the other hand, though we may wish for more systematic and normative validation, little experimental research is available to provide us with systematic tests of the process. The extant research only begins to answer the preceding questions.

Of course, each type of research has advantages and disadvantages. Naturalistic case studies are valuable in providing us with the details of antecedents leading up to play and with the details of the play itself. Naturalistic settings produce valid data on spontaneous play, whereas more contrived laboratory play settings do not lead all children to play as researchers intend them to do. On the other side, experimental studies can add comparisons of larger numbers of children under similar conditions and provide us with more controlled assessments of the frequencies of particular behaviors and the relationships between antecedent conditions and subsequent play. Experimental studies can be used to integrate systematically the results found in case studies, and then therapists, in turn, can assess these new insights in their subsequent case studies. Thus, both research paradigms should be used. By adding systematic, experimental research, we can supplement the information garnered from case studies and have a better grasp of the frequency and factors involved when children use anxiety-invoked play. Assessments of children's dealings with anxiety that has been experimentally induced will be reviewed to provide something of a baseline for children's susceptibility to engage in anxiety-invoked play. However, it should be noted from the outset that these questions are difficult to answer using methods that attempt to induce play in children.

One major difficulty in attempting to assess the relation between anxiety and pretend play is the lack of a standard definition for anxiety, which leads to varied, nonstandard measures. Anxiety has come to mean almost all forms of negative arousal associated with fear, stress, and worry (Lazarus, 1966). Because of the difficulty in defining anxiety, the studies to be reviewed have either neglected to assess levels and types of anxiety altogether or have used behavioral measures that are often crude in differentiating the intensities and nuances of a child's often hidden anxiety. Another caveat to keep in mind is that experimentally induced anxiety will not have the same significance for all children; thus, problems in obtaining equivalent comparisons across all children are created. (These problems in controlled comparisons exist for naturalistic observations as well.)

In perhaps the first study reported, Amen and Renison (1954) used a projective measure to assess children's general anxiety level and correlated anxiety with the overall amount and type of play shown. They found no relation between anxiety and amount of pretend play, but they did find that the most anxious children showed the greatest cognitive maturity in their play and the most goal-oriented play. Because this study did not assess the relation between specific anxiety conditions and play related to the anxieties, it does little to clarify the relation between anxiety and play.

In more systematic research of the relation between anxiety and play, Gilmore (1966) completed three studies. First, he compared hospitalized, school-age children with nonhospitalized children in their play with toys related to hospital settings. He noted the play duration with different types of toys and the toy preferences verbalized by the children. He found that the hospitalized children showed more play and expressed more preferences for hospital-related toys than did the nonhospitalized children. However, this difference could have been due to differences in attention and salience of toys caused by being hospitalized rather than to anxiety.

In the second study, Gilmore manipulated the anxiety of school-age children by telling them that they had the opportunity to join a special club but that the initiation would consist of a painful stimulus. In the first condition, children were led to believe that the anticipated initiation would be a loud, painful noise; in the second condition, the initiation was thought to be a bright, painful light; and in the third, control condition, no painful initiation was anticipated. Children were then left for a period of time to play with toys that involved either noise or light.

The results indicated that the auditory anxiety group played more with the auditory toys, as predicted, and the visual anxiety group and control group showed no differences from each other and played more with the visual toys.

In the third study, Gilmore added an auditory control group to assess whether the play differences were indeed due to the anxiety condition or to differences in toy salience. The procedure for this study was similar to that in the second study, except that one group was led to believe that it would receive a pleasant auditory stimulation for an initiation rather than a painful auditory stimulation. Thus, the effects of auditory salience could be controlled by comparing the negative auditory initiation group with the positive auditory initiation group. Gilmore found that in this study all groups showed a preference for the visual toys over the auditory toys. He concluded that the auditory group expecting the painful initiation, which surprisingly avoided the auditory toys, was made more anxious than the groups in the previous study and that the effects of anxiety showed a curviliniar relation, with extreme anxiety inhibiting anxiety-invoked play and causing avoidance of toys relevant to the anxiety situation (Erikson, 1940).

These studies indicated some relation between anxiety and the type of toys with which the children would subsequently play. In particular, they suggest that there may indeed be an optimal level of anxiety to elicit anxiety-related play. However, there were three major shortcomings in the studies. First, the anxiety measure was not precise in differentiating between anxiety levels in different conditions or individual differences in anxiety. Thus, the precise relation between anxiety and play is unknown. Second, there was no assessment of pretense and fantasy or the themes used in play, only an assessment of the amount of toy manipulation, so no assessment could be made of the kinds of play children used. Third, these studies were carried out with children of school age, who may not readily use pretend play for anxiety reduction. As noted, a major problem with this research, which will also emerge in the research to be reviewed, is that the same situation may elicit vastly different anxiety levels in different children. One child's positive challenge is another child's painful dread.

In more recent research, Gilmore, Best, and Eakins (1980) carried out two studies of play choices after inducing test anxiety, again in school-age children. Children in a high-anxiety condition were led to believe that they had to take an important geography test. In two other conditions, the induced test anxiety was medium and low, respectively. Anxiety questionnaires seemed to show that the induced anxiety level varied from high to low for the conditions as intended, though again, individual within-group differences were not assessed. In a second study, children's intelligence test scores and need achievement scores were also obtained. In both studies, after inducing test anxiety, the researchers observed children in their play choices with jigsaw puzzles that varied in their relevance to the geography test and in their complexity level. As in the previous research, these studies did not assess the relation between anxiety and actual pretense, so that no assessment of the use of repetition compulsion and wish fulfillment could be made. Results from both studies indicated that children's choices and time spent with puzzles did not depend on whether or not the puzzles were related to the geography test. However, in general, as anxiety levels increased, children's preferences for puzzle complexity increased, but the results were dependent on IQ and need achievement. Children who showed high need achievement and high IQ scores also showed an increased preference for complex puzzles as the anxiety level increased (from condition to condition). Children who showed low need achievement and low IQ scores showed no such increased preferences for complexity with increasing anxiety level.

Apparently, brighter, more achievement-oriented children reacted differently to stress, which seemed to increase their preference for a challenging task in this test anxiety situation. This finding suggests that children will show individual style differences in the approaches they take to anxiety-provoking situations.

Whitman (1980) also discussed style differences in individuals he called *repressors* and *sensitizors*. He thought that repressors (perhaps related to the low need-achievement children in the study) were effective in avoiding an anxiety-provoking situation, while sensitizors (perhaps related to the high need-achievement children in the study) were effective in confronting an anxiety-provoking situation (Harter, 1978). It may well be that repressors or children low in need achievement lean toward escape as the kind of play that is elicited by anxiety and that sensitizors or children high in need achievement lean toward repetition compulsion and wish fulfillment as the kind of play that is elicited by anxiety. However, more research is needed to test this hypothesis.

Barnett and Storm (1981) carried out the first experiment in preschoolers concerning anxiety-invoked play. Forty children were randomly assigned to either an experimental group or a control group. The experimental group saw a movie of *Lassie* that included a high adventure theme and ended with the characters, including Lassie, being in danger. The control group saw the same movie, but with the trouble being resolved and the movie having a happy ending. Thus, the researchers held constant the salience of the theme across the movie conditions. Both groups were observed in a pre- and a postmovie, free-play setting in which each child could play with various toys, including a Lassie doll.

The dependent measures were pre- and posttreatment and postplay anxiety scores, as measured by the Palmar Sweat Index (Dabbs, Johnson, & Leventhal, 1968); a happiness–sadness rating made by the children; the duration of play with the Lassie doll; the amount of pretense involving the Lassie theme; and eye contact and vocalizations concerning the toys.

Results indicated that, as intended, the experimental movie significantly increased children's anxiety scores over the scores of children in the control condition. (Again, no individual difference scores were reported.) The experimental group showed significantly more play with the Lassie doll than did the control group. Also, only the experimental group showed a significant reduction in anxiety following play. However, there was no clear relation between specific amount of play and anxiety reduction, so that the higher level of anxiety in the experimental condition could have allowed a greater reduction in anxiety regardless of the children's play. Boys in the experimental group showed significantly more pretense concerning the Lassie theme than did boys in the control group, but there were no differences between girls in the two groups. Rarely did children act out the specific Lassie story that they had observed in the movie.

This study shows a relation between induced anxiety and children's choices of toys and, to some extent, their pretense. It is perhaps significant that this study did not create a frightening condition, but rather one of mild conflict with lack of resolution for the children. The children did not tend to re-create the traumatic aspects of the filmed story but instead changed the play to a pleasant situation; they often hugged the Lassie doll and showed concern for it.

In a follow-up study, Barnett (1984) attempted to assess the effects of a naturally occurring anxiety situation on children's play. She assessed children's play centered on their separation from their mothers on the first day of nursery school. Using the Palmer Sweat Index and a paper-and-pencil test, she divided 3-year-olds into high- and low-anxiety groups. These children were then randomly assigned to a free-play condition or a no-play (storytelling) condition in solitary and group settings.

The results indicated that the highly anxious children in the free-play condition showed a greater decrease in anxiety than did the children in the story condition. Also, the highly anxious children exhibited more pretend play than manipulative or functional play and more pretend play than did the low-anxiety children. In addition, for highly anxious children, peer presence seemed to inhibit the reduction of anxiety, while solitary play seemed to be most effective in reducing anxiety. This study showed that anxiety level influenced the type of play chosen (pretense) and that pretend play was preferred after an anxiety-provoking situation.

In three related studies, our research group also assessed the relation between anxiety and pretend play in preschoolers. Because fairy tales tend to include many anxiety-provoking aspects that are central to the concerns of young children (Bettelheim, 1975; Crain, D'Alessio, McIntyre, & Smoke, 1983), we chose a well-known fairy tale, *Hansel and Gretel*, as the stimulus to induce mild anxiety in children.

Study 1

In the first study, nine 4-year-olds and nine 6-year-olds were tested in their day-care center. One experimenter presented the Hansel and Gretel story to each child individually, with an accompanying picture book. The narration and dialogue were played from a recorder and included music and sound effects. To simplify the story, it began when Hansel and Gretel were lost in the woods and did not include their separation from their parents. The major conflict consisted only of a frightening witch who held Hansel and Gretel captive and wanted to eat them. The story was resolved as Hansel and Gretel managed to push the witch into the oven and escape.

A second experimenter rated the child's anxiety during the story on four levels in each of four categories: body posture, eye gaze, facial expression, and verbalizations. Based on these scores, children were divided into low-, medium-, and high-anxiety groups, with six children in each group. Next, each child was left alone in the room and was told that he or she could play with any toys. Four sets of toys were placed on the floor in front of the child. The toy sets consisted of (1) a fantasy-irrelevant set (i.e., irrelevant to the Hansel and Gretel story) that included an ambulance and doctor dolls; (2) a fantasy-relevant set that included a candy house and Hansel, Gretel, and witch dolls; (3) a low fantasy-irrelevant set that included a picture of a duck to color and magic markers; and (4) a low fantasy-relevant set that included a picture of a witch to color and magic markers. (Drawing and coloring tasks have been found to elicit less pretense than do dolls and other toys; Rubin et al., 1983.)

The observers rated the actual play based on three measures: (1) whether pretense or nonpretense was the modal form of play during the session, (2) whether the modal theme of play for the session was relevant or irrelevant to the Hansel and Gretel theme, and (3) the closeness of the play to the Hansel and Gretel story and whether frightening aspects were included. Interobserver reliabilities for all measures were high.

Results indicated that there were no sex or age differences for any of the dependent variables, and there was no relation between the number of children showing pretend play as the modal form of play and anxiety level. However, anxiety level was related to the number of children showing relevant versus nonrelevant play as the modal form. All six medium-anxiety children showed relevant play as the modal form, compared to only two of the high-anxiety children and three of the low-anxiety children. Also, a correlation of .81 was found between anxiety scores for the low- and medium-anxiety groups and the closeness of the play to the Hansel and Gretel story.

Thus, the results suggest that medium anxiety led to more play relevant to the anxiety-provoking theme than did low or high anxiety. The resulting play was both a direct repetition (repetition compulsion) of the story and a modification of the story (wish fulfillment).

Study 2

In the first study, the effect of anxiety on children's play choices was assessed. In the second study, the effect of play with toys related to the anxiety-provoking situation versus play with toys unrelated to the anxiety-provoking situation was assessed to determine if anxiety-relevant play would reduce anxiety more than would irrelevant play.

The second study was carried out at the same day-care center used in the first study but with 24 children who had not been in the first study. The initial procedure of presenting the Hansel and Gretel story to each child and assessing anxiety level was completed in the same manner as in the first study. After the story presentation, children were randomly assigned to one of the four toy sets used in the first study, so that six children each were allowed to play with each toy set—fantasy-irrelevant, fantasy-relevant, low fantasy-irrelevant, and low fantasy-relevant. After the play session, each child was again rated on the same anxiety-level scale and asked questions concerning his or her preferences. A pre- to postplay, anxiety-reduction score was computed for each child. Results showed no effects of toy set on reductions in anxiety level or on children's preferences for the various parts of the story. There was also no relation between anxiety levels and duration of pretend play shown by the children.

Why didn't the expected results in this study occur? Children in this study showed such low levels of anxiety to begin with that they were probably unable to decrease their anxiety by any significant amount. Although the conditions were similar to those in the first study, it may have been that children from the first study had already discussed the Hansel and Gretel story with the children in the second study and thus had desensitized them to any anxiety-provoking aspects of the story presentation. In any case, this study did not provide any evidence that play with toys (whether relevant or irrelevant to the anxiety-provoking situation) reduced subsequent anxiety.

Study 3

In the previous two studies, the sample size was quite small. In this last study, 45 preschool children were tested individually in a laboratory play room. Each child's parent was present in the play room throughout the session.

Each child was randomly assigned to one of three anxiety conditions, with an equal number of children in each condition. In the first condition—nonanxiety arousal—children observed a story presented on filmstrip. The story was about a monkey that tried on various caps. The story included no anxiety-provoking situations. In the second condition—low anxiety arousal—children observed another story on filmstrip about a witch who tried to frighten people but only made them laugh. This story was added to control for the salience of witches but only in a low-anxiety context. In the third condition—high anxiety arousal—children observed the Hansel and Gretel story on filmstrip. This version of Hansel and Gretel included more anxiety-provoking pictures and sound effects than did the version used in the first two studies. After presentation of the filmstrip, an experimenter asked the child a series of questions concerning aspects of the story. Then the child was allowed to play as he or she wished during a free-play period.

The toys used in the free-play period again consisted of four sets, as in the previous studies, that controlled for relevance of the toys to the filmstrips and fantasy orientation. Scorers rated children's anxiety during the filmstrip viewing, after the filmstrip viewing, and after the free-play period. Also, throughout the free play, scorers rated the fantasy level for each child (from no fantasy to complex and supernatural fantasy) and the relevance of the play to the filmstrip shown. Interobserver reliability for all measures was high.

As was intended, the results showed that, after children viewed the filmstrips, their mean anxiety levels varied from low to high according to the filmstrip viewed. Age was also correlated with anxiety level such that older children showed more anxiety than did younger children. Contrary to expectations, analyses showed no relation between filmstrip viewed and the toy sets preferred, level of fantasy shown, or relevance of the toys preferred. There was a significant condition effect for the amount of anxiety reduction from pre- to postplay. Children in the high-anxiety condition showed the greatest reduction in anxiety. However, because a higher level of anxiety was initially manifest in the high-anxiety condition, there was greater room for a subsequent decrease than in the other conditions. There was no relation of anxiety decrease to amount or type of pretend play.

One important condition effect did emerge. Significantly more children in the high-anxiety condition (i.e., those viewing the Hansel and Gretel filmstrip) than in the other two conditions showed play with the witch doll in which the witch was transformed into a helpless witch rather than simply imitating the story. This finding suggests that when children did use pretend play, they showed wish fulfillment through modifications of the story.

In this last study, the anxiety seemed to be attenuated by the presence of the parent throughout the session. During the filmstrip presentation, most children made verbal and physical contact with their parents and looked at them for reassurance. Although pretend play may function to reduce anxiety, it is certainly not the only means. In this study, children first sought comfort and apparent anxiety reduction from their parents.

Most anxiety-invoked play may occur only after a hiatus from the anxiety-provoking situation rather than directly following it, as was tested in all the studies reviewed. A "cooling-off" period may be necessary for children to be able to use play to process information or to rework the anxiety, because when children do not have control over their immediate anxiety, they may not be able to deal with any additional anxiety, even if it is only in fantasy (see chapter 10 by Fein and Kinney). One example from Study 3 supports this view. One parent brought a second child to the experiment several days after bringing her first child. On the second visit, she reported that the first child, who had seen the Hansel and Gretel filmstrip but had shown little relevant play in the laboratory, had acted out the characters and theme at home over the last 2 days. Future research should assess the effects of anxiety on play after various periods of delay.

Conclusions

This chapter reviewed two bases of information regarding anxiety and pretend play—theoretical explanations of functions and experimental research. It should be clear from this review that the experimental research does not test all the explanations generated by the theories. This research is only a beginning, but although the combined research shows some contradictions in findings, some preliminary conclusions from the research can be drawn to answer the question What kinds of play do children use to deal with anxiety? Our next step should be to substantiate these conclusions through both group and case studies.

1. Regardless of the anxiety produced in a child, simply making a theme or setting salient often increases manipulation and play with toys and objects related to that theme.

2. Anxiety is one form of salience that sometimes increases a child's manipulation and play with relevant toys, but this manipulation does not necessarily include pretense related to the anxiety theme. Some of the research showed an increase in pretend play versus nonpretend play following an anxiety-provoking situation, and other research showed no change in pretend play.

3. Just as anxiety does not necessarily lead to pretending, it does not necessarily lead to children's preferences for relevant props and toys. However, most studies showed a relation between antecedent anxiety and subsequent play relevant to the anxiety-provoking situation.

4. Research does not strongly support the assumption that anxiety is decreased after anxiety-invoked play. Although some anxiety decreases were found, they were often not related to the type of play, the specific duration of play, or the amount of pretense involved. Clearly, more research is needed linking individual anxiety levels to anxiety reduction and assessing under what circumstances anxiety reduction will occur. Indeed, one of the most neglected issues in the research is the relation of individual differences to anxiety levels and subsequent play. The same precipitating

situation can induce vastly different anxiety levels in different children. Some of the research just reviewed suggests that differences such as need achievement and other style differences will determine whether a person finds a situation too anxiety-provoking or about optimum to lead to relevant pretend play or to avoidance. Also, different clinical populations (e.g., sexually abused children) and well children could be compared to assess the relation between individual anxiety levels and amount of external stress as they both influence pretend play.

5. When anxiety-invoked play does occur, it is quite sensitive to subtle differences in anxiety level. There seems to be a curvilinear relation between anxiety level and subsequent play. Low anxiety does not elicit anxiety-relevant play, and high anxiety leads to escape and avoidance of anxiety-relevant play. The view of an optimal level of anxiety to induce play seems to be correct, and thus the need for sensitivity to individual anxiety levels is crucial.

6. When children do engage in extensive relevant play and pretense related to the anxiety-provoking situation, it probably occurs some time after the initial trauma—after a cooling-off period. This may be especially true for situations involving fear or extremely high arousal, in which the negative affect inhibits play rather than motivates it. This conclusion is consonant with the idea that play is used by the child to subdivide negative or confusing stimuli so that they can be processed in smaller doses. In cases of acute fear and anxiety, elimination of highly arousing props or pictures, rather than their use, may allow the child to deal with only a small bit of the traumatic theme. In the initial example in which Nancy refused to play at a Pinnochio theme or even look at the book, a cooling-off period and an elimination of anxiety-related props may have made it possible for her to reenact the traumatic movie. More research regarding delayed pretend play after a cooling-off period would help us to understand the optimal timing of interventions.

7. The frequency of anxiety-invoked play in normal children may not be as high as supposed. It certainly does not emerge with every anxiety-provoking situation. If adults try to channel a child's activities with an eye toward constructing a setting that would facilitate the child's play, what will this intervention do to the optimal amount of such play, as shown by children in spontaneous situations? We simply need more research in this area.

The findings from the experimental studies in many situations add convergent validity to the knowledge gleaned from case studies and in other situations provide an impetus to test tentative conclusions in more detail. The best approach to further our knowledge would be to integrate both group and case studies and, in particular, to apply some experimental methods to play observations in naturalistically induced anxiety situations. Clearly, the questions are complex and could benefit from several kinds of research.

In addition, researchers should not neglect age as a factor because older children seem to be more likely to shift to drawing, stories, and direct discussion as means of processing negative experiences. It would be helpful to have research that would determine the age shifts in children's use of anxiety-invoked play in spontaneous situations.

One final caveat regarding anxiety-invoked play should be considered. For many children, at least some of the time, play seems to serve a communicative function in which the play per se is unimportant. Thus, adults need to be aware of this possible function as well.

A last anecdote illustrates this communicative function in play. A 5-year-old whom I know had been sexually abused by her father when she was 3 years of age. Although her mother had gained some evidence that this had occurred and had involved her daughter in therapy, the girl had not been able to discuss the incidents with her mother. One day the girl pretended that two dolls were having a conversation, and she proceeded to speak so loudly that her mother could hear from another room. She had one doll say, ''My father used to hurt me and touch my body all over and in places where I didn't want him to. Did your father ever do that to you?'' The second doll answered, ''No, mine didn't.'' The first doll said, ''He hurt me, and he told me not to tell my mother or he would be mad at me. I don't know what to do.'' And the second doll replied, ''I think you should tell your mother.'' The girl's mother then entered and told the girl that her friend had been very wise because it was all right to tell her mother anything. This incident allowed the girl to discuss the traumatic experiences directly with her mother but, in a clever way, she had communicated this information without violating her father's prohibitions. This incident suggests that children's use of pretend play as repetition compulsion and wish fulfillment does not exclude their use of play simply as a technique to communicate information in the same way as do the adult specialists who observe them.

ACKNOWLEDGMENTS

Preparation of this chapter was supported by a Mazer Fund Grant administered through Brandeis University. The author wishes to thank Marvin W. Futtersak, Karen Levine, Nathan E. Robinson, Aaron Rapoport, Christine McVinney, Deborah Begner, and children of the Concord Children's Center for their help in carrying out some of the studies reported herein.

REFERENCES

Amen, E., & Renison, N. (1954). A study of the relationship between play patterns and anxiety in young children. *Genetic Psychology Monographs, 50*, 3–41.

Axline, V. M. (1947). *Play therapy.* Boston: Houghton Mifflin.

Barnett, L. A. (1984). Research note: Young children's resolution of distress through play. *Journal of Child Psychology and Psychiatry and Allied Disciplines, 25*, 477–483.

Barnett, L. A., & Storm, B. (1981). Play, pleasure, and pain: The reduction of anxiety through play. *Leisure Sciences, 4*, 161–175.

Bettelheim, B. (1975). *The uses of enchantment: The meaning and importance of fairy tales.* New York: Knopf.

Cline, V., Croft, R., & Courrier, S. (1973). Desensitization of children to television violence. *Journal of Personality and Social Psychology, 27*, 360–365.

Crain, W. C., D'Alessio, E., McIntyre, B., & Smoke, L. (1983). The impact of hearing a fairy tale on children's immediate behavior. *Journal of Genetic Psychology, 143*, 9–17.

Dabbs, J. M., Johnson, J. E., & Leventhal, H. (1968). Palmar sweating: A quick and simple measure. *Journal of Experimental Psychology, 78*, 347–350.

DiLalla, L. F., & Watson, M. W. (1988). Differentiation of fantasy and reality: Preschoolers' reactions to interruptions in their play. *Developmental Psychology, 24,* 286–291.

Ellis, M. J. (1973). *Why people play.* Englewood Cliffs, NJ: Prentice-Hall.

Erikson, E. H. (1940). Studies of the interpretation of play: I. Clinical observations of play disruption in young children. *Genetic Psychology Monographs, 22,* 557–671.

Erikson, E. H. (1963). *Childhood and society,* 2nd ed. New York: Norton.

Freud, S. (1948). *Beyond the pleasure principle.* London: Hogarth.

Geer, J. H., Davison, G. C., & Gatchel, R. I. (1970). Reduction of stress in humans through nonveridical perceived control of aversive stimulation. *Journal of Personality and Social Psychology, 16,* 731–738.

Gilmore, J. B. (1966). The role of anxiety and cognitive factors in children's play behavior. *Child Development, 37,* 397–416.

Gilmore, J. B., Best, H., & Eakins, S. L. (1980). Coping with test anxiety: Individual differences in seeking complex play materials. *Canadian Journal of Behavioral Science, 12,* 241–254.

Harter, S. (1978). Effectance motivation reconsidered: Toward a developmental model. *Human Development, 21,* 34–64.

Lazarus, R. S. (1966). *Psychological stress and the coping process.* New York: McGraw-Hill.

Levin, H., & Wardwell, E. (1971). Research uses of doll play. In R. E. Herron & B. Sutton-Smith (Eds.), *Child's play* (pp. 145–184). New York: Wiley.

Piaget, J. (1962). *Play, dreams and imitation in childhood.* New York: Norton.

Rubin, K. H., Fein, G. G., & Vandenberg, B. (1983). Play. In E. M. Hetherington (Ed.), *Handbook of child psychology,* 4th ed., Vol. IV: *Socialization, personality, and social development* (pp. 693–774). New York: Wiley.

Schaefer, C. E., & O'Connor, K. J. (Eds.). (1983). *Handbook of play therapy.* New York: Wiley.

Singer, J. L. (1973). *The child's world of make-believe: Experimental studies of imaginative play.* New York: Academic Press.

Waelder, R. (1933). The psychoanalytic theory of play. *Psychoanalytic Quarterly, 2,* 208–224.

Whitman, R. D. (1980). *Adjustment: The development and organization of human behavior.* New York: Oxford University Press.

Wickes, F. G. (1927). *The inner world of childhood.* Englewood Cliffs, NJ: Prentice-Hall.

3

Play, Cure, and Development: A Developmental Perspective on the Psychoanalytic Treatment of Young Children

W. GEORGE SCARLETT

Children younger than 4 pose special problems for therapists. Their insecurities about separation make the establishment of working relationships difficult, and their immature language renders "talk therapy" inadequate. Furthermore, their struggles to represent experience overshadow any need they might have to undo old, maladaptive representations. Play provides answers to all three of these special problems because play is the young child's means of relating, communicating, and developing the capacity to represent. So, treating young children depends less on therapists' ability to interpret and more on their ability to play and develop play.

This characterization of therapy with young children may seem obvious and oversimplified. That play is important in treating the very young is indeed obvious. But just why and how play is important is not. Nor is it obvious that interpretation serves only a minor role with this age group since analytically minded therapists often claim otherwise. And though the characterization is simple, what it implies is not. Ability to play in therapeutic ways is both complex and subtle because it demands skill at introducing clinical issues into play while being sensitive to a child's capacity to structure play in collaboration with another.

The discussion that follows offers a developmental perspective on the psychoanalytic treatment of young children. It takes as a given that psychoanalysis has both cured the very young and clarified the nature of their problems. However, it questions the way analysts traditionally have focused on the content of play and its hidden meaning while often ignoring its structure and the degree to which it is shared.

Of course, this distinction between psychoanalytic and developmental perspectives is somewhat arbitrary. Psychoanalysis is itself a developmental theory, one that has provided a wealth of insights into how children come to control impulses, take on identities, and adopt new love objects. However, historically, psychoanalysis has been less concerned about constructing a theory of play and its development and more concerned about interpreting play's content. Winnicott (1986) makes the same point:

> I am reaching towards a new statement of playing, and it interests me when I seem to see in the psychoanalytic literature the lack of a useful statement on the subject of play. . . . The psychoanalyst has been too busy using play content to look at the playing child, and to write about playing as a thing in itself. (p. 39)

Winnicott offers an excellent example of what this discussion is all about. At first glance, his views on play and therapy appear to be identical to those from a developmental perspective. He writes:

> Psychotherapy takes place in the overlap of two areas of playing, that of the patient and that of the therapist. Psychotherapy has to do with two people playing together. The corollary of this is that where playing is not possible then the work done by the therapist is directed towards bringing the patient from a state of not being able to play into a state of being able to play. (p. 38)

However, the way Winnicott understands why even young children sometimes cannot play puts him within the psychoanalytic tradition of focusing on play's content to the exclusion of considering play's structure and the child's capacity to collaborate—as I shall try to demonstrate later in this discussion.

For now, we need to understand more about where differences between psychoanalytic and developmental perspectives on play originate. This requires understanding basic assumptions that analysts have held about fantasy, symbol formation, and consciousness—assumptions that developmentalists have questioned in the course of offering their own view of play.

Assessing Play from a Psychoanalytic Perspective

Let me begin with a brief, very simple summary of two common assumptions that psychoanalytically oriented clinicians have held about play. The first is that play offers a window on the unconscious and its troubling, often conflicting emotions. This assumption underlies Anna Freud's (1965) listing of play and the fantasies behind play as among the principal "items of childhood behavior" to be used to understand a child's unconscious. She writes:

> The well-known sublimatory occupations of painting, modeling, water and sand play point back to anal and urethral preoccupation. The dismantling of toys because of the wish to know what is inside betrays sexual curiosity. It is even significant in

which manner a small boy plays with his railway: whether his main pleasure is derived from staging crashes (as symbols of parental intercourse); whether he is predominantly concerned with building tunnels and underground lines (expressing interest in the inside of the body); whether his cars and buses have to be loaded heavily (as symbols of the pregnant mother); or whether speed and smooth performance are his main concern (as symbols of phallic efficiency). (p. 19)

The second assumption is that children do not know the deeper meaning of their play because they have repressed it, actively kept it out of consciousness to avoid feelings that make them anxious. Melanie Klein (1955) is perhaps the best-known example of a clinician operating under this second assumption. She writes:

Since my earliest case, my interest has been centered on anxieties and the defenses against them. This emphasis on anxiety led me deeper and deeper into the unconscious and into the fantasy life of the child. . . . I also ventured into new territory from another angle; the contents of fantasies and anxieties and the defenses against them, which I found in young children and interpreted to them, were at that time still largely undiscovered. (p. 236)

Taken together, these two assumptions have fostered an emphasis on evaluating the contents of children's fantasies and on treating children by interpreting to them the meaning of their play. But for developmentalists, this psychoanalytic approach presents problems having to do with the underlying assumptions and with the focus on interpreting play's content.

The First Assumption

With respect to the first assumption, most agree that children are often unaware of all that their play symbolizes. However, developmentalists have disagreed with the way that psychoanalysts have sometimes determined play's meaning. At the heart of this disagreement is a distinction between two types of symbols.

This first assumption rests on a distinction between primary and secondary symbols. Children's drinking from empty cups and pretending to sleep may be primary symbols representing nothing more than what they appear to represent and showing themselves to be conscious by the fact that children sometimes announce their meaning ("I'm drinking Kool-Aid") or laugh to show they are "just pretending." In other words, like Freud's cigar, symbols may represent just what they appear on the surface to represent and nothing more.

In contrast, secondary symbols express deeper, largely unconscious concerns, concerns that relate directly to troublesome feelings and hence are significant to the clinician. In Winnicott's (1977) book on his treatment of a 2½-year-old girl nicknamed "The Piggle," he often assumed that the Piggle was producing secondary symbols expressing her concerns over the birth of her younger sister. For example, he writes:

Then she took a round object with a centerpiece that at one time belonged to the axle of a carriage and said: "Where did this come from?" I answered realistically, and then I said, "And where did the baby come from?" She replied: "De cot." At this point, she took a little man figure and tried to push it into the driver's seat of a toy car. It wouldn't go in because it was too big; she tried putting it through the window and tried every way.

"It won't go in; it's stuck." Then she took a little stick and pushed it in the window and said: "Stick goes in." I said something about man putting something into woman to make baby. She said: "I've got a cat. Next time I'll bring the pussycat, another day." (p. 10)

Winnicott's notes on this interview indicate that he took the Piggle's response to his last interpretation as her attempt to change the subject because it made her too anxious. He continued to assume that she had indeed produced secondary symbols representing deeper concerns and troublesome feelings surrounding the birth of her younger sibling.

I give this example because it indicates the developmentalist's problem with the distinction between primary and secondary symbols. The problem is that often it is extremely difficult to identify when symbols are secondary and when they are simply primary. Frequently, there are no tests to distinguish the two. In this example, it appears that Winnicott would have treated both interest and lack of interest in his talk about babies as evidence for the presence of secondary symbols.

The criticism that analysts' interpretations are frequently untestable or ungrounded in observation is old and perhaps tiresome. But it needs mentioning in a discussion of developmental and psychoanalytic approaches to play because it pinpoints where psychoanalysts and developmentalists historically have disagreed. The psychoanalyst's bias has been to attribute more to the child than can be proven and to go beyond observation in an effort to bring the child face to face with his or her problems.

In contrast, the developmentalist's bias has been to attribute to the child only that which can be proven or at least tied to observation. In Stern's words, developmentalists deal with the *observed* child as contrasted with the *clinical* child reconstructed by theory in the course of clinical practice with adults as well as with children (Stern, 1985). So, in the example of the Piggle, a developmentalist might have argued that the little girl's poking a stick through the car window was nothing more than a form of sensorimotor exploration, a holdover from infancy, accompanied by a rudimentary form of symbolizing typical of 2½-year-olds in which realistic props (the toy car and the figure of a man) were used to support a beginning attempt at symbolizing. Developmentalists, then, have been reluctant to attribute deeper meaning to symbols when that meaning is not obvious.

This tendency of developmentalists to resist calling symbols secondary might suggest that they have ignored the affective side of fantasy play. Indeed, they have focused more on cognitive than on affective development, but not by ignoring affectivity altogether. Take Vygotsky (1976) as an example. Vygotsky is known primarily for his insights into cognition, but to him play has its origins in emotions, not thoughts. He writes:

> From the viewpoint of the affective sphere, it seems to me that play is invented at the point when unrealizable tendencies appear in development. This is the way a

very young child behaves: he wants a thing and must have it at once. . . . For example, the child wants to be in his mother's place, or wants to be a rider on a horse. This desire cannot be fulfilled right now. What does the very young child do if he sees a passing cab and wants to ride in it whatever may happen? If he is a spoiled and capricious child, he will demand that his mother put him in the cab at any cost or he may throw himself on the ground right there in the street, etc. . . . If he is an obedient child, used to renouncing his desires, he will go away, or his mother will offer him some candy, or simply distract him with some stronger effect and he will renounce his immediate desire.

In contrast to this, a child over three will show his own particular conflicting tendencies; on the one hand, a large number of long-term needs and desires will appear, which cannot be fulfilled at once but which, nevertheless, are not passed over like whims; on the other hand, the tendency towards immediate realization of desires is almost completely retained.

Henceforth play occurs such that the explanation of why a child plays must always be interpreted as the imaginary, illusory realization of unrealizeable desires. (p. 538)

Vygotsky's belief in the adaptive function of fantasy play has been shared by psychoanalysts. Both he and analysts have agreed that fantasy play serves the important function of helping children cope with frustrations. But as a comparison of Vygotsky and Anna Freud illustrates, analysts and developmentalists have differed over which desires and which frustrations are dealt with in play. Unlike Anna Freud, Vygotsky stayed quite close to what can be observed—so that one might expect him to have interpreted the Piggle's play simply as her realizing a frustrated desire to drive a car.

The Second Assumption

The second assumption, that children do not know the deeper meaning of their play because they have repressed it, also presents the problem of being untestable. But it raises a more fundamental issue concerning the nature of consciousness in young children and the role of fantasy play in the development of consciousness. Furthermore, it brings out the second common criticism leveled at psychoanalysis by developmentalists, namely, that psychoanalysis isn't developmental enough and often attributes more ability to young children than they possess.

This second criticism has been directed at the way analysts have used the concept of repression. The concept of repression provides a good explanation for why adults who are otherwise conscious and self-aware can at times be so unconscious and so unaware. However, repression seems less helpful when applied to young children. To the developmentalist, it is far simpler to assume that the reason young children often do not know the deeper meaning of their play is that their capacity for consciousness is still undeveloped. Piaget (1962) made this argument as follows:

The essential point is that the field of unconscious symbolism is wider than that of repression, and consequently of what can be censored. The question that then arises is whether its unconscious character, i.e., the subject's ignorance of its meaning, does not merely result from the fact that he is incapable of direct and complete consciousness of it. For Freud, censorship is a product of consciousness, and symbolism a product of unconscious associations which elude censorship. In our opinion, it is worth considering whether these two terms might not be reversed, censorship being merely the expression of the unconscious, uncomprehended character of the symbol, and the symbol itself being the result of a beginning of conscious assimilation, i.e., an attempt at comprehension. (p. 191)

From this developmental point of view, then, fantasy play in early childhood is not so much a mask of reality as it is a beginning attempt at understanding reality through re-presenting it on a symbolic level. As symbols of wishes, fears, and conflicts, the symbols of fantasy play may not be completely understood by the child. Nevertheless, by creating them, the child has taken a step beyond the even more unconscious state of infancy.

Certainly, analysts have agreed that fantasy play can function as a step towards consciousness. However, I think it is fair to say that, historically, developmentalists have been less inclined to view unconscious symbols in young children's play as products of repression and more inclined to view them as products of undeveloped capacities for consciousness.

Having looked at basic assumptions underlying the analytic treatment of play, we can turn now to how developmentalists have understood play and its development in early childhood.

Assessing Play from a Developmental Perspective

The developmental tradition has assessed play primarily in terms of its *structural development* and the degree to which it is *shared*. Fantasy play provides the best example—in part because it has received so much attention from developmentalists and psychoanalysts and in part because it is so central to therapy. Let us begin, then, with a developmental perspective on assessing fantasy play's structural development.

Assessing Fantasy Play's Structural Development

The *structure* of fantasy play refers to how characters, events, and scenes are depicted and organized into an integrated whole. Unstructured fantasy play stays close to what is perceived and presents only disconnected events. So, for example, dolls may be pushed and pulled across the floor but never made to ''talk,'' reveal inner thoughts and feelings, or interact. Or the children may play at ironing with toy irons and driving toy cars—without reference to what might be imagined (wrinkled ball gowns, robbers up ahead in their getaway car, etc.), without extending the pretense into a logical sequence of events (iron gown, put it on, then go to the ball; drive car, crash, then go to the repair shop, etc.), and without indicating how they are playing a role or character rather than themselves.

Structured fantasy play, then, is a kind of narrative or story. As an example of structurally developed fantasy play, take the following narrative elicited with props (toy elephant, toy tiger, etc.) after an examiner began a "story" about jungle animals making fun of a purple elephant:

> At 4:6 . . . C makes the elephant cry and wander away saying, "nobody likes me, ooohhh." The other animal figures are made to taunt him. "You are so stupid. Who ever heard of a purple elephant?" The elephant figure is walked to a new spot on the floor; the child speaks to the observer: "Pretend this was a big lake and that he had just got purple paint on him, and he washed it off." The child makes the elephant hop into the lake, where she scrubs at him then walks him over to the group of teasing animals. "Hey, look at me, now I look good so you don't tease me." She makes the tiger figure come over and walk around the elephant. "You are just like the other elephants; we don't tease you anymore." (Scarlett & Wolf, 1979, p. 35)

Here, the structure of the story (fantasy) is clearly developed. Characters are made to talk and interact; events move in a logical sequence. The whole scene is much more than what is conveyed simply by looking at the props and how they are moved around the living room floor.

Recent research on young children's fantasy play provides excellent, detailed descriptions of just how these and other aspects of structural development unfold (Bretherton, 1984; Howes, with Unger and Matheson, 1992; Singer & Singer, 1990; Watson & Fisher, 1980; Wolf, 1981). But this research is motivated by more than the desire to describe. Developmentalists have been keen to assess fantasy play's structure because it reveals underlying thought structures and ways that young children construe the world. So, for example, Wolf (1981) has argued that children start to depict fantasy characters with inner thoughts and feelings at about the age of 3 because it is then that they are first able to think about their own subjectivity and that of others.

More recent research has assessed the structure of fantasy play to measure social and emotional development. For example, Slade (1987) found relations between the structural development of toddlers' fantasy play and the degree to which they were successful at separating from their mothers.

Structural analysis is, of course, known to psychoanalysis—especially in the tradition of psychoanalytic ego psychology. Anna Freud (1965) provides the following example:

> A five-year-old, in his play with "little world" toys, staged the element of "fighting" quite tentatively and soberly by letting the small family dolls engage in quarrels with each other; but as the play progressed, the element of fighting slipped out of control and passed from the people to the inanimate objects until at the climax all the furniture was involved and the kitchen sink engaged in a wild, "hand to hand" battle with the table and cupboards. (p. 100)

Here, then, the boy's losing control over his own aggressive impulses revealed itself in the structure of his play or, more specifically, in the dedifferentiation of animate and inanimate characters.

However, despite ego psychology, examples of structural analysis within the psychoanalytic tradition are few compared to the plethora of examples where analysts have focused on content. The case of the Piggle is more typical of the analytic tradition. In his initial interviews, Winnicott never comments on the Piggle's depicting fantasy characters whose actions are clear but whose thoughts and feelings are not. Nor does he comment on the absence of organized plots and fanciful scenes in the Piggle's play. Content, not structure, remains the focus throughout.

Assessing the Degree to Which Fantasy Play Is Shared

During the past 15 years, developmentalists have focused more and more on early social development (Greenberg, Cicchetti, & Cummings, 1990; Damon, 1983; Richards, 1974). The shift away from focusing on strictly cognitive aspects of development is shown in recent studies of young children's fantasy play, studies that have analyzed the development of joint or cooperative make-believe. For example, Garvey (1976) has provided both an analysis of essential abilities underlying cooperative make-believe play and the following useful definition of such play: ''a state of engagement in which the successive, nonliteral behaviours of one partner are contingent on the nonliteral behaviours of the other partner'' (p. 570). Garvey's analysis and definition indicate what developmentalists have meant by *shared fantasy*. For her, shared fantasy demands coordinating perspectives, developing fantasy in cooperation with another, and a real meeting of minds, not simply acting or talking out fantasies in front of another.

Garvey's definition provides a description of how older preschoolers share fantasy play. Younger preschoolers share in different, less developed ways. Wolf (1981) has described these less developed ways as follows: Initially (around 1½ years) children share simply by playing in front of others, occasionally including others as audiences to their play but not as participants. Around age 2, children begin to encourage others to participate but in very prescribed ways. For example, a child may offer her parent a pretend cookie made from mud. The offering implies a request for the parent to reciprocate by pretending to eat. Children at this stage of sharing may repeat their actions as a response to another's going along with them (e.g., make another pretend cookie), but their fantasies remain *their* fantasies, not products of joining their fantasies with those of others. Truly cooperative fantasy play occurs only toward the end of the preschool years—when children often divide up roles before enacting a dramatic skit or negotiate how some fantasy sequence should be played out (cf. Howes, 1992). Here is an example (Scarlett, 1980) of two 4-year-olds engaged in such cooperative, shared make-believe:

> Billy and Harold are playing with Sesame Street dolls. Harold has the Ernie doll driving a toy truck. A toy mailbox is off to one side. Billy has the Bert doll start to walk; he says to Harold:
>
> B: ''Pretend Ernie gives Bert a ride in the truck.''
>
> H: ''No.''
>
> B: (Billy walks Bert over to the mailbox) ''Pretend the mailbox fell'' (Billy has the mailbox tip over onto Bert. Meanwhile, Harold stops what he is doing and comes

over to Billy). "Pretend somebody trapped Bert in the mailbox. 'Aaah! Get me out
of here!' (Speaking for Bert) "Pretend he pushed the magic button" (Billy has Bert
fly out of the mailbox). "Aaah! Help!" (Billy has Bert get into the truck).

H: "Pretend he got off." (Harold takes the truck from Billy). "Pretend he touched
the secret button" (Harold has the truck touch the mailbox, and then Harold puts
the mailbox on top of Bert. Speaking for Bert, Harold says,) "Oh God, I can't see!"

B: "Pretend Ernie touches the magic button" (Billy has the Ernie doll touch the
mailbox, and then Billy puts the mailbox on top of Ernie. Speaking for Ernie, Billy
says,) "I can't see either!" (p. 238)

In this example, Harold and Billy start off fantasizing separately, but once Harold
becomes interested in what Billy is doing, the fantasy play becomes a joint adventure,
with both boys cooperating to develop what is essentially a common theme.

This, then, is how developmentalists have assessed fantasy play. The assumptions
behind that assessment are that fantasy play both reflects and develops such critical
abilities as the ability to understand and empathize with others. Furthermore, the
developmental perspective suggests that healthy development of fantasy play means
development of joint or cooperative fantasy play.

Interpreting What Analysts Do

This comparison of analytic and developmental approaches to young children's fantasy play leaves us still with the task of determining what developmental theory has
to say about how analytic treatment brings about cure. Again, the case of the Piggle
provides good clinical material to demonstrate the developmental perspective. It does
so for three reasons. First, as has already been shown, Winnicott relies heavily on
interpreting content—so that we have here a case that falls well within the analytic
tradition. Second, Winnicott shows himself here to be a brilliant clinician—so that
we get a picture of the analytic tradition at its best. And third, Winnicott demonstrates
his brilliance by the way he engages the Piggle in the kind of play that allows her
to face and cope with troublesome feelings.

This last reason points to what developmental theory seems to suggest is *most*
important about Winnicott's treatment of the Piggle—*his ability to play and develop
play*, not his ability to interpret. This is my thesis, simply put. In what follows I will
concentrate on Winnicott's first two sessions with the Piggle—enough to make the
thesis clear.

The Piggle came to therapy because her parents were concerned about changes
in her behavior following the birth of her younger sister. After the birth, she became
easily bored and depressed and much more distant from her father. In particular, she
developed a nightmare that kept her awake and caused her great distress. The nightmare was about a "black mummy" who often lived in her tummy and who sometimes came to put her in the toilet. Furthermore, the Piggle talked quite a bit about
a "babacar," where the black mummy sometimes lived. She was very anxious about
the babacar, calling out every night, "Tell me about the babacar, *all* about the
babacar."

During the first session, Winnicott achieved two essential goals. First, he got the Piggle to play with him—by playing alone with toys and a teddy bear and then having the Piggle show the teddy bear the toys. Here is a description (1977) from his notes:

> Already I had made friends with the teddy bear who was sitting on the floor by the desk. Now I was in the back part of the room, sitting on the floor playing with the toys. I said to the Piggle (whom I could not actually see): "Bring teddy over here, I want to show him the toys." She went immediately and brought the teddy over and helped me to show him the toys. (p. 9)

Anyone who has worked with young children will recognize the sensitivity Winnicott showed to the Piggle, especially his sensitivity to her shyness by avoiding eye contact and by engaging her indirectly through directing her to the teddy bear.

The second goal achieved in this first interview is what I will call the introduction of the *clinical theme*. The clinical theme is the fantasy that contains the patient's troublesome feelings; in this case, the clinical theme was the Piggle's fantasy concerning birth—since it was the birth of the Piggle's sister that precipitated her symptoms. Here is Winnicott's (1977) first attempt at introducing the clinical theme into the Piggle's play. It occurred just after he had gotten the Piggle to show the toys to the teddy bear.

> She then started playing with them [the toys] herself, mostly taking parts of trains out of the muddle. . . . Then began something which was repeated over and over again: "Here's another one . . . and here's another one." This had to do mostly with trucks and engines, but it did not seem to matter much what it was that she made this comment about. I took this therefore as a communication and said: "Another baby. The Sush Baby" (the Piggle's name for her little sister). This was evidently the correct thing to say, because now she started giving me an account of the time the Sush Baby came, as she remembered it. What she said was: "I was a baby. I was in a cot. I was asleep. I just had the bottle." . . . [after a sidetrack, Winnicott says] So then I repeated: "And then there was another baby"—helping her on with the story of the birth. (p. 10)

Notice that Winnicott assumes that the Piggle's play is a communication, an instance of secondary symbolizing. He also assumes that the value of his interpretation lies in its helping the Piggle become aware of this symbolizing.

But from a developmental perspective, the Piggle's play is largely nonsymbolic, and the value of Winnicott's bringing up the subject of babies lies simply in his having introduced the clinical theme into their relationship. The next task was for Winnicott to develop the Piggle's play into shared symbolic play so that she could then use play to face and cope with feelings surrounding the clinical theme. This is precisely what he accomplished in the second session.

The second session opened with the Piggle's asking questions about various play objects—much as she had done in the previous session. But then she asked Winnicott, "Do you know about the babacar?" He responded by interpreting, "It's the mother's inside where the baby is born from." She added, "Yes, the black inside."

This is an instance where interpreting paid off. But the payoff was not so much in the interpretation's providing lasting relief as it was in its establishing a line of communication between the Piggle and Winnicott. To provide lasting relief, Winnicott had to incorporate the clinical theme into fantasy play, where feelings could be expressed and managed. Here is how Winnicott accomplished this. After the Piggle played at overfilling a bucket with toys while Winnicott interpreted that she was making a Winnicott baby being sick, Winnicott initiated a new play sequence.

> w. Winnicott is the Piggle's baby; it's very greedy because it loves the Piggle, it's mother, so much, and it's eaten so much that it's sick.
>
> p. The Piggle's baby has eaten too much.
>
> w. The new thing you want is about the Winnicott baby and the Piggle mother, about Winnicott loving the Piggle (mother), eating the Piggle, and being sick.
>
> p. Yes, you do.

After some playing together, the Piggle left the room to join her father. Winnicott remained on the floor next to the toys. When the Piggle returned, she asked:

> p. Can I have one toy?
>
> w. Winnicott very greedy baby; want all the toys.

This round of dramatic play was repeated several times until she left the room to tell her father "Baby want all the toys." She brought her father back into the therapy room, showed him the Winnicott baby, then began her own game of "being born." This consisted of her sliding down from her father's lap, head first, and onto the floor while saying, "I'm a baby too." Winnicott responded:

> w. I want to be the only baby. I want all the toys.
>
> p. You've got all the toys.
>
> w. Yes, but I want to be the only baby; I don't want there to be any more babies.
>
> p. I'm the baby too.
>
> w. I want to be the *only* baby (and in a different voice), shall I be cross?
>
> p. Yes (p. 25)

Winnicott then made a big noise, knocked over the toys, hit his knees and said, "I want to be the only baby." This pleased the Piggle.

It's obvious what Winnicott accomplished by becoming a greedy baby. In this role, Winnicott offered the Piggle a way of confronting her own feelings about the Sush Baby and her desire to have everything for herself. What is not obvious is how a developmental perspective suggests Winnicott's approach.

From a developmental perspective, the immaturity of the Piggle's play indicated that she needed someone to model fantasy play. That is, it would have been too much to expect her to adopt a dramatic role spontaneously, carry out a structured play sequence, and engage in shared fantasy play. She needed help.

She got that help in the form of Winnicott's adopting the role of greedy baby and, in the beginning, giving explicit instructions as to what the Piggle's dramatic role was to be (i.e., instructions that she was to be the mother). Once Winnicott had structured the Piggle's play so as to make it shared dramatic play that incorporated the clinical theme, the Piggle could then go on to adopt a role of her choosing, namely, that of baby. She had been shown that this was possible. Her development of the play, in turn, allowed her to face and begin to manage her desires to be a baby, to have most, if not all, of the attention and love shown to her younger sister. To use Vygotsky's terms, the Piggle now could use play as an *imaginary, illusory realization of unrealizable desires.*

The fact that this fantasy play was shared was important—primarily for the feelings generated *between* the Piggle and Winnicott. From a developmental perspective, to call these feelings *transference* seems unduly complicated and distant from what can be observed. Rather, from this perspective, they are simply feelings of trust and affection that often accompany enjoyable, shared play and that establish a *bond of affection.* For the Piggle, the feelings of trust and affection can be seen in the following sequence: "There was now a lot of face play. She moved her tongue around; I imitated, and so we communicated about hunger and tasting and mouth noises, and about oral sensuality in general. This was satisfactory" (p. 25).

Again, a developmental approach suggests that the term *communication* does not apply. But this is a minor criticism. For what Winnicott achieves in this joint play is a bond of affection. Furthermore, he capitalizes on the good feelings by following the play immediately with a reference to troublesome feelings surrounding the babacar fantasy. Winnicott does this as follows:

w. I said it could be dark inside. Was it dark inside her tummy?

p. Yes.

w. Do you dream about it being black inside?

p. Piggle frightened. (p. 25)

This brief exchange brought the Piggle face to face with her fears. Winnicott surrounded the fear with her newfound relationship to him. He followed this exchange with what he called *consolidating the transference* but with what I will call, more simply, *consolidating the bond of affection.* He writes: "Then there was a period in which the Piggle sat on the floor and was very serious. Eventually I said: 'You like to see Winnicott.' She answered: 'Yes' " (p. 25). From that time on, the Piggle used the bond of affection between herself and Winnicott to face and manage her fears. Winnicott had established a therapeutic relationship by engaging the Piggle in shared fantasy play that included the clinical theme. What followed was more play, more consolidation of the bond of affection, more of what we see here in just two sessions.

Conclusion

My thesis here has been that the analytic approach to treating very young children relies, first and foremost, on the analyst's ability to play and develop play. I have tried to show how this thesis follows naturally from a developmental perspective on young children's fantasy play. This perspective views very young children as needing to develop fantasy play as a means to organize and manage their feelings. Furthermore, the perspective views the process of playing with another and sharing a fantasy as an important means to develop a bond of affection that is itself a means for young children to cope with difficult feelings. Play, then, not interpretation, provides the very young child with ways to face and cope with feelings.

At the risk of confusing the reader, I will end this discussion by quoting from Clare Winnicott's preface to *The Piggle*. In this preface, she says in a very few words what I have been trying to say throughout this discussion. What may be confusing, then, is whether her husband would have said the same thing. From the number of times he interpreted the content of the Piggle's play and from his notes on the sessions, we can only infer from the following that his characterization of what he was doing differed from that presented by his wife:

> Readers will sense Winnicott's own enjoyment in his play with the child. He perceives and accepts the transference, but he does much more; he brings it to life by enacting the various roles allotted to him. The dramatization of the child's inner world enables her to experience and play with those fantasies which most disturb her. This occurs in small doses and in a setting which has become safe enough through the skill of the therapist. The creative tension in the transference is maintained, and the level of anxiety and suspense is kept within the child's capacity, so that playing can continue. (p. vii)

REFERENCES

Bretherton, I. (1984). *Symbolic play.* New York: Academic Press.

Damon, W. (1983). *Social and personality development.* New York: Norton.

Freud, A. (1965). *Normality and pathology in childhood.* New York: International Universities Press.

Garvey, C. (1976). Some properties of social play. In J. Bruner, A. Jolly, & K. Sylva (Eds.), *Play—its role in development and evolution* (pp. 570–584). New York: Basic Books.

Greenberg, M., Cicchetti, D., & Cummings, E. M. (1990). *Attachment in the preschool years.* Chicago: University of Chicago Press.

Howes, C., with Unger, O., & Matheson, C. (1992). *The collaborative construction of pretend.* Albany: State University of New York Press.

Klein, M. (1955). The psychoanalytic play technique. *American Journal of Orthopsychiatry, 25,* 223–237.

Piaget, J. (1962). *Play, dreams, and imitation in childhood.* New York: Norton.

Richards, M. (1974). *The integration of the child into a social world.* London: Cambridge University Press.

Scarlett, W. G. (1980). Social isolation from agemates among nursery school children. *Journal of Child Psychology and Psychiatry, 21,* 231–240.

Scarlett, W. G., & Wolf, D. (1979). When it's only make-believe: The construction of a boundary between fantasy and reality in storytelling. *New Directions for Child Development, 6,* 29–40.

Singer, D., & Singer, J. (1990). *The house of make-believe: Children's play and the developing imagination.* Cambridge, MA: Harvard University Press.

Slade, A. (1987). A longitudinal study of maternal involvement and symbolic play during the toddler period. *Child Development, 58,* 367–375.

Stern, D. (1985). *The interpersonal world of the infant.* New York: Basic Books.

Vygotsky, L. (1976). Play and its role in the mental development of the child. In J. Bruner, J. Jolly, & K. Sylva (Eds.), *Play: Its role in development and evolution* (pp. 537–554).

Watson, M., & Fisher, K. (1980). Development of social roles in elicited and spontaneous behavior during the preschool years. *Developmental Psychology, 16,* 483–494.

Winnicott, D. (1977). *The Piggle.* New York: International Universities Press.

Winnicott, D. (1986). *Playing and reality.* London: Tavistock.

Wolf, D. (1981). *Playing along: The social side of early pretense.* Paper presented at the biennial meeting of the Society for Research in Child Development, Boston.

4

Constructing Metaphors: The Role of Symbolization in the Treatment of Children

JAN DRUCKER

Lizzie, age 13, is reflecting on her early experiences in psychoanalysis, beginning when she was not yet 8. She remembers some of the prominent play themes that formed the content of session after session, month after month. I comment that she always had a special love of playing and an ability to play about those things that were most important to her, even when she could not and/or was reluctant to talk about them. She asks for examples and we discuss a few, including the way she depicted her troubled and painful academic life through our school play. Thoughtfully, Lizzie considers this, remembering that she did not want me to speak to her teachers for fear that I would know how badly things were going and think poorly of her for it. I point out that she was able to tell me what she needed me to know, so that we could work on it through her play. She smiles and says: "I used to wonder how you always knew things when I never told you anything. It seemed so easy."

Allison, age 12, enters the office and considers what she feels like doing. She asks, "Can you tell what mood I'm in by what I choose to do?" Without waiting for an answer, she adds, "Sometimes I don't know myself until I begin doing it or even until I'm done!"

Lizzie and Allison are beginning to understand the role that metaphoric constructions play in the articulation, communication, and mastery of experience. They are somewhat unusual in their ability to talk about this but not in the fact that they use play and other symbolic forms of expression. This chapter considers some of the functions of metaphoric constructions—broadly defined as symbolic play and the uses of language to describe, allude to, and analogize experience—in coping generally and in clinical work with children. A preliminary section will briefly discuss the role of play in child therapy as it has traditionally been conceptualized and will introduce the issues that will be in the foreground of this discussion. Examples of metaphoric constructions created by relatively psychologically healthy children in the midst of coping with traumatic life experiences will be used to illustrate some of the complex roles that symbolization plays in adaptive ego functioning in normal development. Material from the analysis of Lizzie between the ages of 7 and 15 will then be presented and discussed in terms of the evolution of the child's increasing ability to take distance from—that is, to articulate metaphorically—aspects of her ongoing as well as past experience.

Background: Play and Child Treatment

Play as a mainstay in the psychological treatment of children is nearly as old as the use of free association in the analysis of adult patients. Freud's most well-developed statement about the role of pretend play in normal development and the mastery of typical traumatic experiences did not come until 1920, when, in *Beyond the Pleasure Principle*, he took his toddler nephew's play with making a bobbin appear and disappear as paradigmatic of the turning of that which is passively experienced (being left) into that of which the child is the active master (the play disappearance and reappearance). Freud further described the central role he thought such play served in enabling children to deal with life circumstances and used this notion as the basis for his analysis of adult reactions to trauma and the functioning of the ego in attempting to master both everyday and unusual experiences. Even earlier, however, Freud had used the pretend play of children as a medium through which to understand their conscious and unconscious wishes and fears (e.g., in the case of Little Hans in 1905). Jung also drew on young children's pretend play and early on reported cases of what would later be called *play therapy*. The contributions of Anna Freud (1965), Melanie Klein (1932), Erik Erikson (1950), and others to the development of child psychoanalysis, largely via play, are well known, as are some of the points on which these pioneers disagree—how literally to interpret children's play fantasies, how central a role ought to be given to the putting of wishes and fears into words, and how much playing something out can in itself be therapeutic (a question that has continued to be discussed over time, with some later, nonpsychoanalytic therapists—for example, Virginia Axline—working largely without an interpretive process between analyst and child).

It has long been taken for granted that play, if not sufficient, is nonetheless necessary to clinical work with children as a means of revealing, understanding, discussing, and working through troubling ideas and emotions. In a little-known but quite interesting (and surprisingly modern) book written four decades ago, two British psychoanalysts summarized child treatment and the therapy of play this way:

> By making use of play in psychological treatment a double task is fulfilled. The child is set free of his neurosis. . . . At the same time the therapist discovers a new way of access to the child's mind, and . . . extends the knowledge of the structure

and dynamics of the child's rich and complex mental life. The spontaneous play of young children has suggested to us a new method of therapy, while therapy through play has proved to us afresh how necessary for the emotional development of every child is his fantasy and play life; how immensely important at certain stages of his existence it is in enlarging his awareness of the inner and outer world, and in educating the feeling and intuitive aspects of his mind. (Jackson & Todd, 1948, p. 110)

This quotation stands today as a reasonable statement about the centrality of play in development and in therapy. The last sentence hints at aspects of the importance of pretend play that go well beyond the notion of play as the expression of conflict, with its specific content as its most interesting feature. Freud himself saw play as serving much more than an expressive function, and he laid the groundwork within psychoanalysis for the consideration of other aspects of play and symbolization more generally that has evolved over the intervening years. In the academy, developmental psychology, influenced far more by Piaget's early work on play and related symbolic phenomena, has by a separate pathway come to its current great interest in the functions of symbolic play, both inter- and intrapersonally. Piaget's early work has also come to highlight the role of symbolic play in the development and articulation of a sense of self and other, as well as various mental processes long considered more cognitive in the sense of being separate from those considered to be emotional. (The present volume reflects and contributes to the growing interest in symbolization as proceeding at the interface of cognitive and affective functioning.)

If it is assumed that the psychologically healthy child is able to use play to organize, articulate, and master those aspects of his life that would otherwise cause strain, and that play is the medium through which a child's inner world can be seen and better understood, one at once encounters a paradox: As clinicians, we need to be able to draw upon the child's ability to play as a means of communicating with us, facilitating diagnosis, and providing the arena for much of our therapeutic work; yet the children who come to us for treatment are almost always there because the ordinary ways of handling events and emotions, centrally including play, have been insufficient, and symptomatic or other maladaptive means of coping have developed. An inability to play is indeed often one of the reasons for referral for treatment. This may take many forms, of course. The child who has experienced overwhelming trauma, either sudden or continuing, may find ordinary resources insufficient. The child may be deficient in the particular areas that enable symbolic functioning to develop and be put to use—language, pretending, imaginative processes more generally. The child's human and physical environments may have been deficient in those factors that nourish and encourage symbolization. Each of these situations, as it impinges upon the development of play and the means and goals of treatment, has come to be investigated and discussed in the psychological literature. They form an important background to the present discussion in which different, although related, phenomena will be in the foreground.

This chapter focuses on some aspects of children's ability to use age-appropriate, symbolic forms of expression and mastery, and on ways that ability is facilitated in the treatment context. We will consider two situations in which children's highly developed capacities for language and play are available for such functions and one in which those capacities are insufficiently developed and/or deployed to allow the child to live in reasonable psychological comfort. Although the particulars of the cases to be described emphasize some aspects of the evolution of symbolization over others, the material is presented with the aim of posing questions pertinent to a range of clinical situations and carrying implications for theoretical issues as well. To illustrate the multiple functionality and deep complexity of the construction of metaphors of experience in normal development, vignettes drawn from psychotherapeutic work with two girls undergoing considerable life stresses will be described.

Symbolization and Coping: Margaret and Allison

A central aspect of the process of human development from infancy on is the increasing interposition of thought between impulse and action. Freud pointed to the infant's beginning association of the sound of the parent's footsteps with the memory/image of gratification—leading to the ability to stop crying, to calm briefly, on hearing the parent approach when in a state of hunger—as the first indication of ego functioning. The ability to delay gratification even briefly, to take a sound (or other sensory cue) as an index of the situation of need gratification, signals the beginning of the child's ability to function on a cognitively mediated, rather than purely instinctual, level. We know now that the infant at, or even before, birth is a far more competent and responsive—that is, ego-functioning—creature than early psychologists ever imagined. Yet the capacity to be soothed by sounds has to be learned, not in a purely rote associative manner, but through interaction with the social world, and still represents a crucial landmark in human development. The process of development from this point on, then, can be said, from the point of view of mental life, to consist of many elaborations and variations on this theme—the progressive differentiation of the child's experiential world and the increasing ability to take distance from and cognitively mediate one's sensations and reactions. Such achievements as the ability to express one's needs (and later, ideas, wishes, fears, and fantasies) in words and other symbols rather than in body motions are central to the integration of the child into the social world, the elaboration of the child's inner world, and the evolution of the child's ability to master aspects of experience that challenge emotional well-being (see Katan, 1961, for a brief, rich description of the roles verbalization plays in emotional development). As one traces a developmental line from that earliest demonstration of the capacity to delay based on mental activity, through the early use of language for expression and communication, one comes eventually to the emergence and proliferation of the child's ability to symbolize, to articulate in a given medium (whether language, dream images, play, gesture, or drawings) the content of his or her mental life.

Although this schematic overview leaves out much that is important in development, it is meant to highlight the connection between developmentally primitive and developmentally sophisticated aspects of ego functioning that have in common a crucial relationship between action and thought, between experience and its articulation. In the present discussion, *symbolization* and *metaphorizing* are taken as alternative terms for a particular phenomenon: A metaphor here is understood to be the embodiment of a notion in form, a casting of experience from one domain into another. This is a much broader use of the term than one would find in a linguistic discussion of metaphor as a figure of speech. It takes *metaphor* as equivalent to *symbol* in the sense in which that term is used by Werner and Kaplan (1963), with the understanding that one forms symbols in an interaction between referent and vehicle, rather than through a process of matching a label to an already formed content.

The role of symbolization in early childhood has become an increasing focus of developmental psychologists, who variously stress its communicative, interpersonal, and for-the-self functions. I have elsewhere (Drucker, 1979) discussed the affective context of very early symbolization and the processes of endowing, embodying, and representation that progressively characterize the young child's symbolic processes. While acknowledging the multiple functions of symbolization, I focus here on the functions of symbolization for oneself—the articulation of one's own experience in various forms so as to better know and master it. I am now specifically addressing a point in development when the capacity for constructing metaphors in the medium of pretend play is already well established, and I hope to illustrate what a rich resource such activity can be in the process of coping with traumatic experience. The therapeutic context—in which one shares with a special other person the construction of metaphors—contributes a particular flavor and probably import to this activity.

Margaret and Allison are alike in several important respects. They were both between 12 and 13 when faced with significant life stresses. Each is unusually intelligent, with very highly developed verbal/conceptual abilities, and highly imaginative in a variety of media. Although differing significantly in family constellation, specific skills, and academic achievement, they share a quality that may be most significant in the current context: Each has been able, while functioning often on an age-appropriate level in many respects, and occasionally quite precociously in others, to maintain a comfort with and investment in fantasy play and other manifestations of the imaginative inner world (story writing, invention of games and worlds, etc.). For some children of this age, pretend play is no longer an acceptable activity, and Margaret and Allison are each slightly apologetic about their continued delight in play with dolls. Nonetheless, they persist in that pleasure, have found friends with whom to share their interests, and maintain continuity with the rich play of earlier childhood alongside entirely appropriate stirrings of early adolescent interests and themes. (The question of the relation of this continued interest in the forms and process of pretend play to the evident strength of the creative process in these children and others like them is itself an important one, to be left to another context for further exploration.) In any event, it appears to have been fortunate for these particular girls that when they had to deal with unusual stress, they were able to draw on a rich vein of symbolic and imaginative competence, in addition to seeking comfort from friends and family and the direct verbal expression of their thoughts, feelings, and questions about what was happening.

Margaret

Margaret is a tall, attractive, mature-looking girl who has been characterized from early childhood by particular sensitivity and emotional intensity but also by verbal/ conceptual precocity and a zestful engagement in play and interpersonal relationships. She loves horses, dolls, the beach, reading, and, lately, clothes and boys (from afar). An earlier period of psychotherapy, during which Margaret was helped with symptomatic manifestations of her intense emotional reactions (especially temper outbursts and other problems with impulse control), helped to foster a special interest in people's psychological functioning, which she parlayed into both a humorous kind of "psychologist play" and a genuine ability to be seriously sensitive to and helpful with other people's feelings and behavior. It was almost inevitable that Margaret should begin to experience some anxiety when her parents underwent an extremely difficult period in their relationship. Even before her mother had told her father that she intended to get a divorce, and quite a while before Margaret herself was informed of this, she began to experience fear about separation from them. It seemed natural to her to seek help with this symptom by discussing it with her former therapist. Even as this consultation began, the parents' situation worsened dramatically and was brought out into the open.

Within a very short period of time, Margaret and her younger siblings were witness to a near-violent argument between their parents, saw their father become alternately enraged and seriously depressed, with several dramatic departures from the home, and were told that the marriage was indeed in serious difficulty. Margaret in particular was drawn into the discussion of what was happening and was witness to a threat of suicidal action by one of her parents. A great deal of work was done by Margaret, her parents, and me in order to make the frightening events comprehensible, to safeguard the children's welfare, and to assure them that their parents were still committed to them, regardless of the future of the marriage. Margaret made excellent use of opportunities to discuss the situation—with each parent, with me, and with a couple of her close friends whose parents had been divorced. An avid reader, she remembered several novels she had read that dealt with the issue of divorce and she reread them immediately, finding some humor and much comfort in the fact that they described many of her reactions and aspects of her family's situation. She expressed her anger and grief directly to an appropriate extent but was also able to keep some thoughts and feelings to herself when she felt that expressing them would be hurtful or useless. For example, she continued to attend school and carry out her work as usual, yet was able on one occasion to mention the trouble at home to a teacher who was expressing concern. As her birthday approached, Margaret commented that she wished most of all for a reconciliation but would not say this to her parents, as she knew it would only make them sadder and was, by this time, an unrealizable wish.

Just as Margaret was experiencing these very upsetting events in her family life, an external event—the explosion of the space shuttle *Challenger*—occurred, which had an impact on many people her age. Margaret, who is much interested in science and had considered the possibility of being an astronaut, was shocked and saddened. She was with friends when she heard about the disaster and shared her reactions with them and in a school discussion the next day. The next evening, at her therapy session with me, Margaret spoke about the most recent turns in her family's troubles and how she felt about them. She announced a developmental milestone she had just achieved and a social event she was looking forward to. When she then mentioned the space shuttle's accident, she asserted her belief that the space program should continue, marshalling various reasons for this position, and said that she felt she would still consider being an astronaut someday. Without denying the danger or her feelings of fear and sadness, Margaret seemed to be able to see the accident in a longer-range context, something like the broader perspective she was working to achieve about her parents' separation. As she had said, "That first night [of her parents' fight] I couldn't imagine how life would go on, how I could go to school, or ever feel normal again, but now I see that it is going on, even though I feel very sad from time to time." In general, Margaret was coping very well with the breakup of her parents' marriage and the quite disturbing specific events associated with it. She drew on many sources of support and, once she knew what was happening, experienced no further symptomatic or other regression.

In that first session after the space shuttle's explosion, after quite a lengthy period of talking, Margaret had the idea of inventing a "fantasy solution," which she then spun out in words as she built a Lego model of the shuttle. Margaret imagined that at the time of the explosion the shuttle and at least some of its occupants, including the teacher aboard, entered another, parallel time dimension and, rather than being killed, were alive and busy exploring and adapting to life in their new universe. In a sophisticated scientific discussion she explained to me how a parallel present might be conceptualized, but she also took pleasure in building the model itself and began briefly to think about what the astronauts in her fantasy might encounter. In subsequent sessions over a number of weeks, she returned to this fantasy for short periods of time, demonstrating what the people would be dealing with—needs for communication, food, orientation in the new universe, shelter, and so on. She never spent an entire session on this, but she seemed to enjoy keeping the fantasy going (even as she accurately followed the investigations of the accident, recovery of parts of the shuttle, etc.). She herself saw it as a way of "making everything come out all right."

I understood Margaret's shuttle fantasy to be a highly adaptive way of dealing with the dual traumas of her parents' troubles and the shuttle accident. She was dealing both directly, and partially indirectly, with the former in conversation, emotional expression, reading, and a great deal of thinking. She returned to play in the therapeutic context only after the second, lesser but quite dramatic, stressful event. She was able to draw on current events and on her intellectual strength and specific fund of information, as well as her rich imagination and pleasure in formulating and sharing imaginative spheres of experience to create a play episode that condensed many aspects of her current concerns. Not only the shuttle's inhabitants but also she and her family had to deal with a sudden, unalterable shift in reality that they could not prepare for and yet had to adapt to instantly. Through the play, Margaret expressed her understanding of the need to readjust to the altered reality in her family, to find new ways of everyday as well as long-term functioning. She expressed her concerns about the fundamentals of where and how she would live, but also her equally strong need to reconceptualize herself and those closest to her, to reorient herself in an altered universe. The fantasy usefully drew on various other conscious and unconscious aspects of her current psychological reality (including an identification with a scientist/researcher parent). It is this condensation of many levels and themes of psychic life that makes rich play, like dream images, so valuable to the player.

Margaret's ability to create a fantasy articulation and solution of aspects of her life that were troubling to her and difficult to deal with reflects her ego strength. Had it not occurred during a therapy session, it would not have been seen, but I am sure that similar episodes of play and fantasy occur in Margaret's life frequently and serve her well. That she can cast psychic material into another domain and work with it, as it were, at some remove, but without breaking affective connection to it, is a sign of psychological health. That Margaret was not impelled to deal with reality *only* through fantasy is another significant aspect of her maturity and good functioning. In fact, she recognized this herself. Several weeks after the play described, at a time when her parents' situation continued to be unpredictable, but when she was more clear in her own mind about what the outcome would be and more sure that she could survive it, Margaret told me that she had ''found a metaphor to explain my father's behavior.'' He was, she said, like a soda bottle with its lid on. As events occurred and the bottle was repeatedly shaken up, there was no opportunity for the gas bubbles to be gradually released (because, as she explained, he was unable to accept or express feelings), so that the pressure eventually increased until the lid popped off. When I agreed that this seemed an apt way to conceptualize her father as I knew him, and remarked on her use of the term *metaphor,* Margaret casually replied, ''Well, I should know about metaphors. We're studying them in school, along with allusions and other things like that!'' She further commented that it really did help to think of such examples. They made her feel less frightened by what was going on at home.

Allison

Allison is a petite, appealing, young-looking girl who is exceptionally able intellectually and particularly characterized by the richness and diversity of her interests and turns of mind. Like Margaret, she loves to read and write stories and has been an avid doll player. Allison particularly loves and is endlessly inventive in the creation of imaginative worlds—families, personalities, and adventures for her friends, dolls, invented characters, and herself. Even though she had begun to make some tentative strides in the direction of early adolescence, Allison at 12 remained deeply immersed in the style and interests of late latency. This appeared to be a fortuitous factor in her ability to cope with a series of major stresses that occurred between her 11th and 13th birthdays. When Allison was just past 11, her mother became sick with what proved to be a terminal illness. She died when Allison was 12½. During the period between her mother's falling ill and her death, Allison also experienced the sudden death of her maternal grandmother, as well as several other sad and frightening events that, while less traumatic, added to the psychic pain she had to bear.

Over a period of many months during which her mother became rapidly more ill and could no longer be treated, Allison seemed to be working actively on three related tasks that were understood to be crucial by herself and her parents: the gradual awareness, acknowledgment, and acceptance of the fact that her mother was dying; the modulation of the grief and anger she felt to a degree that could be tolerated by everyone and permit her to continue to function at school, with friends, and within the family; and the envisioning and active pursuit of an ongoing life that would continue after her mother's death. Throughout this time, Allison benefited greatly from the fact that she was surrounded by a circle of friends who served as a strong support system for each member of the family. The fact that she was still very much a little girl enabled her to seek and accept nurturance and be taken care of in ways that were comfortable for her, her family, and her friends.

Above all, Allison was helped by the loving participation in her life of her mother, as long as that was possible, and by an intense, devoted relationship with her father, who of course faced the same tasks as Allison, as well as many additional responsibilities. As Allison and her father struggled with the pain and complexities of her mother's illness and of their relationship, they began to weave the tapestry of what would become their life together after the actual death. A final period of many weeks during which Allison's mother was hospitalized and increasingly less able to respond to people created enormous stress but also served as a transitional period in the adaptation Allison and her father had to make.

Throughout this long, hard process, Allison made use of direct, sometimes intense, expressions of a range of feelings, as well as talking to various people close to her about different aspects of what was going on; she also steadily immersed herself in academic and social life, which served as sources of respite, as well as being a way of maintaining continuity amid change and a sense of confidence in her ability to continue to function. Allison seemed to have the capacity to use different people and situations in different ways to find appropriate means of meeting her intellectual and emotional needs; this included a supportive psychotherapeutic relationship that supplemented the crucial family and friendship contexts in which she found solace and specific kinds of help.

Although Allison was able during this difficult period to use pretend play and various other forms of play of the imagination for escape, comfort, and the symbolic articulation (and hence working through) of aspects of her experience, I wish to describe a particular play episode that occurred the day after her mother's funeral. In the preceding weeks, Allison had become interested in a series of books in which teenagers investigated and solved mysteries, including murders. This seemed to correlate with a period of time in which she was, with good reason, confused by an unclear and upsetting situation regarding her mother's hospitalization and condition. On this day, Allison had bought and just begun to read another book in the series. After some discussion of her reactions to the funeral and its aftermath, Allison invented a game for us to play: She would give me clues, and I would try to solve a murder mystery.

Allison constructed and peopled an imaginary setting in which the death (by murder) of a parent occurred. Her clues reflected an intricate mixture of cleverness and mild confusion, so that I quickly felt uncertain about how to begin to reason through the questions of who was guilty and how the death had actually occurred. This was the first aspect of mastery the game afforded Allison; she knew the secrets, was the one who understood, rather than the passive, confused one. The second aspect of mastery involved the content of the game: the death of a parent due to a cause superficially understood intellectually but in a deeper sense mystifying. We played out the process, by which I became confused, sought help via additional clues, gradually understood some aspects of the mystery, misunderstood some clues, and eventually had to have revealed to me the answers to my questions.

Many specific details of the world Allison created served the function of mastery of *particular* aspects of her experience, metaphorically represented not only by being parts of a game, but also in the specific symbolic forms (guises) employed. Several examples will illustrate this point.

• There were several grown children in the family. This made reparation for feelings of loneliness and deprivation that Allison consciously (and fairly frequently) ascribed to being a child—and an only child at that. Further, the different characters of the children offered an opportunity to express different aspects of herself. One was carefree, others serious; one was blind (and thereby spared visual trauma but also acutely emphasizing the role of vision), while another followed an investigative profession not unlike that of Allison's mother. Two had twinlike characteristics and reflected Allison's wish to be very close to someone who intimately understood her, as she had frequently felt her mother did. Some had pure motives (and hence were free of guilt), while others stood to gain by the parent's death and, even if not participating in the murder, might be feeling a good deal of guilt.

• Aspects of the arrangements of the house and of the circumstances of the death subtly reflected aspects of Allison's life and such questions as who slept where, which covered deeper issues about the necessarily shifting relationships in her immediate family.

• Additional twists of fate in the game involved the corpse and were associated with Allison's fantasies about autopsies—who performs them, what they reveal, and, reiterating a theme extremely important to her, what is to be seen, and with what result. (The issue of sensory trauma, especially visual, and defenses against it are long-standing aspects of Allison's psychological makeup.)

There are other levels and types of meaning embedded in Allison's metaphoric construction of which I am aware—including significant aspects of her identifications with each of her parents—and undoubtedly others of which I remain unaware. It is precisely this characteristic of densely packed, highly condensed meaningfulness that makes metaphoric constructions so valuable to their maker and so rich an experience for their audience when (as in the arts) there is one. Like Margaret's shuttle fantasy, Allison's metaphoric working out of her conscious and unconscious thoughts, feelings, and images seemed to serve its own purposes and did not, in my view, call for interpretation. When someone of any age is able to use play or another symbolic medium in this way, in a treatment context or elsewhere, the metaphorizing functions on its own. It is where the process of embodying affectively charged meaning is invaded by anxiety or otherwise disrupted and cannot serve its coping function that intervention, frequently in the form of verbal interpretation, is indeed called for. In these cases, I believe the therapeutic context served as an additional source of support for the symbolic working through of reactions to stress of which these girls were highly capable.

The metaphors created by Margaret and Allison, while occurring in a therapeutic context, responding to trauma, and reflecting very highly developed intellectual and creative processes, have been offered as illustrative of what takes place naturally, and frequently less dramatically, as generally psychologically healthy children or adults articulate ongoing experience, pleasurable or unpleasurable. That articulation always serves the process of knowing for the self, but it also functions in a crucial way in coping when so called upon. In the next section of this chapter I will describe a situation in which this metaphoric capacity was available for relatively conflict-free functioning only after a lengthy treatment process.

The Evolution of Metaphoric Capacity During Treatment: Lizzie

There are many perspectives from which clinical case material can be presented and discussed. To do full justice to any lengthy treatment process would require at least an entire volume, so that any summary must of necessity leave out much that was characteristic and important in the progress of the case. At the beginning of Lizzie's treatment, libidinal and aggressive drive material, as well as issues and modalities from each preoedipal phase, were intertwined in her play. Her ego functioning—at first in active conflict with her drives and then gradually modifying and managing their expression—and the concurrent belated development of a flexible, relatively effective superego were also seen in her play. Shifting patterns of Lizzie's identification with each parent and each sibling, and with new models as they became available—including an important identification with specific aspects of her analyst's personality—as well as the analytic function in general characterized her development over the years of her analysis (four times weekly) and subsequent psychotherapy (twice and then once weekly) from the age of nearly 8 to 16.

The way Lizzie behaved in the sessions—specifically the way she first played, considerably later spoke, and much later achieved a reasonable capacity for metaphoric distance (something Margaret and Allison were able to do much earlier and more easily)—will be described. I will present a series of accounts of individual sessions that occurred at varying times during Lizzie's treatment that illustrate the particular way in which she used pretend play to articulate experience. I will also discuss the gradual process by which she was increasingly able to interpose thought between impulse and action; the inability to do this on an age-appropriate level underlay all of her presenting problems when she began treatment.

Background

Lizzie's mother and father described her as having been an extremely difficult infant, tense and motorically impelled, who slept little, cried a lot, and induced considerable frustration and rage in them. This pattern was in marked contrast to that of her older siblings, who were much easier infants and were doing better in their current development. Lizzie at age 7½ was very immature, doing poorly in school; she had great social difficulty because she was demanding and bossy with other children and was extremely difficult for her parents to manage. She had frequent tantrums and demanded all of her mother's attention, even to the point of screaming if her mother dared to speak on the phone. Her parents had been separated for over a year but were considering trying to reunite (they never did and were subsequently divorced, each remarrying within several years). It was reported that Lizzie had had no overt response to the announcement of the separation, and her parents felt that, as usual, it hadn't really "sunk in." (Much later Lizzie was able to show how much *had* sunk in, as I will describe.)

Lizzie demonstrated a number of difficulties that appeared to be neither purely cognitive nor purely emotional in origin. She had trouble remembering time and date information (although she had an excellent *sense* of time), forgot place and person names, and frequently seemed not to get the point. Much later, when she was much calmer, it was possible to see some primary mild verbal-processing difficulties (particularly difficulty memorizing names, labels, or specific facts) underlying this behavior. Initially we had to understand how dependent she felt on other people to help her stay oriented, and how she used incessant questioning as a form of clinging. Lizzie's mother quite aptly described Lizzie's interest only in people, especially her mother, to the exclusion of interest in toys, clothes, going places, and doing many things (even, initially, watching television). She did not mention any interest in pretend play and expressed her own frustration that, as a preschooler, Lizzie had not seemed to enjoy playing and being read to, as had her older siblings.

The Beginning of Treatment

An adorable little girl with a small but sturdy build and a lively, engaging presence, Lizzie was initially shy about meeting me and coming into my office. Her mother later told me that a huge public tantrum had taken place on the way, because Lizzie did not want to come, and had ended only with the purchase of candy, as usual. Lizzie was demure and interested, however, as she hung on to her mother's hand and then looked tentatively around the office. Characteristically, when asked after a few minutes if her mother could leave, Lizzie replied, "Sure, I don't care." She found it very difficult to acknowledge anxiety or sadness, preferring to deny caring once she had stopped clinging or angrily engaging her mother. While her mother had predicted that Lizzie would leap onto the furniture, she initially sat primly and asked permission to use the toys and other objects she saw. For our first 10 sessions, Lizzie was very controlled, although quite friendly, and sought structured activities including mazes and the coloring of cards for different people. She verbalized very little that was not directly about her activities, even having her mother ask me the one question she had—whether I saw other children. In response to my questions she told me that she hated school and her current teacher, loved to suck her thumb and did it when she was hungry or thirsty but not in a position to eat or drink, and hated her brother, adding, "No matter how much they say I love him, I don't!" This was the last conversation about Lizzie's life we were to have for quite a while, for even on being questioned, Lizzie tended to give very brief, usually rather noncommittal, answers and made it clear that she wanted to play and not talk.

In her mother's presence, Lizzie tended to behave like a toddler, demanding her total attention and preferring direct, especially physical, contact with her to any other activity. (Years later, Lizzie's relationship with her mother remains her arena of least mature, most drive-impelled functioning.) Her analytic sessions proved to be an opportunity for Lizzie to create a pretend play sphere, shared intimately with a caring adult who would not become the direct object of her intense impulses and emotions but who would tolerate and discuss their enactment in thinly disguised play. The following descriptions illustrate the evolution of Lizzie's play, with a focus on the evolution of four phases of that enactment: from a degree of physicality that made it almost lose its play character, to an increasing distance between Lizzie and the characters she played, to the miniaturization and otherwise further distancing of the play, to the gradual ability to talk about the play and then about herself. Eventually Lizzie demonstrated the ability to at least periodically conceptualize her own experience in a verbal metaphoric fashion.

The First Phase: Acting in the Play

In her 11th analytic session, at age 7 years 11 months, Lizzie first introduced the idea of our playing together. After having finished my last maze book and rejected an impulse to play with clay as much too messy, Lizzie took out a doctor kit and a doll and told me I should be the mother of a sick daughter whom I would take to see her, the pediatrician. I was to wait in the waiting room, as my daughter did not want me to see her be checked because I might get upset. Lizzie as the doctor was very bossy and shut the mother out repeatedly but told me what I needed to know. She assured me that "Lots of mothers and fathers find it hard to wait." I was then allowed to visit the hospital only once a week. Between visits, Lizzie, as the doctor, was to work and sleep, but she actually curled up on the couch, thumb in mouth, and closed her eyes. We repeated the basic scenario several times, and when the end of the session neared, Lizzie told me that the daughter would die. She then proceeded to play out the death (my being informed of it and reacting with upset) and the "burial" of the doll beneath a chair. At the beginning of the next session, 4 days later, Lizzie rushed into the office, saying, "I know just what to do—the same game as last time. Do you remember it?" This was to prove characteristic of her involvement with our ongoing play over the next several years. Lizzie always remembered exactly where we had left off and rarely switched the theme or pattern of the play between sessions.

Lizzie's first play theme reflected her fears about the analysis and about me as a doctor. Her mother was relegated to the waiting room and to once-a-week sessions with me in terms almost identical to those she used with me in the play. Some specifics of the pretend daughter's illness also reflected anxiety about a family member who had recently been ill and who indirectly caused a separation of Lizzie from her own mother. The general tone of the play was not only active mastery but even a counterphobic rushing toward anxiety-laden themes; this was characteristic of both Lizzie's ongoing play and her behavior in general. Most striking was the intensity of her investment in the play. Dramatic gestures, intense words, and vivid affect were all conveyed throughout each episode, and a remarkable continuity was maintained from session to session. The daughter, called ''Amy,'' was an ongoing central character for several years, even though the circumstances and events of the play changed dramatically; this, it seemed to me, allowed Lizzie to always have the gratification of playing both herself (via Amy) and powerful other figures in her life. One character did not seem sufficient as a screen for the projection of Lizzie's complex emotions and behavior.

While Lizzie's play in this first phase was clearly pretend, there was also a sense in which it was so vivid as to be practically the repetition of things that had occurred and/or the embodiment of impulses with very little disguise; this is why I refer to it as *enactment*. A few sessions after the first play session described, Lizzie pretended to cut my hair with real scissors in such a way that I felt it necessary to clarify that we were just pretending and that she could not really cut my hair; she accepted this but soon afterward actually cut a doll's hair, testing the limits of what I would allow but also demonstrating how difficult it was for her to ''just pretend'' about a very strong impulse.

The Second Phase: Talking in the Play

Lizzie's 40th session (when she was 8 years 1 month old) represented a shift in the directness of expression and personal contact of our play. In the intervening weeks she had played out many scenarios of life at school, elaborated in wild, rather sadistic ways, and had recently tied herself up and had me hold her on my lap. I found Lizzie waiting for this session lying on the floor of the waiting room, as her mother had done when she had a bad back. She offered me a ''surprise,'' a piece of fruit. She set immediately to continuing where we had left off with her tied up and flailing, helpless and kicking. She then suddenly began to talk, still thinly ''in character,'' about how unhappy she was. She said that she had no mother, father, relatives, or friends. Her father had died of old age; her mother had been shot. Over and over, Lizzie described personal losses and the longing for a parent. She offered many details of how every person had died and reiterated her loneliness, as well as her deliberate wariness of strangers so that she would not also die. She had also lost her apartment and all her money except for a few pennies. My character was no good to her because I did not live at home with her. When I commented on her character's sadness, Lizzie first joked about being, ''sad, mad, bad, cad.'' Then she became serious again, and we discussed how ''someone'' with so many sad feelings would have trouble with friends and how one does get to have friends. Lizzie then asked to take home a little dictionary of mine, and when I said she could read it there, she began to look up words with great enthusiasm. She pushed hard for independence and mastery in this activity, wanting no help with the difficult reading. Finally, she delightedly looked up the words *jerk*, *stupid*, and *brother* in Italian and wrote them down, planning to confront her brother with them at home.

In this session Lizzie demonstrated the means by which she could introduce verbalization of thoughts and feelings into the play. Because it *was* play, she could allow herself to express things she vigorously denied or ignored when being herself. She could by this point allow me to comment on the feelings expressed as long as we were both clearly talking about the characters and not Lizzie. She seemed relieved by the expression of sadness and deprivation and ended the session with a (very rare) direct communication about her sibling—and on a much higher level of ego functioning than the one on which it began.

In the months that followed, Lizzie played out many variations on the themes of abandonment, loss, rage, and revenge. Amy varied from an innocent victim to a provocative participant in sadomasochistic, occasionally overtly sexy interactions. In the guise of a new character, "Baby," nurturant interactions and repeated workings over of the question of whether the child was bad or good were played out. There were occasionally sessions in which Lizzie wanted to play a board game with me, and she was absolutely insistent that I not "let her win" or even play less adeptly than I would otherwise. As strongly as she insisted that play be "just play," Lizzie demanded that reality conform to all of the rules she felt applied. Occasionally also she would speak directly to me, usually in response to a question about her weekend or the like, but she would recount the plot of a movie or describe a sporting event. She never wanted to discuss her feelings about anything or to talk about school at all. The majority of the time was spent in the ongoing pretend play world we had created. The content periodically reflected specific current life events. For example, before she went away to camp, Lizzie and I played many episodes of Amy at camp, writing to her family and having both positive and negative experiences. Characteristically, Lizzie in this phase included a great deal of talking within the metaphor of the play about feelings and thoughts of the characters.

The Third Phase: Increasing Distance from the Play

Over the next months, Lizzie's intolerance of my direct comments on her feelings continued, but she became increasingly focused on *planning* our fantasy play and on its dialogue, rather than on the *action* within the play. In her 163rd session (at age 8 years 10 months), Lizzie began by reminding me of what we had to do to finish what we had left off with last time: writing a letter to "our child." She knew that we also had to decide about the next day's session, which fell on a holiday. She suggested putting off the decision until the end of the hour and planned the letter to be written in considerable detail. She then decided that Amy and her father would themselves devise a plan whereby Amy would pretend to be very sick so that her mother would come. When she learned this, Lizzie told me, she would be so angry that she would die. After planning this scenario, we quickly enacted it as Lizzie had directed, with her dramatically and emotionally depicting Amy's rejection of her mother and subsequent grief. Then Lizzie suggested that we pretend that the *father* died and that Amy and her siblings went to live with another family. She quickly spun out the new scenario: "They will send the boy to camp and then have a baby girl and be very happy with the sister, then send both of them to camp." This continued, with Lizzie deciding that the second mother would then die, and so on.

With much energy, Lizzie created the further fantasy of the boy finding a girlfriend and their courtship and marriage. In the little remaining time after this was planned, she rapidly acted it out, then seemed exhausted and decided to rest while considering the next day's session. We talked about her mixed feelings about it, and I commented that she seemed worried that I would be angry or upset if she didn't come. She seemed to ignore this, but then took a piece of paper and wrote down that she would not come and that she "hops [sic] you are not mad." She then gave me a small drawing as a present—a connect-the-dots picture of a girl with the words *yes* and *no* coming out of her mouth. We agreed that it depicted her uncertainty about the decision.

It is apparent that many of the thematic aspects of Lizzie's play continued to reflect feelings of abandonment and anger, with considerable elaboration, by this point, of her complex feelings of attachment and interest in variations on oedipal dynamics. The shift away from the need actually to carry out the actions represented the increasing distance Lizzie was able to take from her feelings and thoughts. She still had difficulty discussing her feelings about me, but she was able to use symbolic media (writing and drawing) to enrich her relatively meager talk about her decision. During the months that followed, Lizzie occasionally played board games and wanted to be tested on various skills, but she continued to use her sessions primarily for planning and carrying out pretend play themes. She wove fantasies around issues of divorce and remarriage at the time her parents became divorced. As the summer approached, Lizzie said, "We'd better play camp now," her first direct recognition of the fact that playing about things helped her to handle them.

The Fourth Phase: Talking Outside the Play

During the next 6 months, from age 9½ to 10, Lizzie became increasingly able to speak in general terms about things "kids" might think or feel. She was able to discuss something outside of a play context so long as it was not specifically about her. She was also able to some extent to talk about her own life events and a little about her feelings at times, although she would often cut this conversation off abruptly with the demand that we "get down to playing." As the remarriage of Lizzie's mother grew more likely, Amy and her cohorts began to experience remarriages and relationships with their step-siblings. Amy continued to be an alter ego for Lizzie, but other characters took on partial aspects of her reactions to things. The dichotomy between good and bad characters diminished somewhat, and each character became more complex. Occasional sessions occurred during which something pressing was discussed with no play at all, but this remained the exception.

When Lizzie was 11 years 1 month old, she was dealing in an ongoing way with her learning problems, for which she was now being tutored, in ways that included a renewal of school play. However, she was also involved in an ongoing way with games in which we ran shops and restaurants. One day she took time off from all of these games and simply sat and talked. She mentioned some independent, "grown-up" things she had been doing and was able to discuss her conflicted feelings about being more independent of her mother. She wanted to play jacks as we talked. She brought up the question of her continued need for therapy when a friend of hers who "has more problems" was quitting her treatment. At the same time, she planned the continuation of a game we had interrupted. She recounted a movie she had seen with her father, and spoke of his impending move and how often she would see him. She spoke of the fact that he and his second wife were expecting a baby, and we discussed how many big events had occurred in the past year since her parents' divorce.

This conversation led to a discussion of their separation and many aspects of her memories of her new stepfather from the time she was very young. She commented that she didn't like to look at old pictures of herself. When she was a baby she was very cute, but her family had lived together then and it was sad to think about. She didn't like to think or talk about that time. I commented that her mother had thought she didn't react very much to the announcement of the separation, but that I knew she must have had many feelings about it. She replied that she remembered it well and proceded to *act out* her father's departure, with stiff words, carrying a suitcase, kissing each family member. We commented briefly on how hard a time that was, and Lizzie indicated her wish to return to our ongoing play, in which I was working for her at the restaurant. It appeared that recapturing a painful memory led to a temporary regression in which Lizzie could not maintain the distance she had achieved.

The Fifth and Final Phase: On the Way to Verbal Analytic Work

After more than 3 years of analysis, Lizzie was far more able and willing, at least at times, to discuss her life and feelings. Yet despite her greater verbal contributions to our discussions, she was impelled to play-act her father's departure when remembering it. The intensity and immediacy of the memory seemed too strong for her to describe in words, and physical enactment still contributed a great deal to her expressivity. Soon after this, Lizzie began to be increasingly interested in pretend play with miniatures—little dolls to whom she gave names and characters, including Amy. This represented yet another step in the increasing distance she was able to take in the metaphoric articulation of experience. During the next year, she held on to the pleasure in and attachment to pretend play, but in the form of it she continued to differentiate herself from the characters. She devised the idea of writing a play, spending many weeks on lengthy acts, or "chapters," in which she dictated the dialogue and stage directions to me. Eventually we made scenery, costumed the dolls as the actors, and tape-recorded ourselves reading the script. The play was never completely performed, but the tapes were listened to over and over again.

A further step in the direction of distanced metaphoric expression came when Lizzie next decided that we should write and produce our own soap opera. Again she dictated scripts, with complex plots taking several sessions for each episode to be written. This time we recorded the stories but did not act them out with dolls. They were radio plays—far more completely carried out in a verbal mode. Concomitant with this, Lizzie was increasingly willing to discuss her own life without reference to play, and a dichotomy emerged for a while: She would spontaneously report things she was willing to discuss, would tolerate some querying from me, but maintained the play sphere as the domain for dealing with "embarrassing" (at this point largely sexual and interpersonal) themes. During this time, from about age 12 to 13, she also periodically asked about what she had done earlier in her analysis, and when she was 13 she made the comment quoted at the beginning of this chapter, reflecting her eventual conscious understanding of the play as communication.

Soon afterward, Lizzie ceased playing pretend games on a regular basis, although from time to time she would return to them longingly. She came to her now less frequent sessions and either played a board game or sat and talked. In her 14th through 16th years she was able to use the sessions primarily for discussions of what was going on in her life, although she maintained on principle that she shouldn't have to discuss anything she didn't want to, as this was "her time" to use as she pleased. She almost always came with something to discuss, increasingly in direct and vivid emotional terms. The push toward activity continued to be seen in her behavior (in a great desire to be busy and active, not in acting out in undesirable ways) and in the sessions when she would from time to time sprawl on the couch, or sit on the floor, or want to play a board game. Interestingly, a new form of metaphoric communication emerged as Lizzie began to read me magazine articles and recount television movies, with subsequent discussion of the themes and characters and their relation to her thoughts, feelings, and life events, which were typically adolescent by this point. She developed a special interest in television movies that dealt with family/psychological themes and would discuss them avidly with me. As I had sometimes seen them, too, Lizzie came to refer to our common "taste in TV shows," indicating that the shared world she and I had evolved was still an important domain of her experience.

Concluding Comments

The case material that has been described illustrates the adaptive function of the ego capacity to articulate experience in symbolic form. The functions of such metaphorizing for the self have been emphasized. It is important to underline as well unique aspects of the therapeutic session as a locale for symbolization. The presence of the therapist as audience, but also in significant ways as cocreator of the metaphoric world constructed, undoubtedly plays a significant role in the evolving capacity of the patient to express herself symbolically. Likewise, the fact that the imagined world is shared with someone who is neither parent nor peer, but a particularly interested knower of the manifest as well as symbolic content of the metaphor, must be important in the value of the activity. Identification with the therapist as a creator and appreciator of metaphoric expression is an aspect of the therapeutic relationship that is frequently overlooked in relation to the psychoanalytic treatment of both children and adults.

The relative availability and richness of imaginative processes should be considered a central dimension in ego strength as it is assessed before treatment begins. Evolving metaphoric competence should be attended to and fostered during the treatment, rather than being taken for granted. The creation and elaboration of a play sphere in child treatment may be importantly related to what has been described by Spence (1982) as the creation of *narrative truth* in adult psychoanalysis. Further explorations of the role of metaphoric articulation of experience in normal development, childhood psychopathology, and the process of child treatment should prove valuable for theoretical and clinical conceptualizations about this central domain of human experience.

REFERENCES

Drucker, J. (1979). The affective context and psychodynamics of first symbolization. In N. Smith & M. Franklin (Eds.), *Symbolic functioning in childhood* (pp. 27–41). Hillsdale, NJ: Erlbaum.

Erikson, E. H. (1950). *Childhood and society.* New York: Norton.

Freud, A. (1965). *Normality and pathology in childhood.* New York: International Universities Press.

Freud, S. (1955a). An analysis of a phobia in a five-year old boy. In J. Strachey (Ed. & Trans.), *The standard edition of the complete psychological works of Sigmund Freud* (Vol. 10, pp. 5–147). London: Hogarth. (Original work published 1909.)

Freud, S. (1955b). Beyond the pleasure principle. In J. Strachey (Ed. & Trans.), *The standard edition of the complete psychological works of Sigmund Freud* (Vol. 18, pp. 7–67). London: Hogarth. (Original work published 1920.)

Jackson, L., & Todd, K. M. (1948). *Child treatment and the therapy of play.* London: Methuen.

Katan, A. (1961). Some thoughts about the role of verbalization in early childhood. *Psychoanalytic Study of the Child, 16,* 184–188.

Klein, M. (1932). *The psychoanalysis of children.* London: Hogarth.

Spence, D. (1982). *Narrative truth and historical truth.* New York: Norton.

Werner, H., & Kaplan, B. (1963). *Symbol formation.* New York: Wiley.

5

Making Meaning and Making Believe: Their Role in the Clinical Process

ARIETTA SLADE

This chapter is about playing and the clinical process. I began to think about the ideas presented here many years ago, while still in my training and working for the first time with young children in psychoanalytic psychotherapy. These ideas developed in the moments of my sitting with young patients whose play—or lack of it— utterly stymied me. These children did not play in the ways I had expected, and I found myself struggling to make sense of what they were doing. Sometimes their play was highly disorganized, vague, and primitive; at other times, they couldn't make-believe at all. Instead, they immersed themselves in barren, repetitive play that made any attempt at discussion or interpretation impossible. This was hardly how I'd imagined the work of child therapy. Even when there was a point of therapeutic entry, verbal interpretations often fell flat, were disorganizing, or were plainly and simply rejected ("Shut up, Dr. Slade!"). In many instances, I found myself left with no choice but to simply play[1] with the child and—for the time being—to abandon my own need to deduce the meaning of the play and somehow communicate it to my little patient. Often this left me with the uneasy feeling that I somehow wasn't acting like a therapist, nor was what I was doing really therapy.

Simply playing means suspending an interpretive or deductive stance and engaging in the play itself. Contrary to what many case histories might seem to imply, choosing not to use interpretive or deductive language does not mean that therapy per se is not taking place. Serving as an organizing, enhancing, and engaged play partner is hardly a simple task; in many instances, it is of enormous value clinically and developmentally. With children who cannot play coherently or meaningfully, who cannot use the symbols of play and language to make sense of their emotional experiences, who cannot create narratives for their experiences, an essential and prior part of the work of treatment is to help them do so. For children whose representational abilities are immature or compromised by developmental delays, it often seems that the *process of playing itself* is consolidating and integrative; it provides children with the resources to make sense of emotional experiences on their own.

It is only after such consolidations take place that verbal interpretations of repressed ideas or conflicts can be meaningful to the child, for repression and the internalization of conflict *depend* upon organizational capacities that are the result of developing ways of playing. In his book *Playing and Reality*, Winnicott (1971) put it this way: "Psychotherapy has to do with two people playing together. The corollary of this is that where playing is not possible then the work done by the therapist is directed towards bringing the patient from a state of not being able to play into a state of being able to play" (p. 38).

Much of what is written regarding the psychoanalytic treatment[2] of children concerns work with children who are of school age, typically 6 or older. In addition, interpretive or uncovering work is usually the focus of such presentations. However, as children begin to enter treatment at earlier and earlier ages, and as more disturbed children are seen in outpatient settings, questions necessarily arise as to the technical modifications necessary for work with those who are unresponsive to interpretive techniques, or whose play is too primitive or disorganized to make interpretations meaningful or even possible. These are usually children who—either because of their age or their level of psychological development—would be characterized as *preoedipal* in their emotional and object relations development. At the very least, this designation means that there is little evidence of the kind of consolidation and organization of affect and conflict that typify oedipal development, and that—as a consequence—language and other representational processes rarely function to aid in the delay of gratification, in the tolerance of frustration, or as ways of communicating thematic material to others. We can further assume that in such instances the core issues in relationships to others center on separation and differentiation.

My major points are two. First, a clinical picture marked by the predominance of primitive modes of organization requires us to question and to rework the classical *disguise theory* of repression and symbolization. Second, once we go so far as to ask whether the kind of play we see in such young or disorganized children actually serves to disguise meaning, we must also rethink our approaches to interpretation specifically and intervention generally. This chapter will examine the meaning and significance of simply playing for the clinical enterprise. I will use these formulations to suggest modifications in the application to play of classical notions of disguise and repression and to reevaluate the function and therapeutic value of playing in the clinical process.

Jimmy and Nicole: Lessons in Playing

Jimmy, age 3½, was referred for treatment because his mother found him uncontrollable. He occupied himself for the better part of his first 2 months in treatment with the following game: He put on the large duck hand puppets and manipulated his fingers so that the beaks opened and closed rapidly. As he opened and shut the ducks' beaks, he emitted loud, raucous eating/growling noises and grinned mischievously. But it had little of the feel of play: There were no story, no characters, no words, and no feelings. These behaviors went unchanged over the course of numerous sessions. Entry into the play was virtually impossible; he ignored my comments and queries, dismissed my efforts to create a story, and seemed happy just to carry on with the ducks. Given his meager verbal skills and the fact that we had not yet established the words for his feelings, interpretation of the oral aggression in his play did not seem a reasonable option. Besides, repression was clearly not at issue here; if anything, making it possible was. Even if I had wished to interpret the play, its repetitive and driven quality made it impossible for me to figure out the story he was trying to tell me. Any interpretation I made ran the risk of being as disconnected as his play seemed to be.

Nicole, age 7, was referred because of difficulty making friends and adjusting to school. During her first session with me, she chose a family of four squirrels from the toy closet. Heartened by her choice of a make-believe family and hopeful that her play would provide clues to the difficulties I knew she was having, I waited. She carefully took the squirrels out of their cloth house and lined them up on the floor. Discovering that they made a squeaking sound when squeezed, she moved the squirrels up and down and had them talk to each other. The squeaking continued for some time, and I finally asked, ''What are they saying?'' Nicole looked at me dully and replied, with a hint of condescension and a shrug of her shoulders, ''I don't know. I don't speak their language.''

Nicole entered psychoanalytically oriented psychotherapy without the resources to play about or talk about her inner life. As she herself put it, she had no language—make-believe or otherwise—for describing what went on inside her. Her play was fragmented and disorganized, and any discussion of her family, her friendships, or her feelings led to withdrawal at the least and outraged denial at the worst.

In very real ways, Jimmy, Nicole, and children like them introduced me to the issues that are central to this chapter. As I struggled to develop a way of working with them and helping them, I found myself most unclear about how to apply what I'd learned and read about treating children and interpreting play. Both children were seen individually in community mental health settings on a weekly basis. Their parents were seen intermittently for parent guidance sessions. Both families were highly disorganized, and both sets of parents found it very difficult to care for their children responsibly and consistently. The degree of chaos and social isolation in their lives was striking. As a consequence, the parents felt so overwhelmed by their own lives that they found it nearly impossible to follow my suggestions and adopt regular routines and limits. Jimmy's mother allowed him a great deal of freedom and was generally unable to contain him in any reasonable way. For instance, he often chose his own clothes and dressed as he pleased, with little regard for the weather. Ms. A. had been abandoned by her husband and was unable to maintain steady employment. Her child from a previous marriage was profoundly developmentally delayed. Nicole's parents lived separately, and her mother suffered extreme panic attacks and often took to her bed. She avoided relationships except those with her immediate family, and was frightened by even the most routine shopping trips and outings. Nicole visited with her father frequently, although he had little sense of how to spend appropriate time with her and often took her to betting parlors and the racetrack. He was physically overbearing and smothering with her, and expressed his affection in inappropriate displays of caressing and hugging. Nicole was herself quite boyish and scorned activities that were at all stereotypically feminine. This naturally had a great impact on her ability to make friends.

While Jimmy and Nicole would certainly be considered extreme cases, they nevertheless exemplify a set of phenomena that are relatively common in clinical practice with young children. In Nicole's case, play was repetitive and poorly elaborated, and only occasionally did she provide any narration for the overtly violent scenes she played out. When, after some months, she began providing a story line, the actors, relationships, and themes were poorly differentiated and resolution was impossible. The same could be said of Jimmy's play. In both cases, there was an absolute dearth of the richly textured make-believe that we see in neurotic children; instead, it was repetitive and confused. Furthermore, I felt that because of the quality and incoherence of their playing, I had little interpretive leverage. In fact, my efforts to interpret both children's play were most unsuccessful. Often I found that linking the chaos of their play and the strength of their aggressive impulses with their anxiety about the stability and safety of their environments weakened our already tenuous therapeutic alliance.

What I did find helpful, however, was simply playing with them. Over the course of the year of our work together, I tried to help Jimmy learn how to tell a story with his play. He occupied himself throughout many of his early sessions enacting wild crashing scenes with trucks or "eating" episodes with the duck hand puppets. I gradually introduced the notion of telling a story with his play, asking him to name the characters and inquiring about their motivations (e.g., "Why are the ducks doing that?" "Where is the truck going?"). While there were initially few answers to my questions, Jimmy eventually began to supply names and motives for his characters ("It's not a truck, it's an ambulance, and it's going to the hospital in Coney Island"). Stories began to emerge, and feelings were ascribed to characters ("He's hurt. Owwww! He needs a doctor, and has to go to the hospital"). The wild, excited screeching that often accompanied the crash scenes became more differentiated, too, and became clearly delineated ambulance sirens. Eventually, Jimmy began to create coherent scenes of his own accord and to include me in them by spontaneously providing explanations for the characters' actions and behavior. Thus, we were both much closer to the personal and meaningful aspects of his play. I rarely mentioned his real-life pain, nor did I link the violence of his play with the anger and fear I knew he must be experiencing. Instead, we tried to play together. And, over the course of the year, he became more organized, less of a behavior problem, more related, and more relaxed. His mother reported fewer tantrums, he was able to tolerate day care, and he was substantially more accepting of limits.

The same was true of my work with Nicole. For weeks, Nicole acted out scenes of conflict, with squeaks being their only accompaniment. With gentle prodding from me, she finally began to give them speech, to label the actors in her drama, and to tell the story—albeit in a very sketchy fashion—of their battles. The play communicated vividly the chaos of her own home, as well as the fragmentation and overstimulation that were daily realities for her. While she was far from talking about the personal story that lay behind the scenes she was playing out, and responded with notable indifference to any interpretation of her feelings, she was finally beginning to tell a story that made sense to her and to me. She seemed to be learning to describe the pain in ways that were less threatening for her.

Nicole's gradual ability to identify the actors, agents, and feelings in her play narratives brought to light subtle disturbances in reality testing that would have remained hidden had she not begun to tell me about her play. In the early phases of treatment, few narratives were supplied for scenes of a chaotic squirrel family, fighting among superheroes, and the like. Her first attempts at labeling were fairly nonspecific and often preceded wild fighting scenes: "This is a good guy . . . this is a bad guy . . . pow! boom! crash!" The identities of the characters would then shift as the play proceeded: "No, he's a bad guy now, no, he died, no, he's getting up, now he's a good guy." The sources of evil and conflict were for the most part poorly defined, yet men in a number of the scenes were murdered by a "killer tomato." When I asked her about killer tomatoes, she told me that she had seen one in a horror movie; she clearly did not know whether or not to believe in the existence of this terrifying vegetable. Her inability to establish stable identities in play characters, as well as her inability to distinguish fantasy and reality, made it clear that much of our work would have to focus on separating fantasy from reality through the play narratives. To that end, I began focusing quite specifically on the designation of characters and on testing the reality of her stories ("Are there really such things as killer tomatoes?" "Do you think someone can really come back to life once he's dead?" "Which is the good guy and which is the bad one?"). It was my hope that such expectations would permit her to develop play narratives that were more helpful to her, and that would not be as frightening and fragmented as the ones she was presently enacting.

Nicole's treatment continued for several years. Interestingly, she was never able to acknowledge feelings or fantasies verbally, but her play changed considerably over the years. By the time she had been in treatment for over 2 years and was nearing her ninth birthday, she began to look more like a latency-age child, favoring games of checkers and Nerf ball over imaginary play and absorbed in thinking about her favorite boxers and ice hockey players. Her efforts to play out the chaos and disorganization she saw at home had been translated into an interest in violent, highly exciting sporting events. Nevertheless, she had new resources for transformation and sublimation, and although she still lacked the degree of organization necessary to characterize her as neurotic, she had made substantial progress, all of it reflected in the quality of her playing.

Parenthetically, it is important to mention that because of unavoidable limitations on the treatment, I was rarely able to see either set of parents in conjunction with their children's therapy. Thus, it is my strong impression that changes in the children could not be attributed to substantial environmental changes. The success of these two treatments (insofar as Jimmy developed sufficient ego resources to follow simple routines at home and to maintain himself in day care, and Nicole was able to attend school and begin to make friends) raised the following related questions for me: (1) Why were my attempts to link their play with my understanding of their experience so ineffective? (2) What was it about the play itself that was helpful to these children? In other words, why were interventions aimed at linking play with feelings, anxieties, or real-life circumstances less effective than my efforts to join in with and comment upon or expand make-believe and thereby help them in the development of narrative abilities?

Playing and the Clinical Process

Sigmund Freud's particular genius was his recognition that men and women are most pained, and their psychic lives most distorted, by feelings and wishes they cannot accept and cannot express. This vision established the basic mission of psychoanalysis and psychotherapy: to uncover and acknowledge these inner demons so that they may be integrated into the individual's personality in more adaptive and productive ways. The process of bringing to the surface and unmasking is understood by most psychoanalysts to be the primary agent of therapeutic change; it is the interpretation of unconscious, repressed wishes by the analyst that makes structural change possible. While many models have been proposed to understand the change that follows interpretation (Eagle, 1987), the classical position maintains that making the unconscious conscious is among the most important functions of analytic uncovering. Ricoeur (1970) has described this interpretive position as one in which unconscious symbols are invariably viewed as masking a second meaning: "To mean something other than what is said—that is the symbolic function" (p. 12). Thus, interpretation is designed to explicate these second or multiple meanings; in the analytic tradition, according to Ricoeur, overt meanings are treated with "suspicion" by the therapist, who wishes to "substitute for an immediate and dissimulating consciousness a mediate consciousness taught by the reality principle" (p. 35), thereby unmasking, demystifying, or reducing illusions.

Child psychoanalysis began with the pioneering contributions of Melanie Klein (1932) and Anna Freud (1965), who applied these basic principles of unconscious functioning to their work with children and who maintained that the unconscious life of children is revealed through the themes and symbols of play. In particular, it is revealed through the content of their play. Both Klein and Freud—although disagreeing on many critical points of theory and technique—relied upon interpretation of imaginary play as one of the primary means of bringing about therapeutic change in children. In this view of child therapy or analysis, the therapist first deciphers and then interprets the play's true meaning; ultimately, this meaning is verbalized to the child by the therapist or verbalized by the child personally. Together, the child and therapist come to understand that the child's play *means* something. This perspective continues to inform therapists' thinking about what they say to children during the therapeutic hour and what they are trying to achieve with such interpretations.

Emphasis on deciphering the meaning of play content is based on several assumptions that derive directly from Sigmund Freud's writing on the nature and function of symbolization, as explicated in *The Interpretation of Dreams* (1953), as well as his papers on repression (1957a), the unconscious (1957b), and summarized in the *Introductory Lectures* (1961). Freud believed that symbols—whether dream images or fantasies or symbolic reenactments—are directly linked to specific conflicts, feelings, or unconscious fantasies. The assumption of correspondence implies, first, that there exists an explicit one-to-one relationship between symbol and unconscious fantasy, in other words, that play behavior is explicitly referential. In addition to implying a specific relationship between referent and symbol, the assumption of correspondence implies that the underlying conflicts and wishes are themselves consolidated. Freud described the unconscious as a kind of storage container for consolidated ideas that can come to consciousness only in distorted form. Freud believed that the unconscious is comprised of inner images of external veridical perceptions, which by association with the drives acquire a "specific content and become a psychological directional force, the wish for a specific object" (Schimek, 1975, p. 171). Drives then distort these originally objective perceptions; nevertheless, conscious mental representations are directly linked to specific unconscious mental representations. Repression, in the classical sense, pushes aside unacceptable ideas; only if they are consolidated can they be dangerous enough to require distortion.

The assumption of correspondence also implies that symbols as well as many behaviors have specific *meaning*. As he stated in the *Introductory Lectures* (1961), Freud believed that the meaning of a dream may be determined on the basis of knowledge of the "lexicon of ordinary dream symbols," or from the dreamer's associations to specific elements of the dream. In discussing dream symbolism, Freud stated that "the range of things which are given symbolic representation in dreams is not wide: the human body as a whole, parents, children, brothers and sisters, birth, death, nakedness" (p. 153). Thus, a symbol in a dream was understood by Freud to mean something specific and to refer to particular aspects of an individual's psychosexual experience and conflicts. The formal or structural links between a symbol and its referent speak to the cleverness of the unconscious in working its disguise, along with a sort of "will" or purpose that guides the unconscious in its choice of metaphors.

Freud's theory of representation set the stage for therapists' abiding interest in the content and meaning of play. While this has provided generations of therapists with invaluable insights into the meaning of their patients' behavior, it has also led to an overemphasis on deducing the meaning of play through its content. Winnicott (1971) makes this point pungently in *Playing and Reality*: "I seem to see in the psychoanalytic literature the lack of a useful statement on the subject of play. . . . The psychoanalyst has been too busy using play content to look at the playing child, and to write about playing as a thing in itself" (p. 40).

In fairness, there are probably few therapists or analysts who unquestioningly ascribe to Freud's view of symbolism and representation. Similarly, there are probably few child therapists who interest themselves solely in the content of play as a means of uncovering its meaning. Nevertheless, it seems that child therapists are often influenced by Freud's theory of representation in unwitting ways. This *unwitting theory* assumes that the child's play necessarily means something, that that something is relatively concrete, and that the job of the therapist is to figure it out. In other words, therapists are inclined to view play content as a means to understanding the nature of repressed, and necessarily disguised, unconscious experience. This seems especially true of beginning therapists, who have less sense of the function and development of play in treatment. While this approach may often be both meaningful and helpful in working with children, it is important to recognize the developmental assumptions underlying an approach that emphasizes the symbolic meaning of play activity and attempts to uncover the wishes disguised by the child's playing.

An emphasis on the interpretation of disguised wishes that have been repressed implies, first, that the child has developed the ability to make reference to specific experiences. Much of what developmental psychology has taught us over the course of the past decade suggests that the ability to represent specific experience in a stable, meaningful fashion *develops over time*. One of the hallmarks of the psychological functioning of children referred to as *preoedipal*, or in Piaget's (1962) terms *preoperational*, is their striking inability to represent experiences in ways that are coherent and integrated. While the attainment of object permanence certainly indicates that a child has the ability to *represent* an object or experience, ongoing processes of differentiation and integration compromise this process throughout the preoedipal period (Pine, 1985). Certainly, it is some time before young children are able to maintain a sense of the identity of people and things in their world and to understand properly the nature of the relationships between them. These developmental facts raise questions, then, as to when repression proper actually begins to occur; to be able to maintain a specific idea at an unconscious level, one must first have a stable ability to specify experiences. While evidence abounds that preschoolers' representational competence is not to be minimized (Nelson, 1986, 1989), it is nevertheless important not to lose sight of the fluidity and confusion that underlie much of their understanding, particularly in regard to complex emotional events and situations (Pine, 1985).

An emphasis on the interpretation of disguised wishes also assumes that the organizational structures exist to link symbols, which are productions of the conscious mind, to unconscious processes. Freud himself considered this to be a developmental achievement, and one that must have taken place for repression to occur: "Psychoanalytic observation of the transference neuroses . . . leads us to conclude that repression is not a defensive mechanism which is present from the very beginning, and that it cannot arise until a sharp cleavage has occurred between conscious and unconscious mental activity—*that the essence of repression lies simply in turning something away, and keeping it at a distance, from the conscious.* This view of repression would be made more complete by assuming that, before the mental organization reaches this stage, the task of fending off instinctual impulses is dealt with by the other vicissitudes which instincts may undergo—e.g. reversal into the opposite or turning round upon the subject's own self" (1957a, p. 147). In this, and in a second passage where he refers to the unconscious as "organizing itself further" (p. 149), Freud appears to be arguing that the separation of conscious and unconscious, as well as the use of repression as a mode of defending against unwanted impulses, *develop over time*. Furthermore, his indication that more primitive defenses predominate prior to the development of a "sharp cleavage" between the conscious and unconscious underscores the confusion and failures of differentiation that typify early psychic activity.

When we rely upon the interpretation of play in our work with children, then, we assume that unconscious experiences are themselves differentiated, and that the structures that separate conscious and unconscious functioning are in place. However, with some children, such assumptions may not be warranted, depending upon the developmental level of the child. Disguise per se may not be the proper term for describing the relationship between the conscious and unconscious prior to the development of the sharp cleavage Freud delineated. The contents of the unconscious are themselves too diffuse to be specifically disguised, and the modes of organizing against the intrusions of unconscious experiences are themselves less organized and less effective.

Children like Jimmy and Nicole, I would argue, are not hiding/repressing/disguising feelings and fantasies they cannot tolerate. They are living in a chaotic emotional universe that, by virtue of its very disorganization, precludes disguise because it precludes symbolization. Disguise requires psychological structure, the capacity to make reference, and consolidation of internal experience. Disguise requires development that has been lacking in these children. In Freud's terms, disguise requires a cleavage between conscious and unconscious functioning. Jimmy's and Nicole's play does not serve to hide or disguise; rather, their play is a manifestation of the failure to make meaning on any level.

An emphasis on the interpretation of play content further assumes that language has achieved some separation from the domain of action and intention. We use children's play to help them understand their deeper unconscious feelings because—among other things—we believe that the articulation of an unconscious impulse will either provide a modicum of relief from drive tensions or—put differently—give the child tools to organize and integrate internal experiences. However, it is often the case that young or more disturbed children cannot distinguish speaking about an experience from being in it or acting upon it. Thus, even if they can specify an inner experience, its articulation *is* action. The presence of some consolidation does not mean that language is free of its developmental ties to enactment. For more mature children, speaking about emotions makes them seem less live and frightening, whereas for less mature children, speaking about these affects and states can make them seem more real than they already are. In such instances, language does not aid in the defense against uncontrollable feelings, but instead amplifies the sense of lack of control that results from the failure to separate language from action and actuality. Since such actions are often forbidden and the impulses toward them are the cause of deep shame, their articulation by the therapist can be both humiliating and disorganizing. In simple terms, once their feelings have been put into words, these children have few means of protecting themselves from an onslaught of unacceptable and threatening thoughts. For instance, Nicole was unable to respond to any of my comments regarding her feelings about either her parents' or her brother's bizarre behavior and the resultant chaos at home. Only once in 4 years was she able to talk about how embarrassing her brother's odd mannerisms were for her; she was never able to put any of her feelings about her parents into words. Whenever I gently raised the question of her possible worry, fear, or anger (typically in response to a bit of play), she denied such experiences vehemently, withdrew, and stopped playing.

Many of my young patients (I am generally thinking of children under 6) respond with such denial or avoidance when I interpret their feelings to them. Such denial appears to bear little relationship to the depth and stability of the therapeutic alliance or to my cleverness in the timing and wording of the interpretation. It takes many forms. I have been told by 4-year-olds to "shut up!" or "stop wasting my time"; some have simply stamped their feet or put their hands over their ears. One young child regularly locked me in my play closet when I raised issues he could not tolerate. Also the master of the non sequitur, he once responded to my query about a recent bout of rage at his little brother by asking, "Arietta, where did you ever get those beautiful earrings?" Another child, just 5 years old, rebuffed my efforts to talk about her beloved grandfather's moving away, saying, "No talking . . . let's get on with playing!" When I suggested that we could play *and* talk, she said, quite emphatically, "Naaaahhhh." She then used the Ninja turtles and Barbie dolls to tell her story eloquently. I remained silent on the subject of her real life and simply remarked that Barbie certainly had a lot to deal with, given all those scary Ninja turtles trying to get her. In situations like these, I have found that even the introduction of a time limit on talk (Pine, 1985) is of no avail. Sometimes children don't want to talk or to be talked to *at all*.

I do not think that such primitive efforts at denial are responses to premature or overly direct interpretations. Rather, it is my impression that for some young children, the articulation of powerful feelings ("You are feeling so angry at your sister and wish she'd just go away," "You're so angry at your mom for leaving and don't understand why she can't live with you anymore," "You wish you could be a girl so you'd be sure your daddy would love you") brings those feelings to the surface in a way that is overwhelming, shameful, and humiliating. Whether interpretation is liberating or horrifying has everything to do with the degree of consolidation in the developmental picture and with the degree to which language is freed from some of its early ties to the body and to primitive impulses. Only when it has truly become a system of *signifiers* (Piaget, 1962) will interpretation via language be helpful to the child.

The verbal interpretation of unconscious wishes and impulses will be experienced quite differently as a function of the developmental level of the child. The more a child has developed the ability to organize and express internal experiences, has developed the ability to use language in its "signal" functions, and has developed relatively stable abilities to defend against the expression of those that are threatening, the more likely it is that well-timed interpretations will be experienced as illuminating rather than disorganizing. The less mature a child is, the more likely it is that his or her inner life will be experienced as diffuse and unintegrated, and the more likely that mention of such powerful affects and experiences will lead to denial or further disorganization.

One must also consider the role of language in the child's family. Jimmy and Nicole, for example, were growing up with parents who were themselves quite undifferentiated and whose abilities to integrate or express their inner experiences at any level were quite limited. Certainly, the chances of Jimmy's and Nicole's having achieved age-appropriate levels of organization were slim. In addition, both families used language as a means to attack and disorganize other family members rather than to facilitate emotional communication or establish intimacy. For the most part, language functioned to increase conflict and further disrupt relationships. Thus, whatever difficulties Jimmy and Nicole had in freeing language from its developmental links to action and using it as a means of integration were greatly exacerbated by family circumstances.

Finally, the therapist making a verbal interpretation places himself or herself outside the play in a way that is quite different from playing with the child. At the very least, comments about the *meaning* of play assume that the child has the ability to join with the therapist in reflecting either on the play or on his or her inner life. In other words, there is an assumption that together therapist and child can examine the child's inner experience as it is reflected in play or other behaviors and feelings. The ability to tolerate the separation between a feeling and its acknowledgment is a developmental accomplishment; it comes with cognitive as well as ego development, and it cannot be assumed to exist in very young or developmentally compromised children.

The Functions of Playing

When we help children like Jimmy and Nicole learn to play, we help them develop the tools to make sense of things, to link experiences together, and to unravel the tangle of feelings and impulses. We help them to symbolize and to imagine. We tend to think of our work as uncovering meaning, but I think that by learning to play we are helping children to *make* meaning, to make sense of things both consciously and unconsciously, possibly for the first time. It is by means of play that they are *discovering* what they feel, what they know, and what they want. It is also by means of play and imagination that they begin to make sense of what others feel and believe. And as Harris (1989) has so powerfully described it, "[I]magining is a key that unlocks the minds of other people and allows the child temporarily to enter into their plans, hopes and fears" (p. 51). *By putting experiences and feelings into play rather than into words, the child is creating structure.* And by playing with the child, we become a part of the child's discovery of what he or she means to say and means to feel. It is only when experience can be known and represented that it can be hidden; it is only then that deception, repression, and disguise become meaningful terms. And it is only then that interpretation will serve a meaningful function in the treatment. Before these developments take place, language will be experienced as a form of enactment rather than as a form of reference.

Adults figure out how they feel by *talking* it through; very young children figure it out by *playing* about it. The better they are at playing, the more likely they are to tell a story that will be therapeutic for them. Just as adult patients create verbal narratives that pull things together in a way that is clarifying and ultimately curative, children create play narratives that—because they express difficult emotions in a coherent, and fundamentally communicative, fashion—are similarly curative. When our interpretations of such play are disruptive, we can assume that the child does not yet have the resources to distance the self from the play sufficiently to appreciate its meaning. It is the playing itself, the enactment and the discovery, that is mean-ingful. Much the same way that religious rituals such as praying can be experienced as cleansing without our necessarily reflecting on the symbolism inherent in the act, the act of putting things into play and into words can be therapeutic for a child.

Children fail to develop play that is affective, representational, and communicative for different reasons. Jimmy's play made no sense at all. I do not take this to mean that he had no conflicts, but rather that he lacked the capacity to organize his experience in any coherent way. The primitivity of his representational processes reflected an unintegrated, disorganized internal affective experience. He did not know how he felt on any level, nor did he have available the means to create order out of this chaos. Nicole, on the other hand, was more organized internally. Nevertheless, she was unable to tolerate the expression of her feelings, because such expressions threatened her tenuous psychic equilibrium. She could not use representation to organize and integrate her emotional life. With both children, playing provided the most direct means of effecting change in their behavior and relationships. Therapy focused, in effect, upon the playing itself rather than upon the experience it presumably reflected.

What happens in playing that is helpful to children? The process is complex, developmental, and interpersonal and has many aspects. As described by Waelder (1933) and Drucker (1975), play serves a variety of functions for the child. Those I will address here are (1) the development of a narrative, (2) the integration of affect into the narrative, (3) the contextualization of meaning making within an object relationship, and (4) the development of reflective self-function.

The Development of Narrative in Play

One of the first things that a therapist intuitively does when confronted with play that is disorganized, fragmented, and incomprehensible is to label characters, objects, or states in play. This may mean naming the objects or toys a child has chosen or asking the child to name them. Thus, when Jimmy grabbed all the duck puppets and began opening and closing their beaks vigorously, I noted that he'd found the ducks, that they were opening and closing their mouths, and that there was a lot of excitement. Sometimes children spontaneously label their activities and the toys they have chosen, sometimes the therapist will, and sometimes therapist and child work together. (A close reading of Winnicott will reveal how delicately even this simple situation needs to be negotiated. He, for instance, often chose to remain silent.) The goal in labeling is to try to establish who's who, what's what, and what the spirit (excitement, aggression, etc.) of the scene is. In essence, the therapist is letting the child know that there is a stage and that he or she is, in effect, setting it. For children who have rarely had a sense of effectance or control, this itself is a dramatic and powerful intervention.

Once the stage and its players have been set, the emergence of a coherent narrative becomes possible. If the child is to tell a story, objects and players must be related to one another in a meaningful way. A vital part of the therapeutic work is our invitation to link objects and players together. With both Jimmy and Nicole, I asked about the prime players' actions, feelings, and motivations. I remarked that Jimmy's ducks were chewing each other up and wondered if they were hungry. I noted the repeated crashes in Nicole's violent car scenes. I made inquiries about what might be happening and what characters might be feeling, implying that there might eventually be a narrative underlying their actions and that I would be interested in hearing about it. And as the narrative emerged, I tried to expand it and elaborate the story line. For instance, observing a bit of wild ambulance play, I remarked, "Oh, the guy's sick and in the ambulance." As the child then placed the "sick guy" in the ambulance, I added, "Oh, maybe he's going to see the doctor at the hospital," at which point I designated an area in our play space as the hospital. Often these kinds of comments pave the way for the child to create a richer, more dimensional make-believe world. The linking together of events, by making explicit the fact that they are intrinsically and powerfully related to one another, is itself transforming. Children like Jimmy and Nicole have rarely had the experience of an organized, coherent universe and have almost never had the sense that they have any role in creating such organization. They have been constrained in imagining and knowing: in imagining relationships, in imagining inner lives, and in knowing that order can be created.

In work with some children, this is the only kind of play that is possible. And often, play is accompanied by steady improvement in the child, both inside and outside the session. Within the session, play becomes richer and more elaborated, and episodes of play last longer and are more complex. The opportunity to play is greeted with great enthusiasm. Outside the session there is often a decrease in symptoms, as well as reports by parents that their children are less aggressive, anxious, and disorganized.

How can we understand the therapeutic action of this joint, collaborative play? What follows from simply playing with a child? The two most dramatic sequelae are the emergence of narrative and narrative collaboration. The first sequela, the emergence of narrative, has two components: (1) the ability to link action sequences together into a meaningful, *coherent* story and (2) the ability to supply a verbal narrative for such actions. The significance of these two developmental achievements is substantial. In Freud's terms, the development of concrete tools for putting things into action and into words is a pivotal part of the process of developing a cleavage between conscious and unconscious functioning (1957b). As words become means of referencing internal experiences, what is inside and outside, what is wish and what is reality, what is conscious and what is unconscious become more distinct. Children begin to have an affective life that can increasingly be viewed as consolidated and ultimately conflictual (and thereby, finally, interpretable in the classical sense).

More contemporary writers, as diverse in their perspectives as Mahler (Mahler, Pine, & Bergman, 1975), Stern (1985) and Piaget (1952, 1962) have each emphasized the tremendous significance of developing the ability to make sense of the world via symbols and language. For Mahler, it is what makes internalization and object constancy possible; for Stern, it permits new levels of relatedness and interpersonal sharing of meaning; for Piaget, it is the basis of all rational thought. In other words, the development of a separate self capable of choosing to communicate a range of meanings and intentions to another person is contingent upon the ability to use symbols and language in a meaningful way. Recently, developmental psychologists have turned their attention to the specific question of narrative. In *Narratives from the Crib*, Nelson and her colleagues (1989) use the bedtime dialogues and monologues of a toddler named Emily to document the remarkable development of narrative abilities over the second year of life. Emily's talk from 21 to 37 months of age demonstrates her increasing ability to construct a meaningful mental representation of her experience. And it is precisely the ability to represent the world via symbol and narrative that patients such as the ones I have been describing lack.

The level of symbolization ultimately achieved by Jimmy and Nicole was still primitive and basic, that of enactment with a verbal narration. Nevertheless, the significance of their developing the ability to enact experiences coherently cannot be overlooked. As Schimek (1975) notes:

> The different levels at which a concrete experience or object can be represented must not be viewed as merely different codes, different systems of labels attached to the same object. Each level of symbolic representation changes the experience of the object represented, its meaning, function, and relationship to other objects. It is an organizing abstracting process, the construction of a ''higher level of mental organization,'' which cannot be reduced to the distortion or disguise of the contents of a lower level. A dream or fantasy is already a higher level of conscious representation of a motive than the enactment of this motive as concrete action patterns; and the ''interpretation'' of a dream is, in turn, a new, more abstract, higher order construction. Each level makes possible a different way of interacting with the environment, of giving meaning and valence to external events. The kind of symbolic representation or level of consciousness which a motive or drive achieves changes the nature of the motive itself and its influence on behavior. (p. 185)

And just as an interpretation or a fantasy represents a higher-order construction that changes the relationship between the individual and his or her reality, so does enactment. For Jimmy and Nicole, the ability to enact was itself the developmental achievement, the means to consolidation and integration. As language became more directly tied to enactment, it, too, became a means of consolidation and integration. Nevertheless, in cases like these, to engage a child at the level of action is to make the kind of interpretation he or she can understand. The response to a verbal interpretation requires language to have superseded action as a mode of psychological organization. For children like these, enactment *is* their language, and playing with them is our only means of engaging them in a meaningful way.

Play and the Consolidation of Affect

Once a child can tell a story, emotions begin to emerge within the context of the narrative (Bretherton & Beeghly, 1982; Dunn, 1988; Dunn, Bretherton, & Munn, 1987). Characters that had only emitted squeals or sporadic, incomprehensible snatches of dialogue begin to articulate feelings: The man is mad because his car is broken; Barbie is scared; Barbie is happy. The process of naming feelings is a first step in differentiating affect states: distinguishing one affect from another, distinguishing speaking about emotion from acting on it, and distinguishing the emotions of one character from those of another. It typically accompanies the emergence of narrative and is a vital stage in the child's learning how to speak about his or her own feelings, and it is perhaps the first step in discovering how the child feels. It is the beginning of finding sense in terrain that had most likely seemed frightening, overwhelming, and unknowable. It is only after a child has developed the means to express such inner experiences that the therapist can address the child's own feelings. If we ask a child to listen to us talk about his or her feelings before language has taken on an organizing function with respect to emotions, play will be interrupted, behavior will become disorganized, and the child will most likely withdraw.

As just described, addressing the child's *own* feelings can sometimes be quite disruptive; play is interrupted, behavior becomes disorganized, and the child may withdraw. Such disorganization may be attributable to the fact that by asking the child to reflect on personal feelings, we are requiring a level of abstraction that the child is not yet capable of achieving. First, the terrain of emotion has to be established and become familiar; only then will the child have the resources necessary to manage and ultimately reflect upon these experiences. Much in the same way that Winnicott (1965) described children's willingness to adopt a *false self* to protect their core selves from being destroyed by an impinging environment, premature reference to emotional processes can bring about an adaptation that inhibits children from truly making sense of what they feel *on their own*. Collaborative play provides children with the means to discover how and what they feel through play events, characters, and interactions. As explicitly noted by both Freud and Winnicott, the hallmark of primitive disturbances, whether in children or adults, is the *lack of development* both of structures and of the experiences that are ordinarily transformed and elaborated by the development of such structures.

Development of the Therapeutic Relationship

Narratives develop for the *purpose of telling* (Wolf, 1991); when we play with a child, we let the child know that we are there to be told. And as theorists as diverse in their focus as Winnicott (1971), Kohut (1971), and Werner and Kaplan (1963) have noted, symbols emerge within the context of primary object relationships. Children learn to represent internal experiences because these experiences are first made real by another's recognition of them. Winnicott saw the mother's ability to adopt the infant's spontaneous creations, rather than require the infant to adopt her creations, as vital to the infant's experiencing his or her symbols as real and personally meaningful. In Winnicott's view, the child's ego takes over the roles of integrator, synthesizer, and translator that are *first* carried out by the parents. For Winnicott the quality of sharing between mother and child is vital to symbolic development, which takes place as a consequence of the "relaxed self-realization" that follows from trust in the mother's availability. Maternal recognition of the child's gestures and, ultimately, symbols affirms the child in his or her autonomy, yet because the mother has been so intimately involved in the child's symbol making, his or her autonomy does not come at the expense of intimacy and closeness with mother.

Werner and Kaplan (1963) use somewhat different language to make the same point, namely, that symbols emerge in the context of sharing meaning with an "Other"; thus, a critical aspect of the motivation for symbolizing is communication. Werner and Kaplan designate the mother–child relationship as the "primordial sharing situation" and the mother as the individual with whom the child first wishes to share knowledge and meaning: "We may assume that, for the normally developing child, the *sharing* of objects is not simply a secondary condition helpful to the learning about objects or symbols but is rather of vital significance in the child's establishment of a life space, in which he may move with security and confidence" (p. 71). Sharing of contemplated objects with another provides "that necessary primordial basis in which relationships are rooted and from which self, objects, and others emerge and become differentiated from each other without losing their mutual ties" (p. 71). For Werner and Kaplan, objects are first known through sharing them with another and, hence, become "secure-familiar things which can be viewed without fright or fear" (p. 71). They link the calm atmosphere of interpersonal sharing with the capacity to form stable, integrated, and meaningful symbols.

Both Winnicott and Werner and Kaplan see the richness of the symbolic world as inextricably tied to the mother's ability to help the child create meaning within the context of their playing together. Kohut (1971) similarly links early failures in maternal empathy and mirroring to an individual's inability to develop a coherent sense of self and—in particular—a sense of oneself as worthy and emotionally alive. Kohut's reliance on *coherence* as a metaphor for what is lacking in narcissistic patients has much in common, of course, with our emphasis here on narrative and the child's ability to create meaningfully his or her own story. Miller (1981), too, refers to the relationship between maternal responsiveness and an awareness of one's own inner life: "An adult can only be fully aware of his feelings if he has internalized an affectionate and empathic self-object. People with narcissistic disturbances are missing out on this" (p. 21).

Research carried out over the past decade has confirmed that both the ability to express emotions and the ability to tell a story using symbolic play are closely related to the quality of the mother–child relationship. Even in earliest infancy, it is the parents' early designation of the baby's feeling states as meaningful and communicative that makes them real and coherent for the baby (Stern, 1985). Furthermore, which affects mothers choose to attune to are powerfully dictated by their own histories (Haft & Slade, 1989). Virginia Demos (1988), a psychoanalytically oriented infant researcher, offers a wonderful vignette of a mother who perpetually designated her infant's interest as boredom. This child's curiosity and interest generated none of the enthusiasm, excitement, and interest one might expect in a mother who saw her baby as excited and intrigued by the world. Instead it generated frustration, withdrawal, and uninterest in the mother. Demos speculates that this baby's internal experience of "interest" thus becomes associated with a certain kind of empty and unsatisfying exchange, to be experienced in a blunted, vague fashion.

Many empirical studies of early symbolic play have linked aspects of the ability to symbolize with the mother–child relationship. Toddlers whose passage through the separation-individuation process was compromised were found to have fragmented, incoherent, and less sharable symbolic play (Slade, 1986). Research based on Bowlby's theory (1969, 1982) and Ainsworth, Blehar, Waters, and Wall's (1978) attachment paradigm has reported similar findings, particularly that children classified as insecure in their attachment to their mothers derive less pleasure from their play (Main, 1973), have fewer episodes of symbolic play (Bretherton, Bates, Benigni, Camaioni & Volterra, 1979; Slade, 1987), sustain play episodes for shorter periods of time (Slade, 1987), and engage in less complex symbolic play (Bretherton et al., 1979; Slade, 1987). In addition, mothers of secure children were more likely to be actively involved with their children, while mothers of anxious children favored more passive forms of involvement. Interestingly, when engaged in more interactive play, secure children had higher-level and longer play episodes; this suggests that they are better able to use the interpersonal context for symbolic communication. Belsky, Garduque, and Hrncir (1984) reported that secure children were more likely to play at their highest level of competence than were anxious children; thus, while they did not differ from their anxious counterparts in overall ability, they differed in the level of their spontaneous play. Taken together, these results confirm theoretical assumptions regarding the relationship between the history of the mother–child interaction and the child's ability and willingness to symbolize.

The kind of playing we have been describing here is much more like mother–child play than any other kind of playing. Like the mother, the therapist helps the young child make sense of the world by helping the child develop the tools to label and narrate its many dimensions and to give feeling and life to its many inhabitants. In one sense, the therapist is "in" the play with the child; in another sense, the therapist is outside the play, both encouraging and helping the child to expand, elaborate, and define it. When we encounter child patients who lack the ability to enact and narrate the most simple themes at the most rudimentary level, we may not only assume a lack of structure, as well as the absence of emotional development, but also dramatic failures in the environment's ability to create what has been variously called a *holding environment* or a *primordial sharing situation*. For these children, self-discovery has been a lonely and incomplete struggle.

The question of the function of narrative is related to issues of object relations and symbolization. As Wolf (1991) so beautifully describes, telling a story is inevitably a social, communicative act. The development of narratives in treatment cannot be viewed simply as the result of a child's learning to tell a story. He tells his story to another, someone he has come to believe will listen, will engage, and will *play* with him.

The Emergence of Reflection

As play becomes genuinely representational, a story emerges that is imbued with feeling and vitality, and it is comfortably and pleasurably shared with another. For many children, the play becomes a thing in itself: to be repeated, elaborated, and—ultimately—reflected upon. This is the stage at which play can be *examined* by the child along with his therapist, with the shared understanding that it may have meanings beyond its manifest content and the pleasure it affords the players. At a certain point in the treatment, the therapist and child step outside the play *together*; it is then that interpretation may finally become meaningful. The success of this kind of stance depends upon the child's being able to join the therapist in this process; if this cannot happen, interpretations and reflections are experienced as intrusions rather than communications and inquiries.

Sometimes the act of reflecting on a bit of play will free the child to speak of concerns implied by the play. Phoebe, for instance, was having a good deal of trouble managing her feelings of intense rivalry with her younger, charming brother. She was 4 and he was an infant, as sunny and social and she was quiet and intense. One of her favorite games was one we together came to call the "brother game," in which she lined up a series of toy soldiers in a circle and aimed all their guns toward a single figure in the middle. Due to a manufacturer's defect (!), this particular figure had no head; she called it "the brother" and routinely had it destroyed by the circle of soldiers. Interestingly, she usually became very silly and wild as this game progressed. After weeks of commenting on the fate of the brother in the game, I finally shifted from describing the intensity of her rage (which she ignored) and said instead that she kept getting too excited and wild to continue the game. In effect, I reflected on the process rather than the content of her game. She looked at me and smiled. "Do you know what my brother did today? He took my toys. Sometimes I just feel like putting him in a big garbage bag and leaving him out with the garbage!" Together we were able to reflect on the *process* of playing, using it as a means of talking about something painful and upsetting. Drucker's Allison (Chapter 4, this volume) offers an example of more mature forms of reflection.

At a certain point in the treatment, the therapist and child step outside the play *together*. The success of this stance depends upon the child's ability to join the therapist in this process. If this is not possible, interpretations and reflections are experienced as intrusions rather than communications and inquiries.

The functions of play described above are interwoven strands that cannot be separated from one another in practice. Nevertheless, it can be helpful to think of them as distinct entities for the purpose of clarifying component processes. Development along these lines makes the emergence of structure possible and paves the way for the development of more meaningful, communicative, and ultimately healing play.

Simply Playing and the Older Child

It has been my experience over the years that even older, healthier children sometimes find traditional uncovering approaches to play disruptive; they, too, may require a long period of the kind of playing described above. Even if play narratives have been well established and emerge quickly in the treatment, it may be some time before the "calm atmosphere of interpersonal sharing" Winnicott (1971) describes can develop. As the following cases illustrate, work with these types of children raises many complex issues regarding decisions to interpret or comment on play. Clinicians vary in the degree to which they feel comfortable talking about conflicts when the child is overtly resistant to listening or responding; and children differ in the degree to which they *ever* talk about their actual lives and feelings. Sometimes even dramatic developments in play, in symbolization, and in behavior occur without concomitant changes in the ability to express emotional experiences in words. In my view, these symbolic developments are indeed the manifestations of structural change, and we are misled if we await verbal confirmation of them. "It is in playing and only in playing that the individual child or adult is able to be creative and to use the whole personality, and it is only in being creative that the individual discovers the self'' (Winnicott, 1971, p. 54).

Kate, age 6, was the first of her parents' two children. Her brother, two years her junior, had been severely ill with a congenital heart ailment and had required numerous hospitalizations and surgeries. He died when she was 4. As a consequence of the prolonged family crisis, her parents' emotional unavailability during much of the ordeal, as well as the loss of her sibling, Kate was a child unable to openly acknowledge sadness, fear, or vulnerability; what she expressed instead was anger and a need for control. She was intense, demanding, and relentless; her provocations often succeeded in infuriating her parents and driving them away. It was often difficult for them to remember just how vulnerable and needy she really felt. Their anger at her provocations was compounded by their own grief, although both used their own therapy as well as occasional sessions with me to address these feelings. Treatment was initiated because of their feeling defeated by her tantrums and anger, and because they longed to see her happier. Both found themselves engaged in fruitless battles with her, which inevitably left them feeling defeated and helpless. Kate, for her part, denied any reaction to her brother's death and had little perspective on the reasons behind her unhappiness and rage.

Kate was an extremely intelligent but irascible child, with a fierce temper and a loud voice. As might be expected, she tested me aggressively and repeatedly from Day 1. She readily made it clear that she had no intention of talking about her feelings, and that she was going to control the sessions. At the same time, she also *played* from Day 1. Nevertheless, what I found most challenging was finding a way to *play* with her. Because her make-believe was so *apparently* symbolic and her representational abilities were so well developed, it took me a long time to appreciate how much she, too, just needed to play. Only when she was able to enact her struggles within our transferential relationship for a long time did her play begin to change and her ability to reflect begin to emerge.

One of Kate's favorite games was squeeze me into the tiny space between the door to my consulting room and the door to my office waiting room. She would designate me as the pig, herself as the wolf, and the little enclosure as a stove. She would then cook me to a crisp and eat me, one limb at a time. The game would then reverse, and she would be the pig and I the wolf. I would threaten to cook her and make "pig pie," but she would escape every time. I was reduced to being the hapless wolf, unable to trap a wily little pig, which delighted her no end. This eating game emerged around the age of 5 and had many variations. The underlying themes were unchanged, however. What was compelling about these games was how driven and incessant they were. Once she began the cycle, we would repeat it again and again for virtually the whole session. Invariably, I was devoured and she was insatiable, or she cleverly undermined my efforts to eat her and escaped, leaving me hungry and frustrated.

By the time these games emerged, I had been working with Kate for nearly a year. And as they emerged, I began to try to interpret them. Unsuccessfully. Nothing I asked or said about her play changed it (or its aggression or intensity), nor did such efforts yield any change in what she was willing to talk about with me. She vigorously opposed my efforts to talk or understand and once angrily exploded at me——

"You want to know EVERYTHING, don't you?"—making it clear that as far as she was concerned, I was best off knowing nothing. Eventually, I stopped trying to make sense of Kate's play to her and "simply played" with her. The games themselves began to be transformed, with me as a co-player. One day, after eating me up, she sat down in my chair and told me that I was to be a policeman policing the amount of meat she was allowed. Then ensued a long series of games in which I was first the policeman trying to control her eating; she was a wolf with special governmental dispensation to eat as many as 3,000 sheep a day. I, as the policeman, would then take her before the judge to prosecute her rampant sheep eating. I would then switch roles and become the judge, explaining to myself, as the policeman, that she had special privileges and could eat as much as she wanted. Thus, the punishing and nurturing objects battled each other while she watched. The judge always won, and the policeman was always humiliated and was typically fired. Kate, as the wolf, always got to eat her fill.

After many many weeks of this game (interspersed with other games designed to maintain her dominant position in our relationship), a subtle switch occurred and I, as the judge, began to give her dessert. She began to ask for more and more, and the game shifted to my creating and delivering to her more elaborate and substantial desserts: 4,000 chocolate cakes, 1,000 candy bars, and the like. We would then eat these delicious concoctions together. Finally, one day, we were sitting side by side on my couch, having just "consumed" huge quantities of dessert, and she turned to me and said simply, "Do you know that my mother has never let me have a whole ice cream sundae?"

This was the first time Kate had ever shared anything like that with me. We talked about it a bit, and I told Kate I'd see if there was some way I could talk to her mother about this problem. Whatever the truth of this report, Kate was feeling pained by the food battles she was having with her mother. I encouraged Ms. N to let Kate control her own food, assuming that she would eventually regulate herself sensibly. This became a concrete means of addressing Ms. N's unwitting deprivation of Kate and of helping her understand the anxiety underlying Kate's need for control. Her mother agreed to this, and Kate began making her own decisions about what and when she would eat. She gained no extra weight, and the power struggles between them diminished across the board.

The most remarkable change took place in an entirely separate area, however. Kate did not suddenly begin to talk in her sessions with me, but she did begin to choose dolls and figures when she came in rather than long, abusive enactments with me. Shortly after she began to control her own food, she initiated a fight among a group of figures. Kate almost always referred to herself and any toy figures as masculine when she played. Naturally, I spontaneously did so as I narrated her play action. She quickly corrected me and said that some of the figures were female. Several minutes later, she referred to one of the figures as "dudettes," feminizing the popular term "dude." Kate's willingness to endow her play characters with characteristics of femininity and—by implication—vulnerability marked a striking shift. Interestingly and importantly, this shift was accompanied by a move to toys and away from physical enactment. The change did not take place in the realm of talking or understanding but in the realm of playing. It was accompanied in her real life by an increased willingness to allow herself to be more open and vulnerable with both her parents and by a decrease in angry scenes and confrontations.

This "unfolding" took nearly 2 years. The period was marked on my part by gradual relinquishing of a commenting, questioning, interpretive stance and by my becoming more and more actively involved in the play itself. I had a reasonable idea of what the play meant, but there seemed little direct way to discuss such meanings with Kate. In her case, the problem was not one of creating a narrative or of infusing it with affect. There was plenty of that. What was problematic was the driven and ultimately compulsive quality of the play, which effectively severed its tie to the feelings that gave it its shape and intensity. As I became a partner in the play and an object relationship emerged, the play could be transformed and ultimately linked to meaning and feeling.

The Therapist's Failure to Play

It is often the case that children figure things out by playing about them, and that their solutions to their conflicts and concerns can often be dramatically conveyed by shifts in the structure and function of their play. Our playing with them may well help that process. By the same token, our inability or unwillingness to do so may thwart such developmental movement and disrupt play. Two cases serve to illustrate instances in which therapeutic interventions disrupted playing.

After a particularly busy session in which she played the two games that most dramatically conveyed her concerns about maternal abandonment and sibling rivalry, Phoebe pulled out the Legos and began quietly building an elaborate structure. Feeling (as I suspect therapists often do) that I needed to tell her what I thought she had been playing about (and going counter to my own judgment regarding too much talk in therapy), I began to tell her a story about a girl named Lisa. Lisa, I told Phoebe, had some worries that were very much like her own. Sensing her interest, I continued, describing Lisa's feelings in more detail. Phoebe kept listening but seemed more distracted as I continued my story. She, meanwhile, was struggling with the Legos and suddenly exclaimed—apparently to the Legos—"You better shut up!" I laughed and said that I bet she wished I would shut up, too, and she grinned. Undaunted, however, I continued with my story about Lisa. Phoebe's patience by this point was at an end. Turning to me, she said, "I'm working hard on this, and I need QUIET!" Finally, I heard her. She had already played about her feelings about sharing Mommy and hating her sibling, and now she was ready for some quiet time to consolidate.

Another, more serious disruption occurred in my work with Jenny, whom I treated for 2 years between the ages of 7 and 9 and who returned to treatment at the age of 11. The presenting complaint at the time she resumed treatment was an anxious and guilty preoccupation with memories of "doctor" play with a female playmate some months prior to the onset of her anxiety symptoms. She described being unable to get the thoughts out of her mind and worried that she was going "crazy." After talking about the situation for several weeks (she was quite verbal and well past the stage of playing in psychotherapy), she began playing a game of doctor with me. In this case, one of us was alternately designated as the doctor and the other as the patient who was ill and in need of a checkup and medicine. The "doctor" would check the "patient" over, give the necesary medicine and injections, and send the patient home. We would then switch roles. This play went on for a number of weeks without a break, and without any variation in theme or content. Feeling the need to use this play as a means to talk about her sexual preoccupations and her guilt over the doctor play with her playmate, I made what would properly be called an id or content interpretation. I remarked that we were playing doctor, too, but that our play was different from the doctor play she'd been involved in with her friend. I asked her what she thought about it, and wondered if her playing it with me was a way of trying to find a way to talk about it or to do it in a way that felt more safe. Unfortunately (and unsurprisingly, in retrospect), Jenny seemed quite embarrassed by the interpretation and stopped playing the game altogether. She readily acknowledged the link between her play with her friend and her play with me, but she was unable to talk about these links or about the way my interpretation made her feel. It would have been far more useful to help her expand the play or to help her develop it to the point where its meaning became more obvious to both of us.

In our attempts to tell children what we think they mean, we sometimes interfere with their playing in ways that are not at all helpful. These empathic failures seem most likely to arise when interpretation precedes the facilitation of play. This often leads to an overemphasis on the meaning of or motivation behind the play and to an underemphasis on playing itself. Winnicott (1971) makes a similar point:

> Interpretation outside the ripeness of the material is indoctrination and produces compliance. A corollary is that resistance arises out of interpretation given outside the area of the overlap of the patient's and the analyst's playing together. Interpretation when the patient has no capacity to play is simply not useful, or causes confusion. When there is mutual playing, then interpretation according to accepted psychoanalytic principles can carry the therapeutic work forward. This playing has to be spontaneous, and not compliant or acquiescent, if psychotherapy is to be done. (p. 51)

In this same paper, Winnicott discusses the pressure clinicians feel to make "smart" interpretations, even when play is disorganized and apparently meaningless:

> The therapist who cannot take this communication [of nonsense] becomes engaged in a futile attempt to find some organization in the nonsense, as a result of which the patient leaves the nonsense area because of hopelessness about communicating nonsense. An opportunity for rest has been missed because of the therapist's need to find sense where nonsense is. The patient has been unable to rest because of a failure of the environmental provision, which undid the sense of trust. The therapist has, without knowing it, abandoned the professional role, and has done so by bending over backwards to be a clever analyst, and to see order in chaos. (p. 56)

Both the countertransferential need to cure magically with words, as well as the belief that a specific conflict can be deduced from all sorts of play activities, influence therapists in powerful and often unrecognized ways.

Concluding Remarks

Simply playing is among our most valuable clinical tools. For children who lack the ability to make sense of their emotional and social worlds using the tools of representation, or whose abilities are impaired by conflict, playing with another person offers them the tools they need within the context of a safe and benign holding environment. In this setting, knowledge and emotion can begin to be woven together at the representational level and in an object relations context. It is my strong sense that for some children it is the playing itself that is curative, much the way talking with play and finally talking alone are for older children and adults. For young children, playing itself is integrative.

When a child's developmental status requires this emphasis on enhancing and elaborating the ability to play, the therapist's view of his or her own role necessarily changes. The emphasis on facilitating the *discovery* of meaning rather than the *uncovering* of hidden meaning places the therapist in the play with the child, discovering with the child what they mean to play. In this situation, we are no longer purveyors of knowledge or omniscient translators of psychic experience; rather, we are curious co-explorers who have a little more experience at how best to dig. If we accept the notions of Winnicott, Werner and Kaplan, and others, the therapist's willingness to *share* in the discovery of meaning cannot help but move the process along. The therapist's availability as a listening and participating other give coherence and integrity to the child's representations.

It is important to emphasize that I do not mean to offer a formula or strategy for playing with young therapy patients. What I intend is to try to understand better what I think most therapists do intuitively with their patients, and to use such understanding to clarify technical issues in the treatment of young or severely disturbed children. Such notions are applicable to the treatment of older, more integrated children as well, where playing qua playing can be just as important a part of the therapy as talking and understanding. While I think most therapists *know* this from their work, disguise and interpretation have received far more emphasis in the clinical literature. Notable exceptions are the contributions of Drucker (Chapter 4, this volume), Scarlett (Chapter 3, this volume), and Santostefano (1978). Santostefano is one of the few psychoanalytically oriented clinicians working today who has written about the need to help children build cognitive structures and narrative strategies within the context of ongoing treatment.

The prevalent emphasis in the literature on interpretation and meaning does appear to be strongly rooted in classic psychoanalytic notions of the relationship between unconscious mental representation and behavior. As noted above, this emphasis on disguise may be developmentally incorrect for many children and may deflect attention from a consideration of the importance of enactment itself. Enactment is a path to the creation of meaning, not to the discovery of experiences that are already consolidated and have been repressed. Freud's original writings on repression and the dynamic unconscious were derived from his work with adults and with individuals whose development he considered in oedipal terms; consequently, his descriptions emphasize the uncovering of repressed ideas and conflicts. While these notions may be of enormous value in treating children (and adults) whose conflicts are consolidated and integrated around oedipal constellations and subsequent developmental crises, they are of less use in treating children whose capacities for symbolization and abstraction are limited and who, therefore, cannot be viewed as yet capable of either internalized conflict or its disguised expression.

It is particularly important for therapists and analysts to think about the *process* most likely to lead our patients toward the therapeutic "moments" (Pine, 1985) of developmental consolidation. Published case reports often pay great attention to moments of insight or affective consolidation and considerably less to the months of work that make it possible for these moments to happen. In instances where the development of well-articulated narrative modes is often the aim of treatment, what are so often considered the "background" moments of therapy deserve as much careful consideration as the "foreground" moments of consolidation. The notion that therapeutic change resides in moments of insight resulting from verbalization (either the analyst's or the patient's) derives from early psychoanalytic notions of the relationship between verbal interpretation, catharsis, and structural shifts. The issue of whether or not this model is applicable to the treatment of older children and adults cannot be addressed more completely here. However, it does seem likely that this model is useful only some of the time and then only with some children.

These considerations raise important questions regarding the training of child therapists. The experience of waiting for weeks or even months for a piece of interpretable behavior, or of being puzzled by a child's fantasies or play constructions, is common for child clinicians. Nevertheless, the *process* of creating meaning is rarely addressed in the literature. As a consequence, this aspect of the work is particularly difficult for the neophyte, who will have read numerous accounts of therapists' creative responses to their patients' equally creative symbolic play and are likely more than a little unsettled by the dearth of such material in their own work, especially in the early phases of treatment. It may also help temper and contextualize some of the anxiety and boredom that are often part of the work of helping the child find a way to play. Even experienced therapists feel a pressure to interpret and make sense of play for their patients; somehow, such exchanges seem like *real* therapy, whereas playing per se does not. I still find myself feeling uneasy and guilty when a child and I have been "simply playing" for a long time, and I often begin wondering how I can bring us back to what we're *really* supposed to be working on. Winnicott was right: It is sometimes safer to be clever than to play.

The position I am arguing has much in common with the latter-day emphasis on narrative within developmental psychology and psychoanalysis. Bruner (1990) has argued that the representation of an experience in narrative serves "cooling" functions and contains otherwise disturbing or disruptive affective states. Main and her colleagues (Main & Goldwyn, in press; Main, Kaplan, & Cassidy, 1985) have linked the quality and coherence of narrative with the integrity and level of attachment and object relationships. In his writings on narration in psychoanalysis, Schafer (1983) has emphasized the critical role played by the analyst as "co-author" in the creation of a meaningful, synthetic, and ultimately healing narrative. Spence (1982, 1987) has also emphasized the curative value of patient and analyst creating a narrative that is emotionally vital and coherent. He, too, sees the aim of analysis as discovery rather than uncovering, and he stresses the vital role of telling a story that makes emotional and personal sense to the patient.

Once we view the therapeutic milieu as necessarily analogous to the early parent–child dialogue, where meaning and symbols are created rather than uncovered, our views of the therapeutic process and of our role as therapists must change. We are "coauthors" of the patient's narratives (Schafer, 1983), using language as much to enrich dialogue as to generate insight. While clinicians cannot lose sight of the *possible* meanings of play, it is just as important to help the child figure out ways to bring these meanings into focus and be able to play in ways that are rich and consolidating. The more unable a child is to play, the more it is necessary to help him or her find ways of playing by helping to create stories, infuse them with feelings, and share them with another. Clinicians who work with young or very disturbed children do so naturally; nevertheless, we must begin to broaden traditional views of the meaning and function of play by incorporating our experience with young or prerepresentational children into the psychoanalytic literature on play and playing.

ACKNOWLEDGMENTS

I would like to thank Lisa Marcus, Irving Steingart, and Dennie Wolf for their generously taking the time to read and thoroughly comment on several earlier versions of this chapter. Their input truly helped me find and make meaning. I would also like to thank the students who attended my graduate seminar on symbolic processes from 1987 to 1991 for their help in developing and thinking through the point of view presented here.

NOTES

1. This term is borrowed from Drucker's (1979) description of an infant and mother "just playing." This exceptional paper was one of the first of its kind to address directly the relationship between object relations development and symbolization, and powerfully influenced my thinking on the subject.

2. The term *psychoanalytic treatment* will be used to designated psychoanalytically oriented psychotherapy as well as psychoanalysis. The term *therapist* will be used to designate an individual who conducts either psychoanalytically oriented psychotherapy or psychoanalysis. The differences between these two modes of treatment are complex, particularly in childhood, and will not be dealt with due to space limitations.

REFERENCES

Ainsworth, M., Blehar, M., Waters, E., & Wall, S. (1978). *Patterns of attachment: A psychological study of the strange situation.* Hillsdale, NJ: Erlbaum.

Belsky, J., Garduque, L., & Hrncir, E. (1984). Assessing performance, competence and exec-
    utive capacity in infant play: Relations to home environment and security of attach-
    ment. *Developmental Psychology, 20,* 406–417.
Bowlby, J. (1969). *Attachment.* New York: Basic Books.
Bowlby, J. (1982). *Loss.* New York: Basic Books.
Bretherton, I., Bates, E., Benigni, L., Camaioni, L., & Volterra, V. (1979). Relationships
    between cognition, communication and quality of attachment. In E. Bates, L. Benigni,
    I. Bretherton, L. Camaioni, & V. Volterra (Eds.), *The emergence of symbols: Cognition
    and communication in infancy* (pp. 223–270). New York: Academic Press.
Bretherton, I., & Beeghly, M. (1982). Talking about internal states: The acquisition of an
    explicit theory of mind. *Developmental Psychology, 18,* 906–921.
Bruner, J. (1990). *Acts of meaning.* Cambridge, MA: Harvard University Press.
Demos, V. (1988, October). The affective self. Paper presented to the Annual Meetings of
    the Association for Self Psychology, New York City.
Drucker, J. (1975). Toddler play: Some comments on its functions in the developmental
    process. *Psychoanalysis and Contemporary Science, 4,* 479–528.
Drucker, J. (1979). The affective context and psychodynamics of first symbolization. In N.
    Smith and M. Franklin (Eds.), *Symbolic functioning in childhood,* (pp. 27–40). Hills-
    dale, NJ: Erlbaum.
Dunn, J. (1988). *The beginnings of social understanding.* Cambridge, MA: Harvard University
    Press.
Dunn, J., Bretherton, I., & Munn, P. (1987). Conversations about feeling states between
    mothers and their young children. *Developmental Psychology, 23,* 132–139.
Eagle, M. (1987). *Recent developments in psychoanalysis: A critical evaluation.* Cambridge,
    MA: Harvard University Press.
Freud, A. (1965). *Normality and pathology in childhood.* New York: International Universities
    Press.
Freud, S. (1953). The interpretation of dreams. In J. Strachey (Ed. and Trans.), *The standard
    edition of the complete psychological works of Sigmund Freud* (Vols. 4 and 5, pp. 1–
    723). London: Hogarth Press. (Original work published 1900.)
Freud, S. (1957a). Repression. In J. Strachey (Ed. and Trans.), *The standard edition of the
    complete psychological works of Sigmund Freud* (Vol. 14, pp. 141–158). London:
    Hogarth Press. (Original work published 1915.)
Freud, S. (1957b). The unconscious. In J. Strachey (Ed. and Trans.), *The standard edition of
    the complete psychological works of Sigmund Freud* (Vol. 14, pp. 159–216). London:
    Hogarth Press. (Original work published 1915.)
Freud, S. (1961). Introductory lectures on psychoanalysis. In J. Strachey (Ed. and Trans.),
    The standard edition of the complete psychological works of Sigmund Freud (Vol. 15,
    pp. 3–234). London: Hogarth Press. (Original work published in 1916.)
Haft, W., & Slade, A. (1989). Affect attunement and maternal attachment: A pilot study.
    Infant Mental Health Journal, 10, 157–172.
Harris, P. (1989). *Children and emotion.* Oxford: Basil Blackwell.
Klein, M. (1932). *The psychoanalysis of children.* London: Hogarth.
Kohut H. (1971). *The analysis of the self.* New York: International Universities Press.
Mahler, M., Pine, F., & Bergman, A. (1975). *The psychological birth of the human infant.*
    New York: Basic Books.
Main, M. (1973). *Play, exploration and competence as related to child–adult attachment.*
    Unpublished doctoral dissertation, Johns Hopkins University, Baltimore.
Main, M., & Goldwyn, R. (in press). Interview based adult attachment classifications: Related
    to infant–mother and infant–father attachment. *Developmental Psychology.*

Main, M., Kaplan, N., & Cassidy, J. (1985). Security in infancy, childhood and adulthood: A move to the level of representation. *Monographs of the Society for Research in Child Development, 50* (1–2, Serial No. 209).

Miller, A. (1981). *The drama of the gifted child.* New York: Basic Books.

Nelson, K. (1986). *Event knowledge: Structure and function in development.* Hillsdale, NJ: Erlbaum.

Nelson, K. (1989). *Narratives from the crib.* Cambridge, MA: Harvard University Press.

Piaget, J. (1952). *The origins of intelligence in children.* New York: International Universities Press.

Piaget, J. (1962). *Play, dreams and imitation in childhood.* New York: Norton.

Pine, F. (1985). *Developmental theory and clinical process.* New Haven, CT: Yale University Press.

Ricoeur, P. (1970). *Freud and philosophy.* New Haven, CT: Yale University Press.

Santostefano, S. (1978). *A biodevelopmental approach to clinical child psychology.* New York: Wiley.

Schafer, R. (1983). *The analytic attitude.* New York: Basic Books.

Schimek, J. (1975). A critical re-examination of Freud's concept of mental representation. *International Review of Psychoanalysis, 2,* 171–187.

Slade, A. (1986). Symbolic play and separation-individuation: A naturalistic study. *Bulletin of the Menninger Clinic, 50,* 541–563.

Slade, A. (1987). The quality of attachment and early symbolic play. *Developmental Psychology, 23,* 78–85.

Spence, D. (1982). *Historical truth and narrative truth.* New York: Norton.

Spence, D. (1987). *The Freudian metaphor.* New York: Norton.

Stern, D. (1985). *The interpersonal world of the infant.* New York: Basic Books.

Waelder, R. (1933). The psychoanalytic theory of play. *Psychoanalytic Quarterly, 2,* 208–224.

Werner, H., & Kaplan, B. (1963). *Symbol formation.* New York: Wiley.

Winnicott, D. W. (1965). *Maturational processes and the facilitating environment.* New York: International Universities Press.

Winnicott, D. W. (1971). *Playing and reality.* London: Tavistock.

Wolf, D. P. (1991, June 7). Narrative, narration and narrators in childhood. Paper presented at the Eighth Annual Lee B. Macht Series, Harvard Medical School, Department of Continuing Education.

II

RELATIONSHIPS
AND
SYMBOLIZATION

Although play is often compared to fantasy and dreams, it is fundamentally unlike those private forms of reverie. Symbolic play, in particular, is deeply social. Even the earliest forms of pretense—''gotcha'' and ''peekaboo'' games—depend on a shared conspiracy between self and other. They involve, at the very least, a pact to drop immediate concerns and to transform or ignore reality. Equally, many forms of playful inventions—like 2-year-olds' going-away games or 5-year-olds' animations of toy dinosaurs—require another to be amazed or delighted, even if just as a witness. Even when play occurs in solitude, in the middle of the kitchen floor, or in a corner, it remains social: Its routines and its symbols were once, and often still remain, stamped with the delight, intensity, or indifference with which they were once greeted. The chapters in part II explore this aspect of playing, asking how the presence or even the recollection of another person structures, sustains, or infiltrates the conduct and the content of the child's play.

6

The Leaving Game, or I'll Play You and You Play Me: The Emergence of Dramatic Role Play in 2-Year-Olds

ELSA FIRST

This chapter describes a typical child–parent game of hiding and leave taking discovered in a naturalistic study of the home play of children during the third year of life. The unfolding of this game revealed the capacity for dramatic play *in statu nascendi*. To see how a 2-year-old plays depends on the child's having an older, willing coplayer (e.g., a parent or other caregiver or older sibling or friend) rather than agemates only to play with. By witnessing these joint productions, I was able to ask: What might we properly consider the earliest forms of dramatic play, and what do these forms have to teach us about the nature and significance of the capacity to pretend to be someone else? Given that what I collected were samples of child–parent co-productions, I was also able to examine the interpersonal origins of dramatic play.

The game, which I call the *Leaving Game*, is made up of the conjunction of two motifs initiated by the child: "I'm leaving" and You cry." In this study the game emerged around age 2.4. The game is of intrinsic interest as a spontaneous family ritual that appeared to mark a particular developmental stage, as did other common games found in the collection (e.g., a game of refusals found at ages 2.8–2.9). It also proved to be a "window" through which one could focus back on the even earlier forms of dramatic role play, which seems to emerge between ages 2.0 and 2.4 as a distinctive mode of aesthetic-symbolic expression in its own right.

As a result of my observations, and throughout what I have to say here, I consider drama, and with it dramatic play, as a distinctive and not a hybrid mode, with its own elements, methods of composition, and unique evocativeness, just as verbal narrative or representational drawing are distinctive modes of representational expression. I am proceeding, in a sense, as Freud did when he considered dreams as a distinctive, though unconscious, expressive mode constrained by its own "considerations of plastic representability." Briefly, I suggest that drama has to do with what can effectively be represented by actors on a stage (or play space).

It is not easy to define precisely what one would recognize as dramatic role play in the play of 2- to 3-year-olds. The familiar dramatic roles that 3- to 5-year-olds play (e.g., fireman, king, princess of power, etc.) already draw on quite abstract and generalized concepts, or borrow from preexisting fictive characters located in a social realm. The 2-year-old, however, is only just moving from pretend action sequences or pretend action-with-dialogue sequences to more elaborated and more thoroughly imagined play, which involves both two pretend roles as well as plot and dialogue, in which the roles may or may not be explicitly named. Sometimes the roles are ambiguous or indicated only by the plot. But the point is that the child now is playing at representing a person (or another creature) rather than simply pretending to perform an activity, and that pretend character is found in a dramatic relationship with another pretend character. It is the emergence of this sort of pretending, and the meaningfulness of these transient dramatic scenes in their momentary family context, that I wish to examine.

Whether the role was verbally labeled or not did not seem the best criterion for this sort of pretending. Instead, what I decided to take as a distinct marker of pretending to be someone other than oneself was a moment first appearing at around age 2.4 when the child is able to reverse roles explicitly with a co-player, as in the form of "I'm Mommy and you are me." A later ability, appearing at around ages 2.6 to 2.8, to rotate pretend roles between two or more co-players also indicates that a density of imagining had been reached, since roles cannot be switched around at will unless they are imaginative constructs.[1]

Reversibility: Playing Each Other

These nodal points suggest a way of describing three phases in dramatic play that mark its increasingly formal sophistication over the course of the third year. The first stage, the focus of this chapter, is characterized by the formula "I'll play you (Mommy) and you play me (child)." It will be termed *reversed roles*. This is the point at which a child moves from playfully representing a creature who is like herself to representing fairly explicitly designated dyadic roles, which often take the form of mother–child role reversal. At this point the self represented in play (by the parent who is playing the child) is the child's current child self, and the role reversal is now to I ↔ you.

The next phase, located at around ages 2.6 to 2.9, is termed *reversibility of roles* and can be characterized formulaicly as "I'll play X and you play Y, but also you could play X while I play Y." This phase features a variety of dyadic roles conceived in complementary or reciprocal pairs or polar opposites (e.g., doctor/patient, repairperson/person with damaged vehicle, cook/eater, mother/baby, big one/little one). It is characteristic that these roles may be rotated between co-players in the course of the same play episode. I will argue that the self that is represented in such play is no longer simply the child's whole current self, but rather aspects of the self that are understood as partial and transient aspects (as the baby, for example, represents a former wished-for or repudiated state). That is, roles at this stage now afford the representation of *aspects* of the self. I will further argue that the complementary or polar conception of these roles, when examined in context, suggests that what the child is symbolizing is not characters or character traits per se but *aspects of two-person relationships*. The reversibility of the roles will be explicated as showing that the child now understands that different family members can participate at one or the other pole of the relationship (e.g., giver/receiver, rejector/rejected) at different times.

The third phase, located at around ages 2.9 to 2.11, I term play with *multiple reversible roles*. More characters are now on stage at once, but their relation is still dyadic. For example, within the same episode the child might be ticket seller, pilot, and airline steward, but the co-player is always the passenger. Here the formula might be "I'll be A or B or C while you are X." Alternatively, as in the game of exclusions, a typical game in this period, there may be three characters, A, B, and C, but the dialogue and action are only between A and B or B and C at any given time, which still distinguishes it from triadic or so-called oedipal play. I will argue that this represents the child's understanding that A could be to B as B is to C, or A and B could be to C as B and C are to A.

The observations on which the study is based come from a year of visits with five families who participated in a study of their 2-year-olds' home play. The children clustered in the age range from 2.0 to 2.4 when the observations began, except for one boy who was 2.7. Three of the children were girls and two were boys. All were firstborns except for one girl, who had a brother 4 years older. The parents, middle-class professionals, ranged in age from 34 to 47, with a median age of 40.

A distinctive methodological feature of the study is that I enlisted parents as the primary observers and reporters of whatever naturally occurring play episodes they happened to notice in the course of a given week. I interviewed the parents at irregular intervals varying from weekly to monthly, and they occasionally volunteered more frequent phoned-in reports. I also observed the children at home periodically. Interview questions were "What is your child playing now, that is, this week?" "What's new (in play and in general)?" "Are there any favorite kinds of play?" "Is there anything your child especially likes to play alone?" "Is there anything you especially tend to play together?" "What is the child playing with the other parent or other household members?" Follow-up questions were "Do you remember when, where, and how this game started?" "Do you remember who started this or that element of the play?" "Do you remember what you had in mind or what the mood was when this play occurred?" Using the parents as participant observers weighted the reporting in favor of recent novel events and play in which a parent had been involved.

The conditions of the naturalistic study fostered consideration of dramatic role play as something that emerges out of a matrix of child–parent pretending. This brought the observations into the perspective we associate with Winnicott, in which play and playfulness are recognized as capacities that arise in the context of a relationship (Winnicott, 1971, 1977). It also brought the study in line with the attention that has converged on the "peekaboo" game as a paradigmatic example of play, whether from a cognitive, developmental, or psychoanalytic point of view (Bruner & Sherwood, 1976; Kleeman, 1967; Stern, 1981). The peekaboo game, like Freud's paradigmatic example of symbolic toy play, the *fort/da* game, is a game about disappearance and reappearance, absence and presence. It is, par excellence, the game in which we can watch the capacity for object constancy (in both the Piagetian and the psychoanalytic sense) being played with. But, as Bruner seems to have had in mind when he considered it as a game in which the rules of play are learned, and as Dan Stern had in mind when he defined a play episode as turn taking in the regulation of mutual attention (Stern, 1981), peekaboo is also a good game for studying how mother–child interaction facilitates or diminishes the capacity for play and, by implication, for symbolic expression and participation in a world of shared cultural meanings, which is what Winnicott (1971, 1977) had in mind. It is in this framework that I have used observations of the Leaving Game to illuminate the origins of the ability to put oneself in another's place.

The Notion of Cross-Identification

Looking at early proto–role play as revealing something of the child's sense of self and other during the third year, and using reversed roles and reversibility of roles as milestones, I realized that the capacity to assume a pretend role has to do with the ability to put oneself in another's place. Here the Winnicottian concept *cross-identification*, is suggestive (Winnicott, 1971). He defined it only as the wholesome or creative aspect of introjective/projective processes, but what it refers to, in a broader way, is the capacity to put oneself in another's place, to understand the other's experience. For Winnicott an essential aspect of the capacity to relate to others is involved here. It is a capacity that is glossed over by the usual notion of empathy or imaginative sympathy (because we treat empathy as though it were a discrete minor talent, like musical pitch). The Kleinian notion of projective identification loosely covers the territory of being able to feel for, with, about, and through others. But the Kleinian term brings with it many complexities and unresolved difficulties, especially if we wish to distinguish wholesome fellow feeling from pathological attributions. By contrast, Winnicott was trying to indicate a basic capacity to understand others and to feel understood, which continues to develop throughout life and which depends on the ability to experience similarity to others. He characterized a patient who lacked the capacity for cross-identification as being unable to realize that anyone could understand or feel for her.

One gets the best glimpses of what Winnicott took as examples of early childhood cross-identification in his notes on treatment sessions with a child between ages 2.4 and 4.1 (Winnicott, 1977). He clearly felt that the capacity to be someone else *playfully* (not delusionally or obsessively) correlated with a consolidation of the sense of self that occurred soon after the middle of the third year, and that the other side of this consolidation is an increasing ability to put oneself (unenviously) in the place of others on the basis of an empathic or intuitive understanding of common-alities of inner experience. This, then, is the full meaning of cross-identification.

This turning point in the consolidation of a sense of self has been spoken of variously in psychoanalytic theory. It has been described as achieving a capacity for ambivalence or emotional object constancy. It has also been conceptualized as com-pleting the separation-individuation process (Mahler, Pine, & Bergman, 1975) or as working through the *depressive position* (Klein, 1932). I avoided the familiar psy-choanalytic language of wish and defense in looking at 2-year-olds' dramatic play. What was cognitively and emotionally new about such play as a novel mode of symbolic expression and communication was likely to be overlooked, I felt, if one focused on the content only as the expression of a fantasy (a wish) or subsumed these new skills under the heading of intrapsychic defense mechanisms (e.g., iden-tification, reversal of role, etc.).

The notion of cross-identification is helpful in elucidating the 2-year-old's often fluid or ambiguous efforts at pretending precisely because it helps to avoid confusing ambiguity with pathology. The general working notion that there are wholesome as well as unwholesome introjective and projective processes can help one explore the world of dyadic role play, with all its complementary or reciprocal roles (leaver/left, healer/hurt, nourisher/hungry one, etc.), with more respect and curiosity. Instead of seeing that world as confused or fundamentally sadomasochistic, we can appreciate in it the child's increasing ability to symbolize aspects of relationships, and to see himself in others and others in himself.

The Leaving Game

The Leaving Game was the first highly salient child–parent game in the entire home-play collection. It appeared in remarkably similar form and at the same age (2.3–2.4) in all three of the girls. (The two boys showed elements of the game at the same age but, as will be exemplified later, a full-fledged Leaving Game as dramatic role play did not emerge in their families.) The simplest general characterization possible of the game is as follows: The child plays at (pretends) leaving the co-player, while having the co-player play at (pretend) being left, by pretending to cry.

> Jane, by age 2.4, had a game in which she'd announce, "I'm going. You be alone. You cry." She would play this game with her mother or her father, and also with her au-pair. A week after this game became established, she began a variant of it with her mother: "I'm going to the office. You cry."

This game was the first dramatic scene involving two characters, dialogue, and plot, which a cluster of children had in common and which appeared at the same age in each child. Once it appeared, it became prominent and was played with peak intensity for a distinct period, usually about 3 weeks.[2] Across the families, the dia-logue was strikingly similar in two respects: In the earliest appearances of the game, it always included the instruction "You cry." And the "I'm going" statement usu-ally was put in terms of going to work. The child also seemed to be playing a *mother* leaving for work (as indicated by the tone of voice, choice of phrase, or costume). The game had evidently not arisen in response to current external events (e.g., a mother's return to work), as there had been no changes in the parent's work schedules in any of the families in the study at the time the game appeared.[3]

The game was, surprisingly enough, played with enjoyment, that is, playfully, not anxiously, in all three families. The parents evinced pride in the child for coming up with the game. They seemed to feel that communication with their daughter had been increased and enhanced in some unspecified way.

In the general welter of other play material, the shapeliness of this game was striking. That shapeliness made for focus on the imaginative *form*: two-person role play in which the pretend roles were apparently mother and child, with the child and mother playing in such a way that their roles were reversed. How did this form arise? At what point could it be said that the players were playing pretend *roles*, in the sense that they had assumed pretend characters who were subjectively or explicitly not themselves?

A Case Example

Bonnie's protocol offered the most thorough account of the emergence of the Leaving Game. One could trace the emergence of the elements of the game in terms of *content*: the motifs "I'm leaving" (for work) and "You cry." The emergence of the *form* of dyadic role play could also be traced.

Bonnie's role play developed in a manner that may be fairly typical, at ages 2.0 to 2.3, out of a matrix of two-person dramatic pretending in which Bonnie *played at mothering* the mother. But while Bonnie was thus turning a passive experience into an active one *in dramatic pretending* for the first time, she wasn't yet playing an imaginary role. There is a distinct progress in her record from pretending to *do* what mother does to pretending to *be* mother. In her earliest proto–role play (whether the theme is nurturing or leaving), Bonnie was evidently still subjectively herself, and mother remained mother. The experience is reversed (from passive to active), but the person is not. Only gradually does the child move into pretending to be the mother while having the mother pretend to be the child. This crucial transition may remain ambiguous for a while to observers, though it may be sensed by the players. One can certainly say that it has been reached when it is made verbally explicit by the child. In Bonnie's case, it was only in and through the playing of the Leaving Game that she reached an explicit formulation equivalent to "I am pretending to be you, and you are pretending to be me."

Phase One: Reversal of Activity

In these games, the child does to the mother what the mother usually does to her in regard both to nurturance and to separation (leaving). Also notable in this phase are the first played-at aggressive acts done to mother in the first transient or ambiguous pretend personae (Cookie Monster and Bonnie-as-doctor).

> Bonnie, age 2.0, begins playing taking care of her mother. A favorite pastime is a game that *reverses* Bonnie's bedtime ritual: Bonnie has her mother lie on the bedside rug with a bottle, pretending to fall asleep, while Bonnie sits in the rocking

chair, singing lullabies. (This, like other first mothering games, strikingly dramatizes reversal. Outwardly, it might look as if the players were portraying each other, but this never crosses the mother's mind in her reporting; evidently it is not yet the mother's subjective experience.)

Bonnie, age 2.0 (a bit later in the month), also starts directing, "Mommy cry," to have her mother pretend to cry. The sense of the game is that Bonnie is leaving her mother, but this is only minimally enacted by Bonnie's taking a step or two away and is not verbalized. This is the first adumbration of the content elements of the Leaving Game, that is, instructions to cry in the context of being left. "Mommy cry" shows that it is Bonnie making her mother cry. "You cry" would be a more flexible direction, allowing the mother's role to be imagined more ambiguously.

Bonnie, age 2.1, walks around wearing the shoes her mother usually wears only to work, announcing to mother, "I going to the office and the movies." (This marks the appearance of what will become the "I'm leaving" motif of the Leaving Game in verbal form. Mother here is still the audience, not the coplayer who is being left. How much Bonnie is subjectively Mother is unclear. Most likely she is playing at being like Mother. Her tone is affirmative and pleasurable. (She makes this move in the direction of identification on the basis of her mother's being active, purposeful, and free to go out and enjoy herself.)

Bonnie, age 2.2, plays mothering games that become more various and include dialogue (e.g., "Too hot; can't eat it yet"). Bonnie pretends to be diapering her mother, giving her "medicine" because her bottom hurts, combing her mother's hair, and putting in barrettes. But in all this play *she refers to herself as "Bonnie," and her mother is still "Mommy."*

Bonnie, age 2.2, announces, "I Cookie Monster," and then bites her mother. Her mother says that she should only pretend to bite. Bonnie becomes briefly frightened that Cookie Monster is in the house and will bite her. It is notable that this first effort at a pretend identity has an aggressive content and that her mother accepts the aggression—with qualification. Bonnie's anxiety exemplifies the lability between not quite successful pretending and a transient symptom, here on the cusp of being able to symbolize aggression in dramatic play.

Bonnie, age 2.2, after an office visit to the (female) pediatrician, pretends to give her mother a shot. She also tests her mother's reflexes so aggressively that it hurts. In terms of affective content, retaliation and the need for mastery are obvious. In terms of form, this is the first play in which Bonnie might appear to be playing an imaginary character. Indeed, she uses a doctor kit she was given for her second birthday and hadn't played with before. *But she is still Bonnie doctoring Mother and refers to herself as "Bonnie."* The game of giving shots recurs. Sometimes the context shows the content to be retaliation for some frustration; at other times, it seems merely an enjoyable conventionalized motif in which she rehearses the form of pretending.

Phase Two: Proto-Drama

In a subsequent phase of play development, the child pretends to be a creature who is somewhat like herself, while her mother is cued to play at being herself or pretends to be a person somewhat like herself.

Bonnie, age 2.2 (last week of the month). The doctoring game is elaborated into a version of a hiding game. Mother plays a doctor who listens to Bonnie's heart; Bonnie plays a frisky little dog (probably a puppy) who runs around, crawls under furniture, and enacts running away and playing freely and happily by herself in inaccessible places. Occasionally she returns to be examined and have her heart listened to again.

In terms of thematic content, this is a most interesting kind of game; each mother–daughter pair in the study developed an analogous but idiosyncratic one. It is a dramatization that somehow captures and expresses characteristic qualities of Bonnie and her mother's relationship at this moment in the separation-individuation process. The frisky puppy exults in independence and in being able to have adventures and play by herself, out of her mother's sight, but with the assurance that her mother calmly supports this activity. Both players agree that the puppy should be periodically checked by the mother-doctor to see that the freedom hasn't been too stressful or harmful. Something of the harmonious relationship of this pair is unwittingly expressed here, as is Bonnie's characteristic playful rebelliousness and the mother's typical conscientious concern.

(Here two pretend roles are adumbrated for the first time in a game that will lead into the Leaving Game. But the roles are indicated only by props and action, and any naming of the roles was done by the mother. In this step into pretend roles, Bonnie's mother is still a character who symbolizes mother, for example, mother as doctor, and Bonnie is still a character who symbolizes Bonnie, for example, Bonnie as frisky puppy.)

Phase Three: Two-Character Drama (Reversed Roles)

In this phase of the game's development, the child plays a character who is Mother, while the mother plays a character who is the child.

Bonnie, age 2.3. The Leaving Game proper appears. Bonnie walks in mother's work shoes and *announces explicitly for the first time*, *"I'm Mommy."* Mother asks who she is, and Bonnie tells her, "You're Bonnie." Bonnie then says, "I going to work now." Mother replies, "Don't be gone long. I'll miss you," and Bonnie says, "I be back soon."

(In this couple, Bonnie's mother turns the earlier "You cry" motif into an explicit verbal expression of the idea of missing the absent person. Together they move into verbally explicit reversal of roles at the same time that they move into the final or fully achieved stage of the Leaving Game. This version of the game contains the shared understanding that the person who is left will miss the one who leaves, and the reassurance that this missing is tolerable and will be followed by reunion.)

Bonnie, age 2.4. The Leaving Game, played with peak intensity and frequency the week it appeared, gradually subsided and had temporarily disappeared only 3 weeks later. Instead, Bonnie began actively ordering mother to leave whenever mother was about to go to work, saying, "You go now."

The ability to play at reversed roles explicitly now becomes a basic element in Bonnie's repertoire. She starts many pretend games by announcing, "I'm Mommy and you're Bonnie." The two then converse in these roles, and the play content is mostly nurturance: As "Mommy," Bonnie cooks, puts on her "daughter's" bib, and so on. This game lasts for about 2 weeks.

Bonnie, age 2.4 (last week) to 2.5. "I'm Mommy and you're Bonnie" now is proposed by Bonnie predominantly when her mother is about to leave for work, at which point Bonnie engages her mother in a more elaborated version of the Leaving

Game. They have extended conversations about how "Mommy" has to go to work, and about how she and "Bonnie" will miss each other while they are apart and look forward to seeing each other again.

Bonnie, age 2.6. At this point the Leaving Game is forgotten and a phase of reversible roles begins. Bonnie and her mother play a variety of pretend roles based on characters from *Sesame Street*, including parents with a baby, a big girl and a baby, and so on, with Bonnie rapidly switching and rotating the roles between the players.

But what does the Leaving Game mean? What does it express aesthetically? What is its function if we see it as a temporary family ritual? Anthropologists working out the meaning of a ritual might first trace the provenance of its elements. I tried to trace the provenance of the Leaving Game's motifs.[4]

Origins of the Motif "I'm Leaving"

The motif "I'm leaving," elaborated as "I'm going to work," often had an affirmative connotation in its origins. It could be traced to statements the children had made as early as age 2.0 in which they conveyed their awareness of a new capacity to be alone in a positive sense, to be autonomously occupied. And indeed, at about this age, all the children took a distinct developmental leap seen in a marked, if small, increase in their ability to be happily engrossed in solitary play, as if there had been a sudden burgeoning of an inner world.

These statements of wanting to be left alone seemed, in context, often as much a celebration of independence as an attempt to master or retaliate for being left. For instance, the proud tone of Bonnie's "I'm going to the office and the movies" suggested more of an identification with a purposeful mother who enjoyed life than an affiliation with an abandoning mother. This independence is not unique to Bonnie:

Sasha, age 2.0. Sasha first said, "I'm busy," with the implication that she wanted to be left alone while defecating. From age 2.0 she began declaring, "I'm busy, go away," or "I'm busy, don't look at me," quasi-playfully, in other contexts: when she didn't want to be interrupted in her play to comply with her mother's requests.

Sasha's "I'm busy" then became her Leaving Game dialogue:

Sasha, age 2.0 to 2.3. Hide-and-seek games with her mother began to include the element that the mother should cry when she couldn't see Sasha. This was initiated by Sasha: "You cry." Sasha then added the motif "I'm busy, I'm working" while she hid.

Similar elements appeared at this period in other families even where the playful drama of a Leaving Game did not develop:

Sam, by age 2.3, would regularly remark proudly to his father or mother, "I'm busy doing *my* working," as if he himself were pleased, as the parents were, by his newfound ability to be engrossed in play on his own. Sam also sometimes said this in a retaliatory way when one of his parents returned from work.

An original game Jane developed with her mother supports the inference that part of the foundation for the Leaving Game is a newly consolidated sense of independent selfhood and agency. This sense of self involves a new consciousness of the ability to have wishes and make choices, even if they are not the parents'.

> Jane, age 2.3, a week or two before her Leaving Game appears, develops a game called "What does Jane want?" It consists of Jane's asking this question repeatedly in a tiny, playfully diffident, almost sly voice while her mother first pretends to give a variety of improbably exotic answers and then finally divines the ordinary thing (e.g., orange juice) Jane really wants.
>
> This game, in which the mother parodied her own failures of attunement and Jane dramatized her own diffidence about expressing needs, played out something as characteristic for this pair as the conscientious doctor–frisky puppy game was for Bonnie and her mother. Like the doctor–puppy game, it was a spontaneous dyadic creation that was evocative of separation-individuation issues in this couple: Would the mother allow Jane to make independent demands, and would she allow Jane to individuate as a nonideal (nonexotic) child? Like many parent–child games, it also served to repair some discord in the relationship. In fact, Jane's mother suggested that the game served to make her aware that she had not been taking enough account of Jane as someone who increasingly had divergent wishes of her own. (Possibly these realizations can occur because Jane and her mother are themselves in this game but also playing at being themselves—in a manner analogous to mother as doctor and Bonnie as puppy.)

Hide-and-Seek as a Background Element or Precursor of the Leaving Game

The derivation or emergence of the Leaving Game from games of hide-and-seek is particularly clear in the report on Sasha (see earlier) and was also present in Jane's case. If the Leaving Game commonly emerges partly out of a revival and elaboration of the typical simple games of hide-and-seek popular in the second half of the second year, what does this suggest? In terms of content, it points, of course, to themes of separation, absence, and mutual re-finding. Hide-and-seek, as children play it with peers and siblings as well as with parents during the last quarter of the second year, increasingly involves *turn taking* at hiding and finding, as well as longer hiding intervals and more complete or remote hiding. On the plane of action (not yet quite of symbolic drama), what is played is that *both* players can and do alternately have the experience of losing track of the other, and both also actively hide from the other. Hide-and-seek also, as part of the derivation of the game, reminds us to consider that even when the Leaving Game scene only portrays departure, implicit in the cognitive–affective background is the understanding that departure may be followed by return. But the new thing I wish to suggest by harking back to the Leaving Game's origins in hide-and-seek is that just as hide-and-seek players alternately exchange experiences, something of this mutuality may be found at a higher level in the Leaving Game, in that each player plays the part of the other.

The importance of turn taking in hide-and-seek (as in peekaboo) suggests that another genre of game, which I call *mirroring games*, should be included in the line of development leading to the Leaving Game, although this takes us back to the presymbolic period. For example, from 15 to 22 months, Bonnie and her mother played a mirroring game that was a kind of nonverbal, kinesthetic form of Simon Says: The mother would initiate some funny, fairly complex gesture, which Bonnie would then playfully copy. Bonnie then would take a turn at initiating a funny gesture to be copied by her mother. Sasha and her mother, from around 20 months at least, had an analogous kinesthetic mirroring game: taking turns at improvising and copying dance movements.

But both the elements of hiding and being busy may be found without a Leaving Game.

> Josh, age 2.4. Games of hiding from his mother become prominent, particularly after any short absence by the mother. Josh also begins complaining freely at this point about his parents' spending so much time at work. For several weeks, Josh will pointedly ignore one or the other parent when either of them returns from work, saying that *he* is busy. (The prevailing mood is of a frankly retaliatory communication.)

The "You Cry" Motif

The pivotal element that creates a playful drama is the instruction "You cry" *and* its acceptance by the coplayer. "You cry" sets up a dramatic scene with two players who have separate, conflicting, but interrelated intentions (one wants to leave, the other laments being left).

The provenance of "You cry" could not be directly traced in these families. This is partly because the data collection did not start before age 2.0. The parents were all mildly surprised at the "You cry" game, as if something qualitatively new had happened. But the portrayal of crying was already familiar. Representations of distress or sadness by crying seem to be common in doll and puppet play in the 18- to 24-month period, judging by the subjects' younger siblings who were followed peripherally in the study:

> Alan, age 19 months, begins imitating and naming the affects of animals in picture books, such as "Cat sad."
> Kathy, age 2.0. Her first recognizable toy story is a much-repeated favorite: Kathy has a toy dog trip and fall. Then she represents the dog as crying by shaking it and imitating crying herself.

Nor is it novel to show one agent affecting another, since such action–reaction sequences are also a feature of under-2 doll and puppet play.

> Max, age 20 months, has a crocodile puppet pretend to gobble up everything. His father takes this action as a cue to pretend to act frightened.

The provenance of the crying motif doesn't specify its affective connotation in the game and doesn't explain the leap into drama. It may be that what is new about "You cry" is the representation of crying in the context of separation and the fact that this did not appear in prior doll play. However, there is no evidence for this conclusion. It may be helpful to remember that if Punch bashes Judy and Judy cries, this is not drama but farce. Action and reaction alone are not drama.

I think that what is significantly new is the instruction, which is also a request, that the co-player accept representation of an *internal* reaction that has meaning because of the *relationship* between the players (e.g., it is implicit that the co-player cares enough to cry over being left). In cognitive terms, it might be said that the child can now predict the other's reaction. But this prediction is only a hypothesis to be tested in play.

The child who first proposes, however tentatively, "You cry" in this context is testing whether the co-player can playfully acknowledge sadness over being left. If so, it means that the co-player not only acknowledges this experience but can accept and contain or tolerate it. Moreover, the foundation is already laid for the question "Can you realize that the feeling I am asking you to play is what I feel when you leave me?" In short, the proposal "You cry" already sets up the possibility of what Winnicott meant by cross-identification (in the form of "I could imagine that you could feel toward me—missing me—what I feel toward you).

The Leaving Scene as Drama

We find the Leaving Game is about *missing* another if we consider it, a bit playfully, as a scene of primitive drama. Indeed, this little scene contains two, if not all three, components of the tragic action of Greek drama: *poeima, pathema, mathema*— purpose, passion (or suffering), and perception. An intention or purpose is declared, its consequences are suffered, and (perhaps, as we'll see later) some new perception or insight is reached (the perception that missing is mutual).

One character announces an intention to leave and leaves; the other is left alone and laments the departure. The game portrays a moment of departure and the moment afterward. (As soon as I leave, you will start to cry.) It thus manages to put on stage departure and the subsequent experience of being left while sadly missing the absent person, telescoped into a very short scene. It is, we could say, a representation of the experience of *missing* someone (absent but remembered) in a very short play.

In the language of separation-individuation theory, and in both the cognitive and psychoanalytic notions of object constancy, we might suppose that it marks a developmental moment at which the experience of missing an absent loved one can be not only tolerated but anticipated. But this account still does not adequately explain the leap to two-person dramatic play.

The Meaning of the Game

In the preceding section, we have traced the provenance of the motifs, considered the game phenomenologically as a piece of drama, and noted Bonnie's protocol showing the gradual emergence of role play. It is a game about being able to miss someone and also about being able to assert independence (given the prevailingly positive tone of the earlier versions of the "I'm leaving" motif). It is also a game in the course of which the child becomes able to pretend explicitly to be someone else. One line of development leading to the game involves turn taking in games of hide-and-seek. It makes the leap from hide-and-seek to symbolic drama in that the child instructs the co-player to show an internal response to the child's (verbalized) action.

Why is the Leaving Game co-emergent with the move to explicit dyadic role play in the form of reversed roles? The meaning of the game must lie in the answer to this question. Hide-and-seek has not been raised to drama merely by the addition of dialogue. It is also not enough to say that the game is about missing and independence. This is a comment from the point of view of the spectator or the visiting anthropologist who hasn't yet figured out the function of this ritual game in the family. We must inquire into the experience of the players, for the meaning of the game resides in what occurs for and between the players in the course of playing it, with increasing playfulness, and in the fact that missing and independence have become playable between child and parent.

The Leaving Game and Role Play

I propose that a shift in the nature of proto–role play occurs in the course of playing the Leaving Game. To spell out in schematic and linear fashion what may be more shimmering and simultaneous or dialectical in the playing: There is a shift on a continuum from primarily retaliatory or mastery or identificatory play to play involving what Winnicott meant by cross-identification: the capacity to realize that what you feel toward the other the other may also feel toward you.[5]

In terms of thematic or affective *content*, the game starts: I want to put you through the experience of missing me when I leave you, just as I miss you when you leave. It comes out at the end something like this: "I know that you can miss me as I miss you" (with both players exchanging this communication) and "I'm willing to let you leave me to have your own life" (with both players exchanging this communication too).

In terms of *form*—that is, in terms of the capacity for imaginative role play or for pretending to be another—there is progress on a continuum (which is also a qualitative leap) from "I will play at doing to you what you do to me" to "I can pretend to be a character who represents you while having you play a character who represents me." Note that one implication is: I can imagine/understand that you could imagine what it is to be me, and I know that you know I can imagine what it is to be you.

Again, schematically (the inner experience will be considered in more detail later), there are the following formal stages: When the child first indicates, "I'm leaving, you cry," the child is subjectively herself and her mother is also subjectively herself. Objectively, also, the child is seeing her mother as the mother, and the mother is seeing her child as the child.

As the mother realizes she is playing the child's experience, she may begin to represent the child more clearly. And as the child discovers that her mother is playing the child, the child may begin to represent the mother more clearly by her tone of voice or choice of phrase (e.g., when Jane moves from "I'm going" to "I'm going to the office"). Thus the game is mutually defined, with a process of interactive change on both sides.

They thus arrive at a middle or transitional phase. At this point the child is subjectively still herself, leaving her mother and making her mother cry, but she is also subjectively beginning to be her mother leaving the child. Conversely, the mother is subjectively both her current self *and* the child having the experience of being left behind. During this transitional phase, each may see the other player in this ambiguous double way. The child sees the mother crying as the mother and child at once. The mother experiences the child's leaving as the child's leaving her and as herself leaving the child both at once. This back-and-forth communication may then culminate in the child's verbalization "I'm Mommy, you are me," and the role reversal is complete: The child has learned to role-play in a new way based on the understanding that the self can be imagined by another.

This middle, or transitional, passage may be exemplified by one final play report. I did not at first include this interesting transitional play sequence in my reflections on the Leaving Game because it was not clear to which category it belonged. It starts by belonging to the genre of Bonnie's frisky puppy play: Sasha plays an elusive, cuddly little animal hiding from her mother. In keeping with that genre, this report expresses characteristics of this dyad's relationship in regard to separation-individuation. It thus represents the phase in which the child plays a creature who represents herself and the mother also plays herself as a pretend character. The sequence then also develops into a Leaving Game, as marked by the motifs of announcing that the child is going to work and having the mother cry. It does not, at least as reported, reach a clear outcome of verbalized role reversal. But it does reach the farther shore of the Leaving Game in that it contains the reassurance of happy re-meeting in dramatized form.

SASHA, age 2.4. A game is played with her mother every evening for a week, becoming gradually more elaborate. Sasha pops out from a hiding place behind the sofa for a brief visit with her mother, then abruptly and blankly disappears, returning to her hiding place. She hides for fairly long periods and then abruptly reappears. As the game goes on, it is emphasized that she reappears with cheery aplomb, as if nothing questionable had happened.

Sasha says at first that she is playing a "little animal," soon characterized, evidently on her mother's inquiry, as a "cuddly creature" and then named Wully Wully after a character in *Babar* ("an animal that is seldom seen"—the mother thinks this must have been her contribution).

Sasha's disappearances are soon announced as "Back to my home!" and then also as "Back to work!" In the later stages she announces only "Back to my work!"

Meanwhile, Sasha's mother is instructed to cry at each disappearance and then to "cry more" while the creature hides. Mother then adds some dialogue, complaining about the shortness of the visits. (Note: Here the mother seems to have begun playing Sasha.)

In the final elaboration, Sasha instructs her mother to be happy to see her again each time she reappears and to ask for a cuddle, which Sasha then gives willingly. (Note: By this point, Sasha evidently was representing an affectionate mother, albeit a mother who leaves. She was also being an affectionate child reassuring mother, by playing the game, that she could tolerate her mother's absences, as well as her mother's oscillations of mood from availability to unavailability.)[6]

To summarize, Sasha starts out as a *little* animal, evidently representing herself. In the middle she seems still to be partly herself, wanting to turn the tables on her mother *and* to communicate how she feels. Increasingly, she adopts her mother's characteristic style and tone on departure and reappearance (the briskness of back-to-work and the cheery aplomb of reappearance). Her mother starts (by her retrospective account) by feeling that this is a game in which Sasha willfully disappears. After "Cry more," as she remembers it, she has the idea, which makes her feel somewhat guilty, that Sasha is reacting to a temporary change in the mother's work schedule, which means that the mother has more frequent but shorter play times with Sasha. At this point the mother begins playing Sasha. Finally, Sahsa returns in a nonretaliatory mood as a loving mother who willingly consoles the child.

This prompts further schematic spelling out of the inner experience of the players of such games. In accepting the crying role and playing it, a mother begins to realize that she is playing the child. To do so, she must contain her own guilt over her wishes to leave the child and over the harm she may have done, and in that sense to acknowledge her own aggression without feeling it as too destructive. At the same time, or even before realizing that she is playing the child, she may get in touch with her own experiences of missing, including missing the individuating child. At this point, the mother might subjectively be both herself missing the child and the child missing her.

The child, to start with, sees the mother accept retaliation and feel the pain of it without being too hurt. This helps the child contain her own guilt over retaliatory wishes or wishes for independence and allows play to continue. Even if the mother is not yet mainly portraying the child, the child realizes: Mother knows what it is like to miss someone; she is like me that way. Here the child's capacity to identify with the mother on a tender basis is enhanced, and this leads to the child's representing the mother more clearly in the game, moving from retaliation to communication.

As the child moves to representing the mother, the mother may be further helped in containing her guilt by her enjoyment of the child's capacity to play, and also by her enjoyment of the child's positive identification with her as an active, purposeful mother who has a right to a life of her own. The identification may feel positive because the feeling tone of the game is already less retaliatory and more playfully expressive. The mother may be put in touch with her own wishes for the child's independence, and this appreciation of the active, aspiring child may be communicated. The child, in response, portrays a caring mother who can miss the child and realize that the child will miss her, but who also has her own wishes for a life of her own, without this being a rejection of the child (see Bonnie's "I be back soon").

We can now try to answer the question with which we began: Why is "I'll play you and you play me" coemergent with the Leaving Game? The message exchanged in the playing of the game is: I know that you could miss me as I miss you. And: I know that you could wish to have a life of your own, apart from me, just as I wish to have a life of my own. And: I know this because *I can feel while we play the game that we are like each other* (cross-identification) *in being able to miss and in wanting to leave.*

The child's ability to cross-identify is facilitated by the parent's ability to play the game. And the child's ability to play may help the mother deepen *her* sense of cross-identification—for example, to accept the increasing separation without feeling merely retaliated against or abandoned or guilty.

I propose that it is cross-identification—indeed, probably *mutual* cross-identification—that is the springboard in the capacity for a certain kind of role play. In the schematic, if necessarily labored, analysis of the steps illustrated by the Wully Wully game, there is a transitional period in which both players are, I hypothesize, subjectively at once both themselves and the other. This is the turning point that frees the child to play the mother in a way that is explicit and eventually also nonretaliatory. "You could miss me as I miss you" becomes the basis for "I'll play you and you play me"—and vice versa. (I do not mean that the child's relational experience before this point is purely retaliatory. I only want to highlight a step in symbolic representation: the symbolization, in dramatic play, of mutual understanding.)

Role Play, Self–Other Boundaries, and Cross-Identifications

Once a child can do something, we tend to take it for granted. Only when we catch it *in statu nascendi* do we tend to appreciate it as an achievement. The intention of this chapter is to show this particular step into role play (e.g., the capacity to play at reversed roles) in slow motion so that readers can begin to consider it as a distinctive creative step. A qualitative leap in the capacity for symbolic (aesthetic-expressive) representation occurs here, along with a leap in the capacity for interpersonal play and communication. Insofar as the move into role play is mediated by this step of playing at dyadic reversed roles, I would suggest that it also calls for a reconceptualization of the separation-individuation process.

It has long been assumed that being able to pretend a role requires a consolidation of the sense of self and other, as well as a sufficient sense of the difference between fantasy and reality so that the child is not too threatened by anxieties over loss of identity. (Such anxiety is familiarly exemplified in the literature by the child under age 3 who is afraid to put on a Halloween mask.) This way of thinking implies a conceptual model in which internal self and object representations become increasingly discrete, bounded, unitary, and permanent. But looking at role reversal play as involving processes of cross-identification suggests another dimension: Pretending to be someone else may be based not only on *wishing* to be someone else (or on being able to symbolize aspects of the self, e.g., a frisky puppy), but also on an understanding that self and other may be similar in having similar relational experiences. So, while we may think of self-other boundaries as consolidating at this point (as Winnicott also did), in another dimension the sense of self and other is also moving in the direction of becoming more fluid and imaginatively *exchangeable*: Now that I am I, I can realize that we share similar affective experiences without being afraid of turning into you.

Cognitive Basis of Dramatic Character: The Self as Subjective and Objective

Pretending to be a character is not something the child does in isolation, and it involves more than the child's constructing and sustaining an imaginative schema of a character on his or her own, insofar as it is arrived at by the route outlined earlier. Early dramatic play is a co-production; early dramatic characters are conceived as relational—that is, as participating in a relationship; and who the character is or what the character means depends on the relationship. This is true of drama in general: no Lear without a Cordelia. Pretending to be someone else while that other person pretends to be you signals that personhood or identity has now become something that can be played with imaginatively. Is it an overstatement to say that the concept of dramatic character begins here?

The child's ability to pretend to be another person is grounded in the child's experience that the coplaying parent can also conceive of the child's identity as a separate identity that can be understood, held in the imagination, and played with. This could be considered a kind of higher-level mirroring, on a line with the earliest mirroring of the infant's affects, and through the various kinds of presymbolic mirroring games.

In role reversal, a more complex intrapsychic process is modeled and mirrored: the process of being able to think about, imagine, and then pretend to be the other. Instead of just remembering and reproducing a gesture, one reproduces another's being and inner experience. This is the cognitive dimension of the play of cross-identification.

The doll and puppet play that children are capable of from 18 to 24 months of age has recently been studied (Stern, 1985) as evidence of the child's ability at that point to conceive of the self as an objective entity, and to represent self and others symbolically in toy play. It has been noted that in such play the child can understand the symbolization not only of how things were or are, but how the child might, counterfactually, wish them to be (e.g., as when Herzog's 18-month subject is relieved by the representation of the return of the absent father doll to the mother's bed) (Herzog, 1980). It is worth contrasting such doll play with the role play at age 2.4 in order to grasp more thoroughly what has been added by the step into role play. Here is one example from the children in this sample:

> Sasha, age 23 months, has a surprise visit from an au-pair who had left 2 months earlier (having lived with the family from the time when Sasha was 11 months old). Sasha refuses to get out of her crib or engage with the visitor until she deliberately performs the following wordless scene with toy animals for the au-pair to watch: Teddy and Cat kiss. Cat throws away Teddy. Teddy and Cat kiss. Cat throws away Teddy. Teddy and Cat kiss. Teddy throws away Cat.

Presumably this means: You threw me away (the repeats would equal intensively or once too often), and now I want to throw you away. What ingredients are added in the Leaving Game that are not already found here?

In terms of the argument of this chapter, there are two significant additions. Though the Teddy–Cat scene is surely a communication, the affective tone is a retaliatory one. The Leaving Game constitutes a passage out of a retaliatory world, that is, a world in which people act upon and react to each other but without the symbolic representation (dramatization) of mutual understanding. Teddy does not know how Cat feels except in terms of what Cat has done to Teddy. But Bonnie and her mother have pretend conversations about how they will miss each other.

In playing at reversed roles, Bonnie is saying, "I know you know how I feel." The self is symbolized not by a toy, but by another person who is expected in the course of the game to become able to play the child's self. In the step taken from 18 months on, the self is conceived by the child as a subjective entity that can now also be *objectively* experienced by others and objectively thought about, symbolized, by the child. In the dramatic play at age 2.4, the self is a simultaneously subjective and objective entity that can also be both objectively *and* subjectively experienced by the other. The child now knows this because of the child's own capacity for cross-identification. ("You could miss me as I miss you" has replaced "I'll reject you as you rejected me.")

A final clinical vignette from the treatment of an 8-year-old girl who was not quite able to play at reversed roles should add perspective. In psychoanalysis, a child's relative inability to play has always been taken as an index of relative pathology. Similarly, an adult patient's relative inability to play within the transference is also an index of relative illness. To *play* in the transference means to be able to imagine the therapist's reactions hypothetically, conditionally: "You might feel this way or that way" rather than "I'm sure you are reacting this way or that way." The degree to which the patient cannot play relates to the degree to which the patient is then living, relatively speaking, within a retaliatory world, a world in which people can only exploit, manipulate, or punitively compete with each other.

A Note on Gender

It was striking that in this very small sample the girls developed a Leaving Game, whereas the boys did not. The two boys did enter the phase of reversibility of roles ages at 2.6 to 2.8, but without going through role reversal with a parent at age 2.4, at least as reported and reconstructed. (They had the possibility of doing so, because in the boys' families, though not in the girls', the parents were sharing parenting time equally.) Was gender a factor? If so, the route into role play outlined here might be a female route. I have gotten the impression that mothers play mirroring games more intensively and through a later age with girls than with boys. If the Leaving Game were to prove gender specific, it would have interesting ramifications in terms of the social psychological construction of gender differences. This hypothesis would, of course, require much further investigation.

Rosa

Rosa, age 8, in the eighth month of analysis, "won" the therapist's office in a board game and was thus offered the option of pretending to be the therapist. At first she had no idea how to assume ownership and pretend to be Dr. L., except to rearrange and clean things and make free use of the desk and materials. When Dr. L. offered to play the child-patient, Rosa addressed her by Dr. L.'s first name, Peggy. It did not occur to her that Dr. L. could play Rosa. The only bit of the therapist's role she took on was to announce the session's end.

"Dr. L." and "Peggy" continued sessions in these nominal roles, but very awkwardly. The roles were brittle, often broken, and bore little relation to the session's activities. Rosa used her privilege of being Dr. L. to raid the cupboard (covertly) for sugar cubes, while Dr. L., often confused as to who was supposed to be whom or whether a pretend game was being played, also broke the frame of pretending by sneaking in exploratory questions while she was supposed to be only Peggy. Rosa then forbade Dr. L. to ask questions and scotch-taped her mouth. Meanwhile, however, in the course of their then frequent hide-and-seek games, Rosa began to take on more of Dr. L.'s manner, imitating her style of searching the room. Dr. L., in response to this action, began playing at hiding in Rosa's manner, pretending to sleep under the sofa cushions.

Giving and receiving communication had been difficult from the start. Rosa warded off any acknowledgment of a relationship to the therapist by denials and distracting behavior. Her first ventures into puppet play were broken off if the therapist commented, and she retreated into obsessive mending of materials or trying to use up all the office supplies.

Around the time of short holiday breaks, Rosa had begun hiding from the therapist (e.g., in the waiting-room closet), and this had gradually shaded into games of hide-and-seek. Hide-and-seek seemed to establish a climate in which Rosa's first dramatic pretending could appear. Rosa's anxieties about giving or receiving were shown in store and rummage sale games, as well as in games of gift giving that appeared particularly whenever her mother paid the (low-fee) clinic. It was always unclear whether the gifts exchanged (office materials cursorily wrapped) were supposed to be good or insulting, just as in the store games it was very confusing who was getting the better deal or who was getting gypped. Rosa also played a telephone operator or airline booking agent who summarily disconnected customers or put them on hold. (The therapist verbalized the theme of people disconnecting from each other.) Rosa then asked Dr. L. to play the disconnecting operator. Later she asked Dr. L. to play the act of calling up her patients and canceling their visits.

This confusing period, in which it was unclear whether gifts were good or bad, who was giving or getting more or less, and who was disconnecting from whom, can be contrasted with what I've called the transitional period of the Leaving Game. In Rosa's play, the insulting gift giver or the uncaring operator might have been an aspect of herself or of the other, or of both at once. But this is an example of *projective and introjective processes* in their unwholesome aspect: Rosa could not or would not distinguish herself from the bad other, and the other also was projectively construed as being like Rosa's bad sense of herself. In the Leaving Game, when it started to become ambiguous who was whom, this was because more positive and wholesome cross-identifications were beginning, providing a bridge to empathic role reversal. At the same time, it had already been established in mutual play that the mother could accept symbolic aggression from the child and could accept some representation of what she did to the child as aggressive or hurtful.

When Rosa asked Dr. L. to play at disconnecting, she may have been asking, "Can you accept that disconnecting is part of something you do?" This may have been a helpful step in separating out what felt bad, so that Rosa did not have to take full responsibility for all bad experiences.

A store game, when they were later in the nominal roles of "Dr. L. and Peggy," enabled the two to take a further step toward a more meaningful role reversal. After a long holiday weekend, Rosa skipped several sessions. She then played she was Dr. L. phoning Peggy to say that the store was open again and having a wonderful sale, but that Peggy should bring a lot of money. Peggy arrives. "Dr. L." acts bored and indifferent, but then sells her some quite nice things and throws in a free gift of a pillow. At this point the therapist relaxed and felt free to begin to play the child/patient/customer as if she were Rosa rather than "Peggy," choosing Rosa's favorite pillow. "Dr. L.," the storekeeper, asked for a gift in return, namely, the raisins she'd been promised in reality before the holiday as a more healthy substitute for the sugar cubes she'd kept stealing. Raisins were produced and appreciated. (Note that now good free gifts had been exchanged.) Frankly speaking as Rosa, the therapist asked: "Do you want me to tell you why I skipped sessions? I felt you didn't care about me on your vacation, so I did the same to you." (The therapist was still unable to let this emerge in the game, but she was becoming more comfortable playing Rosa, now that both players had become more benign figures.)

At this, Rosa said that she wanted to "change parts" and *pretend* to be Rosa, while Dr. L. should pretend to be Dr. L. (Here Rosa, struggling toward a conception of reversibility of roles, had arrived at something rather like the stage of the frisky puppy game: She was pretending to be someone like herself. As "Rosa," Rosa cuddled the free gift cushion and complained of anxieties about physical injuries, of feeling tired and wanting to stay in bed, rather than come to her session. Dr. L., pretending to be herself, made an interpretation linking the anxiety and tiredness with the holiday break, and Rosa, for perhaps the first time, freely said, "Yes, that's true," thus accepting the gift of the interpretation as good.)

Here role reversal was not complete. But there was a move to playful dramatic *communication.* Some of what still lay in the way was suggested by a subsequent session in which Rosa played a psychiatrist interviewing a child patient's mother. Rosa had come a long way from being able to play the therapist only in concrete terms, using up desk supplies. The burden of the scene was that the psychiatrist guessed that the mother was abusing her child, but the mother denied it. The coplayer was instructed: "Keep on lying."

Rosa had been referred for learning difficulties and because traumatic aspects of her early history were known from her preschool day-care center. Her thinking at the start of treatment often seemed overly concrete, confused, or blocked. The steps she is going through in learning to play in a way she never had are not an exact recapitulation of the stages of role play I have located at ages 2.0 to 2.5, but they illuminate that development.

At first, communication is blocked due to anxiety that giving or receiving communications means that one person will be taken over by the other. Confused and negative self and object representations (the insulting, cheating gift givers) gradually yield to representations that suggest a dawning understanding that each player might be both someone who leaves (becomes unavailable, disconnects) and someone who gives good gifts—and there is the beginning of trust that this can be safely and mutually acknowledged. The idea that Rosa is afraid of the pain involved if she allows herself to miss the therapist could also begin to be acknowledged.

Conclusion

The Leaving Game is a dyadic process of mutual cross-identifications that facilitates the child's emergence into role play. Indeed, I hope my analysis of the Leaving Game may serve to exemplify what Winnicott meant by cross-identification. This chapter may be read as simply an expansion of Winnicott's intuition that linked the arrival at dramatic play with the capacity for cross-identification. It is also an elaboration of his sense (which can be traced in the Piggle case [Winnicott, 1977]) that a developing capacity for cross-identification, shown in a disturbed child's newfound capacity for dramatic play, amounts to a move out of a retaliatory world.

What did Winnicott mean by the *wholesome* aspect of projective/introjective processes? If the Leaving Game may serve to exemplify this aspect, it points to the enrichment of a person's sense of selfhood through the finding of commonalities. In the Leaving Game, we see the child consolidating a richer as well as more flexible self by discovering and symbolizing, in the process of playing, that he or she shares certain relational experiences with the coplayer.

Self–other differentiation is generally supposed to occur on the basis of finding differences. And it has been conceptualized as the establishment of increasingly firm boundaries in the inner representation of self and other. The Leaving Game suggests that we should look at another dimension: an increasingly discriminating fluency in being able to find kinship with the experience of others. Paradoxically, the very young child becomes a more individuated self through playing at being other selves.

NOTES

1. A few weeks before what I term role play proper appeared, children in this sample might announce pretend identities (''I'm a horsie'' or ''I'm Cookie Monster''), but the accompanying play was only fleeting despite the verbal labeling. And some recognizable roles were found, after 2.6, in families that played the dialogue from a favorite storybook scene without needing to name the characters.

2. This periodicity was characteristic of other prominent or favorite games, whether typical or idiosyncratic, in the collection.

3. This, together with the distinct timing of the game, first suggested that its inception might mark some critical period or turning point in the process of separation-individuation and that something had been satisfactorily worked through or played through in the course of the game's peak period.

4. I was trying to think as naively as possible, by which I mean something like phenomenologically, without giving special priority to developmental, cognitive, psychoanalytic, or anthropological points of view, though of course questions hovered in the background: Was it a developmental marker or even an organizer in Spitz's sense? What cognitive abilities— for example, in the sense of time and ability to conceptualize and symbolize the continuing existence of an absent object—correlated with the ability to play the game? What capacities to modulate and symbolize aggression were manifest in the children's other play at ages 2.0 to 2.4? Why did the families relish the game?

5. This would be the simplest form of cross-identification. A fuller form, seen around age 2.8, would be: What I can feel toward you in relation to X, you can feel toward me in relation to Y, as in Piggle: Mommy is jealous of Daddy's love for me the way I am jealous of Mother's love for Baby. (See Winnicott, 1977, pp. 55–65, esp. p. 61.)

6. It may be that the fact that this game did not yet have the outcome of explicit verbalized role reversal relates to the fact that in this couple the child partly takes the task of consoling mother, while in the Bonnie–mother dyad, the mother takes the initiative in presenting a reassuring solution.

REFERENCES

Bruner, J. S., & Sherwood, V. (1976). Peekaboo and the learning of rule structures. In J. S. Bruner, A. Jolly, & K. Sylva (Eds.), *Play* (pp. 277–285). New York: Basic Books.

Herzog, J. (1980). Sleep disturbance and father hunger in 18- to 20-month-old boys: The Erlkoenig syndrome. *Psychoanalytic Study of the Child, 35*, 219–236.

Kleeman, J. A. (1967). The peekaboo game: Part I. Origins, meanings, and related phenomena in the first year. *Psychoanalytic Study of the Child, 22*, 239–273.

Klein, M. (1932). *The psychoanalysis of children.* London: Hogarth.

Mahler, M., Pine, F., & Bergman, A. (1975). *The psychological birth of the human infant.* New York: Basic Books.

Stern, D. (1981). The early development of schemas of self, of other, and of various experiences of ''self with other.'' In S. Kaplan & J. D. Lichtenberg (Eds.), *Reflections on self psychology* (pp. 49–85). New York: International Universities Press.

Stern, D. (1985). *The interpersonal world of the infant. A view from psychoanalytic and developmental psychology.* New York: Basic Books.

Winnicott, D. W. (1971). *Playing and reality.* New York: Basic Books. (See especially chapter 10.)

Winnicott, D. W. (1977). *The Piggle. An account of the psychoanalytic treatment of a little girl.* New York: International Universities Press.

7

Self–Other Action Play: A Window Into the Representational World of the Infant

ANNI BERGMAN
ILENE SACKLER LEFCOURT

From early on, babies, by virtue of their babyness, elicit playfulness in others. Smiles special for baby, unique tempos of speech and body movement, and games passed down through the generations comprise the first mother–infant play. The mother of a 2-month-old baby recently asked us: "Would you like to see our first game?" She and her infant, gazing into each other's eyes and smiling, became engaged in a dialogue. She lifted the baby from her lap, raised him slightly above her head, and said, "bouncy, bouncy!" She then returned him to her lap. The baby moved his body upward and looked at her expectantly. This provided the signal for her to lift him again. After several repetitions he stopped signaling; she was immediately sensitive to the change in his behavior, and the game ended.

The first play experiences, between mother and baby, promote the baby's most rudimentary sense of self and other within the context of an intimate, affectively attuned relationship. The games of early infancy create a mutually regulated action dialogue between mother and infant. The earliest mutually regulated dialogues provide the foundation for what we will describe as *self–other action play*. Self–other action play is play in which themes of self, other, and self with other predominate and in which the formation, transformation, and interrelatedness of self and object representations take place. We refer to these interactions as self–other action play because the baby playfully enacts many of the salient experiences of self, other, and self with other. We believe that such play contributes to the formation and integration of self and object representations in a unique way. Self–other action play eventually leads to the capacity for role play, which requires at least a rudimentary ability to take the perspective of another. When it emerges, role play becomes a new interactional language. Like spoken language, ideas and feelings are expressed. However, while in internalized language, or thought, ideas and feelings are internally processed, during role play they are enacted. The capacity to role-play indicates that interactions with others have been internalized; that is, they have become part of the child's representational world.

Our understanding of the representational world of the infant before symbolic capacity is established has been enriched by researchers who have studied in detail how infants organize their experience internally (Stern, 1985). A young infant's representational world is organized by interactions, memories, and expectations (Stern, 1985). Recent mother–infant interaction research indicates that interaction structures are represented in a presymbolic form and lay the foundation for symbolic forms of self and object representations (Beebe & Lachmann, 1988). In addition to the formation of progressively organized images of self and other, several theoretical constructs of the infant's intrapsychic organization of lived experience with an emphasis on interaction have been proposed: *scripts* by Nelson and Gruendel (1981), *generalized episodes* by Bretherton (1984), *internal working models* by Main, Kaplan, and Cassidy (1985), and *representations of interactions that have been generalized* (RIGs) and *prenarrative envelopes* by Stern (1985, 1992). All of these formulations refer to the infant's intrapsychic organization and memories of lived experience, and provide babies with a way of preserving the structure and quality of interactions, specific memorable events, and the likely course of events based on average experiences.

Here we will focus on a particular aspect of the infant and toddler's representational experience: the way in which playful interchanges, occurring in the context of the mother–child relationship, provide the scaffolding for evolving representations of both self and other and self with other. Our work draws on that of a number of authors who have argued that significant relationships are the foundation for successful symbolic growth. For example, research growing out of attachment theory (Sroufe, 1979) has demonstrated the relationship between the presence of the mother in the child's life and the amount and quality of the child's play. It further demonstrates a connection between the quality of the relationship to the mother and the quality of play. Slade has done extensive research on the influence of maternal involvement on the quality of symbolic play in toddlers. She has shown that "interaction with another appears to bring out higher performance and to provide a critical context for the elaboration and expression of symbolic processes" (Slade, 1987a, p. 374). Her data demonstrate the importance of mothers and caregivers' playing with their children. In particular, Slade found that children whose move to the phase of object constancy was compromised were limited in their capacity to maintain the organizational structure or conceptual underpinnings of a play scene. She says: "The failures of internalization which inhibited the resolution of rapprochement were reflected in the structure, coherence, and integrity of play" (Slade, 1986, p. 548).

Essentially, Slade's work draws attention to the social construction of the play process, particularly the connection between maternal participation and availability and the success of eventual symbolic representation. Our work is complementary; we are interested in showing how prototypic games played by mothers and infants during each subphase of the separation-individuation process contribute to the formation of internal representations of self, other, and self with other (Drucker, 1979; Mahler, Pine, & Bergman, 1975). While this process of forming representations proceeds outside of the play situation as well, we believe that special qualities and characteristics of play make a unique contribution to the representational world of the infant. Garvey (1977) notes the following characteristics of play:

> (1) Play is pleasurable, enjoyable. . . . (2) Play has no extrinsic goals . . . it is more an enjoyment of means than an effort devoted to some particular end. . . . (3) Play is spontaneous and voluntary. . . . (4) Play involves some active engagement on the part of the player. . . . (5) Play has certain systematic relations to what is not play . . . play has been linked with creativity, problem solving, language learning, the development of social roles, and a number of other cognitive and social phenomena. (pp. 4–5)

These characteristics color playful interactions with delight. These highlighted moments of pleasurable play, often part of basic caretaking activities, are an essential part of mother–infant interaction. In what follows we will look at these kinds of play exchanges (self–other action play) that occur during the successive phases of the separation-individuation process as described by Mahler et al. (1975).

Separation-individuation theory, which is based on detailed observational study of the developing mother–infant relationship, enriches our understanding of how play may contribute to the formation of self and other representations during the preverbal and earliest verbal periods of development. Consequently we will examine shifts in play behaviors that occur during the subphases of the separation-individuation process as it unfolds across the first 3 years of life (Mahler et al., 1975). In so doing, we will show that self–other action play serves different representational functions at different ages and promotes the linking and integrating of existing simple representations to form new, more complex representations. Using the subphases of the separation-individuation process as an organizing prospective for the description of self–other action play does not imply that one kind of play or representation is replaced by another. The subphase theory takes into account the overlapping and complex layering of the development of the representational world.

Play with Objects Connected to Mother: Linking Representations (5 to 9 Months)

A baby at 5 months is clearly attentive to the outside world. This marks the beginning of the differentiation subphase, the first subphase of separation-individuation, which takes place from about 5 to 9 months. We will describe two kinds of play during the differentiation subphase that we relate to the formation and integration of self and object representations and thus describe as self–other action play.

The first of these types of play is with objects that belong to mother, such as her jewelry, keys, and eyeglasses. Originally initiated by baby, this play is quickly responded to and elaborated by mother. These objects are of interest to infants at this age because of certain physical attributes that appeal to babies: For example, they are shiny or make special sounds. However, we assume that they are also of special value to the baby because of their connection to mother's body. They belong to mother; they are part of mother; yet they can be taken by baby and thus become baby's. Playing with these objects in mother's presence promotes the mental processes that create a relationship between an inanimate object and the specific person with whom it is associated. It is the relationship, created by the infant between mother and the objects that belong to her, combined with the intrinsic pleasure derived from the manipulation of these objects, that gives the object special meaning. Mental processes imbue the objects that belong to mother with "momminess." This begins when infants cherish and love to play with objects that belong to mother and continues in a variety of ways throughout life. This is play in Winnicott's *intermediate area*:

> The intermediate area to which I am referring is the area that is allowed to the infant between primary creativity and objective perception based on reality-testing. The transitional phenomena represent the early stages of the use of illusion, without which there is no meaning for the human being in the idea of a relationship with an object that is perceived by others as external to that being. (Winnicott, 1953, p. 90)

Play with inanimate objects that belong to mother reveals the emergence of the mental capacity to invest an object with feelings one has toward another and transfer attributes of one object to another. This capacity to link and integrate representations is the first step in the developmental pathway to symbolic functioning.

Separation and Reunion Play: Linking Representations of Interactions

The second kind of self–other action play that begins during the differentiation subphase is more clearly interactional. We refer here to games of peekaboo and what we call "I give it to you—you give it to me" and "I drop it—you pick it up." "I give it to you—you give it to me" is the game in which baby hands an inanimate object to mother and mother hands it back to baby. This self–other interaction is repeated several times and is usually accompanied by a singsong phrase. This mother–infant play activity seems to provide the baby with an experience of separateness and connectedness. "I drop it—you pick it up" is the familiar, endlessly repeated activity, initiated by babies, in which the baby drops, and eventually throws, an object and mother retrieves it. We believe that repetition of this sequence— holding on to an inanimate object, letting go of the object, and having the object returned—promotes the formation of representations of expected sequences.

Games of "I give it to you—you give it to me" and "I drop it—you pick it up" deal with issues of letting go and repossessing of inanimate objects that we think are related to issues of separation and reunion with loved ones. When the baby's actions are responded to with playfulness, these activities become pleasurable games of mastery.

The classic game of peekaboo is typically introduced by mother into the mother–baby play repertoire at this time (Bruner & Sherwood, 1976). Mother, while pulling a sweater over baby's head, may elaborate the activity of dressing into a game of peekaboo. In another form of peekaboo, mother covers baby's face with a diaper and baby learns to pull it off, or mother covers her own face. The external, self–other action often changes in games of peekaboo as mother and baby interchange roles of hiding and finding. The specific games of peekaboo played by each mother and baby, including the roles played by each, will have their own personal signature and reveal aspects of their relationship.

One special characteristic of these games that deal directly with appearance and disappearance is that they typically are accompanied by crescendos and decrescendos of excitement. The increase and decrease of arousal are mutually regulated and result in an experience of fluctuating, moment-to-moment state sharing (Stern, 1985). The reappearance after a brief disappearance evokes the joy of refinding, that is, rediscovering mother. Furthermore, the experience of "making" mother retrieve the lost object enhances the feeling of the self as agent. At a time when babies are increasingly confronted with feelings of loss and separateness, and just on the brink of becoming capable of more independent activities, in particular locomotion, we believe that the emergent experience of self as agent and highlighted experiences of state sharing, that is, attunement (Stern, 1985), may be particularly exciting. We are reminded here of Pine's concept of *moments*, which he believes to be structure-building (Pine, 1985).

At about 8 months there is a marked change in baby's reaction to mother's absence for even brief periods. Momentary losses of mother elicit a variety of distress reactions (Mahler et al., 1975). In his presentation entitled "The Origin of Conflict During the Separation-Individuation Process," McDevitt (1988) traces the development of anxiety and conflict throughout the separation-individuation period and notes that play becomes an important part of active coping behavior in response to separation toward the end of the first year. Games of peekaboo and "I drop it—you pick it up" after the onset of separation anxiety can provide the baby with experiences of control and mastery over loss and retrieval and over separation and reunion. In the presence of mother, these games promote the formation of representations related to separation and help transform painful experiences into pleasurable play.

A representation of mother as permanent (i.e., a sense that mother exists even though out of perceptual awareness) is promoted by experiences of separation followed by reunion and enables baby to tolerate separations from mother. The expectation during separation that separation will be followed by reunion is a result of the integration of the representation of mother, the representation of separation from mother, and the representation of reunion with mother. These newly integrated representations form the expectation that separations from mother will be followed by reunions with mother and the sense that mother exists even though out of perceptual awareness. These early representations and the ways they are linked together, with both their cognitive and emotional components, contribute to the eventual ability of the baby to tolerate separations.

Transitional Phenomena: Evoking a Representation of
Mother in Her Absence

Gradually baby's mental representation of mother may be evoked in her absence. For example, upon awakening a baby may coo or babble, possibly evoking mother's presence. Or baby begins to be able to soothe himself as he has been soothed by mother. Sucking his fingers or making tongue and lip motions and sounds might evoke the feeling of sucking the breast; the blanket or cuddly toy has aspects of the mother's soft body. This process of being able to derive comfort from something that reminds one of mother begins as early as 5 to 9 months and continues in various forms appropriate to the child's developmental stage.

A dramatic and poignant example of the capacity for self-soothing and the way in which transitional phenomena promote self-soothing occurred when Jessica McClure, an 18-month-old girl, was trapped at the bottom of a well for 58 hours (Shapiro, 1987). After moments of crying for her mother, she began to sing to herself the songs that her mother sang to her, thus evoking a representation of mother that may have helped her to endure the traumatic separation. The process of attaching aspects of the mental representation formed from knowledge of the actual mother to the representation of an inanimate object (or, in the case of Jessica, a song) contributes to the capacity to evoke the representation of mother during her absence. We are describing a presymbolic process by which not only lived experience determines the formation of representations but also the linking of already existing simple representations, which then form new, more complex representations. The process of linking representations of inanimate objects to representations of mother is an internal activity in which the baby becomes invested. This process contributes to the developing sense of self. Stern (1985) states: "Each process of relating diverse events may constitute a different and characteristic emergent experience. . . . I am suggesting that the infant can experience the process of emerging organization, as well as the result, and it is this experience of emerging organization that I call the emergent sense of self'' (p. 45).

We are suggesting that emergent experiences result in the emotional investment of the internal world. Self–other action play constitutes a kind of emergent experience and may in this way contribute to the uniquely human capacity to form symbols. It is not simply that the representation symbolizes the actual object, but also that the emotional investment in the inner sense or feel of mother eventually enables that inner experience or representation to substitute for the actual mother. This is similar to the way in which an emotional investment in representations is necessary for the creation of a transitional object: "It is true that the piece of blanket (or whatever it is) is symbolical of some part-object, such as the breast. Nevertheless, the point of it is not its symbolic value so much as its actuality. Its not being the breast (or the mother) is as important as the fact that it stands for breast (or mother)'' (Winnicott, 1953, pp. 91–92). The attachment to the transitional object results not only from the fact that it symbolizes the love object, but also that it is an external manifestation of the emotional investment in the developing representational world.

Play Away from Mother and the Internal Sense of Being with Mother (10 to 15 Months)

The next subphase of separation-individuation is practicing (10 to 15 months). During the practicing subphase, there are dramatic increases in physical ability and a great upsurge of pleasure in locomotion and functional play. Infants of this age practice, with great interest and compelling motivation, their quickly emerging capacities to crawl, climb and walk and their rapidly increasing manipulative skills. Enthralled with their play activities, infants vigorously begin to explore the other-than-mother world and at times appear oblivious to mother.

During this subphase, physical distance between mother and infant can be initiated by baby. The infant no longer has to endure passively being left, but can actively begin to leave and in this way practice separations and reunions. Mahler et al. (1975) observed that as long as the mother is not too far away, the infant's practicing subphase behavior continues with exuberance. If the distance is too great or mother is away for too long, the joy in practicing wanes and the infant becomes subdued.

Babies this age crawl and then walk away from mother, returning often, not with the intent to play with her but rather to facilitate their own play. At these times, babies may use mother's body as if it were an inanimate object to climb on, step on, push, and pull—a stepping stone to the world to further baby's activities and to extend baby's reach. The infant's external obliviousness to the actual mother is accompanied by an intrapsychic way of being with mother, and it is this internal sense of being with mother that enables the infant to separate from her.

This internal way of being with mother is related directly to actual experiences with mother. The memories of actual experiences of being with mother are retrievable, when separated from her, when an attribute of the memory is present (Stern, 1985). Perhaps the bodily pleasures and elation that accompany play activities during this subphase are the attributes that evoke the internal sense of being with mother. But the reverse is also true: The inner sense of being with mother increases the pleasure in play activities and the mood of elation characteristic of this subphase. Optimal amounts of the actual mother's presence and emotional availability are required in order for the baby to pursue these play activities and to derive pleasure from them. Although exceedingly interested in the other-than-mother world, the infant needs to reestablish frequent eye or physical contact with mother. Furer called this touching base with mother *emotional re-fueling* (Mahler et al., 1975). There is an ongoing interplay between actual experiences of being with mother, the internal sense of being with mother, play in the other-than-mother world, and the pleasure and mood of elation. The interrelatedness of these experiences suggests the integration of inner and outer reality and of self and object representations.

It is central to our thinking that the spontaneous, inner sense of being with mother that enables the baby to separate physically from her is itself an important intrapsychic phenomenon that promotes development. This inner sense of being with mother during the practicing subphase lays the foundation for the later mental capacity to create or evoke the inner sense of being with mother, as desired or needed, when there is a greater displeasure in separateness. (This was seen in the previously noted case of Jessica McClure.) The ability to evoke and sustain representations increases with development and facilitates the formation of psychic structure.

During the practicing subphase, intense pleasure in independent locomotion and newly acquired motor capacities propels the toddler to embrace a new separation and reunion game. Chase and reunion games are a new form of the earlier peekaboo game and serve a similar function. They are initiated by both mother and baby, and often involve a rapid alternation of roles of chasing and being chased. Peekaboo, a self–other action game of separation and reunion, becomes infused with the functional pleasure derived from motor capacities.

Play Re-Creating Essential Ways of Being with Mother: Fluidity of Representations

A commonly observed game during the practicing subphase that further suggests the integration of self and object representations is baby feeding mother playfully. This self–other action play suggests an experience of self–other ambiguity, as well as the emergence of self and object representations during play. How does one interpret this play—"I, baby, do to you, mommy, as you have done to me" or "I am now mommy and you are baby; therefore, I feed you as you have fed me"? This game and similar ones provide an actual experience of being with mother while evoking representations of mother, of self, and of self with mother. The ambiguity inherent in this play of who represents whom suggests the fluidity that is inherent in the process of integrating representations.

The use of the pull toy, another favorite play activity during the practicing subphase, raises similar questions about the meaning of play at this age (Shopper, 1978). Baby walks proudly, with his pull-toy behind, and looks back at the toy frequently. How do we understand the meaning of this play—"I am mommy, with a pull-toy baby who goes everywhere with me" or "I am baby and have a mommy pull-toy who will go wherever I go"? One might ask similar questions about riding on kiddie cars, which begins to be a favorite activity. Riding on his own car, does the child feel strong and powerful, like his mother? Or does the child now have a pretend parent always available on whom to ride? We believe it is the ambiguity about self–other symbolic meaning that gives these games special power and makes certain possessions coveted in special ways. Once again the very uncertainty of who represents whom reveals an essential fluidity and simultaneity of representations, and the process of linking and integrating representations, forming new representations.

Games of Sharing: Integrating Representations of Self and Mother (15 to 24 Months)

During the rapprochement subphase (around 15 to 24 months), another important change occurs: the child wishes to share objects and activities directly with mother and to engage mother in play. As the toddler becomes increasingly aware of his vulnerability, helplessness, and smallness, his relative obliviousness to mother demonstrated during the practicing subphase begins to wane. In an attempt to bridge the separation between self and other, children of this age bring many things to be touched and held by mother. During the early rapprochement subphase, a child literally fills his mother's lap with the other-than-mother world. A common playground activity is to wander from mother and return with "treasures" that the child demands to be held and kept by mother. These things range enormously in size and can include everything from favorite toys to objects such as pieces of wood, scraps of paper, metal, and bottle tops. "Each time the toddler finds her he brings along a new piece of the world outside, and each time he leaves her he takes with him a part of her. Increasingly this part is an image. . . ." (Bergman, 1978, p. 158). In this way the child creates a physical bridge between mother, self, and the other-than-mother world and facilitates the formation of a psychological bridge. The psychological bridge we refer to is constructed of representations of mother, self, and self in relationship to mother, as well as of representations of inanimate objects. This self–other action play adds to the stability and integration of developing representations of self, other, and self with other.

During the rapprochement subphase, the toddler's newly acquired and valued skills are repeatedly demonstrated for mother in order to receive her admiration and approval. The coming together of mother and toddler in this mutually pleasurable and gratifying way helps the child to tolerate his feelings of vulnerability, helplessness, and ineptness by having his competence mirrored and admired. These shared moments also help bridge the gap of separateness. While observing a toddler jump up and down with mastery and delight, his mother looking on with admiration, one gets the feeling that the child becomes "filled" with mother's admiration and love. This is reminiscent of the way in which inanimate objects touched by mother seem to be transformed by momminess. It is not uncommon during the rapprochement subphase for a child to refuse a cookie unless first touched by mother or to have a hurt healed by mother's magical kiss.

The child's conflicting wishes for autonomy, on the one hand, and for mother to be ever-present, on the other hand, culminate in the rapprochement crises. Attempts at omnipotent control of both self and other are the way in which the toddler tries to solve this inherently insoluble problem. A great need for mother's emotional availability (Emde, 1980; Mahler, 1963) combined with frequent outbursts of anger often make even brief separations stressful. We will attempt to show how self–other action play helps the child to deal with the conflicts that arise during the rapprochement crisis.

Beginning Role Play Between Mother and Baby: Representations of Empathic Exchanges (22 to 26 Months)

During the rapprochement subphase, a maturational leap in symbolic functioning and important developments in play occur. Although we believe that precursors to symbolic functioning or more rudimentary forms of symbolic functioning are evidenced in earlier play, the symbolic meaning of a child's play gradually becomes clearer. The unfolding of this process is revealed during the rapprochement subphase when self–other action play actually takes the form of role play.

In beginning role play, mother often takes a fairly passive role as the child tells her what to do. She allows herself to be used to meet the needs of the toddler's inner life. A common script enacted by children of this age requires mother to cry when baby leaves or to cry when she has been hurt. For example, toddler leaves the room and says, "Mommy cry." Toddler then returns and says, "Here I am. Mommy, stop crying." They hug. This role play is less ambiguous in terms of role designation than the play described during the practicing subphase. Baby plays mommy, and mommy is supposed to play baby. Typically this kind of game is repeated over and over and represents active, pleasurable mastery in play of the painful situation of being left. In a slightly more complex scenario, the mother of a 20-month-old boy reports that he bites her playfully but sometimes quite hard. She pretends to cry. He runs and brings her his blanket, the beloved transitional object, to comfort her. He shifts from being the playful biting baby, or the aggressive hurtful baby, to the comforting caretaker. This game is repeated over and over. Such early forms of role play typically involve the exchange of roles between mother and child addressing issues of vulnerability, separation and aggression, and experiences of empathy, reparation, and love. The ability to play these games, that is, to put oneself in the role of another, requires the beginning ability to objectify the self (Piaget, 1962; Stern, 1985) and the capacity to link and integrate representations. The representations integrated include representations of mother, self with and without mother, actions of mother, and self performing the actions of mother. This kind of role play reveals early identifications with mother and the working through of issues and conflicts related to separation and reunion and to aggression and reparation. Role play further promotes the integration and elaboration of self and object representations. The integration of self and object representations will eventually result in a self that can be both similar to and different from mother, both complying with and opposing mother, and both loving and hating mother. Role play, with its expansion and elaboration of representations, promotes identification that will be instrumental in the resolution of the rapprochement crisis.

Further Development of Role Play: The Consolidation and Expansion of Representations (24 to 30 Months)

As rapprochement conflicts begin to be resolved (around 24 to 30 months), the *on the way to object constancy* subphase begins. With self and object representations now more firmly established, the child is further able to enact a wide range of needs, impulses, and conflicts through role play. Therefore, during this phase, our ability to learn about the representational world of children through their play is dramatically increased. Now role play begins to include characters from the outside world. It is no longer limited to role exchange between mother and child; it begins to include the child's everyday experiences with people such as the mail carrier, bus driver, repairman, police officer, and doctor.

We wish to emphasize that role play that includes characters from the other-than-mother world begins when the self is firmly enough established to be able to put itself in the place of the other; this is the hallmark of the *on the way to self and object constancy* subphase. This expanded role play enables the child to elaborate and consolidate aspects of development that were first established during earlier developmental phases when issues and conflicts were negotiated within the parent–child context. Now the child is able to extend characteristics of self and other, and the relationship between himself and significant others, to the widening world. The roles that are enacted express the child's knowledge of the people who surround him, help the child expand that knowledge, and represent important aspects of the now more consolidated and ever-expanding inner representational world. Such role play reinforces both connections with and separations from emotionally significant others because each role enactment embodies a crucial aspect of the self and the other. We suggest that this kind of role play is directly related to self–other action play that occurred earlier and continues to deal with the basic themes of self–other interaction.

We believe that the internal experience during role play can be best understood in terms of Winnicott's intermediate area of experience (Winnicott 1953). Both a certain fluidity and constancy of self and object representations remain characteristic of role play, and a particular kind of integration of self and object representations and of inner and outer reality occurs. Role play serves the child's simultaneous needs to both express and disguise his impulses, anxieties, and conflicts (Bornstein, 1945).

"Mail carrier" is a favorite game of children on the way to object constancy. This role play allows children to continue the pleasure of bringing treasures to mother, a pleasure that began during the early rapprochement subphase. Mail carrier role play, a game that has anal phase components, puts giving and receiving of valued things into a context that assures the child that his gifts will be received with approval and delight. Children of this age have observed that adults are often excited about getting mail and that it connects them with people who are somewhere else. Thus the child not only reinforces the bridge between self and mother, but also acknowledges the relationship between mother and others.

"Doctor," a popular game throughout childhood, begins at this age. Doctor play usually originates as a reenactment of the child's visits to the doctor and gradually is elaborated. Many children alternate between the roles of doctor and patient, while others consistently choose one role or the other. Doctor play provides the opportunity to explore the body, a self–other action play activity that began during the differentiation subphase, and to address concerns about the integrity of the body and the genital difference that become important during the second year. Both passive wishes and sexual and aggressive impulses are expressed. Doctor play is self–other action play that often involves direct and intimate body contact between self and other.

Playing doctor also enables many children to reconstruct and work through traumatic experiences of illness and injury. A 22-month-old girl who suffered a severe injury to a finger that resulted in losing a great deal of blood, an emergency visit to the hospital, injections in her finger and buttock, and a huge bandage that covered her hand completely frequently played doctor in the following weeks. She alternated between playing the role of the frightened, crying patient; the angry, defiant patient;

the detached, hurtful doctor; the concerned, healing doctor; the frightened, guilty mother; and the comforting, loving mother. The enactment of self and other roles related to the accident facilitated the integration of representations and the resolution of the impact of the traumatic experience.

Sometimes role play can serve the integration of both masculine and feminine identifications within an appropriate gender role. For example, a 2½-year-old boy whose father was in the construction business chose the role of repairman. He loved tools and was not satisfied with toy imitations. The boy was clearly identifying with his father as he walked around the house with his little tool box, talking to his mother about all the things he was fixing. His collection of favorite tools included the vacuum cleaner, which was regularly used by his mother. Thus the role of repairman included both male and female identifications within a male role. The incorporation of a female identification into a male gender role supported this little boy's growing masculine identity without relinquishing the identification with his mother. In addition, role-playing a repairman probably helped him cope with the discovery of anatomical difference, an important developmental issue of children his age.

"Bus driver" and "elevator operator" are favorite games of separation and reunion. Issues and conflicts from earlier subphases of separation-individuation, as well as oral and anal phase development, are addressed. The child controls the make-believe mechanical door that enables passengers to leave and enter the bus; passengers are dropped off and must wait (and often pay) to be picked up. In this way, the child may be dealing with issues of what goes into and out of the body, as well as issues of separation and reunion with love objects. Perhaps this game of separation and reunion is a new edition of the earlier games of peekaboo. The small toddler feels powerful as he pretends to drive the huge bus and in this way continues to work on rapprochement subphase issues of feeling relatively small and helpless.

"Police," "cops and robbers," "superhero and villain," and variations thereof include the enactment of aggressive impulses or references to them and reveal beginning superego structure formation. Many children alternate between the police and criminal roles, while others exclusively play one role or the other. The good–bad split in roles is a significant aspect of this play and promotes the integration of good and bad, self and object representations. In addition, the police in pursuit of the criminal may be an elaborated version of the earlier game of chase and reunion. Within the child's life experience, the authority of the police is understood to be more powerful than that of his mother and is to be respected by him as well as his mother. This aspect of police play enables aggression mobilized toward mother in response to her limit setting to be modulated, thereby facilitating object constancy.

Role play that includes characters from the outside world captures essential aspects of love objects and simultaneously promotes separation from them. This type of role play integrates and expands representations of self and mother, and reveals the consolidation of representations created by linking representations of mother with representations of self. Because of more advanced symbolic functioning and greater integration of representations, developmental issues and conflicts are addressed in more derivative form, thus facilitating development.

Many of the issues and conflicts addressed in role play during the *on the way to self and object constancy* subphase originate in earlier developmental phases and continue to be issues for life. Many role-play games appear to be elaborated versions of earlier self–other action play. The roles enacted have been observed by the child in his ever-widening world and in some way capture not only internal conflicts seeking resolution or developmental issues to be negotiated, but also significant aspects of the adult that the child is aspiring to be and is already becoming, as well as elements of the external world within which he lives. Role play moves this process beyond the parent–child relationship while simultaneously incorporating it. Resolution of issues and conflicts that first emerged in infancy need no longer be exclusively bound to the parent–child relationship. In this way, role play serves a unique function in development.

Summary

During the separation-individuation process, self–other action play promotes the child's formation and integration of self and object representations and his adaptation to those conflicts and losses that are part of normal development. The capacity to role-play, that is, the capacity to reenact one's own lived experience or one's own experience of another, is the culmination of a process that is rooted in earlier forms of self–other action play and, further, promotes the integration of self and object representations. In addition, role-play games seem to share action themes in common with earlier play.

The ability to create relationships between objects, between representations and objects, and between representations is a mental capacity that is required in order to role-play. We believe that this occurs for the first time in play during the differentiation subphase when a relationship is being created between mother and those objects that belong to her—her jewelry, clothes, and so on. This developing mental capacity, the capacity to link and integrate representations, is next revealed during the rapprochement subphase during play that creates a bridge between mother and self and between mother and the rest of the world. The second mental capacity essential to role play is the ability to evoke a representation when desired. This capacity is first revealed during the practicing subphase and was described as an inner sense of being with mother that enables the infant to separate from mother. Furthermore, this inner sense of being with mother promotes the integration of self and object representations.

We have suggested that the linking and integrating of representations occurs in self–other action play throughout separation-individuation. During the differentiation subphase, play with mother's possessions facilitates the linking of representations of mother with things that belong to her. During the practicing subphase, the fluidity of representations of self and other inherent in certain play activities, and the ongoing mutual regulation of and reciprocity between actual experiences of being with mother, the internal sense of being with mother, participation in play activities in the other-than-mother world, and the pleasure and elation that is derived from those activities, suggest the integration of self and object representations. During the rapprochement subphase, play activities in which child fills mother's lap with inanimate objects, thereby filling mommy with the world and the world with momminess, and play in which the child performs skills for mother, thereby filling the self with mother's loving admiration, promote the integration of representations of mother and inanimate objects and of mother and self. These play activities create a psychological bridge through representations that can connect the separate mother and self.

During the fourth subphase, *on the way to self and object constancy*, play that includes roles from the outside world begins. This occurs when the self is firmly and flexibly enough established that the child not only can put himself in the place of emotionally significant others, but can also extend this capacity to include persons beyond parents and other family members. This kind of role play is related to self–other action play that occurred during earlier phases and continues to deal with the basic themes of self–other interaction. It enables the child to elaborate and consolidate aspects of development that were first established during earlier phases when developmental issues and conflicts were negotiated almost exclusively within the parent–child relationship. During this phase of development, because of more advanced representational and symbolic capacities, those same issues and conflicts can be addressed in more derivative form allowing for the further elaboration and consolidation of development. Resolution of issues and conflicts that first emerged in infancy need no longer be exclusively bound to the parent–child relationship.

ACKNOWLEDGMENTS

We wish to thank those colleagues who have made valuable comments on earlier versions of this chapter, and in particular to acknowledge the contributions of Drs. John McDevitt, Robert Michels, and Ethel Person.

Throughout this chapter, *mother* is used to refer to the caretaking other, regardless of gender, and masculine pronouns are used to refer to the child. This has been done to distinguish clearly references to the mother and references to the baby. The unique aspects of the father's role in the processes discussed will not be addressed here.

REFERENCES

Beebe, B., & Lachmann, F. (1988). The contribution of mother–infant mutual influence to the origins of self and object representations. *Psychoanalytic Psychology, 5*, 305–337.

Bergman, A. (1978). From mother to the outside world: The use of space during the separation-individuation phase. In S. Grolnick & L. Barkin (Eds.), *Between reality and fantasy* (pp. 147–165). New York: Jason Aronson.

Bornstein, B. (1945). Clinical notes on child analysis. *Psychoanalytic Study of the Child, 1*, 151–166.

Bretherton, I. (1984). Representing the social world in symbolic play: Reality and fantasy. In I. Bretherton (Ed.), *Symbolic play: The development of social understanding* (pp. 3–41). Orlando, FL: Academic Press.

Bruner, J. S., & Sherwood, V. (1976). Peekaboo and the learning of rule structures. In J. S. Bruner (Ed.), *Play, its role in development and evolution* (pp. 277–285). New York: Basic Books.

Drucker, J. (1979). The affective context and psychodynamics of first symbolization. In N. R. Smith & M. B. Franklin (Eds.), *Symbolic functioning in childhood* (pp. 27–41). Hillsdale, NJ: Erlbaum.

Emde, R. (1980). Emotional availability: A reciprocal reward system for infants and parents with implications for prevention of psychosocial disorders. In P. Taylor (Ed.), *Parent–infant relationships* (pp. 87–115). Orlando, FL: Grune & Stratton.

Garvey, C. (1977). *Play.* Boston: Harvard University Press.

Mahler, M. (1963). Thoughts about development and individuation. *Psychoanalytic Study of the Child, 18,* 307–324.

Mahler, M., Pine, F., & Bergman, A. (1975). *The psychological birth of the human infant.* New York: Basic Books.

Main, M., Kaplan, N., & Cassidy, J. (1985). Security in infancy, childhood, and adulthood: A move to the level of representation. *Monographs of the Society for Research in Child Development, 50* (1–2), 66–104.

McDevitt, J. (1988, May). *The origin of intrapsychic conflict during the separation-individuation process.* Paper presented at the Margaret Mahler Symposium, Medical College of Pennsylvania, Philadelphia.

Nelson, K., & Gruendel, J. (1981). Generalized event representation: Basic building blocks of cognitive development. In A. Brown & M. Lamb (Eds.), *Advances in development and psychology* (Vol. 1, pp. 131–158). Hillsdale, NJ: Erlbaum.

Piaget, J. (1962). *Play, dreams and imitation in childhood.* New York: Norton.

Pine, F. (1985). *Developmental theory and clinical process,* New Haven, CT: Yale University Press.

Shapiro, W. (1987). One went right: Woes from Wall Street to the Gulf—but a happy ending in Texas. *Time, 130,* 30.

Shopper, M. (1978). The role of audition in early psychic development with special reference to the use of the pull toy in the separation-individuation phase. *Journal of the American Psychoanalytic Association, 26,* 283–310.

Slade, A. (1986). Symbolic play and separation-individuation. *Bulletin of the Menninger Clinic, 50,* 541–563.

Slade, A. (1987a). A longitudinal study of maternal involvement and symbolic play during the toddler period. *Child Development, 58,* 367–375.

Slade, A. (1987b). Quality of attachment and early symbolic play. *Developmental Psychology, 23,* 78–85.

Sroufe, L. A. (1979). The coherence of individual development: Early care, attachment and subsequent development issues. *American Psychologist, 34,* 834–841.

Stern, D. N. (1977). *The first relationship: Mother and infant.* Cambridge, MA: Harvard University Press.

Stern, D. N. (1992). Pre-narrative envelope: An alternative view of "unconscious fantasy" in infancy. *Bulletin of the Anna Freud Centre, 15,* 291–318.

Stern, D. N. (1985). *The interpersonal world of the human infant.* New York: Basic Books.

Winnicott, D. W. (1953). Transitional objects and transitional phenomena. *International Journal of Psychoanalysis, 34,* 89–97.

8

Play: A Context for Mutual Regulation Within Mother–Child Interaction

LORRAINE McCUNE
DONNA DIPANE
RUTH FIREOVED
MARY FLECK

Mothers and their infants are linked in a process of interaction whereby each continually affects the other (Maccoby & Martin, 1983). The characteristic of mutual regulation within mother–child interaction can be addressed by focusing on two dynamic aspects of the interchange. The first aspect deals with the child's developing maturity, as evidenced by level of cognition, language, and independence. The second involves the mother's calibration of her own role in relation to the child's level of functioning, which can be seen in her responsive and initiating actions with the child (Clarke-Stewart, Vanderstoep, & Killian, 1979; Rocissano & Yatchmink, 1983, 1984). Play situations provide the ideal opportunity for such mutual regulation to grow because rules, goals, and limits are established by the play partners rather than by external experiences. The goal of this chapter is to explore these two aspects in relation to their influence on the process of mutual regulation within the mother–child interaction in a play setting. We will describe developmental trends in the character of mutual regulation and examine individual differences that are not immediately apparent in group findings.

Play can be viewed as a window on the cognitive language and social development of the child. From the cognitive perspective, observing play allows us to infer the child's emerging ability to symbolize internally and through the manipulation of objects in pretend sequences (Nicolich, 1977). Several lines of research suggest that symbolic play may be a good predictor of language skills; McCune (McCune-Nicolich, 1981) has described correspondences between level of play and language. In contrast to routine daily care such as bathing and dressing, play offers an opportunity for communication and for closeness in the mother–child interaction by providing a unique context in which the child can be a more equal partner with the mother.

The notion that experiences with the social partner play a critical role in the child's motivation to symbolize has been raised by researchers in this area (O'Connell & Bretherton, 1984; Dunn & Wooding, 1977; Rogoff, 1990; Slade, 1987; Werner & Kaplan, 1963), but to date there have been relatively few empirical studies that address these phenomena.

The Mutuality of Symbolic Play Development in Late Infancy

During the first 2 years of life the child undergoes a series of developmental transitions. The major cognitive achievement of this period is the gradual emergence of the ability to represent experience symbolically (Piaget, 1962). This particular transition is evidenced in both the child's play and language. Play evolves from object exploration and realistic object use to extended pretend sequences and then to planned pretend (Nicolich, 1977). Both the duration and the level of play episodes increase with age (Slade, 1987). Language proceeds from preword vocalizations and gestures to early sentences. McCune (1993) has reported that symbolic play levels are predictive of language transitions. Socially, the infant's capacity for self-regulation is limited in the first year of life, but begins with the ability to inhibit reaching movements (at approximately 8 months) and continues to expand, so that a shift occurs from parental regulation to coregulation (Maccoby & Martin, 1983). Physically, the child develops the ability to move away from the mother, but can use language and play to maintain contact with her (Clarke-Stewart & Hevey, 1981). These emerging abilities are critical factors in the child's navigation of the separation-individuation process (Mahler, Pine, & Bergman, 1975; Slade, 1986) and makes it possible for the child to establish a sense of independence and autonomy.

Inferential evidence suggests that play with mother, particularly pretend play, provides a critical vehicle for the child's transition to symbolization. Dunn and Wooding (1977) first observed that in the home, children sought out their mothers to demonstrate pretend play, although they were content to play alone at other activities. Slade (1987) investigated the effect of different amounts and styles of maternal involvement on toddler symbolic play and found that the symbolic play level for the child was highest in an active maternal involvement condition when the mother initiated, suggested, and joined in play with the child. However, even when the mother just commented to her child but remained essentially uninvolved, the duration and level of play were increased. Using only child-initiated episodes to eliminate the possible effect of mother's directing the play also revealed that both conditions— the mother involved and the mother commenting—were associated with longer and higher-level play episodes than when the mother was not involved. These findings highlight play as a unique opportunity for mothers' role in mutual regulation to enhance development.

Developmental transitions experienced by the child both influence and are influenced by the content and style of the mother–child interaction. During the first 2 years of life, children become vastly more effective social partners (Clarke-Stewart & Hevey, 1981). By 2½ years, children and mothers are equal partners in initiating interactions. And because children are clearer in their bids and initiatives, mothers become more responsive over time (Bronson, 1974). Bakeman and Adamson (1984) found that as infants become older (i.e., by approximately 18 months of age), they are more likely to combine object and social play: They spend more time in coordinated joint play involving a triadic interaction of the infant, an object, and a partner; less time engaged with just the partner; and less time unengaged. These studies indicate that emerging abilities and competencies of the developing child to attend and coordinate social and object realms have a clear effect on the style of the mother–child interaction.

Developmental change is also evident in the way the mother anticipates, responds to, and adjusts to the infant's developmental level. As the mother witnesses an increasingly complex and capable child, her role in the interaction changes. The child who experiences increasing expectations from the parent is stimulated to progress. Thus, the spiral of mutual regulation proceeds. Mothers have been found to employ various strategies in matching their behaviors to the developmental level of their children. A play setting puts the mother in a more responsive role in relation to the child since there is no real goal for play. Play allows the child to take the lead, and the mother is able to reflect on what the child is doing on his or her own. The mother is far more likely to take the lead in activities such as meals or bath times.

Hodapp, Goldfield, and Boyatzis (1984) examined maternal activities preceding and following developments in their infants' skill-related behavior and found that mothers alter their behaviors in ways that seem supportive of their children's developing skill. Behaviors that mothers used included gaining the child's attention prior to beginning gestures, to indicate the expected behavior, and reinforcing increasing approximations of the targeted game behavior, suggesting that such maternal scaffolding behavior helps the child to acquire necessary game skills. Bakeman and Adamson (1984) investigated the role mothers play in fostering forms of coordinated attention with their 6- to 18-month-old infants. They found that mothers positively influence joint engagement states by capturing their infants' attention to an object/event as a prelude to a period of mutual exploration. This may provide an implicit social context for nonverbal referential communication as the infant develops the ability to coordinate attention across social and object domains.

Qualities of Dyadic Interaction Affecting Play Development

A question of particular interest to clinicians working with mothers and infants is the relationship of the mother–child interaction to developmental outcomes for children. In her longitudinal study of infants between 9 and 18 months of age, Clarke-Stewart (1973) found that the child's overall competence was related to the mother's effectiveness, positive and responsive language, and amount of interaction with the child. The variable most highly correlated with child competence was maternal verbal stimulation. Maternal effectiveness was positively related to child's early test performance and negatively related to infant irritability. A group of maternal behaviors termed *high stimulating/high responsive* were associated with the highest Bayley scores. Those labeled *low stimulating/low responsive* were associated with the lowest Bayley scores. Clearly, qualitative features of the interaction were related to the child's developmental outcome.

Clarke-Stewart et al. (1979) used the same cross-dimensional approach with a different group of children at 24 months of age. In this sample, child IQ correlated with the following maternal behaviors: descriptive speech, positive play, nondirectiveness, and nonrestrictiveness. Maternal language level directed to the child was found to have a high positive correlation with child language level. In their study of the relationship between mother–child interaction variables and child linguistic skills among 24-month-old children who had been born prematurely, Rocissano and Yatchmink (1983) found child linguistic skill to be associated with the maintenance of joint attention in the mother–child interaction. Among children who frequently engaged in interactions where they attended to the same aspect of the environment as their mothers (termed *synchronous*), linguistic skills were described as robust. The linguistic skills of children in less synchronous dyads were less strong.

Joint attention has two important aspects: its maintenance in mother–child interaction and differences among dyads in negotiating joint attention. In a sample of 17- to 25-month-old infants and their mothers, Rocissano and Yatchmink (1984) found that 75% of their interactive turns were synchronous. When the asynchronous turns were examined, three distinct styles of interaction emerged for mothers with their children: directing, uninvolved, and equal numbers of both directing and uninvolved behaviors. The authors pointed out that mutuality was achieved either through a symmetrical exchange in which each member contributed equally or through a reciprocal exchange in which one member became more active to maintain a matched level. Instead of dyads using predominantly one pattern, patterns were used in different ways by different dyads.

The issue of predicting outcomes for children by examining the influence of the mother–child interaction is related to the stability of infant and maternal characteristics. In their investigation of continuity in individual differences in mother–child interaction, Pettit and Bates (1984) observed 128 dyads at 6 and 13 months. Individual differences in the relationship at 6 months were predictive of individual differences at 13 months. The authors found that mothers who showed interest in their babies and who directly stimulated cognitive growth had a pattern of interaction that was predictive of infants who at 13 months were more likely to be involved in object-oriented communication and to have higher Bayley scores than infants in a nonstimulating dyad. Although play was not the focus of this investigation, maternal variables included play-associated behaviors such as giving, demonstrating, and returning toys to the infant. Another pattern of interaction that emerged was of a mother using control strategies and an active, unresponsive child. The authors suggest that this relationship may be an early indicator of a conflicted mother–child interaction pattern.

Thus, current work in the area of mother–child interaction, as reviewed here, demonstrates that as children proceed through developmental milestones in cognitive, language, motor, and social–emotional abilities, mothers respond and adjust to their changing children in ways that facilitate the children's growth. At the same time, there are clear and consequential differences in the styles of playing developed in individual dyads. Clearly, play provides a social context within which such differences in interaction may be appropriately examined and understood since many of the studies reviewed involve play, showing investigators' implicit recognition of the value of the play setting for observing both developments and differences in interaction patterns (Adler, 1982; Bakeman & Adamson, 1984; Crowley & Spiker, 1983; Hodapp et al., 1984; Mahoney, 1983; Pettit & Bates, 1984; Rocissano & Yatchmink, 1983).

Capturing Interactive Play Data: The Implicit Theories of Different Approaches

Among studies of mother–child interaction, two major methodologies have been employed: microanalytic techniques (Brazelton, Kozlowski, & Main, 1974; Stern, 1974a, b; Wasserman & Allen, 1985) and checklist procedures (Bronson, 1974; Clarke-Stewart & Hevey, 1981; Escalona, 1973). With microanalytic coding, observations are recorded on the basis of time of events. A limitation of time-sequential methods is that one cannot determine whether a particular action is a continuation of a sequence begun in an immediately prior interval or occurs in response to the behavior of the partner in a earlier time interval. This method is better suited for early mother–infant interactions characterized by relatively simple, rapidly changing behaviors of shorter duration. With toddlers, analysis of longer behavioral units is necessary. Checklist procedures involve checking off similar types of behaviors as they are observed. These procedures have the disadvantage of losing the effects of one partner's actions upon the other.

Both of these techniques are an effective means to analyze specific segments of naturally occurring behaviors. However, they are limited in their ability to capture the impact of the context of the interaction. One method to retain the interdependence of the interaction is to use procedures that record, in addition to the content of the interaction, responses that are dependent or contingent upon those of the partner (Adler, 1982; Crowley & Spiker, 1983; Rocissano & Yatchmink, 1984).

Adler's (1982) work, which encompasses aspects of previously cited investigations of mother–child interaction, was developed to record the specific behavior and its function within the social context of play. The following areas were examined: (1) the structure of the exchange, (2) the content of the interaction and the functions of the behaviors, (3) the individual dyad's interaction style, and (4) the relationship between interaction style and the child's symbolic development, as expressed in play and language. Adler used a cross-sectional sample of infants 19 to 24 months of age and developed a methodology for coding interaction during a play session on the basis of meaningful segments of interaction termed *moves*. Mothers assumed an active role in play activities with their children, carried major responsibility for keeping the interaction going, and used techniques that varied in directiveness and attention to the children's goals. Behavior styles of mothers and infants varied along two continua: maternal directiveness and child demand strength.

Although mothers were always contingent to children, children were less contingent when mothers were directive and more contingent when mothers facilitated children's goals. Combinations of individual styles contributed to interesting dyad differences. When the interaction was related to symbolic development, it was found, in general, that low-symbolic children were less responsive to their mothers' initiations, had mothers who were more dominant, and were themselves low in demand strength. However, when individual cases were examined, the relationship among the variables appeared to be highly complex.

Adler's procedure segments observation on the basis of events described as codable moves rather than of time. In order to allow for analysis of longer units of interaction, large, continuous behavior units (such as getting a mop and mopping the floor) are coded as a single event rather than as separate behaviors. This allows longer samples of interaction and play to be analyzed. These events, or moves, are then assigned codes. Duration is ignored while the order of the behaviors, the assigned code, and the partner's response are recorded. To determine infant and mother responsiveness, the codable moves are classified as either obligatory or nonobligatory. Obligatory moves are verbalizations or actions that convey an expectation of response from the other person. Examples include the child motioning for help, the child showing the mother a toy, and the mother asking the child a question. Nonobligatory moves are actions or utterances that place no response demand on the partner. For example, comments on the ongoing activity ("You found a shoe") or confirmation of the child's actions ("That's right") would be coded as nonobligatory.

Adler's system consists of 4 nonobligatory and 14 obligatory moves for the mother. Of the 13 child move categories, 5 are nonobligatory and 8 are obligatory (Table 8.1). Obligatory moves vary in the amount of participation demanded from the partner. Of the maternal obligatory moves, *suggest symbolic play, suggest nonsymbolic play, prohibit, direct, disconfirm* and *attention* are considered to be stronger than other moves. These moves tend to direct the child in some way toward the mother's agenda rather than putting her in a responsive role for the child. The ratio of these directive moves to the total number of maternal moves is an index of maternal directive strength. The child's moves vary from *reach* or *show* (e.g., show a toy) to *request help* or *request joint nonsymbolic play*, which demand more participation from the mother. The child moves *request information, request help, request joint nonsymbolic play*, and *request joint symbolic play* are described as strong moves. The ratio of these strong moves to the total number of child moves is an index of the child's demand strength.

Since not all codable moves require a response from the partner, only obligatory moves were coded for contingency. By their nature, nonobligatory moves do not require a response and therefore were not coded for contingency. If all moves were coded for contingency, we would not be able to distinguish between cases where a partner received few demands to respond to and cases where there was very little responding when responding was expected or required. Contingency is broadly defined as any response that relates to the partner's obligatory move. This includes all forms of acknowledgment (nodding, answering, accepting) as well as relevant new moves, such as when the mother encourages independence in response to the

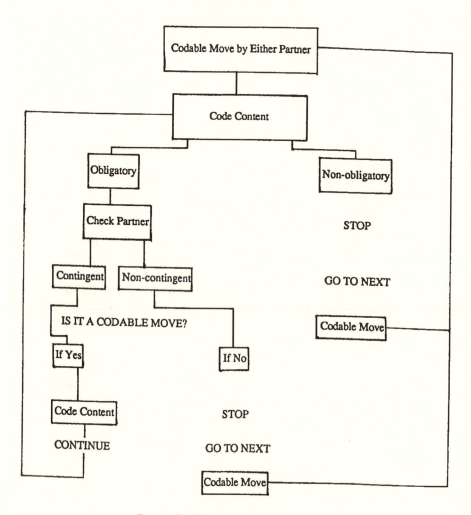

FIGURE 8.1 Flowchart for Adler coding.

child's request for help ("I think you can do it yourself. Push here."). If both partners are involved in the activity, they are considered to be operating contingently. Social contingency is possible even without compliance. Children who respond to directions by doing the opposite of the request are rated as contingent, providing that they acknowledge their mothers in some way. A noncontingent response is one that neither acknowledges nor relates to the partner's obligatory move. For example, the mother may tap the toy basket and call to her child, who continues to walk away. If the partner is contingent, the partner's move is also coded, if codable. If the partner

TABLE 8.1.   Categories of Mother and Child Moves

Mother	Child
Nonobligatory	
Comment	Comment
Confirm	Physical contact
Physical contact	Symbolic play
Correct	Nonsymbolic play
Obligatory	
Directive	*Strong*
Direction	Request information
Prohibit	Request help
Disconfirm	Request joint symbolic play
Attention-getting device	Request joint nonsymbolic play
Suggest symbolic play	
Suggest nonsymbolic play	
Facilitative	*Weak*
Independence	Reach
Help	Request object
Structure	Give/show/offer
Joint nonsymbolic play	
Joint symbolic play	
Demonstrate symbolic play	
Demonstrate nonsymbolic play	
Other	*Other*
Request information	Look

is noncontingent, the next codable move is identified from either partner (Figure 8.1). The codable moves are divided into directive and facilitative moves for the mother and into strong and weak bids for the child (Table 8.1). From these, the child strength index and maternal directive index are computed.

Thus, the Adler system allows a researcher to describe the many independent aspects of mother–child dyadic play that determine both the flavor and the outcomes of those interactions.

The Study

The purpose of the current study is to explore the character of mutual regulation during play by describing developmental trends and examining individual differences. To accomplish this, the method developed by Adler (1982) was applied to a longitudinal sample of mothers and infants at ages 9, 12, 18, and 24 months. Specific questions addressed in this study included the following: (1) What is the role of each partner and the content of the mother–child interaction at each age? (2) How does the interaction change from 9 to 24 months? (3) How do the dyads differ from each other in their interactive styles at each age? (4) What variables are related to these observed differences both within and among dyads?

Subjects

The subjects were 10 Caucasian infants, 5 males and 5 females, who were part of a larger study. The infants were selected for participation from advertisements placed with the local radio station and a local daily newspaper. In all cases, the mother was the primary caretaker, as defined by responsibility for daily care at least 50% of the time between 7 A.M. and 7 P.M. The children were unselected for social class. The educational level of parents ranged from high school completion to doctoral degrees.

Procedures

The subjects were videotaped monthly, beginning at 9 months of age and continuing until they reached 24 months of age. Data available on these infants include object permanence measures, Bayley scales scores, symbolic play levels, and mean length of utterance assessed at 9, 12, 18, and 24 months.

The play sessions were 30 minutes in length. In these sessions, the mother and child were seated on the floor with a collection of toys. The mother was instructed to allow the child to take the lead in playing with the toys but to respond as the situation warranted. Structuring the play sessions for the dyads provided freedom from other activities, thus allowing the partners to focus on the interaction as much as they were able.

The first 10 minutes of the interaction were used for analysis in this study for infants aged 9, 12, 18, and 24 months. The instrument used to code mother–child interaction was developed by Adler in collaboration with McCune (Adler, 1982; Massing & McCune, 1986), as described previously.

Written transcripts were prepared for each videotape of each child at each age, which included a description of child and maternal behaviors and exact vocalizations and verbalizations. To determine function, it was necessary to note the context in which each behavior, vocalization and/or verbalization occurred. The transcript and coding sheet were then reviewed by the other coders to check for agreement on both moves and codes. Reliability measures were taken among the three coders for the behaviors selected as codable moves, for the codes assigned, and for whether the move was contingent or noncontingent. The reliability measure yielded a range from 76% to 92% agreement for move identification and from 78% to 95% agreement for the codes assigned. Any disagreements were discussed and resolved by consensus.

Results

We will first present results concerning the children as a group, followed by details of three cases in order to clarify the implications of this study of play interaction. For each pair at each of the four ages, proportions were calculated using the codes obtained from videotapes and transcripts. Using repeated measures, these percentages were compared across the four age periods under study. When the results were tested for sex differences, none were found. When significant differences were found, Tukey's Honestly Significant Difference (HSD) test was used as a post hoc procedure to isolate the means that contributed to the differences.

The proportion of child activity was defined as the number of child moves divided by the total number of moves for the interaction; likewise, the proportion of maternal activity was the number of mother moves divided by the total number of moves. The total number of moves increased significantly over time for the sample ($F = 5.88, p < .01$), indicating that both members became more active as the infants matured. The infants became increasingly active at later ages, so that by 18 and 24 months, the relative contribution to the total number of moves was balanced between members of the dyad. As the infants contributed more at 18 and 24 months, the maternal activity significantly decreased at these ages (HSD, $p < .05$). The number of moves contributed by the infants increased significantly from 9 and 12 to 18 and 24 months (HSD, $p < .05$), the same ages at which the percentage of moves contributed by the mothers showed a significant decline. This balance can be illustrated by looking at the means for the total number of moves and the mean percentages contributed by mothers and infants at the ages studied (Table 8.2).

In addition to considering the number of moves for each member, the number of moves that attempted to engage the partner was studied. These moves are defined as obligatory moves. The proportion of mother or child obligatory moves was the number of that partner's obligatory moves divided by the total number of the his or her moves. The proportion of obligatory moves changed significantly over time for both mothers and infants (child obligatory moves: $F = 12.55, p < .01$; maternal obligatory moves: $F = 3.29, p < .05$). The actual differences were not large, with the exception of the few numbers of obligatory moves exhibited by the 9-month-olds. The infants placed more response demands upon their mothers as they matured. However, these results were not linear. Rather, as a group, the infants had the most obligatory moves at 18 months, with the mean number of obligatory moves being about the same for the 12- and 24-month-olds. The mothers, on the other hand, were the least likely to obligate their infants at 18 and 24 months. The means for the proportion of maternal and child obligatory moves are reported in Table 8.3.

The codes most frequently assigned to the child's behavior are two nonobligatory

TABLE 8.2.   Means (and Ranges) for Activity Level

	9 Months	*12 Months*	*18 Months*	*24 Months*
Total moves for	103.50b	121.20ab	155.50a	160.40
interaction	(70–141)	(81–169)	(82–214)	(95–259)
Maternal activity	60.84a	55.29ab	50.45b	49.93b
	(39–72)	(47–64)	(37–57)	(40–60)
Child activity	39.26b	44.71ab	49.55b	40.07b
	(28–61)	(36–53)	(43–63)	(40–60)

Note: Means with the same subscript did not differ significantly.

TABLE 8.3. Percentages (and Ranges) of Obligatory Moves

	9 Months	12 Months	18 Months	24 Months
Maternal obligatory moves	65.87a	65.52a	53.19a	53.08a
	(48–87)	(41–83)	(16–70)	(12–76)
Child obligatory moves	4.39b	19.30a	24.58a	18.03a
	(0–14)	(4–16)	(8–33)	(5–37)

Note: Means with the same subscript did not differ significantly.

moves: nonsymbolic play and symbolic play. Nonsymbolic play is characterized by recognizing and exploring object use. Symbolic play is characterized by using objects to pretend at self-related activities, as well as activities with others, and combining pretend sequences. In this sample, the average proportion of nonsymbolic and symbolic play moves to the total number of moves was .57 (range = .26 to .89). At all ages, these children engaged in more nonsymbolic than symbolic play, particularly at the younger ages, with more evidence of symbolic play emerging in the 24-month-olds.

Both mothers and infants were highly contingent at all ages. The infants were 87–91% contingent, and the mothers responded contingently over 97% of the time to their infants' obligatory moves. The mothers exceeded the children in their tendency to keep the interaction going by responding contingently to their partners more often than did the infants at every age.

The maternal directive strength index was related to the mutual contingency or joint focus of the pair. This was the percentage of directive moves made by the mother divided by her total number of moves. As a group, the mothers were low in their directive strength. In Adler's cross-sectional study using the same coding system, a mother was considered to be directive if the directive index was greater than .60. A low directive index was one below .40. Except for one mother who attained a directive index of .45 at 24 months, all of the mothers exhibited a directive index below .40 regardless of the age of their infants. If a threshold exists for directive strength, then all of these mothers fell below the threshold, indicating that they exhibited a less directive style. The maternal directive index did not change significantly as a function of the age of the infant. Though the group as a whole would be considered nondirective, the variation among the individual mothers, and among the ages, was broad, as will be discussed below.

The child strength index, or demand strength, also changed significantly over time. Once again, the data do not have a straight linear progression. As a group, the infants were higher in bid strength at 18 months. No infant evidenced strong moves at 9 months. By 12 months, half of the sample had strong bids. All of the children employed some strong bids by 18 months. There were no clear developmental trends due to individual differences. Seven children were highest in bid strength at 18 months and then decreased by 24 months.

While as a group the mothers and infants maintained a high level of contingent responding or joint focus, differences emerged when the dyads were studied individually. Closer examination revealed the contingency of the individual pairs to be

TABLE 8.4.   Individual Differences at 24 Months

Child No.	Contingency (Rank)	Maternal Directive Index (Rank)	Child Obligatory Moves (Rank)	Mean Length of Utterance (min.)	Symbolic Play
02	81.03 (8)	45.24 (1)	28.07 (9)	1.0	4.3
07	75.86 (9)	31.58 (2)	36.84 (10)	1.0	4.2
04	95.00 (2)	29.93 (3)	12.90 (4)	1.2	5.0
10	73.53 (10)	22.92 (4)	18.48 (6)	2.2	4.3

related to other factors. At 24 months, the toddlers who maintained the lowest contingency with their mothers were the least verbal, as measured by mean length of utterance. They also tended to have lower levels of symbolic play. Another variable that was related to the mutual contingency or joint focus of the pair, was the maternal directive index. At 24 months, the children who were least verbal and lowest in contingent responses had mothers who were most directive. These infants and their mothers were partners in interactions where the mother attempted to keep the interaction going by maintaining a higher level of contingency, and by being more directive with infants who were withdrawing and exhibited lower verbal skills. However, this pattern was not completely consistent. With one pair, though the mother ranked as the third most directive, the child was second highest in contingency. Even though the low-contingent infants were less responsive to their mothers' obligatory moves and had less verbal ability, they tended to obligate their mothers more. The contingencies—mean length of utterance, maternal directive index, and level of symbolic play—for the children who were lowest in contingent responses and for the mothers who ranked highest in directive index are illustrated in Table 8.4.

In summary, while the mothers were nondirective in their overall style as a group, the most directive mothers at 24 months tended to be in partnership with infants who exhibited lower levels of language development and fewer contingent responses and who obligated their mothers more. Further, significant Spearman rank correlations resulted when the maternal directive index was compared with the Bayley scale scores at 24 months. The direction of the correlation was negative. That is, the mothers who were most directive had infants at 24 months with significantly lower Bayley scores ($r = .55$, $p < .05$). An exception to this general trend is illustrated by one pair where the child of a directive mother was second highest in contingency. This child also placed less obligation on the mother and exhibited a higher symbolic play level. Adler found a similar pattern with highly contingent children who were matched with more directive mothers. These children also demonstrated a higher level of symbolic development.

Discussion: The Dyadic Nature of Play Styles

This methodology reveals how mutually regulated play behaviors are. For example, the group scores for maternal directive index did not change significantly over time, but the means for the group indicate a relatively lower level of directive strength on the part of the mothers at 18 months. The mothers of the 18-month-olds tended to become less directive at a time when their infants had the higher bid strength or were stronger in their demands. Thus, the mothers' ability to lead or to direct the interaction appeared to be highly sensitive to the infants' increasing ability to make demands in return. As the infants became more active, stronger in their types of bids, and better able to place response demands upon their mothers, the mothers correspondingly dropped back. The mothers made proportionately fewer moves when interacting with 18- and 24-month-olds. They also obligated their infants less at these ages. While the mothers tended to be as directive with 12-month-olds as they were with their 24-month-old toddlers, they were less directive when interacting with the 18-month-olds.

Similarly, the correlations between the coding and other variables reveal what may be some of the consequences of different play experiences. At 24 months the toddlers who demonstrated the lowest contingency were also the least verbal. Since according to this coding system contingency is not dependent on verbal ability, alternative explanations for this finding need to be explored. Factors to consider include the following: (1) The child's level of comprehension may be delayed, limiting his or her ability to understand the mother's request, and (2) the child's lack of expressive language may place added stress on the dyad, contributing to the mother's assuming a more directive role.

Due to the intrinsically dyadic nature of mutual regulation, it is virtually impossible to apportion effects of mother and child variables in the interaction. In an attempt to sort out variables that might account for a correlation between maternal behavior and child cognitive competence, Olson, Bates, and Bayles (1984) noted the following variables that interact with each other and contribute to the mother–child interaction to varying degrees: quality of attachment, level of maternal restrictiveness, level of child social responsiveness, level of child intelligence, and socioeconomic status.

As a further illustration of the mutuality of play styles, consider the following accounts of the play sessions of three dyads at 24 months. While all three of the children demonstrated appropriate language development and symbolic play levels, their mother–child interaction styles are quite different and therefore provide an interesting contrast in the range of dyadic styles that can foster growth.

Dyad 6

Although both members of this dyad contributed a relatively equal number of moves, when paired together they illustrate a somewhat asynchronous interaction. The mother obligated her child in the majority of her moves, and many of those bids for interaction were directive in nature. She was one of the mothers with the most obligatory moves at 9, 18, and 24 months and was also rated as one of the most directive mothers at 9, 12, and 24 months. In response to these obligatory moves, her child, J., ranked as one of the lowest in contingent responding at 12, 18, and 24 months. In comparison to the other children, he evidenced a low ratio of obligatory moves at 9, 12, and 24 months. The percentage of obligatory moves he did make ranked as one of the lowest in bid strength at 12, 18, and 24 months. While his mother employed directive attempts to engage J., he appeared to prefer to play alone and did not actively attempt to engage his mother.

The following segment of play from their play interaction at 24 months illustrates the mother's directive and the child's less contingent, nonengaging style. While J. was involved in a symbolic play act, his mother continually directed him toward another activity that he failed to acknowledge. The mother commented on J.'s activity instead of joining in his play or acknowledging its symbolic nature.

> J. takes a coffee pot from the toy basket and says, "Baby, baby."
>
> In response, his mom says, "Find the baby."
>
> J. does not respond to mom's direction, and he continues to play with the coffee pot.
>
> He takes the lid off and begins to put it back on.
>
> J. then holds the coffee pot up and shows it to his mom, saying, "Baby, baby."
>
> Mom watches and says, "Find the baby."
>
> J. fails to acknowledge his mother's direction and continues to play with the coffee pot, placing the lid back on. Once again, he says, "Baby."
>
> Mom comments, "The baby's not going to be in there." She once again directs J., saying, "Find the baby."
>
> J. says, "Coffee," and pretends to drink from the toy coffee pot.
>
> Mom questions J., saying, "Coffee?" and then "Does J. drink coffee? J. drink coffee?"
>
> J. shakes his head yes in response.
>
> Mom says, "No, J. doesn't drink coffee. Nanny drinks coffee."
>
> J. says "No" and continues to pretend to drink from the coffee pot.

Dyad 10

In contrast to the previous pair, Dyad 10 evidenced a more harmonious interactional style. While this mother is also characterized as directive, her child actively attempted to engage her in his play, using strong bids for interaction. The mother ranked as one of the most directive at 12, 18, and 24 months. The child, P., ranked as one of the highest in demonstrating obligatory moves at 9, 18, and 24 months and in bid strength at 12, 18, and 24 months. He also played a slightly more active role in the interaction than his mother at 12, 18, and 24 months.

The following segment of play, taken from an interaction at 24 months, illustrates their interactional style. The mother's behavior is directive but focused on the child's activity. The child's behavior demonstrates his strong effort to obligate and to engage his mother in his play.

> P. pretends to eat some plastic food. He hands a bunch of grapes to his mother and says, "Mom, eat some of that."

Mom pretends to eat some grapes and says, "Oh, thank you. Very good. They're nice and sweet."

P. holds up the corn to show his mother and says, "Corn."

Mom acknowledges his label, saying, "Um hum."

P. hands the corn to his mother and says, "Eat."

Mom joins in the symbolic play, saying, "Will you put some butter on my corn? Can you find the butter?"

P. picks up an object (not the butter) and rubs it on the corn.

Mom questions, "Where's the butter?"

P. locates and picks up the butter.

Mom confirms, saying, "There you go."

P. rubs the butter on the corn and continues to request that his mother join in his symbolic play.

Dyad 9

Interaction in this dyad is characterized by a mother who obligated her child during much of the interaction but used more of a facilitative rather than a directive style. L. is highly contingent and becomes stronger in her bids for interaction over time. Her mother played an active role in the interaction and was ranked as one of the most active mothers at 12, 18, and 24 months. She ranked as one of the highest in demonstrating obligatory moves, yet was least directive in all four sessions. L. ranked as one of the most contingent children at 12, 18, and 24 months. At 24 months she ranked as the highest in strongest moves.

The following segment of play from their 24-month session characterizes the synchronous interaction of this dyad and illustrates the mother's active, facilitative style. She often keeps the interaction going by joining and extending L.'s play. L.'s style includes contingent responding to her mother's obligatory moves and strong bids for keeping her mother involved in the play.

Both Mom and L. have been involved in a symbolic play sequence in which they pretend to enjoy a meal of plastic food.

Mom continues to eat her fish and says, "My fish is very good."

L. pretends to eat corn and says, "That hot."

Mom continues to eat and says, "That good? Mmmm, good. Oh, but now I'm thirsty."

L. picks up a plastic piece and questions, "Milk?"

Mom replies, "That's a banana. No, let me have some milk."

L. holds up another plastic piece and says, "Milk?"

Mom comments, "Yeah, some milk."

L. pretends to pour the milk into her mother's cup, makes pouring sounds, and says, "Chocolate."

Mom pretends to drink the milk, complete with drinking sounds, and says, "Hmmmm, that's better. I was very thirsty."

The key point is that in examining mother–child interaction, one cannot focus on the behavior of one partner in isolation. While the mothers in Dyad 6 and Dyad 10 are similar in their directive, active style, their interactions are quite different. A directive mother paired with a less active and less contingent child, as in Dyad 6, resulted in a somewhat asynchronous interaction. A similar directive, active mother paired with a child who played an active role in the interaction and used strong bids to involve his mother in his play, as in Dyad 10, resulted in a more harmonious interaction. The point here is that maternal behaviors similarly described can in fact be associated with quite different dyadic styles, depending on how they interact with child variables.

The Implications for Intervention

Because there are many healthy patterns, any intervention should be undertaken with extreme caution. Evidence does exist that certain aspects of the interaction facilitate learning for the child. For instance, Olson, Bayles, and Bates (1986) found that maternal responsiveness and maternal verbal stimulation were each positively correlated with child vocabulary size, while restrictive maternal behavior was associated with immature speech development in the child. Slade (1987) reported a similar finding: Mothers actively joining their children in play enhance the duration and level of pretend play. When mothers engage in interactions appropriate to the child's developmental level and focus of interest, this reduces the child's cognitive workload, freeing the child's cognitive resources for development and learning (Howes, 1992; Rocissano & Yatchmink, 1983, 1984).

Individual differences in dyadic interaction and maternal adjustment to developmental level also affect dyads when the child has a disability. Investigations of mother–child interaction among children with Down syndrome indicate that mothers are able to match their interactions to a level appropriate to their child's development (Buckhalt, Rutherford, & Goldberg, 1978), and the linguistic style of mothers of children with disabilities changes as they continually adjust to their children (Mahoney, 1983). Crowley and Spiker (1983) found that individual differences in mother–child interaction patterns among 2-year-old children with Down syndrome were related to children's level of mental development. While neither sensitivity, elaborateness, nor directiveness alone could account for higher functioning among the children, it was concluded that the optimal combination of all three may provide the environment most conducive to the development of these children.

Although these studies often conclude by implying that there are potential benefits for applying findings to intervention, specific techniques are not outlined. In order to begin to develop some strategies for intervention, it is important to get a flavor for the content of specific interactions. It is not the case that maternal behavior affects the child in a one-way causative form. Rather, the actions of both members interact to form a particular style, many patterns of which may represent healthy-enough or outright healthy patterns. Possibly the most important intervention is to interact with individual dyads, to characterize the dyad style, and to assist mothers in understanding their characteristic interactions with their children.

In precisely this way, the procedures used in this research can also be helpful in an intervention setting. Play as an intervention approach enhances the interaction of the dyad by providing opportunities for each partner to initiate. Related to this is the benefit of the potential for joint activity such that when distractions are reduced, the dyad is freed to become engaged in a common agenda. For the child, the agenda is play; but such play provides the context for cognitive, social, and language growth. Using videotapes of play sessions, mothers can be assisted in understanding their interaction with their children. In order to establish the play session, the following guidelines are suggested:

> 1. Prepare for the play session by "childproofing" a room or area so that there should be no need to prohibit the child from engaging in any activity, and the mother can be free to become engaged with the child.
>
> 2. Assemble a few toys (appropriate types and number depend on the child's maturity) that will form a focus for the session.
>
> 3. Avoid having specific expectations for the child's performance. Instead, encourage the mother to allow the child to take the lead in choosing toys and activities and to interact as they would normally.

By viewing the videotape collaboratively with the mother and guiding her observations of both her and her child's actions, it should be possible to help her to identify various aspects of the interaction. For example, she can observe how her child requests joint play, how her child responds to her suggestions or directions for play, and/or how her child demonstrates contingency. Additionally, she can observe the behaviors she uses to engage her child in play. The videotape needs to be viewed in a nonjudgmental manner, respectful of the mother's insights and avoiding any notion of what is right or wrong. Through such a feedback technique, mothers can learn about their children's developmental level and mode of communication and their own contribution to the interaction. Only then will they be in a position to change their interactive style and thus eventually modify the patterns of joint exchange.

REFERENCES

Adler, L. (1982). *Mother–toddler interaction: Content, style and relations to symbol development*. Doctoral dissertation, Rutgers University, New Brunswick, NJ.

Bakeman, R., & Adamson, L. (1984). Coordinating attention to people and objects in mother–infant and peer–infant interaction. *Child Development, 55,* 1278–1289.

Brazelton, T. B., Koslowski, B., & Main, M. (1974). The origins of reciprocity: The early mother–infant interaction. In M. Lewis & L. A. Rosenblum (Eds.), *The effect of the infant on its caretaker* (pp. 49–75). New York: Wiley.

Bronson, W. C. (1974). Mother–toddler interaction: A perspective on studying the development of competence. *Merrill-Palmer Quarterly, 20,* 275–302.

Buckhalt, J. A., Rutherford, R. B., & Goldberg, K. E. (1978). Verbal and nonverbal interaction of mothers with their Down's syndrome and nonretarded infants. *American Journal of Mental Deficiency, 82,* 337–343.

Clarke-Stewart, K. A. (1973). Interactions between mothers and their young children: Characteristics and consequences. *Monographs of the Society for Research in Child Development, 38* (6–7), 917–999.

Clark-Stewart, K. A., & Hevey, C. M. (1981). Longitudinal relations in repeated observations of mother–child interaction from one to two and one half years. *Developmental Psychology, 17*, 127–145.

Clarke-Stewart, K. A., VanderStoep, L. P., & Killian, G. A. (1979). Analysis and replication of mother–child relations at two years of age. *Child Development, 50*, 777–793.

Crowley, S., & Spiker, D. (1983). Mother–child interaction involving two-year-olds with Down syndrome: A look at individual differences. *Child Development, 54*, 1312–1323.

Dunn, J., & Wooding, C. (1977). Play in the home and its implications for learning. In B. Tizard & D. Harvey (Eds.), *Biology of play* (pp. 45–57). London: Spastics International Medical Publications.

Escalona, S. K. (1973). Basic modes of social interaction: Their emergence and patterning during the first two years of life. *Merrill-Palmer Quarterly, 19*, 205–232.

Gunn, P., Clark, D., & Berry, P. (1980). Maternal speech during play with a Down's syndrome infant. *Mental Retardation, 18*, 15–18.

Howes, C. (1992). *The Collaborative Construction of Pretend.* Albany: State University of New York Press.

Hodapp, R. M., Goldfield, E. C., & Boyatzis, C. J. (1984). The use and effectiveness of maternal scaffolding in mother–infant games. *Child Development, 55*, 772–781.

Lerner, R. (1976). *Concepts and theories of human development.* Reading, MA: Addison-Wesley.

Maccoby, E., & Martin, J. (1983). Socialization in the context of the family: Parent–child interaction. In E. M. Hetnerington (Ed.), *Handbook of child psychology: Socialization, personality and social development* (pp. 1–101). New York: Wiley.

Mahler, M., Pine, F., & Bergman, A. (1975). *The psychological birth of the human infant.* New York: Basic Books.

Mahoney, G. (1983). A developmental analysis of communication between mothers and infants with Down's syndrome. *Topics in Early Childhood Special Education, 3*, 63–76.

Massing, L., & McCune, L. (1986). Relations among mother and toddler interactive behaviors and child developmental level. Unpublished manuscript, Rutgers University.

McCune, L. (1993). Normative study of representational play at the transition to language. Unpublished manuscript, Rutgers University.

McCune-Nicolich, L. (1981). Toward symbolic functioning: Structure of early pretend games and potential parallels with language. *Child Development, 52*, 785–797.

Nicolich, L. M. (1977). Beyond sensorimotor intelligence: Assessment of symbolic maturity through analysis of pretend play. *Merrill-Palmer Quarterly, 23*, 89–101.

O'Connell, B., & Bretherton, I. (1984). Toddlers' play alone and with mother: The role of maternal guidance. In I. Bretherton (Ed.), *Symbolic play: The development of social understanding* (pp. 337–368). New York: Academic Press.

Olson, S., Bayles, K., & Bates, J. (1986). Mother–child interaction and children's speech progress: A longitudinal study of the first two years. *Merrill-Palmer Quarterly, 32*, 1–20.

Olson, S., Bates, J., & Bayles, K. (1984). Mother–infant interaction and the development of individual differences in children's cognitive competence. *Developmental Psychology, 20*, 166–179.

Pettit, G. S., & Bates, J. E. (1984). Continuity of individual differences in the mother–infant relationship from six to thirteen months. *Child Development, 55*, 729–739.

Piaget, J. (1962). *Play, dreams and imitation.* New York: Norton.

Rocissano, L., & Yatchmink, Y. (1983). Language skill and interactive patterns in prematurely born toddlers. *Child Development, 54*, 1229–1241.

Rocissano, L., & Yatchmink, Y. (1984). Joint attention in mother–toddler interaction: A study of individual variation. *Merrill-Palmer Quarterly, 30*, 11–31.

Rogoff, B. (1990) *Apprenticeship in thinking*. New York: Oxford University Press.

Slade, A. (1987). A longitudinal study of maternal involvement and symbolic play during the toddler period. *Child Development, 58*, 367–375.

Slade, A. (1986). Symbolic play and separation individuation: A naturalistic study. *Bulletin of the Menninger Clinic, 50*, 541–563.

Stern, D. N. (1974a). The goal and structure of mother–infant play. *Journal of the American Academy of Child Psychiatry, 13*, 402–421.

Stern, D. N. (1974b). Mother and infant at play: The dyadic interaction involving facial, vocal and gaze behaviors. In M. E. Lewis & L. A. Rosenblum (Eds.), *The effect of the infant on the caretaker* (pp. 187–214). New York: Wiley.

Wasserman, G., & Allen, R. (1985). Maternal withdrawal from handicapped toddlers. *Journal of Child Psychology and Psychiatry.*

Werner, H., & Kaplan, B. (1963). *Symbol formation*. New York: Wiley.

III

DIFFERENCES AND DISTORTIONS IN SYMBOLIC FUNCTIONING

How can we understand the differences between one child's make-believe and another's? What can we learn from the study of symbolic play in children whose development is profoundly delayed or impaired? These questions are linked, for in answering either one, we must examine the many profound connections between levels of cognitive maturity and emotional development *as they are integrated* into familial, social, and educational environments. The chapters in part III compare the play of girls and boys, of master players and poor players, and describe the impact of maternal depression, child deafness, and autism on symbolic development. The final chapter here examines the play development of a child with a shy or inhibited temperamental style. Each of these chapters is an attempt to investigate imaginary play in light of a number of complex interactive contexts and, in so doing, to provide a more complete and dimensional view of the nature and function of symbolic development.

9

Windows on Social Worlds: Gender Differences in Children's Play Narratives

LOUISA B. TARULLO

Hal's Story
An then he came to the bad one's house/
An then they/he killed him/
An then he was dead/
An then he took the women/then he killed the women/
I mean he took the guard and put him to bed/
An they took they hat off/
An then they prayed for him/
An then they made a sound with the trumpet/
And then the women had the hat/An then she put it right here/
An then she was cryin'/
An then he was wavin' his trumpet like this/
An then they buried him/

Maggie's Story
Green figure: "Oh boy/I'm going to take a bath/
I'm taking it into the/woopsie/I forgot to take off my hat/
Oh, nooo/
Yikes/he'll be mad at me"/
Green figure to Blue figure: "Ah, here's your hat/
Sorry I got it all wet"/
Blue figure: "Hey you/why did you forget to take it off when you got up?"/
Green figure: "I don't know"/
Blue figure: "Wanna come with me on a boat ride?"/
Green figure: "Okay, your turn to wear the hat"/
Narrator: It's too hard for him to keep on the hat/*He* better/

Each of these brief stories paints a world of human relationships. But in the first story, life is perilous; there is more concern with ritual after death than with motivation for violence. The vivid scene is external, focusing on action rather than psychological experience. In the second story, we hear the conversations, internal and mutual, of the characters; we are privy to their worries and to their reconciliation. The first narrator is a boy, the second a girl. Their sharply contrasting narratives are not necessarily average, or typical, of their gender and social groups. Instead, they are narratives of a boy and a girl "at the extremes," who let us see the subtle differences that may grow into different adult orientations toward relationships and morality.

By the time most children are 5 years old, they have acquired an impressive level of knowledge about how people relate to each other. They can interpret the thoughts and feelings of family and friends, and express their own ideas and emotions in words. They are familiar—either as actors or as audience—with the scripts that shape the dramas of everyday life: scenes of anxiety, sorrow, conflict, forgiveness, compromise, and joy. Through their play, and the internal or spoken narrative that accompanies it, children reenact these scenes with more or less verisimilitude in autobiographical or fictionalized versions. Through this narrative language, children express what is on their minds—to themselves and anyone else who will listen.

Developmental psychologists have begun to chart the patterns by which children come to master and use psychological concepts in their social interactions. Recent developmental research suggests that among normally developing children, there are many commonalities in the steps toward this proficiency. Developmental linguistics has shown that young children come to comprehend and apply emotion-descriptive (affective) language in a common developmental sequence. From early on, children's speech reflects an "extremely adaptive" ability to understand the psychological workings of other family members (Dunn, 1986). By their third year, children already have a fairly well-developed capacity to analyze the goals and motives of others, particularly as they impinge on the child's own. Once this "rudimentary theory of mind" has developed, it is through speech that children acquire further information about how people interact (Bretherton & Beeghly, 1982). Dunn (1986) suggests that during periods of emotional urgency, a child is particularly attuned to the behavior of those nearby. Bretherton and her colleagues (1986) believe that such emotion-arousing events bring out the child's affective vocabulary, "illustrating that the ability to discuss emotions fulfills a significant regulative and clarifying function even in very young children's conduct of interpersonal relations" (p. 545).

The rate of acquiring an affective language may vary with social class and gender, although the sequence is similar across groups (Ridgeway, Waters, & Kuczaj, 1985). By the time children reach school age, they have mastered two essential concepts: that human beings are alike in being both agents of external events and experiencers of internal events, and that human beings are different in their experience of events. One's own internal states may not accurately predict those another person would experience in the same situation (Wolf, Rygh, & Altschuler, 1984). Children's narratives demonstrate that by the early school years, boys and girls across social classes have acquired a basic, common vocabulary for describing internal states (Tarullo, 1988).

At the same time, given an equal range of vocabulary about what people see, feel, and know, narratives also reveal a good deal about individual differences among children in their expression and integration of psychological understanding. Clinicians have long viewed doll or replica play as providing a window into a child's understanding of human relationships; in this context, play narratives have been seen as an expression of what a child finds most salient in his or her experience of living with other people. For Vygotsky (1978), play is "a recollection of something that actually happened . . . more memory in action than a novel imaginary situation" (p. 103). The study of children's narratives to reveal individual differences is, in essence, borrowed from clinical work, where the intense focus on individuals and the particularities of single lives—leading either to health or to pathology—has long led clinicians to be interested in variation. It is the premise of this chapter that such differences are the result of choice: that children tell or act out stories that have meaning *for them*, in words that they have made their own. As Labov (quoted in Peterson & McCabe, 1983) has described them, narratives serve two basic functions: reference, or relating information, and evaluation, or giving the meaning the narrative has *for the narrator*. It is this evaluative aspect of a child's language—why the narrative is told—that can reveal the patterns and emphases of his or her psychological understanding and interest.

Whether children express interest in or identification with the affective states of others in an experimental situation may depend on many factors: the research protocol, their verbal facility, the sex of the experimenter, and their ease in talking with an adult about personal concerns. One of these factors is certainly the culture in which a child grows up—a culture shaped by the interaction of social class and gender. Boys and girls grow up in different relational cultures, and the communicative patterns they internalize and perpetuate may shape the contrasting moral views of the men and women they will become. Research has shown that adult men and women are most differentiated by their conceptions of human interactions, suggesting gender-linked, though not gender exclusive, differences in perspective. These differences have emerged most dramatically in the research of Gilligan (1982) and Lyons (1983), who have used extensive, open-ended interviews to study such phenomena. When men and women are asked to tell stories about their moral conflicts and about their relationships with other people, two differing perspectives on self and morality come to light. Men are more likely to see relationships in terms of duty and rights, and to think of themselves as essentially separate individuals, whereas women are more likely to see themselves as connected to others through bonds of responsibility and mutual care.

The two perspectives on relationships and morality that Gilligan and Lyons have delineated as rights and care stem from the child's earliest experience of relationship. Mothered by a person of the same gender, "girls come to experience themselves as less differentiated than boys" (Chodorow, 1978, p. 167). Because boys are treated as other from the start and must later repress their attachment to their mothers, Chodorow believes that boys' "relational potential" is inhibited by this process; as a consequence, they come to see themselves as "more separate and distinct from others" (p. 207). Eichenbaum and Orbach (1987) agree, and suggested that a girl's search for identity is through connection with others, through becoming "like but separate from mother'' while boys ''search for self through distinguishing themselves from others'' (pp. 121–122).

As girls move into the world outside the family, they carry with them the seeds of a female culture that has led them to value empathy, caretaking, and orientation to the needs of others. Chodorow has argued that as long as women are the sole primary caretakers, girls will grow up to reproduce the mothering role. In their clinical investigation, Eichenbaum and Orbach have seen women seek to reproduce the mother–daughter relationship in their adult friendships. It is not necessary to wait until adulthood to see these patterns. From the time of their earliest friendships, girls reproduce a female culture of relationship; through behavior and, most important, through language, they carry and share in a distinctly ''girls' world.''

Many researchers studying children's play have commented on the dichotomy between girls' more intensive, or particularized, relationships and boys' more extensive, or generalized, relationships with their peers. Language plays sharply different roles in girls' and boys' cultures. As Goodwin (1980) has noted in a study of girls' and boys' social groups, different male and female speech patterns are ''not only indicative, but also constitutive of characteristically different social organizations'' (p. 172). Maltz and Borker (1982) agree that males and females have ''cultural differences in their ideas about how to engage in and interpret friendly conversation'' (p. 200). Boys' play is more likely to take place in large groups, outside, and in public places, and to involve competitive games with contingent rules of strategy and a high ceiling of skill (Lever, 1976). A boy uses language to assert a dominant position in a hierarchy, to draw and hold an audience, or to compete with another person for the floor, thereby expressing his individual identity within the group (Maltz & Borker, 1982). Since the rules are a crucial aspect of many boys' games, dispute resolution is a frequent type of conversation in which wielding power and control—without bullying—is an important skill.

Developmental psychologists from Piaget (1965) to the present have noticed this aspect of boys' play, though not all have agreed with Piaget's interpretation that boys have a more highly developed sense of justice and law. Girls are just as concerned about fairness—and just as likely to experience conflict—but the playing field is the more intimate one of the small group or the best-friend dyad. Girls are more likely to play inside or in the confines of their own yards; their nonimaginative games like jump rope or hopscotch feature indirect competition and unchanging rules of procedure. Disputes are unlikely, but when they do occur, girls have little experience in resolving them according to a legal formula, and the game may break up while conflicting allegiances are sorted out. According to Lever (1976), ''girls' behavior is directed less toward resolving problems and conflicts than toward maintaining the relationship among the players . . . focusing less on the development of an abstract rule system than on the development of empathy and sensitivity to the feelings of others'' (p. 482). For girls, conversation and confidences are the stuff from which friendships are woven. According to Maltz and Borker (1982), it is not power that differentiates between girls, but relative closeness. While for boys the focus of interactions is usually objective—a ball game, a computer program—for girls the focus is subjective. The conversation is, in a sense, the relationship. The exclusive nature of girls' friendships can lead to emotional breakups, and the ''ideology of equality and cooperation'' that marks female friendships must be carefully balanced with "a social reality that includes difference and conflict" (Maltz & Borker, 1982, p. 205).

Relationships are defined and maintained through forms of communication; differences in language use are the shaping force in these male–female relational contrasts. Because of the importance of how children talk *in* their relationships, how they talk *about* relationships—in autobiographical or fictionalized accounts—can reveal their psychological understanding and interests. Researchers grant communication the major role in developing social cognition (Bretherton & Beeghly, 1982; Bretherton, Fritz, Zahn-Waxler, & Ridgeway, 1986). Speech can be observed both in actual social interactions and in symbolic play situations that provide a window into a child's social understanding (Pitcher & Prelinger, 1963; Rheingold & Emery, 1985; Wolf, Rygh, & Altschuler, 1984).

Children's narrative representations of human actions, experiences, and interactions can identify the categories of human behavior that individuals find most salient or significant, in much the same way moral dilemmas do for adults. Boys and girls seem to be speaking in different voices about different ways of experiencing the world. Yet these dimensions have proven difficult to capture in frankly experimental situations with children and rarely translate into significant differences in group means. For most socioaffective measures, (aggression being a notable exception), boys and girls look more alike than different on average. While boys are more likely than girls to show verbal and physical aggression toward peers (Maccoby & Jacklin, 1980), male and female distributions on experimental measures of empathy and perspective taking overlap considerably (Eisenberg & Lennon, 1983). However, the study of children's narratives of real or fictionalized events reveals a rich range of male–female differences that have much in common with children's conversations and children's games. Such narratives are the focus of the current study.

The Study

The current study considers differences in boys' and girls' narrative descriptions of their social and emotional worlds. The research extends previous work on girls' and women's personal conversation to the consideration of narrative language. We will diverge from more traditional experimental approaches to the study of gender differences in social class in two ways: (1) naturalistically gathered stories and narrative accounts will be used, and (2) only those boys and girls who lie outside the overlapping male and female distribution of responses will be studied. Children who are placed at the extreme end of their own gender's continuum by virtue of the type of story they tell and the kinds of experiences they describe may not be typical of their gender group overall and yet may give it its characteristic flavor or reputation. Their patterns of telling are particular to their own gender; they do not have counterparts in children of the other sex. We believe that the study of these outliers provides the most direct access to the kinds of contrasts that distinguish the narratives of young boys and girls. One particular aspect of this difference will be studied: the construction of human interactions as portrayed through their characters' relationships, conflicts, and motives. It is precisely these dimensions of human experience that have been found to be so different in adult males and females.

The data for this analysis are drawn from a longitudinal study of children's narratives told from kindergarten through second grade (ages 5 through 7). Children's stories—one an autobiographical tale, the other a fictional story enacted with small models or replicas of people and props—were collected from 52 children at two schools. One is a small, primarily middle-class urban private school with a religious affiliation, and the other is a public school in a working-class urban neighborhood. These schools provide contrasts of social and educational environments that foster different perspectives on gender roles. Thus, the study deliberately sampled situations in which gender might be constructed variously. (See Tarullo, 1988, for details of study.)

In this chapter, two groups in which gender differences were most pronounced will be closely studied: public school boys and private school girls. Many of the public school boys were marked by their high use of references to conflict, especially physical conflict, lack of explicit motivation for conflict, and a tendency to resolve conflict negatively or not at all. In this sense, they were extreme among boys. By contrast, private school girls (as well as many of their public school counterparts) were characterized by high use of dialogue, low use of references to conflict, use of psychological conflict and explicit conflict motivation, and positive conflict resolution. These, too, were extreme for their gender group. These extreme contrasts suggest the convergence of social class and gender roles in shaping children's conceptions of the social world.

Boys at the extreme represent a social group that is lower in socioeconomic status and more likely to have authoritarian relationships with adults, both parents and teachers, than the children at the private school. Bernstein (1971) suggests that such role-bound social development has differential effects on males and females that serve to reinforce sex-stereotypical behavior and speech. For example, according to Bernstein, the function of language is markedly different for a working-class girl in a positional or role-based family than for her brothers, in part because of the social uses of language. While she learns the complex nuances of control, mediation, and nurturance among parents and siblings, his communication is primarily within an activity centered, peer group–based environment.

If his peer group tends to value aggression or antisocial behavior as a form of male gender identification (Ullian, 1981), a boy at the extreme may indeed "behave in a way atypical of most children of both genders" (Henshall & McGuire, 1986, p. 142). Such children may not only affect the mean of aggressive behavior, they may also change the emotional climate around them, causing their peers to become more likely to be involved in combative situations (Henshall & McGuire, 1986). Children who are labeled aggressive at an early age tend to retain that categorization, and those tendencies become more marked with age (Cummings, Hollenbeck, Iannotti, Radke-Yarrow, & Zahn-Waxler, 1986; Loeber, 1982). These boys at the extreme, whose language shows a preoccupation with aggressive themes, may interact with others in a pattern that becomes amplified with age, as "the social structure becomes the child's psychological reality through the shaping of his acts of speech" (Bernstein, 1971, p. 144).

Case Studies

Ruthie and Eddy: A Study in Contrasts

In the case studies that follow, contrasting gender-related patterns of language and play will be traced in boys' and girls' narrative representations of behavior. One such contrast is provided by Ruthie and Eddy, two public school students who represent the extremes. In their second-grade year, both children appear to be relaxed and confident storytellers. The narratives analyzed here were enacted using a set of small, androgynous figures and props, including a crown, trees, and a wooden structure. The children were asked by the experimenter to make up a story and tell it using the toys. Like many 7-year-olds, Ruthie and Eddy are competent users of affective language; they can refer to a full range of social interactions; and they can each tell fully elaborated narratives. Since they share this common repertoire, it is a difference in choice, not competence, that leads them to tell such different stories.

At first glance, the players and the stories in which they figure appear similar. Both Ruthie and Eddy use the idea of a king and his subjects. Both children are talking about relationships: Approximately half of their narrative clauses are about characters interacting with one another. Both children's narratives portray a significant amount of conflict, defined in this study as having at least 20% of narrative schemes about conflict. Thus, the comparison is not between "shoot-em-up" and "playing house," but between two ways of talking about trouble in relationships.

On closer examination, there are sharp contrasts between these stories. Eddy's relationships are almost twice as conflict-filled and tend toward violent physical conflict, while Ruthie's are conflicts over goals and desires. In addition, Ruthie grounds her conflicts in explicit motivations. She commits to words the reasons behind the characters' different perspectives, as well as their efforts toward compromise. Through two narrative devices, the use of character dialogue and references to the characters' internal states (feelings, thoughts, and motives), Ruthie presents the conflict from the inside—from the viewpoints of her characters. In contrast, Eddy takes an externalized view of his characters' conflict. He tells the story almost entirely through third-person narration, and while he also employs a range of internal state language, he uses approximately half as much as Ruthie does.

Ruthie draws a complex world of relationships in which individuals' needs conflict and loyalty clashes with personal desires. Although in a position of power, the king admits to his "partner" who works for him that he needs his help and company. The seed of the conflict emerges in this interchange:

> The king was talking to his partner/
> And the partner said he wanted to quit/
> but the king said um/the king didn't want him to quit

The king then engages his three guards to persuade the partner to stay. They face a conflict between their allegiance to the king, in fulfilling their duty to him, and their loyalty to the partner, one of their own:

They said the king/We're not supposed to call/tell you
But the king wants you to stay cause/he/he can't
just have three men/he needs one more man like you

That the partner may not be entirely honest is portrayed in the changing reasons he gives for leaving: "I gotta go get/find my wife" and, later, "I want to go on a vacation." The king is skeptical and confronts the partner: "Then you want to find your wife/and now you want to go on a vacation." Eventually the partner admits the real reason he has to leave the king's service, and concedes that he has been less than forthright:

Partner: "I have another job"/
King: "I thought you told me that you didn't have a job"/
Partner: "That day when I was on the phone I didn't tell you/
I told you that was my wife/
But it was really/um that guy to give me a job/
And I took it/
Now I have to go today"/

Despite the partner's possible lack of trustworthiness, the king accedes to his request: "Alright, you may go today/But come back tomorrow." The partner agrees to these terms. Thus both characters show a willingness to compromise. In addition, the king tries to secure the future of the relationship by letting go in the present. However, in a later chapter of the story, the king shows the emotional costs of letting go, of the conflicts between his needs and those of his men. The ending is not "happy ever after," but bittersweet, as the king hides his own wishes and feelings in order to satisfy others:

And the king started crying/
Because he knew he really wanted them to have a vacation/
But it didn't always work/
So the king started crying cause they want to go/
Then they came out/
And he wiped his tears real fast/
And then he (partner) said "King are you crying?"/
He (king) said "NO/no no"/

Ruthie's world of the king and his subjects is drawn primarily through dialogue, which may reveal or hide a character's true purposes. Wolf et al. (1984) have attributed girls' propensity for conversation between characters to a sense of identification with those characters. As Maltz and Borker (1982) have noted, girls' relationships focus on the subjective; the conversation is the "currency" of the relationship. In narratives such as Ruthie's, girls portray relationships not through third-person narration, but largely through conversations like the ones that make up their friendships.

The interpersonal struggle at the core of Ruthie's story is a classic one of conflicting needs that must be taken into account. Power brings with it a responsibility to be just, despite the personal sacrifices. Another theme is the loneliness and isolation of being in command: Despite his power, the king cannot command the affection of his workers. When the partner returns a day late, the king is willing to forgive him and asks him to have breakfast, but the partner declines; he will only "go do the work I'm 'sposed to do." Ruthie's story of truth and duplicity, trust and skepticism, duty and care reveals an understanding of the inherent difficulties of relationships.

The replica play narrative told by Eddy in his second-grade year depicts a clearer dichotomy between black and white, bad and good. The story is told through action more than speech or introspection. Like Ruthie's it focuses on issues of trust, but the message is that appearances are deceiving; you cannot trust those close to you who may want to seize your power and position.

> He's really a bad guy/He's really the black knight/
> And he looks like a white knight/
> And he's trying to steal the gold/

Another issue in Eddy's story is the nature of identity. When the false knight dethrones the king, he is able to impersonate him without even the queen's taking notice.

> And then went up to the king and queen/
> And took the king while she was looking over there/
> . . .
> And took the king away/
> And took his suit/And put his suit on/
> And put him/sat back down/

Posing as the king, the black knight then betrays him, blaming the king for the violence he himself has caused. The knight points at the king, saying, "I'm the king/ that's the one you're looking for." The real king then is forced to fight with his own guards to regain his rightful place. The battle rages for a while, with action and sound effects. Finally the king wins, although there is no real explanation given as to why he is victorious or what becomes of the usurper.

> And they switched clothes again/
> And put the real king back up/
> And that's the end/

Eddy's imaginative world is filled with violent action that is not grounded—at least explicitly—in psychological motivation. The characters are identified not through their voices or thoughts, but by externals. If the bad knight appears as a white knight, he is trusted to be close to the king. If he wears the king's suit, even the queen does not question his identity. The true king must resort to violence to combat violence, since his own guards do not recognize him when he speaks. Aggression proves to be the means by which the king regains his throne; he appears to be physically stronger than the usurper. Eddy's story can be considered to have a positive outcome, since the king is restored, but there is no mention of the fate of the black knight. We do not see below the surface of these characters to understand why they act as they do.

A look at the earlier kindergarten narratives of Ruthie and Eddy offers a developmental perspective on the different paths they have taken. At age 5, Ruthie tells a story based on having seen a short silent film, a tale of a boy whose hat is taken by two others. In this earlier story, conflict is also central, and motives for the disagreement are spelled out:

> They found some hats/
> An the other boy wanted them/
> An he wouldn't give it to them/

There is some hiding and hitting. Finally the first boy taunts: "An you can't find those hats." The other boys offer a resolution: "If you give 'em to me/then we will give one to you." When this swap is accomplished, a conventional happy ending results:

> An they were all friends/
> Then they went home together/

Both Ruthie's kindergarten and second-grade stories require compromises for a resolution; although the kindergarten effort is neatly resolved, the second-grade story shows the cost of balancing conflicting needs. At the age of 7, Ruthie shows a complex understanding of conflicting motives and compromise.

Eddy's kindergarten narrative is picaresque in structure, with episodes of fighting among the various characters. The fighting may be "play fighting" or real violence, but it is hard to tell since no motive is given for the scuffling. The fighting breaks up when the "blue guy" is hurt and "goes crying to his mother." There is a lull in which the fighters rest and do exercises together. But then the green figure ambushes the blue and shifts his allegiance:

> And now he ain't his friend anymore/
> Now he's *his* friend/
> Now the green guy and the white guy are friends/
> But nobody doesn't love the blue guy anymore/
> An then he went into the bushes like that/
> To find another friend/

The rejected character "thinks that he's Superman, but he ain't." Even though he thinks he has "the power," he is continually beset by foes throughout the remainder of the narrative. Certainly Eddy has developed a more structured sense of a good story by second grade, but the early glimpse of psychological suffering and rejection is not present in his later narrative. Perhaps at age 7 Eddy is unwilling to reveal so directly how it feels to be rejected and bullied. The second-grade story gives a material motive for the violence—stealing the gold and regaining the throne—as well as a discrete resolution. Common to both stories is a reliance on physical aggression to settle conflicts and a third-person narrative voice.

The boy and girl whose narratives have been discussed represent different developmental trajectories. Both children show development from ages 5 to 7—in their vocabularies, in their imaginative capabilities, in their sense of what makes a good story. However, Ruthie's second-grade story shows an additional psychological dimension that is absent from Eddy's: a concern for the internal experiences that motivate behavior and a realization that different people may not see things in quite the same way. She also shows a concern for avoiding violence and aggression while not denying the reality of conflict. Eddy's kindergarten story gives a glimpse of a character's feelings of hurt and powerlessness, but these insights are not developed in his second-grade story. Instead the narrative appears more removed from personal concerns.

The course of development of altruism and aggression appears to follow a different path for boys and girls, according to Cummings and associates (1986). For 2-year-old boys, intense aggression was correlated with a response to others in distress. Such boys appeared to be emotionally sensitive; their social environments could determine whether they would ultimately become sympathetic or antisocial (Cummings et al., 1986). Boys have the potential for psychological understanding and expression, but this ability may develop or atrophy, influenced in part by their social and educational environments.

The play narratives of Ruthie and Eddy are reminiscent of the adult contrasts in perspective found by Pollak (1985) and Pollak and Gilligan (1982). Using the Thematic Apperception Test (TAT) with adolescent and adult subjects, Pollak and Gilligan (1982) found marked differences in how males and females interpreted depictions of intimacy and solitude. In response to picture stimuli, male subjects found danger in intimate situations, while females saw threat in competition or isolation. In other words, the projective tests revealed "how women seek safety in the very situations in which men perceive danger and how men seek safety in the very situations in which women perceive isolation" (Pollak, 1985, p. 54). Pollak found women more likely to name their characters and portray intense and complex emotions, while men's characters were insubstantial and remained detached both from emotion and from the consequences of violence. Pollak gave women credit not for denying the fact of violence, but for trying to avert it, using their "knowledge of how connection and communication can mediate against the dangers of life" (p. 128). These issues of safety or danger in relationship and of relative willingness to identify with characters in conflict are vividly borne out in the stories of these young boys and girls.

Donald: Charting a Moderate Course

Boys who seem to combine psychological insights with references to aggressive behavior may develop along different trajectories. Donald, a private school boy, appears to be taking a different path from Eddy's. While Donald's kindergarten replica play narrative shows a slapstick approach to conflict, he produces a very different story 2 years later. At age 5, Donald's story is filled with sound effects and random action, yet he does mention internal states and motivations:

> (One figure knocks down the other two)
> "You don't DO that"/
> "I didn't do it/HE did/OOOH"/
> "You feel guilty, guy?"/
> The king and the white guy got knocked down/
> (figures piled atop one another)
> "I never really liked these circus acts"/
> AAAAHHH/
> (one figure falls to floor)
> "What happened?"/
> "Why did you make me fall into a thirty mile down pit?"/

By second grade, Donald displays ways of settling disputes that do not require physical combat. One character who is climbing a tree brags to his friend below:

> And he said to his friend that he was a good guy
> because he could climb a tree/
> And the other person was a bad guy/
> And the other person didn't like that/
> So he said, "Could you teach me how to climb a tree?"/

The friend's refusal to rise to the taunt, and instead to ask for lessons in tree climbing, serves to defuse the conflict situation. The result is beneficial to both parties:

> And the guy that just learned to climb a tree practiced
> climbing trees alot until he was just about perfect/
> And then they met again/
> And they played tree tag/
> (holds figures together in a hug)
> That's the end of the story/

Donald's resolution displays a sophisticated understanding of how others think and feel and a willingness to portray affiliative relationships. It is atypical for its conflict avoidance. The use of a wider range of psychological references is especially apparent in personal narratives told by private school boys at age 7. When asked to tell a story about something that actually happened to them, not a made-up story, second-grade private school boys are more willing than their public school counterparts to let their internal states show and to discuss friendships in a positive fashion. This pattern suggests that the private school boys respond differently to the demands of different tasks, while the public school boys—boys at the extreme—do not. For the boys at the extreme, narrative depiction of affiliative relationships and psychological motivation is not evident by the second-grade year.

Maggie and Tess: Conflict Avoidance

Conflict avoidance is usually more common in girls' narratives, as it is in girls' play. Numerous researchers have commented on the indirect nature of girls' conflict. Since girls are socialized against expressing their anger and aggression, these surface in indirect ways. The result is talking behind each other's backs and social ostracism rather than direct accusations and confrontation (Cairns, 1986; Goodwin, 1980). In the intense, dyadic world of girls' friendships, conflict can be devastating, resulting not in a scuffle or a legal dispute, but in a betrayal of trust and confidence. Girls may, by being more personally invested in their friendships, have more to gain in interpersonal sensitivity training but more to lose if the relationship is severed. When defining herself through a relationship, a girl risks losing her identity when losing the connection.

In this study, only girls, including Ruthie in the narrative discussed earlier, displayed a particular concern for a breakdown in a relationship. Two of these narratives, both by private school girls, highlight the importance of trust and of maintaining connections in both peer and family relationships. Every relationship carries with it the possibility of misunderstandings and isolation, making the world a frightening place. However, in the stories that follow, there is the security of a "safety net" in the form of another caring person who fills the gap.

Maggie and Tess, both second graders, tell autobiographical stories of being left alone. For Maggie, the problem arises when her car pool leaves her at school; the members are convinced that "she does something else on Thursdays." Maggie tells this story twice, once as a report and again in a dramatized version. In the latter story, the character playing Maggie arrives on stage to find that her car pool has left:

"Where are they/
I just can't imagine where they went/
I know this is the second time/
They ought to remember"/

Luckily there is still someone in the school office; Maggie calls her mother, who picks her up and offers consolation: "I'm sorry they left you at school." Back home again, Maggie's character confronts her car pool members:

"You left me at school again"/
"But you do something different every Thursday!"/
"Uh-uh/Tuesday"/
"Alright/We won't forget you again"/
(whispers) "At least I hope we won't"/

Maggie has projected herself into the inner workings of both the victim and the guilty parties. Those who abandoned her were not malicious, just mistaken, but the possibility of harm is equally real. In the first-person version of this story, Maggie admits, "Boy, was I scared." In her fictionalized version, however, the character takes charge of a difficult situation, going to responsible adults for help and clearing up the misunderstanding so that it is not likely to happen again. The real Maggie is not so sure: She admits to the experimenter that she is afraid there is no driver available for the car pool today. While Maggie the storyteller constructs a happy ending, Maggie the child knows that real life is not always subject to such a comforting resolution.

Tess's second-grade autobiographical story is also about a misunderstanding that leads to being left alone. One evening when she was 5 years old, a friend walked her partway home. But when she knocked on her front door, no one answered:

I knock on/ and no one came/
And I thought that something bad had happened to my parents/
And it got me really, really scared/
Cause I was five when this happened/
And then I sat on the front porch/
And I started to cry/
And then someone/some people came out and they said/
"What's the matter?"/
And I said/"No one's home/and I think they all died"/

These neighbors wait with her until her mother returns. In explaining what happened, the child does not blame the mother but complains that her friend let her down: "I said/'It wasn't my fault, Mom/It was my friend's fault because she didn't walk me all the way.'" Her mother does not explicitly apologize but soothes her:

It's okay dear/now you're home/
And don't worry about anything/
And that's the end of what happened/

As in Ruthie's and Maggie's stories, the happy ending does not seem entirely satisfactory. Although everything is all right now, there is a sense that these missed connections can happen again, that the world is not entirely safe. For the child who depends so much on the balance and harmony of her relationships, this is a hard lesson.

At one point, however, Tess offers a story in which this relational balance is achieved.

Once upon a time there was a Rainbow/
And the Rainbow had two best friends/
The Rainbow's two best friends were named Rain and Sun . . .
One day the Rainbow didn't come out/
The Rainbow wasn't feeling very well . . .
So Rain got a cup/and poured his water in the cup/
And Sun shined . . .
(Rainbow said) "You ought to leave now/
Because you might get sick yourself"/
So Rain and Sun left . . .

This was the next day/and what happened was/
Rainbow came out and spread its beautiful colors into the world/
And everybody was happy/

Rainbow has two best friends, Rain and Sun. One might say that Rainbow depends on these friends for its very existence. When Rainbow is sick, the two friends come and give of themselves, water and sunshine, in an effort to cheer up their friend. But Rainbow shows concern for them as well, warning that they had better leave to avoid getting sick, and they comply. The next day, the two friends are rewarded by the return of Rainbow's beautiful colors to the sky. Tess's fantasy story provides a model of harmonious interdependence that her real-life experience cannot quite match.

Conclusion

Children's autobiographical stories and play narratives are not samples of actual social interactions. They are not direct statements of aggression or conciliation between friends. Instead, they offer a child the ability to be dramatist, director, and all the actors in a representation of such interactions. Through such dramas, a child can consider all perspectives on a situation or focus on just one. The child can project himself or herself into the characters or maintain distance from the figures set in motion. Because of its concentrated form, such narrative language is richer and more revealing than a sample of everyday speech. It contains clues that we can use to understand how a child sees the world and how she or he interacts with the people in it. Language is the vehicle through which children learn about the psychological dimension of human experience. Socialized in a particular culture, identified with a gender, children assimilate particular expectations about the limits of self-expression. If their social and educational environments constrain this expression into stereo-typical patterns, both boys and girls are shortchanged.

Perhaps the more obvious losers are boys like Hal and Eddy, who must maintain a masculine image through their forms of discourse: being assertive, boasting, never admitting uncertainty. While they may develop skills in settling disputes about rules, holding the floor in a discussion, and organizing people to complete a task, they are less experienced in understanding a particular other or their own unique emotions. Erikson's (1968) developmental model describes the task of the school-age child as *industry*, learning "to handle the utensils, the tools, and the weapons . . . used by the big people" (p. 123). A child's failure at this stage is categorized as a sense of *inferiority*, "an estrangement from himself and from his tasks" (p. 124). For Erikson, the work of adolescence is ego integration, and only in young adulthood is true intimacy possible. This story of development, seen through masculine experience, offers a limited model of emotional growth.

It is important to note, however, that being male is not equated with being aggressive or antisocial. The boy who acts or talks aggressively—or who tells stories about characters who do—is not typical of his gender. The presence of a cluster of these outliers among boys suggests that there are different developmental trajectories, not just for boys and girls, but for boys from different social worlds. Some boys, while biologically male, seldom manifest the stereotypical masculinity that includes aggression in language and behavior. While capable of telling an action-packed fictional story, they may reveal a more thoughtful, emotional side in autobiographical narratives. Other boys may seldom risk expressing their affection or concern for other people, possibly fearing that they will be branded as "girlish." Falling into gender stereotypes can only be limiting to boys and girls alike; learning descriptively about all possible roles, rather than having narrow, prescribed roles assigned by gender, is beneficial to both sexes.

Theories of how children form their gender schema once pictured males and females as polar opposites. More recently, however, masculinity and femininity have been seen as representing "interpersonal styles or clusters of attributes that are not mutually exclusive" (Hall & Halberstadt, 1980, p. 270). Gilligan (1982) and Lyons (1983) have often cautioned that their evidence shows two orientations toward relationships and morality that are gender related, though not gender exclusive. A child should not be limited to the behaviors considered most acceptable to one gender, but should "possess attributes or have behaviors in his or her repertoire that are valued for both sexes" (Hall & Halberstadt, 1980, p. 270). This more descriptive, rather than prescriptive, attitude toward gender identity is a product of gradual social change. However, its effects and promises may not be equally felt in all school contexts. While boys at the private school, influenced by a curriculum that stresses gender equality, may feel the freedom to talk positively about relationships in a personal story, their public school agemates may feel constrained. If boys at the extreme have been labeled as antisocial, or if their peer relationships are built on speech patterns of action, boasting, and hierarchy (Maltz & Borker, 1982), they may not feel comfortable talking about affiliative relationships in their narratives.

Gilligan (1982) suggests that the missing character in Erikson's developmental story is the female, who fuses identity with intimacy, who "comes to know herself as she is known, through her relationships with others" (p. 12). These narratives suggest that girls at both schools, through their identification with characters and their avoidance of conflict, express similar concerns. This reliance on relationships can put girls at risk for emotional turmoil if they have not learned how to balance conflicting needs. As Gilligan has warned, the care perspective, taken to extremes, can lead to caring for others at the expense of the self.

Putting the needs of others above her own, a girl can become a victim of her own unselfishness. Recent clinical research on the effects of divorce on children has suggested that girls who seem to cope at the time of their parents' divorce may suffer a "sleeper effect" (Wallerstein & Blakeslee, 1989). As they enter adulthood, young women may be beset with fears of betrayal or commitment that they attribute to being children of divorce. Faced with making decisions with long-term implications, two-thirds of the young women (ages 19–23) in Wallerstein's study confronted anxieties that had been suppressed for years. Wallerstein also documents cases of "overburdened" children who take over the caretaking functions for distraught parents and risk losing their own identity. Girls whose mothers suffer from affective disorders are also thought to be at greater risk than sons for the development of later psychopathology, perhaps because of their close identification and emotional involvement with their mothers (McGrath, Keita, Strickland, & Russo, 1990; Zahn-Waxler, Kochanska, Krupnick, & McKnew, 1990). These extreme cases represent the nature of the risks for girls who define themselves through relationships. If a parent is in crisis, girls may take over parental functions, or they may appear to cope by blocking out their own emotional needs—only to find themselves unable to enter confidently into adult relationships. To grow up healthy in the ethic of care means avoiding enmeshment while maintaining a sense of interdependence between self and other.

Pollak (1985) has noted that males and females see threat and danger in anti-thetical situations, a finding that has its roots in children's same-sex friendships and has implications for the ways adults relate to one another. While men fear intimacy, women fear competition and isolation. Experienced in close relationships with their mothers and girl friends, school-age girls may lack the psychological resources to take individual initiative, the strength to care for themselves as well as other people, or the ambition to compete. Adept at orchestrating a challenging task or game, boys may see emotional vulnerability as a threat to their hard-won individualism. Achieving a balance of intimacy and identity is the developmental task facing children of both sexes as they move into the social world of school. Their stories tell us that this is a difficult transition. Eddy may be less afraid of fighting a neighborhood bully than of admitting his anxiety. Maggie may find it easier to blame herself than to confront a friend who has been cruel. The voices of these children at the extremes of their gender groups inform us of gender differences in the way children perceive themselves in relation to others: differences that foreshadow their adult orientations toward relationships and morality.

ACKNOWLEDGMENTS

I appreciate the assistance of Dennie Wolf and Sharon Grollman in conducting this study. This study was carried out at the Harvard University Graduate School of Education.

REFERENCES

Bernstein, B. (1971). *Class, codes and control.* Vol. 1, *Theoretical studies towards a sociology of language.* London: Routledge and Kegan Paul.

Bretherton, I., & Beeghly, M. (1982). Talking about internal states: The acquisition of an explicit theory of mind. *Developmental Psychology, 18,* 906–921.

Bretherton, I., Fritz, J., Zahn-Waxler, C., & Ridgeway, D. (1986). Learning to talk about emotions: A functionalist perspective. *Child Development, 57,* 529–548.

Cairns, R. B. (1986). An evolutionary and developmental perspective on aggressive patterns. In C. Zahn-Waxler, E. M. Cummings, & R. Iannotti (Eds.), *Altruism and aggression: Biological and social origins* (pp. 58–87). New York: Cambridge University Press.

Chodorow, N. (1978). *The reproduction of mothering: Psychoanalysis and the sociology of gender.* Berkeley: University of California Press.

Cummings, E. M., Hollenbeck, B., Iannotti, R., Radke-Yarrow, M., & Zahn-Waxler, C. (1986). Early organization of altruism and aggression: Developmental patterns and individual differences. In C. Zahn-Waxler, E. M. Cummings, & R. Iannotti (Eds.), *Altruism and aggression: Biological and social origins* (pp. 165–188). New York: Cambridge University Press.

Dunn, J. (1986). Growing up in a family world: Issues in the study of social development in young children. In M. Richards & P. Light (Eds.), *Children of social worlds* (pp. 98–115). Cambridge, MA: Harvard University Press.

Eichenbaum, L., & Orbach, S. (1987). *Between women: Love, envy and competition in women's friendships.* New York: Viking Press.

Eisenberg, N., & Lennon, R. (1983). Sex differences in empathy and related capacities. *Psychological Bulletin, 94,* 100–131.

Erikson, E. H. (1968). *Identity: Youth and crisis.* New York: Norton.

Gilligan, C. (1982). *In a different voice: Psychological theory and women's development.* Cambridge, MA: Harvard University Press.

Goodwin, M. H. (1980). Directive-response speech sequences in girls and boys' task activities. In S. McConnel-Ginet et al. (Eds.), *Women and language in literature and society* (pp. 157–173). New York: Praeger Press.

Hall, J. A., & Halberstadt, A. G. (1980). Masculinity and femininity in children: Development of the Children's Personal Attributes Questionnaire. *Developmental Psychology, 16,* 270–280.

Henshall, C., & McGuire, J. (1986). Gender development. In M. Richards & P. Light (Eds.), *Children of social worlds* (pp. 135–166). Cambridge, MA: Harvard University Press.

Lever, J. (1976). Sex differences in the games children play. *Social Problems, 23,* 478–487.

Loeber, R. (1982). The stability of antisocial and delinquent child behavior: A review. *Child Development, 53,* 1431–1446.

Lyons, N. P. (1983). Two perspectives: On self, relationships, and morality. *Harvard Educational Review, 53,* 125–145.

Maccoby, E. E. (1985). Social groupings in childhood: Their relationship to prosocial and antisocial behavior in boys and girls. In D. Olweus, J. Block, & M. Radke-Yarrow (Eds.), *The development of antisocial and prosocial behavior* (pp. 263–284). New York: Academic Press.

Maccoby, E. E., & Jacklin, C. N. (1974). *The psychology of sex differences.* Vol. 1. Stanford, CA: Stanford University Press.

Maccoby, E. E., & Jacklin, C. N. (1980). Sex differences in aggression: A rejoinder and reprise. *Child Development, 51,* 964–980.

Maltz, D. N., & Borker, R. A. (1982). A cultural approach to male–female miscommunication. In J. A. Gumperz (Ed.), *Language and social identity* (pp. 196–216). New York: Cambridge University Press.

McGrath, E., Keita, G. P., Strickland, B. R., and Russo, N. F. (Eds.) (1990). *Women and depression: Risk factors and treatment issues.* Washington, DC: American Psychological Association.

Peterson, C. L., & McCabe, A. (1983). *Developmental psycholinguistics: Three ways of looking at a child's narrative.* New York: Plenum Press.

Piaget, J. (1965). *The moral judgment of the child.* New York: Free Press.

Pitcher, E. G., & Prelinger, E. (1963). *Children tell stories: An analysis of fantasy.* New York: International Universities Press.

Pollak, S. (1985). *A study of gender differences in violent Thematic Apperception Test stories.* Unpublished doctoral dissertation, Harvard University Graduate School of Education, Cambridge, MA.

Pollak, S., & Gilligan, C. (1982). Images of violence in Thematic Apperception Test stories. *Journal of Personality and Social Psychology, 42,* 159–167.

Rheingold, H. L., & Emery, G. N. (1985). The nurturant acts of very young children. In D. Olweus, J. Block, & M. Radke-Yarrow (Eds.), *The development of antisocial and prosocial behavior* (pp. 75–96). New York: Academic Press.

Ridgeway, D., Waters, E., & Kuczaj, S. A. (1985). The acquisition of emotion-descriptive language: Receptive and productive vocabulary norms for ages eighteen months to six years. *Developmental Psychology, 21*, 901–908.

Tarullo, L. B. (1988). *Patterns of gender difference in two schools: A comparison of children's personal narratives.* Unpublished doctoral dissertation, Harvard Graduate School of Education, Cambridge, MA.

Ullian, D. Z. (1981). The child's construction of gender: Anatomy as destiny. In E. K. Shapiro & E. Weber (Eds.), *Cognitive and affective growth: Developmental interaction* (pp. 171–184). Hillsdale, NJ: Erlbaum.

Vygotsky, L. S. (1978). *Mind in society.* Cambridge, MA: Harvard University Press.

Wallerstein, J. S., & Blakeslee, S. (1989). *Second chances: Men, women and children a decade after divorce.* New York: Ticknor and Fields.

Wolf, D. (1985). Ways of telling: Text repertoires in elementary school children. *Journal of Education, 167*, 71–87.

Wolf, D., Davidson, L., Davis, M., Walters, J., Hodges, M., & Scripp, L. (1988). Beyond A, B, and C: A broader and deeper view of literacy. In A. D. Pellegrini (Ed.), *Psychological bases for early education* (pp. 123–152). New York: Wiley.

Wolf, D. P., Rygh, J., & Altschuler, J. (1984). Agency and experience: Actions and states in play narratives. In I. Bretherton (Ed.), *Symbolic play: The development of social understanding* (pp. 195–217). New York: Academic Press.

Zahn-Waxler, C., Kochanska, G., Krupnick, J., and McKnew, D. (1990). Patterns of guilt in children of depressed and well mothers. *Developmental Psychology, 26*, 51–59.

10

He's a Nice Alligator: Observations on the Affective Organization of Pretense

GRETA G. FEIN
PATRICIA KINNEY

Five children—Sally, Jill, Chris, Alison, and Marge—are sitting under the climbing tower in a classroom of 4-year-olds. The teacher reminds them that only four children are permitted to be there. As the children discuss who will leave, Mark enters, announcing that he is a police officer. There are now six children under the tower. The original group persuades Mark to leave:

> MARK (to the group): I'm an alligator. (He crawls out. Chris and Mark chat about being alligators and police officers between the slats of the tower.)
>
> MARK (to Chris): I'm gonna bite you!
>
> CHRIS (to the others): Don't stick your head out!
>
> SALLY (leaving the tower, says to Mark): Hi, alligator.
>
> (The children under the tower approach Mark. They challenge, tickle, and tease him. He growls and looks angry. Jill and Marge run back to the tower in pretended fright.)
>
> SALLY (to Mark): Don't eat yourself up! Alligators are nice. Alligators are nice. (Mark crawls on all fours, growling.)
>
> SALLY (to Jill and Marge): He's silly. He's not eating anybody up.
>
> (Marge and Sally join Mark and crawl on the floor as alligators. Jill, alone, watches from the tower. After about a minute, she crawls out of the tower and joins the alligators crawling after Mark.)
>
> SALLY (reassuringly, to Jill): He's a nice alligator.

It's as easy as child's play. Or is it? For all its assumed simplicity and universality, *play* has as many as 51 possible definitions and the term appears in over 16 idiomatic expressions conveying many different shades of meaning. Although a source of frustration for scholars, these definitional vagaries do not bother children. When asked to define play, children as young as 5 years of age point to its nonobligatory features (Fein, 1983; King, 1979). As one child succinctly put it, "Play is doing what you want to do," while "work is doing what you gotta do."

Children apparently define play according to the normative context in which it occurs. The same activity may or may not be play, depending on whether it is freely chosen or required. In a normative definition of play, children's notions about permission, obligation, and penalty are central. Matters pertaining to these notions fall within the purview of deontic logic, a formal system describing the rules and derivations of relations between and among normative concepts. In the system described by Anderson and Moore (1957; Anderson, 1967), permission is viewed as a primitive construct. Notions such as obligatory, forbidden, and indifferent are derived from the concept of permission. For example, an act is obligatory if and only if one is not permitted not to do it. In such a system of deontic logic, children's definitions of play would be deontically "indifferent" because the children define play as a context in which they are permitted to do a variety of activities and also permitted not to do these activities.

Suppose, then, that we have a classroom in which free play is defined by the teacher as a time in which children may choose what to do and what not to do as long as certain safety rules are respected. In this classroom, a popular choice is social pretense. However, some children engage in social pretense on a regular basis, others choose to do so less frequently, and a few never make this choice. This variation, observable in many preschool and kindergarten classrooms, poses some interesting questions about differences between players and nonplayers and about the rationale of interventions designed to convert nonplayers into players.

Because pretend play often deals with the ludicrous and the absurd, with seemingly distorted and half-baked ideas, children who engage in this activity might appear to be socially immature, confused about the world, or emotionally unstable. Certainly, when development is viewed as the acquisition of conventional referential categories, factual knowledge, and a realistic self-appraisal, an activity in which referential categories are often unconventional, conceptual categories counterfactual, and self-appraisals improbable might be construed as regressive, expressing children's limited grasp of real-world relationships. The research, however, says otherwise. Children who spontaneously engage in this activity, when compared to their less playful peers, tend to be more friendly, popular, expressive, cooperative, verbal, and creative, less impulsive and aggressive, and more likely to take the perspective of others (see Fein, 1981, and Rubin, Fein, & Vandenberg, 1983, for a review of this literature.) Other studies confirm this optimistic profile of the high-play child (Connolly & Doyle, 1984). More impressive, kindergarteners' participation in sociodramatic play predicts their social and social-cognitive maturity in first and second grades (Rubin, 1985).

While participation in social pretense augers well for young children, the failure to participate in this activity bodes less well. Nonparticipants tend to be socially isolated, unhappy children, at least in classrooms where pretend play is encouraged and is an active part of the free-play curriculum (Rubin, 1985). However, because this research is correlational, it is not possible to decide whether competent children choose to play or whether participation in this play actually enhances social competence. Play training studies indicate that children who do not play spontaneously can be taught or encouraged to do so and that enhanced social competence may result from this effort (see Fein, 1981, for a review). These findings, of course, do not preclude the possibility that socially competent children may also display a preference for pretend activities.

This research raises some fairly substantial issues. First, our notions about the difference between participating and nonparticipating children are fairly limited. For example, these children may differ in basic cognitive, symbolic, or verbal abilities. Certainly some investigators have advanced this position (e.g., Smilansky, 1968). Another possibility is that the difference is a stylistic one; some children—for example, the dramatists described by Wolf and Gardner (1979)—may prefer this expressive mode, while other, equally capable and mature children do not. Children who do not participate in sociodramatic play may have as much social contact as they desire and may gravitate to other activities.

A third possibility is that high- and low-play children differ neither in their cognitive abilities nor in their personal style if, by ability or style, we mean enduring individual dispositions. Rather, play is suppressed by fairly immediate affective factors at home, in school, or in the child. Erikson (1940) observed that therapeutic play is disrupted when children become overly anxious, an observation in keeping with the idea that play is associated with an optimum level of arousal (Hutt, 1979). If, as psychoanalytic theory maintains, pretense is about emotion, a dispassionate and deliberate return to emotionally charged, drive-related impulses and ideas (Erikson, 1963; Kris, 1952; Peller, 1954), a precondition for this return might be a moderately low level of immediate anxiety or distress (Gould, 1972). In the previous episode, Sally, a skilled pretend player, seems to understand that the alligator play requires the players to realize that the alligator is "really" nice. Her message is directed to Jill, who is reluctant to participate, and to Mark, whose anger at being excluded from the tower must be contained within a symbolic expression.

A second question concerns play *intervention*. In intervention research, one or more standard training procedures are typically applied to all children in a group. In some studies, the intervention occurs in the classroom; a teacher or researcher steps in to expand the child's play when it occurs, efforts often accompanied by planned experiences aimed at increasing children's knowledge of playable themes (e.g., Rosen, 1974; Smilansky, 1968). In other procedures, children are taken, singly or in groups, from the classroom to a secluded area, where adults encourage them to play with materials provided for this purpose (Freyberg, 1973; Saltz, Dixon, & Johnson, 1977). Regardless of the procedure, play enhancement occurs fairly quickly. The second question, therefore, is why these interventions work at all, and why they work so rapidly.

Smilansky (1968) suggested that if children lacked information about playable themes, an enriched curriculum would be the most effective remedy. In contemporary terms, these children might be said to lack the scripted knowledge required for play (Bretherton, 1984). If, however, children lacked techniques for elaborating play themes and sharing them with others, that is, if they lacked procedural knowledge, training in the use of play techniques would be the most effective intervention procedure. In the Smilansky study, technique training was more effective than an enriched curriculum, but a combination of these procedures worked best. Conceivably, nonplayers in the Smilansky study lacked procedural as well as declarative knowledge.

Other interpretations of intervention outcomes are possible. One possibility is that adult efforts to encourage play tell the children, "This activity is permitted here." If nonparticipating children feel apprehensive about play's apparent rulelessness, lack of predictability, and affective content, the message might also be that these "alligators are really nice." This interpretation assumes that children who do not play have the conceptual and technical knowledge to do so. Play is inhibited because the children are unsure whether the fantasy and disorder embedded in the play can be contained. According to affective theory, pretense involves the expression of emotionally consequential issues without a direct experiencing of the emotion (Fein, 1987, 1989). Play will not occur if there is any doubt about the derivative, nonreal status of the expressed affect or about its acceptability in a given situation.

The following analysis is based on in-depth clinical case studies of 30 children. Fifteen children were master players and 15 were nonplayers or novices. Teachers in 15 preschool and kindergarten classrooms were asked to nominate two children from their class, one whose dramatic play was rich and frequent and another whose play was either limited or nonoccurring. After 5 weeks of observation to confirm these nominations, individually tailored interventions were designed. The children were observed during intervention and for 1 or 2 weeks after intervention was terminated. The purpose of the study was to compare high- and low-play children, to evaluate children's response to the intervention as it was occurring, and to assess their postintervention behavior. Two of these comparative case studies are summarized here.

The Children

Annie and Kirsten

Annie, 5 years old, was attending kindergarten in an independent school. Her light brown hair was usually in pony tails fastened by barrettes the color of her immaculate designer outfit. Her features were finely detailed and her complexion was delicately colored, reminiscent of a porcelain collector's doll. The following observation, the first, is typical of those recorded over the first few weeks:

> Annie is sitting alone at a table, chin in hands, chewing on her fingers. Gracie leaves the table and Annie follows her to the doll corner. Gracie begins a pretend game with Kate. Annie sits on the couch alone, watching them intently. She slowly slips off the couch, bringing herself closer to Gracie and Kate, watching but not participating. She moves back to the couch, putting herself close to Kirsten and Lisa, whom she also watches. She returns to the table and sits alone for a few minutes. She returns to the now vacant doll corner, where she methodically removes both

chairs from the top of the table. She then fingers her hair, yawns, and meanders back to the table.

Kirsten, the high-play child, was also 5 years old. She had blond hair, tied in two disorderly pony tails above her ears. Her clothing was casual: jeans, T-shirt, and sneakers that were clean but looked as if they were worn and enjoyed. The first observation found her snuggled in a bean bag chair in the housekeeping corner at the beginning of an elaborate pretend episode:

> KIRSTEN: Pretend you brought me some meat loaf. I'm the sister. Bring me a spoon.
>
> LISA: No, you have to be the baby.
>
> KIRSTEN: No, I'm the sister.
>
> LISA: Here, baby.
>
> KIRSTEN: Thanks. Bring me another plate and spoon. I want to have a fruit cocktail.
>
> LISA: Here, baby.
>
> KIRSTEN: Get me some aspirin. I have a headache.
>
> LISA (pretending to hand Kirsten aspirin): Here, baby. I mean, sister.

Note that Kirsten escalated her sisterly characteristics until Lisa agreed to the role. Kirsten does not typically claim the motherly role, but whatever her role, she actively orchestrates the action. The following transcript is only part of a much longer 45-minute episode. Note that for Kirsten there are two themes—"parties" and "telephone conversations." These themes weave recursively in and out of the episode, but each repetition introduces a variation on the central theme:

> (Kirsten, Lisa, and Colleen are playing a game at the table.)
>
> KIRSTEN (to Lisa): You're not my friend.
>
> LISA (to Kirsten): Well, you're not my friend.
>
> KIRSTEN (to Lisa): Hey, Lisa. Me and Colleen talked on the phone. I'm having a party.
>
> COLLEEN: What do you want? I'm gonna give you something you've never had before—a teddy bear—a mommy teddy bear.
>
> KIRSTEN: No! Don't tell me! I don't want to know.
>
> (They move to the housekeeping area.)
>
> KIRSTEN: (to Lisa): Pretend your name is Kathy. My name is Mary. We're not going to dress up. (to Colleen, who is playing with a fire truck): Hey, brother, brother, what are you going to be?
>
> COLLEEN: Bauser.
>
> KIRSTEN (to Colleen): I'm Mary. Let's pretend I woke up in the morning. (to Lisa): Go to bed. Go to bed. (to Colleen): Pretend you gave me a present and it was a telephone.
>
> COLLEEN: Okay. Here's the phone. I'll fix it. Pretend I fix telephones.
>
> KIRSTEN: Okay. I'll call my friend. 2-3-4-4-5-9. (to Colleen): Want to talk, brother?

COLLEEN (taking the phone): I've got a couple of things to do. I can't hear anything. It's unplugged. She plugged her thing out.

KIRSTEN: Too bad.

COLLEEN (talking into the phone): Hello. Hi there, Mary. Want to come over and party? Everybody plugs out their plug. I can't stand it!

KIRSTEN: You can't stand it? (Kirsten goes to the table where Lisa is playing with the dolls. She picks up a doll.) I want to be the mommy, though. (Kirsten blows up a plastic cube.)

COLLEEN (to Kirsten): C'mon. Let's go to the movies. Let's have a date.

KIRSTEN (ignoring Colleen, says to Lisa): Hey mom, anybody call me?

LISA: Yes, Susan did.

KIRSTEN (to Colleen): Hey, brother, I'm gonna call Susan. (She picks up the phone and begins to dial.)

Note that this sequence began with a nonplay, negative interaction with Lisa, one of Kirsten's regular play partners. Kirsten quickly converted her hostility into a pretend event marked by social compatibility. Colleen responded as if such a conversation had occurred and a party was indeed in the offing. As if hearing Kirsten's underlying message, she offered a gift. At a manifest level, the themes are parties and phone conversations. But at an affective level, Kirsten's fantasies deal with the feeling of self-worth and its confirmation by the receipt of gifts and phone calls to and from attentive friends. Note also Colleen's pretense that Mary (Kirsten), on the other end of the line, pulled the phone plug and therefore did not hear Colleen's message. At this, Kirsten almost switched to the less vulnerable role of mom, but, changing her mind, deciding to try again with a pretend friend who was not one of the players.

During the first 5 weeks of observation, the contrast between Annie and Kirsten was stable and striking. Kirsten was a master player, skilled in communicating and coordinating pretend sequences. She was articulate and approached classroom life with competence, confidence, and a sense of humor. Kirsten's play reflects what Miller (1973) would view as *galumphing*. As indicated in the preceding exerpts, she was able to manipulate the process, guide it, and shape it. But she was also able to let loose and dangle if that's where the play took her.

By contrast, Annie approached the world in a literal way. During free play, Annie typically drew with crayons and built with tinker toys or small colored cubes. Her self-chosen tasks were finite, controlled, and product oriented. Her play choices were limited to safe, structured materials that required no participation with others or teacher guidance. These activities took place as she sat in a chair at a table, an arrangement that seemed to protect her from the intrusion of other children and defined an unambiguous space within which she could safely busy herself. When not at the table, she wandered around the room, often twirling her pony tail as she watched the other children play. By the fourth week of observation, she had developed a tenuous relationship with Gracie, an assertive, commanding child. Annie trailed after Gracie, echoing her activities until Gracie found another partner.

Kirsten was among the top students in her class in language and social development, self-confidence, and overall competence in academic tasks. Annie was at the bottom of the group in some areas, but not all. Her academic skills were as good as Kirsten's. However, when she spoke, her voice was barely audible, and she did not make eye contact when speaking to a peer or to an adult. Annie seemed to be at the periphery of classroom life, while Kirsten often created it. While Kirsten seemed comfortable in the school setting, Annie seemed apprehensive, tentative, and withdrawn. The difference between the two children extended to their appearance. Kirsten's casual attire was in marked contrast to Annie's ordered, put-together, and not-to-be-disturbed appearance.

As far as the school knew, neither child was experiencing an especially traumatic home life, and they both came from intact, seemingly well-functioning families. Even though Kirsten frequently played the role of sister, she was actually an only child, as was Annie. Annie's mother, a dancer, was a reserved, refined, immaculately dressed woman who looked elegant even in jeans. Kirsten's mother was socially active, outgoing, and often in a breathless rush to get from one place to another.

Jill and Ellen

Jill, 4 years old, was attending a private nursery school for the second year. She had dark brown curly hair and usually wore a dress and sneakers to school. The following observation is fairly typical of her preintervention behavior:

> Jill and Alison were sitting on the rug, working shape puzzles. Alison put her puzzle away, and Jill did so too. Alison wandered over to a group listening to a story on the record player. Jill followed. Alison sat down at the table with paper and magic markers. Jill wandered to the play beauty parlor, sucking her thumb and twisting her fingers in her hair while watching the active play going on there. She roamed around the room to the birthday chart, then to the book corner, still sucking her thumb and fingering her hair. Slowly she wandered over to Alison at the table:
>
> Alison (sternly, to Jill): I'm doing this.
>
> Teacher (bringing another chair and extra markers and paper to the table): Now someone else can come and draw. (Jill continued to watch Alison, sucking her thumb and twirling her hair.)
>
> Alison (to Jill): Aren't ya gonna do this? Sit in the chair. (Jill smiled and sat down.)
>
> (Alison has printed GSHASO at the top of her page. Jill copies the same letters, frequently checking Alison's paper.)
>
> Alison: That's an f. F starts with chicken. (Alison prints her name on the next line.)
>
> (Jill said nothing, copying Alison's name on her own paper.)
>
> Alison (pointing to Jill's paper): That's not an A. (It was.)
>
> (Alison went to the easel. Jill finished copying Alison's paper. When finished, she stood up, looking unhappily at the blue ink on her finger. She wandered to the rug area, to the paint jars stored on a shelf, and then to the easels where she watched Chris paint. She wandered to the carpet, sat down, and rubbed the carpet with her

hand. Jill rested her head on the carpet, sucking her thumb. She then sat up and looked around the room.)

Jill's behavior stands in marked contrast to that of Ellen, one of the several master players in this 4-year-old group. Ellen has dark brown hair cut in a bilevel hair style. She, too, wears dresses to school, many of which are dressy and frilly. She has an extensive wardrobe of shoes, some of which have tiny heels. She often comes to school adorned with jewelry, but even when she doesn't, she borrows jewelry from another child or from the housekeeping corner. In these observations, Ellen was involved in dramatic play every day, carrying play themes into most other activities:

(Ellen and Betsy finish painting at the easel. They go to the play beauty parlor, where they load rollers and other equipment into buckets.)

Ellen: Look at us, we're packing. (Ellen and Betsy carry their loaded buckets to the white shag rug, singing, "do, dee, dumm, dum.")

Ellen (to Betsy): Here we are. We're at the special hotel now, right? (To Alison who is sitting on the rug): Let's say you broke into the house.

The play continued, shifting in location from slide to rug, then from chairs to rug, which were incorporated into the vacation theme as "cars" and "water," respectively. The girls joined Chris under a large table covered with a drop cloth, at which point the teacher invited Ellen and Betsy to the table, where drawing paper and magic markers were available. Themes touched upon earlier returned in this new activity.

Ellen: I'm 16.

Betsy: I'm 16, too.

Ellen (to Betsy): Oh, my God! There's the bad guy. (to Danny, who had stopped to watch the drawing): You're bad to us. (She returns to her drawing.) Hey, look at my dress.

Betsy: My dress is like this.

Ellen: Look at me. My mommy has short hair today. She's gonna have green today. I asked Mommy, and I'm older than her today. Now I'm gonna write my daddy on this side (the other side of the paper). He's gonna be this big. I'm gonna write his long hair. (to Betsy): Did your mommy pack? (to the teacher): We work here in the computer center. (to Betsy): Do we work here? Let's take our shoes off. (Betsy didn't respond, and neither girl did anything with her shoes. Ellen began to sing.) Well, we'll decide, sebin, sebin, sabalc, bella, hella, bella, bula, soway, soway.

Betsy: I got recognition.

Ellen (to the teacher): Look at us, teacher. We're playing we work here. (She resumed singing.) Oh, be shella, she a let.

Jill and Ellen are of interest because they were comparable in their ability to work complicated puzzles, understand directions, match and write letters, and engage in other activities that do not require speech or imaginative behavior. In other respects, the two children were strikingly different. During free-play time, Jill stood apart from the other children, sucking her thumb, twirling her hair, or jumping from one foot to the other as she watched the others play or as she aimlessly wandered about. If explicitly invited, she would join another child and, as in the episode presented earlier, imitate the other child's behavior. She did not respond verbally to the other children, and when the teachers tried to initiate conversation, she responded with a nod or with a smile but never with words.

In contrast, Ellen was cheerful and lively, her play swiftly paced and vivid. Dating, going to a dance, and taking trips were recurring themes. She assigned roles to other players and skillfully drew them into her activities. And yet, her approach to the dramatic play was permissive; often several themes were going on concurrently. For example, a couple of players might go shopping while she and some others went to a dance, with the entire group converging in the "car" (a row of chairs) as they traveled together to their various destinations. Although often the source of a play theme, Ellen did not insist that her peers fall in line. They often did so when she made an intriguing suggestion, but just as often they elaborated on their own, while she picked up different thematic strands. Using Parten's (1933) descriptors, her play was often cooperative but just as often associative. At times, the thematic parts resembled a fugue; at other times, a sonata.

Each of these children had a fairly stressful home life. When Ellen was 3 years old, she moved into the area with her mother and a male friend whom the mother subsequently married. Ellen's natural father lived in San Francisco, and her visits to him were opposed by her mother. During the week of this observation, Ellen's mother was experimenting with various hair colors that changed daily, although never to green. From Ellen's perspective, this, too, could happen; after all, life was unpredictable. Ellen's mother was portrayed on one side of the page, her father on the other. Each parent was deftly caricatured as she struggled to bring the complexity and conflict in their tense relationship into balance.

Jill's home life was also stressful, although the stress was from a different source. Jill's mother, who had had a miscarriage the previous year, was again pregnant. In Jill's presence, she announced to the teacher that the doctors considered this a high-risk pregnancy, but that she didn't want to discuss the upcoming event with Jill for fear of another miscarriage. According to the mother, Jill reacted to the miscarriage with thumb sucking, bed wetting, and clinging to her mother. Jill was enrolled in the nursery school shortly afterward; at that time, she had difficulty separating from her mother.

When the teacher first discussed Jill's unhappy school behavior with her mother, the mother reported that Jill enjoyed school; every day, she and Jill spent much time reviewing everything that happened in school. Jill's accounts were careful and accurate. According to the mother, Jill loved letters and numbers, and her parents frequently worked with her on these things. One unfortunate consequence of the teacher's attempt to discuss Jill's withdrawn behavior was the mother's increased pressure on the child. When picking Jill up at school, she would ask, "Did you tell the teacher what we did yesterday? Did you tell the teacher what you brought?" When Jill was mute, the mother pressed: "Why didn't you tell the teachers?"

Intervention

Here then are two high-play children, master players who were zestful, expressive, and liked by their peers. Each may have experienced stress at home, although in greatly varying degrees. Whatever the source of intensity of stress, neither child was immobilized by it. Their emotional experiences, whether literal or nonliteral, were woven exuberantly into their pretense. As we studied their play transcripts, it soon became clear that these master players, for all their organizing skills, were amazingly undemanding of their play partners. As a result, several different personal themes often developed concurrently, interspersed periodically with coordinating efforts.

We have also described two low-play children, withdrawn and tense, wistfully observing their peers and gaining some measure of comfort from hair twirling, thumb sucking, and other self-stimulating behavior. Perhaps life for these low-play children was experienced as more stressful, even though to an outside observer the home lives of high- and low-play children do not appear to differ greatly in this respect. Conceivably, the difference is not in the external source of stress, but rather in the resources available to these children for coping with the tensions and discomforts that are an inevitable part of growing up.

In considering strategies for intervention, the children's teachers were consulted and the classroom environment was evaluated. Possible interventions were reviewed in the light of situational factors, the attitudes of cooperating teachers, the importance of maintaining a warm and flexible climate, and the possible impact of the intervention on other children in the classroom. The strategy developed for each child attempted to take into account their special interests and concerns, practical limitations imposed by the school setting, and the fact that one of the interveners was a school administrator and the other was one of the classroom teachers.

Annie

The intervention designed for Annie was built on the notion that her central preoccupation at the time was to hold herself together, behave properly, and conform to whatever was expected of her. And so, it was decided not to add anything new to her life, but rather to take advantage of the interests she had already expressed. The play theme chosen—a supermarket—was familiar and lent itself to structured roles and schoollike activities. The idea was to set up a supermarket in the classroom, and to call upon Annie's interest and skill in writing numbers and in orderly activity to involve her in the play. The props consisted of assorted empty food boxes, a small shopping cart, an ancient adding machine, aprons, a cash box with Monopoly money and real pennies, plain white stickers, and magic markers. These new items attracted a large group of children that grew when the adding machine began to clickety-clack as white paper spewed forth. The teacher announced that everyone would have a turn working in small groups with the new material. Kirsten, Kate, and Annie (who at this point was outside the supermarket area looking in) were designated as the first group. Annie quietly walked into the area.

Annie immediately gravitates to the adding machine. She hits the numbers, but nothing happens. The teacher asks her if she wants to be shown how it works. Annie nods. One demonstration and Annie understands. She hits a number and then the total bar, then repeats this over and over. In no time at all, a long trail of paper begins to stream out of the machine. Kirsten tries to organize a role-play situation. Kirsten and Kate approach the adding machine, pushing Annie aside. Annie backs away, returning to her customary role of onlooker. Once again, Kirsten tries to organize the play, this time with herself as manager, cashier, or some other high-status role:

Kirsten: Who's gonna be the person to buy?

Kate: I'm not.

Kirsten: How much does this (a box of graham crackers) cost? It costs $1.50. (She return to the adding machine and hits some numbers, but the tape gets stuck.)

Annie (to Kirsten): I'll do it.

(Kirsten and Kate return to their discussion of pricing items in the basket. Arms loaded with items, they charge the adding machine. Annie leaves, once again assuming the role of observer. She then walks over to the basket and pulls out a can of beans.)

Annie (in a whisper): How much does this cost? (She reaches into the basket again, coming up with a box of Cup-a-Soup.)

Annie (still almost inaudible): How much does this cost?

Kirsten (to Annie): Please, be the one who buys it.

(Annie shakes her head, no. Kirsten looks to Kate. No, again.)

Kirsten (disgustedly): If nobody wants to be the person who buys, we're not playing.

And they didn't. Annie tried to join the play, imitating Kirsten and Kate, as if she were trying to rehearse the lines that would integrate her in the play. But when invited to assume an unrehearsed and apparently undesirable role, she flatly refused.

The supermarket turned into a great success with the group, but Annie remained on the periphery. At this point, the decision was made to add greater participation by the teacher and the realistic mechanics of operating a supermarket. Because the children had shown spontaneous interest in the cost of the items, they were invited to help price items with the teacher. When Annie was invited to help, she refused at first. Three other children and the teacher sat down to price the items. Annie hovered near the group and then joined them.

Teacher (holding up a box of graham crackers): How much do these cost?

Liza: $21

Annie: That's too much. (The teacher asks her how much she thinks it should be.) $8

The teacher shows the children how to make a dollar sign. Annie writes an 8 on a sticker, copies the dollar sign backward, and puts the label on the box. This activity continues for about 20 minutes. Soon, Annie is laughing, suggesting prices in an audible voice, and even making eye contact with peers and the teacher. The teacher then suggests that the items be placed on the shelves, and the children eagerly do so. Annie then asks if she can be in charge of the cash box. Liza says she wants to work the adding machine. The teacher elects to be a shopper and asks Betsy to help with the shopping. The teacher then suggests that she and Betsy pretend to shop for a birthday party. The teacher offers to be the mother, and Betsy agrees to be the sister. They both enter the shopping area and pick out some items. Annie is watching.

Teacher (to Annie): Will you help me find some candles for a birthday party? (Annie quickly responds.)

Annie: Do you need some coffee? (She hands a can of coffee to the teacher.)

Annie goes to the cash box. The teacher and Betsy, finished with their shopping, move to the checkout counter. Annie takes items out of the basket while Liza rings them up. No dialogue occurs.

In this episode, the roles were understood, but the play was simply a realistic replication of supermarket behavior. Annie, however, became an active participant in this literal, teacher-supervised episode. It was the first time during the school year that Annie had engaged in a spontaneous verbal exchange, and the first time her behavior was animated and involved. Episodes of this nature continued for two more observations. Although the play slowly moved out of the realm of safe, adult-sanctioned activity and into child-generated peer encounters, Annie's play continued to reflect her meticulous, precise style. There were still no signs of galumphing.

Two weeks later, a week after intervention had stopped, Annie took her first step toward spontaneous pretense with a peer. The encounter occurred as she became engaged in an interaction initiated by Erika, an expert pretend player. Erika had suggested that a house be built from blocks so that food purchased at the supermarket could be used at home:

Erika (to Annie): Let's pretend it's your birthday party and we can make a play dough cake.

Annie: Let's pretend that the straws are the candles.

With the phrase "Let's pretend," Annie signaled her readiness to become an active participant in social pretense. In this postintervention period, the teacher was no longer directing or suggesting play themes. The supermarket remained a popular play area, but by this time Kirsten, Kate, Erika, and Annie had abandoned it for the blocks. The postintervention period was marked by observations such as the following:

Annie was in the center of a block structure that extended to the middle of the classroom. This elaborate structure, made of both cardboard and unit blocks, was populated by stuffed animals. Gracie and Annie were together. The teacher asks what they are making:

Gracie: A house, I think.

Annie (laughing): No, it's a barn.

The remainder of this episode was rich in pretense dialogue, transformations, and metacommunicative statements. Annie and Gracie were equal partners in the elaboration of the pretend episode. Other children joined them, and Annie continued to be an active participant.

In this particular intervention, the teacher accomplished two things. First, she reassured Annie that play was permitted in school. Second, she created a safe social situation in which playful interactions could occur. Annie then took over, managing the rest on her own. The data provide little evidence that Annie lacked information about the real world. If she lacked knowledge of play techniques, she acquired it in a few days.

Jill

The intervention developed for Jill consisted of pairing her with a skilled player during free-play time. The child chosen for this purpose was Sally, a warm, friendly, easygoing youngster who had spontaneously shown concern for Jill. When free play was announced, the teacher took both children aside and suggested to Jill that she could "be with Sally." Sally seemed pleased by this arrangement and quickly became Jill's partner. For 4 weeks, 5 days per week, twice each day, Jill was paired with Sally. Observations of Jill's behavior continued during this period. At the end of 4 weeks, the teacher-promoted pairing ceased. Jill was then observed for an additional 2 weeks.

During the first week of intervention, the following episode was recorded:

(Jill is stretched out on the slide, surrounded by Sam, Peter, Ellen, Billy, and Patrick)

Peter: We're doctors.

Sam: We're pretending these (stickers) are Band-aids. (He puts stickers on Jill's arms and head.)

Ellen: Look what we're playing. We're playing it for real. She's got another mark right here. (She puts a sticker on Jill's hand.)

(Patrick puts a stretch belt over Jill's forehead. She is very still, saying nothing.)

Billy: She got hurt from being a bad guy.

Peter (to Ellen): Nurse.

Ellen: I'm the nurse. You're supposed to call me nurse.

(Billy places an empty picture frame over Jill's face. Jill looks straight ahead with a blank stare.)

Peter (to Billy): Okay, what really happened?

Ellen: Well, I think she was hit by . . .

Peter (feeling Jill's forehead): Her temperature is up.

Sam: I think she must be mysterious.

Peter (to Jill): Open up! (Jill opens her mouth.)

Billy: Go aaaaah. (Jill says nothing.)

Peter: Her temperature is very high.

Sam: She has a temperature again.

Peter: She's gotta stay here for a few days.

Ellen: She can't go home because she was hurt in her house. She fell down and burned herself.

Sam: So how did she get here? Well, she gotta have an operation. (Jill abruptly gets up.)

Unfortunately, this observation started after the play sequence had begun, so we don't know how the children maneuvered this retiring child into the role of patient. However it happened, Jill willingly submitted to their ministrations, allowing the play to center on her without protest. She played the willing and submissive patient until an operation was announced. Jill terminated the play.

Although Sally was not a participant in the previous episode, Sally and Jill were together much of the time. Jill's first active participation in pretense occurred a week later, when Jill and Sally pretended to eat and drink in the absence of any objects. The alligator scene, which occurred later that week, was the first instance of active participation in group play. Note that Sally's reassurance to Jill was couched in such a way as to remind her that the alligator was not at all like a real alligator, that the play was nonviolent and under control in spite of its noise and movement. From a psychoanalytic point of view, it is provocative that these early pretend activities (and the one to be presented) focused on eating and being eaten.

For Jill, a peer protector and mentor permitted her to become a part of the group's social and fantasy life. Over the 4-week period, Jill became more joyful and verbal. Observations from this period contain countless examples of laughter, silliness, and spontaneous, fast-paced play. Although unlike Sally, Ellen, and many of the other children Jill did not initiate play themes, she enthusiastically endorsed those of her peers. In this period, she was never observed sucking her thumb or twirling her hair. In the postpairing period, while often with Sally, Jill interacted with other children as well. Here is a glimpse of Jill during the postintervention period:

Jack, Sally, and Jill are on the rug, sorting cards with pictures of different foods on them. There is much giggling as they say silly things about the pictures.

Sally: This food is makin' me hungry.

Jill: I wanna eat those cookies. (Laughing, she grabs the cake card and pretends to eat the picture, repeating the pretense with the sandwich picture and the milk picture.

Sally: Were's the bananas?

Jill (Shrieking with laughter): Oooh, hot dogs. Ooooh, eggs. (She goes from one card to the other, giggling, as she pretends to eat the pictures.)

Jack: You ate them all up. And you made a mess.

Jill (giggling): Let's eat the clothes.

Some Conclusions

Annie and Jill are not unusual children. We were able to find one or more nonplayers in each of the 15 classrooms, just as we were able to find one or more master players in each classroom. Some interventions produced more striking changes than others, but because these efforts were designed as clinical case studies rather than as controlled experiments, we can make no claims about the magnitude of the effects or even about whether the changes we observed might have happened if no deliberate interventions had occurred. However, the effort suggests some useful notions about why some capable children do not play even though they are in daily contact with peers who do (Fein & Stork, 1981).

Our analysis begins with the issues of permission and obligation and with the idea that some young children are overly sensitive to the obligatory aspects of their environment. These children, who desperately want to do what they are supposed to do, come to school burdened with an inordinate sense of duty to meet adults' expectations. These expectations, which stress academic achievement and obedience, promote an image of school as a sedentary, teacher-organized place. Each of our low-play children performed well in teacher-led group activities and in well-structured, teacher-assigned tasks. However, the schools attended by the children stressed experiential learning and autonomy. Upon finding themselves in a classroom in which nonsedentary, peer-organized activity was actively pursued and endorsed by adults, these children faced the discrepancy between the expectations of home and those of school. Presumably, this discrepancy produced considerable anxiety.

In effect, the children came to school expecting to work, only to find that they were expected to play. However, the notion of expectations fails to convey the depth of the dilemma faced by the children. In order to understand the source of their near-paralysis, it is necessary to examine the implications of the children's definition of play as deontic indifference. These children were comfortable when told what to do; they became paralyzed when told to do what they wanted to do. Most young children enjoyed the idea of choice; most of our low-play children seemed to find this idea frightening. Unlike Ellen, they were not able to play "we work here." The freedom to choose brings with it the freedom to choose wrongly; our low-play children did not enjoy the emotional luxury of being wrong.

This interpretation touches, of course, on other issues. It implies that some low-play children have been asked prematurely to develop self-control and adultlike behavior. For these children, the spectacle of other children noisily engaged in messy and imaginative activities must be overwhelming. As they roamed the classroom, our low-play children studied the chaos and then withdrew as if fearful of being caught up in it. Interestingly, they paused longest at groups engaged in dramatic play, fascinated and yet repelled by what they observed. After these sorties, they sought the safety of the tables providing crayons, small building toys, or puzzles—familiar, easily controlled activities. Their social contacts occurred there and, prior to the intervention, ended there. Each child tried to solve the problem of social isolation by finding a domineering peer to copy, but these peers rarely used this opportunity to extend the relationship. For these low-play children, peer observation and modeling were not the pathway to social participation. Although they seemed to desire social involvement, the play involvement fostered in the classroom threatened their precarious hold over the impulses, angers, and affections they were trying so hard to contain. These children had much to fear from the unruly, disequilibristic aspects of play (Sutton-Smith, 1986).

The nonplayers in our sample seemed to come from families in which impulse control and adultlike behavior were highly valued. Psychoanalytic concepts of the ego and its functioning offer one way of thinking about the meaning of these values for preschool children. From this perspective, play involves the regression to primary process modes of thinking in the service of ego processes (Kris, 1952). For play to occur, ego processes must relax their containment of primitive impulses while controlling their expression. As play may be disrupted when the expression of dangerous feelings can no longer be controlled (Erikson, 1940), play may also be suppressed when control over these feelings is too fragile and yet too important to be relaxed.

Conceivably, the behavior of these stiff, orderly children may reflect difficulties in the parent–child relationship. For example, anxiously attached children show lower levels of pretense and peer interaction than do securely attached children (Lieberman, 1977; Matas, Arend, & Sroufe, 1978; Slade, 1987). At the same time, children who are apprehensive about separation show elevated levels of pretend play (Field, 1984), and the opportunity to play may reduce separation anxiety (Milos & Reiss, 1982). One interesting issue is whether insecure attachment is one of several particular sources of anxiety that inhibit the use of pretense as a coping mechanism (Singer, 1979). If so, a secure attachment relationship may be one of the prerequisites for the use of pretense to cope with separation and other sources of anxiety.

For both children, the first impact of the intervention was to end their social isolation. The active participation of the teacher might have done for Annie what Sally did for Jill, that is, offer reassurance that pretense activity could be contained and controlled, and that it was sanctioned in the classroom. For Annie, the path to social participation and play was through her skills and interest in the academic part of school (reading and writing numbers) and through her interest in controllable materials (in this case, the adding machine) that do her bidding and bring no surprises. For both children, entry as a passive participant preceded the active adoption of roles. Jill was perhaps the more venturesome of the two, submitting herself to the passive role of patient without being sure where the activity would lead. When the play became alarming, however, she successfully terminated her participation. Her success may have confirmed the deontic principle that in play the individual is permitted not to do as well as to do.

The analyses offered here suggest some additional directions for future research. First, play interventions might be distinguished according to whether one assumes that the children lack procedural or declarative knowledge, or that they lack the emotional ease needed to engage in pretense. The latter assumption was explored in the case studies reported here. Also of interest is what is meant by play recovery. As our children changed from nonplayers to players, a passive play role preceded an active one, and responsiveness to others' play ideas preceded the introduction of their own play ideas. Psychoanalytic theorists have long stressed the notion that pretense is an active process in which the ego becomes receptive to instinctual pressures and internalized prohibitions (Peller, 1954). Sampling the concerns of one's peers may be safer than sharing one's own concerns. But if pretense is to facilitate mastery, each child must connect with those things that matter most to her. Play interventions might be evaluated according to the nonplayer's role in the initiation and orchestration of play themes.

In sum, we think that some children are nonplayers for three related reasons. One concerns the expectations they bring to the play setting. A second concerns the threat of choice. A third concerns the primacy of impulse control in the organization of these children's behavior, the significance of choice, and the primacy of impulse control. When these children come to a school in which play is a planned part of the curriculum, they must deal with a risky activity that exposes sensitive emotional issues to public scrutiny. That these low-play children required so little encouragement to undertake the risk may reflect their willingness to gamble on a benign public. Perhaps reassurance from teachers and peers helped them to recognize that children other than themselves were also coping with the tribulations of growing up. After all, if make-believe alligators can be tamed, why not real ones too?

ACKNOWLEDGEMENT

We wish to thank Loretta Lage for her contributions to this chapter.

REFERENCES

Anderson, A. R. (1967). Some nasty problems in the formal logic of ethics. *Nous, 1*, 345–360.

Anderson, A. R., & Moore, O. K. (1957). The formal analysis of normative concepts. *American Sociological Review, 22*, 9–17.

Bretherton, I. (1984). Event representation in symbolic play: Reality and fantasy. In I. Bretherton (Ed.), *Symbolic play: The representation of social understanding* (pp. 3–41). New York: Academic Press.

Connolly, J. A., & Doyle, A. (1984). Relation of social fantasy to social competence in preschoolers. *Developmental Psychology, 20*, 797–806.

Erikson, E. H. (1940). Studies in the interpretation of play: I. Clinical observations of play disruption in young children. *Genetic Psychology Monographs, 22*, 557–671.

Erikson, E. H. (1963). *Childhood and society.* New York: Norton.

Erikson, E. H. (1977). *Toys and reasons.* New York: Norton.

Fein, G. G. (1981). Pretend play: An integrative review. *Child Development, 52*, 1095–1118.

Fein, G. G. (1983). Play: Surfaces of thinking and feeling. In J. L. Frost & S. Sunderlin (Eds.), *When children play* (pp. 45–53). Wheaton, MD: Association for Childhood Education International.

Fein, G. G. (1987). Pretend play: Creativity and consciousness. In D. Gorlitz & J. Wohwill (Eds.), *Curiosity, imagination, and play: On the development of spontaneous motivational and cognitive processes* (pp. 281–304). Hillsdale, NJ: Erlbaum.

Fein, G. G. (1989). Mind, meaning, and affect: Proposals for a theory of pretence. *Developmental Review, 9*, 345–363.

Fein, G. G., & Stork, L. (1981). Sociodramatic play: Social class effects in integrated preschool classrooms. *Journal of Applied Developmental Psychology, 2*, 267–279.

Field, T. (1984). Separation stress of young children transferring to new schools. *Developmental Psychology, 20*, 786–792.

Freyberg, J. T. (1973). Increasing the imaginative play of urban disadvantaged kindergarten children through systematic training. In J. L. Singer (Ed.), *The child's world of make-believe: Experimental studies of imaginative play* (pp. 129–154). New York: Academic Press.

Gould, R. (1972). *Child studies through fantasy.* New York: Quadrangle.

Hutt, C. (1979). Exploration and play. In B. Sutton-Smith (Ed.), *Play and learning* (pp. 175–194). New York: Gardner Press.

King, N. (1979). Play: The kindergarten's perspective. *Elementary School Journal, 80*, 81–87.

Kris, E. (1952) *Psychoanalytic explorations in art.* New York: International Universities Press.

Lieberman, A. F. (1977). Preschooler's competence with a peer: Influence of attachment and social experience. *Child Development, 48*, 1277–1287.

Matas, L., Arend, R. A., & Sroufe, A. (1978). Continuity of adaptation in the second year: The relationship between quality of attachment and later competence. *Child Development, 49*, 547–556.

Miller, S. (1973). Ends, means and galumphing: Some leitmotifs of play. *American Anthropologist, 75*, 87–98.

Milos, M., & Reiss, S. (1982). Effects of three play conditions on separation anxiety in young children. *Journal of Consulting and Clinical Psychology, 50*, 389–395.

Parten, M. B. (1933). Social participation in preschool children. *Journal of Abnormal Social Psychology, 28*, 136–147.

Peller, L. (1954). Libidinal phases, ego development, and play. *Psychoanalytic Study of the Child, 9*, 178–198.

Rosen, C. E. (1974). The effects of sociodramatic play on problem-solving behavior among culturally disadvantaged preschool children. *Child Development, 45*, 920–927.

Rubin, K. H. (1985). Play, peer interaction and social development. In A. W. Gottfried & C. C. Brown (Eds.), *Play interactions: The contribution of play materials and parental involvement to child development* (pp. 120–148). Lexington, MA: Lexington Books.

Rubin, K. H., Fein, G. G., & Vandenberg, B. (1983). Play. In P. Mussen (Ed.), *Manual of child psychology* (Vol. IV, pp. 693–774). New York: Wiley.

Saltz, E., Dixon, D., & Johnson, J. (1977). Training disadvantaged preschoolers on various fantasy activities: Effects on cognitive functioning and impulse control. *Child Development, 48*, 367–380.

Singer, J. L. (1979). Affect and imagination in play and fantasy. In C. Izard (Ed.), *Emotions in personality and psychopathology* (pp. 13–34). New York: Plenum Press.

Slade, A. (1987). Quality of attachment and early symbolic play. *Developmental Psychology, 23*, 78–85.

Smilansky, S. (1968). *The effects of sociodramatic play on disadvantaged preschool children.* New York: Wiley.

Sutton-Smith, B. (1986). The spirit of play. In G. G. Fein & M. Rivkin (Eds.), *The young child at play: Reviews of research* (Vol. 4, pp. 3–16). Washington, DC: National Association for the Education of Young Children.

Waelder, R. (1933). The psychoanalytic theory of play. *Psychoanalytic Quarterly, 2*, 208–224.

Wolf, D., & Gardner, H. (1979). Style and sequence in early symbolic play. In N. R. Smith & M. B. Franklin (Eds.), *Symbolic functioning in childhood* (pp. 117–138). Hillsdale, NJ: Erlbaum.

11

Symbolic Development in Children with Down Syndrome and in Children with Autism: An Organizational, Developmental Psychopathology Perspective

DANTE CICCHETTI
MARJORIE BEEGHLY
BEDONNA WEISS-PERRY

Goals of the Chapter

In this chapter, we argue that the study of atypical populations can enhance our understanding of the ontogenesis of normal symbolic processes. Specifically, we demonstrate that if a basic social-communicative system is in place, even if it is developing more slowly and somewhat aberrantly (as in Down syndrome), then it will yield a very coherent pattern of symbolic development in both linguistic and nonlinguistic domains. If this social-communicative system is disordered (as in autism), a very different picture emerges.

First, we describe the theoretical framework that guides our work—the discipline of developmental psychopathology and the organizational approach—and highlight how this perspective is an ideal one for studying symbolic development in atypical populations. We accomplish this by reviewing the studies on the development of play in two groups of atypical children—youngsters with Down syndrome (DS) and autistic children. Before documenting what these studies tell us about normal and pathological symbolic development, we state why we chose these two specific groups of children as exemplary populations to enhance our knowledge of normal and deviant ontogenesis. Subsequently, we examine the interrelations among symbolic play and other developmental domains, such as language, cognition, and social interaction, to learn how symbolization is organized in these special groups. The role that the social-communicative system plays in the organization of symbolic development in these and other populations is then examined.

The Organizational Developmental Psychopathology Perspective

The field of developmental psychopathology has begun to emerge as a logical extension of the outgrowth of thinking that emphasized that the developmental approach can be applied to any culture or population, normal or otherwise deviant (Werner, 1948). Nearly all of the great systematizers in psychology, psychiatry, and psychoanalysis and the neurosciences have argued that we can learn more about the normal functioning of an organism by studying its psychopathology and, likewise, more about its psychopathology by studying its normal condition (Cicchetti, 1984). Numerous others, trained in a variety of disciplines and conducting research on an array of different populations, have espoused a similar philosophy (see Cicchetti, 1990a, for an overview). Because historical and contemporary theorists have argued that psychopathology is a distortion of the normal, the study of psychopathology is thought to throw into sharper relief one's understanding of normal processes. Moreover, the investigation of psychopathological processes and outcomes from a developmental perspective is believed to lead to a greater understanding of psychopathology than would be the case if the disorder were studied from a nondevelopmental perspective (Cicchetti, 1984; Sroufe, 1989; Sroufe & Rutter, 1984).

The theoretical perspective that guides and influences our thinking and research is one that is closely aligned with Werner and Kaplan's (1963) organismic-developmental approach. The organizational perspective consists of a set of regulative principles that can guide research and theorizing concerning human behavior (Cicchetti & Beeghly, 1990b; Cicchetti & Schneider-Rosen, 1986; Cicchetti & Sroufe, 1978; Santostefano, 1978; Sroufe, 1979; Sroufe & Rutter, 1984).

According to the organizational approach, development may be conceived as a series of qualitative reorganizations among and within behavioral and biological systems, which take place by means of differentiation and hierarchical integration (see also Sameroff, 1983; Weiss, 1969). Variables at many levels of analysis determine the character of these reorganizations: genetic, constitutional, neurobiological, biochemical, behavioral, psychological, ecological-environmental, historical, and sociological. Moreover, these variables are conceived as being in dynamic *transaction* with one another (see, e.g., Gollin, 1984; Gollin, Stahl, & Morgan, 1989; Sameroff & Chandler, 1975).

The organizational approach conceptualizes human development in terms of an hierarchical organization of transacting and interrelated behavioral and biological systems (Weiss, 1969). In psychology three general behavioral systems—cognitive, affective, and social—have been proposed by investigators adopting an organizational approach. The hierarchical integration that occurs with development takes place *within* each behavioral system; additionally, competencies in each system become integrated *between* behavioral systems (Cicchetti, 1990b). The organization and integration of these behavioral systems in normal development and the observed lack of organization and integration, or integration of pathological structures, in pathology then become two of the most central concerns of developmentalists. Of particular importance are advances and lags in one behavioral system with respect to the others because the presence of capacities of one behavioral system may be a necessary condition for the development or exercise of capacities of another system. For example, in infancy certain social capacities (i.e., those associated with a secure attachment) may be necessary for the age-appropriate development of cognitive abilities (Gersten, Coster, Schneider-Rosen, Carlson, & Cicchetti, 1986). Likewise, certain cognitive skills may be necessary for the development of particular affective expressions and experiences (Cicchetti & Sroufe, 1976, 1978; Hesse & Cicchetti, 1982; Mans, Cicchetti, & Sroufe, 1978). Lags in these systems may then result in compensatory development, which may in some instances leave the child vulnerable to psychopathology (Cicchetti & Schneider-Rosen, 1986).

In formulating the orthogenetic principle, Werner and Kaplan (1963) argued that development was characterized by progression from a state of relative globality and undifferentiation to one characterized by increasing articulation, complexity, differentiation, and hierarchic integration. In a later article, Kaplan (1966) argued that psychopathology was characterized by dedifferentiation and disintegration of functioning. Kaplan described five polarities that occur in the course of ontogenetic growth. He stated that *functions* or *ends* progress along a dimension labeled *inter-fused-subordinated*. As will be the case for the remaining polarities, the first polar opposite mentioned is the more primitive, undifferentiated state of affairs. *Means* are said to develop from a state of *syncresis* to one of *discreteness*. The *structure* of an act proceeds ontogenetically from a *diffuse* to an *articulate* pole. Finally, the ability to *maintain integrity* and to *adapt* to the biological and experiential vicissitudes of life is thought to develop along two independent but related courses: *rigid–flexible* and *labile–stable*. Thus, in pathological development, one would expect an *interfusion* of ends or goals, a *syncresis* of means, a *diffuseness* in acts and their products, and a *disintegration, rigidity*, and *lability* in an organism's adaptation attempts.

Applying these principles to the normal development of symbolization, at the beginning the symbol is thought to be syncretically fused with other acts at primitive levels of functioning (Kaplan, 1966). Over the course of development, as levels of functioning become increasingly differentiated, there is more individuation and articulation of distinct activities. Consequently, the process of symbolization attains autonomy, and the self becomes more cognizant of its symbolic activities (Kaplan, 1966). Psychopathology in symbolization would presumably be revealed by functioning that is largely primitively organized and syncretically fused. By exploring the emergence of symbolization in children with DS and those with autism, we will elucidate this process.

An Organizational Approach to the Study of Symbolic Development in Children with Down Syndrome and in Children with Autism

In normal children, development often occurs so rapidly that the simultaneous emergence of behaviors or competencies in various domains may be epiphenomenal rather than indicative of structural or functional interrelations. However, in developmentally heterogeneous populations, such as children with DS and autistic children (Cicchetti & Beeghly, 1990a; Cicchetti & Sroufe, 1978; Cohen & Donellan, 1987; Mundy & Sigman, 1989; Wing, 1981), true developmental convergences and discontinuities may be more readily ascertained. In addition, both of these groups of children reveal a marked language delay (Beeghly & Cicchetti, 1987a; Cicchetti, 1990c; Lord, 1984; Mervis, 1990; Rutter & Garmezy, 1983; Tager-Flusberg, 1988, 1989). Moreover, both children with DS and autistic children are organically impaired, though there are many dissimilarities within the functioning of their autonomic and central nervous systems (Cicchetti, Ganiban, & Barnett, 1991; Cicchetti & Sroufe, 1978; Coyle, Oster-Granite, & Gearhart, 1986; Dawson & Lewy, 1989; Ganiban, Wagner, & Cicchetti, 1990, Rutter & Garmezy, 1983). Furthermore, both groups of children have cognitive deficits, with the vast majority of them functioning in the retarded range of general intellectual functioning (Cicchetti & Beeghly, 1990b; Hobson, 1986; Rutter, 1983; Rynders, Spiker, & Horrobin, 1978; Wing, 1981).

Nonetheless, the specific types of deficits differ and the constellations of cognitive characteristics associated with the cognitive deficits are very different (Hermelin & O'Connor, 1970; Mundy, Sigman, Kasari, & Yirmiya, 1988; Prior, 1979; Rutter, 1983). Autism appears to have a specific *social-cognitive* deficit (Baron-Cohen, Leslie, & Frith, 1985; Frith, 1989; Hobson, 1982, 1983, 1989; Langdell, 1978; Leslie, 1987; Ricks & Wing, 1976; Riguet, Taylor, Benaroya, & Klein, 1981; Rutter, 1983; Sigman & Mundy, 1987; Wing, Gould, Yeates, & Brierley, 1977). Moreover, the pragmatic-linguistic asynchronies found in the course of autistic development should provide additional insight into the source of these social-cognitive deficits (Mundy & Sigman, 1989; Sigman & Mundy, 1987). Children with DS, in contrast, manifest gross lags in expressive language even when one controls for their mental age (Beeghly & Cicchetti, 1987a; Fowler, 1990; Mervis, 1990). Thus, it would be interesting to determine what consequences this particular *décalage* might possess for other aspects of their symbolization. In contrast, the reverse condition is true for autistic children. Although their language is often severely delayed and abnormal when it emerges, autistic children are *especially* delayed in pragmatics and communication—the social uses of language (Cantwell, Baker, & Rutter, 1978; Curcio, 1978; Landry & Loveland, 1988; Rutter & Garmezy, 1983; Tager-Flusberg, 1988, 1989, 1992). Nonverbal communicative skills such as symbolic miming or gestures are also strikingly impaired in these children (Rutter & Garmezy, 1983).

The study of symbolization in children with an array of cognitive deficits, especially children who possess different but clearly identifiable etiologies and symptom pictures, could make a major contribution to the developmental–difference controversy extant in the field of mental retardation (Cicchetti & Pogge-Hesse, 1982; Zigler

& Balla, 1982). Because the study of symbolic development in normal children has been intensively studied (Bates, Bretherton, & Snyder, 1988; Bretherton, 1984; Rubin, Fein, & Vandenberg, 1983), research on children with DS and autistic children will allow us to add precision to the developmental theory of symbolization. Since the process of symbolization crystallizes more gradually in atypical children, we will have the opportunity to observe in microgenetic fashion what unfolds much more rapidly in normal children.

Symbolic Development in Down Syndrome

Why Down Syndrome?

Children with DS are a particularly interesting population of organically retarded children to study. First, infants with DS are etiologically homogeneous and detectable from the time of birth. Thus, their development can be assessed and followed from the beginning. Second, although infants with DS develop at a slower pace, they are strikingly heterogeneous in functioning, ranging from severely delayed to near-normal. Their delayed but heterogeneous development allows for a more precise examination of ontogenetic sequences in various psychological, biological, and social domains and of assessing interrelations among these systems at a particular point in ontogenesis (Cicchetti & Beeghly, 1990b; Hodapp & Zigler, 1990).

During the past two decades, a growing body of research has documented that infants with DS undergo developmental patterns and sequences that are highly similar to those of normally developing children, particularly during the sensorimotor period. For example, the following domains of development look remarkably coherent for children with DS: sequences of Piagetian stages of sensorimotor development (Cardoso-Martins & Mervis, 1985; Cicchetti & Mans-Wagener, 1987), interrelations between cognitive and affective development (Cicchetti & Sroufe, 1976, 1978; Thompson, Cicchetti, Lamb, & Malkin, 1985), organization of attachment, affiliation, and wariness behaviors (Cicchetti & Serafica, 1981; Serafica & Cicchetti, 1976), emergence of visual self-recognition (Loveland, 1987; Mans, Cicchetti, & Sroufe, 1978), negativism (Spiker, 1979), the development of eye contact (Berger & Cunningham, 1981; Jones, 1980), and maternal referencing (Sorce, Emde, & Frank, 1982). These similarities are especially noteworthy given the well-documented developmental delays of these children and certain abnormal features, such as motivational and attentional aberrations (Ganiban et al., 1990) and dampened affectivity, delayed responsivity, and slowed information processing (Cicchetti & Sroufe, 1976, 1978; Emde & Brown, 1978; Ganiban et al, 1990; Thompson, Cicchetti, Lamb, & Malkin, 1985; see Cicchetti & Beeghly, 1990b, for a review).

Fewer studies utilizing a developmental approach have focused on the transition from sensorimotor to representational functioning in infants and toddlers with DS. The marked expressive language delays in children with DS noted earlier make the investigation of the nature of this crucial transition, as well as the effect of this language delay on the emergence of symbolic play, especially important to examine in children with DS.

Symbolic Play Development in Children with Down Syndrome

According to the organizational perspective of development, it is important to assess a child's functioning in multiple domains and on stage-salient developmental issues (Cicchetti & Wagner, 1990). As such, the play context is excellent for elucidating developmental organization. Play is one of the most important tasks of the preoperational period, and it taps the intersection of cognitive, social, emotional, motivational, and linguistic development. As one illustration of these organismic developmental principles, it has been shown that play is a window on social understanding in both normal (Bretherton, 1984) and pathological (Beeghly, Weiss-Perry, & Cicchetti, 1990) groups of children.

The majority of previous studies of children with DS have focused primarily on the cognitive deficits of these children (Hodapp & Zigler, 1990). In addition, until recently, much of the extant data on play in children with DS have been seriously flawed on a number of methodological grounds and thus difficult to interpret (Quinn & Rubin, 1984). Recently, however, several investigators have focused on the study of children with DS from a developmental perspective, both to illuminate processes of normal play development and to uncover more specific information about the development of DS children. In support of the findings of previous play research in normal populations, these investigators have found significant positive correlations between symbolic play maturity and level of cognitive development, as assessed by standardized, psychometric tests (see, e.g., Beeghly & Cicchetti, 1987a; Hill & McCune-Nicolich, 1981; Motti, Cicchetti, & Sroufe, 1983; Riguet et al., 1981; Sigman & Mundy, 1987). Similarly, in a study of handicapped children of varying etiology, Wing et al. (1977) reported that no child with a mental age under 20 months engaged in symbolic play. Moreover, among the organically retarded subgroups studied, children with DS exhibited the most fluent and flexible symbolic play.

The *sequence* of early symbolic play development in children with DS also appears to be markedly similar to that observed in normally developing children (e.g., Beeghly & Cicchetti, 1987a; Hill & McCune-Nicolich, 1981; Motti et al., 1983). Although unfolding at a delayed pace, the play of children with DS progresses through the same sequences of decentration, decontextualization, and integration in object and social play that characterize the play of normally developing children, at least during early childhood (Werner & Kaplan, 1963).

In a recent study of symbolic play in our laboratory (Beeghly, Weiss-Perry, & Cicchetti, 1990), the development of four different aspects of symbolic play was examined in 30 children with DS. Each child with DS was individually matched to two nonhandicapped children for sex and for mental age or chronological age. Children and mothers were videotaped during a 30-minute free-play situation with a standard set of age-appropriate toys. Children's play was coded using four developmental play scales derived from empirical data reported in the play literature. The first scale focused on the increasing complexity and integration of action schemes ranging from single schemes to hierarchically integrated, multischemed play. The other scales were concerned with role representation. The first of these scales was concerned with social roles depicted in play with small figures (toys), and the second dealt with social roles in play with human partners. Scores on both of these social role scales ranged from self-related pretend behavior to integration of the roles of several actors. The last scale measured children's increasing decontextualization of object use, ranging from use of prototypical objects during play to gestural miming and verbal ideation of nonpresent objects. Two scores were derived from each of the four play scales: the highest level of play observed and the average level observed. In addition, the density (number of symbolic schemes per play bout) and complexity (number of different symbolic schemes per play bout) were assessed.

Results indicated that, for all children, mental age was significantly correlated with play maturity (both average and highest play levels) on each of the four scales, as well as with play density and play complexity. These findings support those reported in previous studies of both normal and delayed populations and attest to the developmental validity of the play scales.

Although the children with DS and their mental-age matched controls did not differ significantly on the highest level of play observed for each scale, for play density, or for play complexity, they had significantly lower *average* scores on each of the four play scales. Their lower average scores may be attributed to the tendency of children with DS to repeat the same schemes more often (a finding also noted by Kopp, Krakow, & Vaughn, 1983, and by Riguet et al., 1981). Specifically, it is likely that the different strategies utilized by the older children with DS reflect their slower information processing abilities. However, the fact that they attained symbolic play levels that were not significantly different from those of mental-age matched non-handicapped youngsters suggests that their alternative strategies did not interfere greatly with their ultimate play achievements.

Thus, despite certain differences, these results suggest that the symbolic play of children with DS, while delayed, continues to develop similarly in sequences to that observed in normal children during the transition from the sensorimotor to the pre-operational period. These findings also confirm and extend prior research with both normal and atypical populations documenting the relationship between symbolic play and cognitive development in early childhood.

Symbolic Play, Cognition, and Affect in Children with Down Syndrome

Piaget stressed that although the structure of play may be linked to emerging cognitive abilities, the motivational force behind play is often affective in nature (Piaget, 1981; Piaget & Inhelder, 1969). For normally developing children, correlations among measures of cognitive and affective dimensions of object play have been regarded as signs of *mastery motivation* (e.g., Jennings, Harmon, Morgan, Gaiter, & Yarrow, 1979) or *play style* (e.g., Fein & Apfel, 1979). In these studies, enthusiasm and persistence in object play have been associated with the complexity and maturity of object play. Similar interrelations between cognitive and affective dimensions of object play have been observed in children with DS. For example, in a longitudinal study of 31 children with DS, Motti and her colleagues (1983) found that the symbolic play of 3- to 5-year-old children with DS was qualitatively similar to that observed in cognitively comparable nonretarded children (e.g., Nicolich, 1977). Moreover, marked individual differences existed among these children. Children with higher levels of cognitive development engaged in more mature levels of symbolic and social play, explored toys more actively and thoroughly, were more enthusiastic during play, and exhibited more positive affect than less cognitively advanced children. The marked coherence of these children's affective–cognitive development was highlighted by the fact that both symbolic play maturity and affective play behavior were significantly correlated with cognitive and affective assessments that were collected in the first and second years of these children's lives. Specifically, affect ratings of these children at 10 months and scores from the Bayley mental scales made at 24 months both predicted later symbolic play maturity and affective-motivational play behavior at 3–5 years. Moreover, coherence among cognitive and affective behavior was observed in this sample throughout infancy. For example, cognitive developmental status at 16 months was predicted by affective ratings made at several earlier developmental points during the first year of life (Cicchetti & Sroufe, 1976, 1978).

These findings were partially replicated in a second study of symbolic play development in children with DS conducted in our laboratory (Beeghly, Weiss-Perry, & Cicchetti, 1989). In this study, developmental trends in play and children's affective and social behaviors during play were assessed in 35 children with DS. The behaviors of the children with DS were compared to those observed in two groups of nonretarded comparison children: one group individually matched to the DS children for sex and mental age and the other matched for sex and chronological age. A time-interval coding system assessing categories of object and social play found to follow developmental sequences and to be highly related to cognitive development in the play literature (e.g., Belsky & Most, 1981; Nicolich, 1977; Ungerer, Zelazo, Kearsley, & O'Leary, 1981) was used to assess the maturity of the children's spontaneous play. In addition, dimensions of affective-motivational play behavior (from Motti et al., 1983) and aspects of dyadic social behavior were rated independently from the videotapes by a second coder.

Significant intercorrelations among symbolic play maturity, level of cognitive development, affective-motivational play style, and social interaction skills were observed within each group of children (children with DS, mental-age controls, chronological-age controls), supporting and extending those reported by Motti et al. (1983) and Hill and McCune-Nicolich (1981). Moreover, developmental trends in object play that were similar to those reported for nondelayed children (Belsky & Most, 1981; Ungerer et al., 1981) were observed both in children with DS and in the nonhandicapped control children. For all children, the proportion of time spent in symbolic and structured social play increased significantly across cross-sectional age groups, whereas the reverse trend was observed for less mature forms of object play (e.g., simple object manipulation). Moreover, between-group comparisons revealed that children with DS did not differ from their mental-age–matched controls on any object play category.

However, as a group, children with DS did differ significantly from cognitively comparable controls on several measures of *social* behavior. DS children were found to engage in less social referencing with their mothers during object play (i.e., object sharing, joint attention seeking) and were rated as being less socially responsive and less initiating during the free-play period than were mental-age–matched controls. Similar unique characteristics have been reported in other studies of social behavior in infants with DS (e.g., Jones, 1980; MacTurk, Hunter, McCarthy, Vietze, & McQuiston, 1985; Mundy et al., 1988). However, despite these differences, within each group of children these social variables were significantly correlated with level of symbolic play maturity, affective-motivational style, and mental age. Thus, it appears that both DS and nonretarded children exhibit a similar organization of the social, affective, and cognitive domains of symbolic functioning.

Implications of Aberrant Social Development for Play Development in Children with Down Syndrome

Hypotheses concerning the nature and content of parent–child interactions in dyads with DS children are similar to those held in research with normal parent–child dyads. For example, both assume a bidirectional influence (e.g., Bell, 1968; Lewis & Rosenblum, 1974; Schaeffer, 1977). The role of parental support in guiding, stimulating, and supporting normal children's emerging symbolic abilities has often been stressed (e.g., Bruner & Sherwood, 1983; O'Connell & Bretherton, 1984; Vygotsky, 1962). Children with DS exhibit certain unique cognitive, physiological, and perceptual difficulties that place such interactions in jeopardy. For example, children with DS display delayed and dampened affect and social responsivity, which impairs the establishment of turn taking and reciprocity during play interactions (Cicchetti & Schneider-Rosen, 1984; Emde & Brown, 1978; Hesse & Cicchetti, 1982; Jones, 1980). These and other difficulties (e.g., decreased parental referencing during object play and social interaction and fewer social initiating behaviors—see Mundy et al., 1988) allow caregivers fewer opportunities to read, mark, and reward the behavior of children with DS (Berger, 1990). Taken together with their delayed developmental progress, play interactions with children with DS are often exhausting and unrewarding. Parental beliefs about their DS children's developmental delays or passivity may also elicit excess stimulation and directiveness on the part of the parent, an interactive strategy commonly used by parents of handicapped children of varying etiology (Cardoso-Martins, 1984; Cross, Nienhuys, & Kirkman, 1985; Cunningham, Reuben, Blackwell, & Deck, 1981; see also Bell & Harper, 1977).

It was usually assumed that an overly directive interactive style is detrimental to children's cognitive and linguistic development, since it is parent contingent rather than child contingent (e.g., Cardoso-Martins, 1984; Jones, 1980; Mervis, 1990). This interactive strategy may also be less than optimal for supporting symbolic play development. In one study, mothers of infants with DS who were most controlling and explicitly directive had children who took the least initiative and were less independent during play.

However, these findings are qualified by other research. Crawley and Spiker (1983), for example, examined the relation between maternal interactive style and 24-month-old DS children's interactive behavior and play maturity. Although they found that a significant number of mothers were rated very high on directiveness, interestingly they also found that many of these mothers were also rated high on sensitivity. Moreover, there were marked individual differences in social behavior among both children and mothers. Importantly, mothers who were both highly sensitive and highly directive were also rated as high on *stimulation value*, a dimension that was most highly correlated with children's play maturity, level of cognitive development, and social responsiveness.

Similar results were reported by Beeghly and her colleagues (1989). In this study, described earlier, mothers of children with DS were also found to be more directive and more assisting than mothers of nonhandicapped children. However, these mothers did not differ in rated dyadic harmony, positivity, or contingent responsivity to their children from mothers of nonhandicapped children at a similar level of cognitive development. Moreover, rated dyadic harmony was correlated with mental age for both children with DS and nonhandicapped children in this study, as Crawley and Spiker (1983) reported in their investigation. It appears that mothers of children with DS are able to overcome interactive difficulties with their children (see also Sorce & Emde, 1982). These findings have implications for intervention strategies. Instead of emphasizing parental stimulation or focusing solely on infant deficits, programs should attempt to improve the quality of social interaction and collaborative play between parent and children (Cicchetti & Mans-Wagener, 1987; Crawley & Spiker, 1983; Kennedy, Sheridan, Radlinski, & Beeghly, 1991).

Language and Symbolic Play Development in Children with Down Syndrome

The search for associations and dissociations among linguistic and nonlinguistic domains of symbolic development has long been of interest to developmental theorists (see Bates et al., 1987, 1988, and Rice, 1983, for reviews). More recently, practitioners working with language-delayed children have implemented research findings concerning early language–cognition relationships in an attempt to improve their diagnostic and treatment services (e.g., Kennedy et al., 1991).

Although the classical developmental hypothesis of a strong, generalized association among language and cognition in early ontogeny (the *semiotic function*: Piaget, 1962; Werner & Kaplan, 1963) has largely been discredited (see Bates et al., 1988; Bates, Thal, Whitesell, Fenson, & Oakes, 1989; and Rice, 1983, for reviews), a growing body of evidence for more limited and specific associations among aspects of language and symbolic play (*local homologies*: Bates, Benigni, Bretherton, Camaioni, & Volterra, 1979) has been reported for both normally and abnormally developing children.

For example, in studies of normally developing children, significant correlations between language and symbolic play have been reported by several investigators. In one longitudinal study of children from 9 to 13 months of age, symbolic play measures were the strongest predictors of communicative gesture and language ability (Bates et al., 1979). Other investigators also reported significant associations of symbolic play with language development (e.g., Fein, 1979; Largo & Howard, 1979).

Similar evidence from studies of children with delayed linguistic and cognitive development, such as children with DS or autistic children, also supports this local homology view. Wing and her colleagues (1977) found relationships between language comprehension and play maturity in a mixed group of retarded and autistic children. Similarly, Sigman and Ungerer (1984) reported significant correlations between receptive language and symbolic play maturity in mentally retarded (including children with DS), autistic, and normal groups of children. They also reported significant interrelations between receptive language and the ability to imitate gestures and vocalizations among all three groups (see Riguet et al., 1981, for similar findings).

In their longitudinal study of play–language relations in language-delayed preschoolers of varying etiology, Kennedy et al. (in press) found associations between specific aspects of early language development and symbolic play over time, confirming those reported in the literature for normally developing children. However, the variability of language and play behaviors across observations was more marked than was typically observed in normally developing children.

In our own studies of symbolic development in children with DS, we found evidence for both associations and dissociations among domains of symbolic play and language development in children with DS (see Beeghly & Cicchetti, 1987a; Beeghly et al., 1990, for reviews). Like other investigators (e.g., Mervis, 1990), we found that children with DS were markedly delayed in expressive language relative to their level of cognitive development. Syntactic development was most delayed, followed, in turn, by lexical and pragmatic development. Nonetheless, striking parallels between spontaneously occurring symbolic play and expressive language were observed, as follows: (1) no prelinguistic child engaged in any symbolic play; (2) children in the one-word stage of language development produced only single schemes in symbolic play; (3) children in early Stage I of language development (mean length of utterance [MLU] = 1.01–1.49: Brown, 1973; Miller, 1981) were beginning to combine simple symbolic schemes during play; and (4) children with more advanced language (i.e., in late Stage I or higher) produced planned, hierarchically integrated symbolic play bouts. Moreover, both MLU and mental age were significantly correlated with indices of symbolic play maturity for both children with DS and their cognitively matched, nonhandicapped controls. Specifically, the complexity of children's play schemes and their depiction of social roles during pretend play were closely tied to mental age, MLU, and pragmatic skills.

One exception to this remarkably coherent pattern was noted, however. Children with DS had particular trouble using objects in decontextualized ways during pretend play. Recall that these children also had particular difficulties in the acquisition of syntax. A problem with abstract symbol use may underlie both areas of relative deficit. In support of this notion, Bates et al. (1987, 1988) reported that normally developing children who engaged in frequent object substitutions during symbolic play were more likely to use a style of language acquisition (*analytical*) most predictive of later grammatical development.

Symbolic Play, Language, and Social Understanding in Children with Down Syndrome

In normally developing populations, children in the second and third years of life become increasingly aware of themselves as agents and recipients of action and of self–other differences (Kagan, 1981). Children manifest this emergent awareness in their use of language and symbolic play (Bretherton, 1984). For example, frequencies of self-descriptive utterances, personal pronouns, self-naming, and internal state words (used to label the emotional states, intentions, and volitions of self and other) increase dramatically during this period (Bretherton & Beeghly, 1982). In symbolic play, children also represent their early concepts of self and other. In both play and language use, children undergo a process of decentration, decontextualization, and integration (Fenson, 1984). That is, children first tend to refer to self and other in the here and now in both language and play, and later begin to use these domains to refer to past, future, hypothetical, pretend, or other decontextualized events.

In our laboratory, we investigated longitudinal changes in these aspects of play and language in children with DS during mother–child free play and during a structured mother–child picture book task (see Beeghly et al., 1990). We compared their performance with that observed in three groups of nonhandicapped children matched to the children with DS for mental age, chronological age, and MLU. Results indicated that in both DS and control groups, children underwent similar processes of decentration, decontextualization, and integration in both language and play. One exception was noted, however. Children with DS were more likely to use internal state language and utterances describing actions to refer to others, as opposed to themselves, relative to developmentally matched controls. In addition, only the most cognitively mature children in each group used language and play in hypothetical or nonpresent contexts. Despite developmental delays and certain aberrant features of DS symbolic processes, these results attest to the striking coherence of play, language, and social understanding in young children with DS.

Symbolic Development in Autism

Why Autism?

Autistic children represent another important group to study from an organizational, developmental psychopathology perspective. Like children with DS, most autistic children exhibit marked linguistic and cognitive retardation, show difficulties in specific social behaviors, and manifest wide individual differences in functioning (Cohen & Donellan, 1987; Dawson, 1989; Hobson, 1986; Ricks & Wing, 1976; Rutter, 1978; Rutter & Garmezy, 1983). However, the *specific* patterns of cognitive, socioemotional, and linguistic differences clearly differentiate autism from other handicaps (DeMyer, Hingten, & Jackson, 1981). In particular, three severe deficits in behavioral functioning distinguish autistic children from other retarded and psychiatric groups: (1) symbolic play, (2) communication and language, and (3) social interaction (Baron-Cohen, 1989; Hobson, 1986; Rutter & Garmezy, 1983; Sigman & Mundy, 1987). All of these primary deficits can be characterized by postulating a *social-cognitive deficit* in autistic children (Dawson, 1989; Rutter, 1978, 1983) that involves the serious impairment of symbolic skills such as symbolic play, language, and other related representational and metarepresentational domains (e.g., self vs. other) (Baron-Cohen, Leslie, & Frith, 1985; Leslie, 1987; Leslie & Frith, 1990). Many autistic children never develop language or symbolic play, but even in those who do, symbolic play is most often rigid, repetitive, and stereotyped, lacking the complexity, fluidity, and creativity observed in normal or mentally retarded children's play (Black, Freeman, & Montgomery, 1975; Riguet et al., 1981; Sigman & Mundy, 1987; Sigman & Ungerer, 1981; Wing et al., 1977).

Symbolic Play, Language, and Cognition in Children with Autism

As in most studies of handicapped children, until recently, investigators of symbolic development in autistic children rarely adopted a developmental framework. Instead, deficits in symbolic behaviors were assessed or physical similarities among behaviors alone were measured (e.g., Tilton & Ottinger, 1964). In the past 15 years, however, research on symbolization in autistic populations has approached the problem developmentally, resulting in findings that have important ramifications for the process and nature of symbol development in both normal and abnormal populations.

Deficits in both symbolic play and language were reported for autistic children by Sigman and her colleagues (Sigman & Mundy, 1987; Sigman & Ungerer, 1981). In one study, 16 autistic children showed less symbolic play (both spontaneously and after prompting) and more immature play than did 16 normal children at a similar level of cognitive development (mean mental age = 24.8 months). However, as reported for children with DS and for nonretarded children, play maturity was significantly correlated with mental age in both groups. Interestingly, autistic children with higher receptive language abilities exhibited more mature symbolic play, as well as longer sequences of integrated play, than did autistic children with low receptive language. Similarly, Riguet et al. (1981) assessed symbolic play in 10 autistic children, 10 children with DS, and 10 normally developing children of equivalent verbal mental age (mean mental age = 2.6 years) in both structured and free-play contexts. Results indicated that autistic children engaged in less symbolic play, produced fewer different symbolic uses of objects, and engaged in more off-task behavior than did either the children with DS or the normal children. However, symbolic fluency was significantly correlated with verbal mental age within each child group.

Autistic children also evidenced a marked impairment in their capacity to imitate (a deficit observed in autistic children by other investigators; see, e.g., DeMyer et al., 1972). Dawson and Adams (1984) reported similar findings and noted that many preschool-age autistic children functioned socially at a level comparable to normal 1- to 4-month-old infants. Interestingly, Dawson and Galpert (1987) later designed and implemented an intervention technique for promoting social effectance in autistic children based on the recognition that the emergence of early abilities needed to be promoted. Specifically, parents were taught to imitate the vocalizations and facial expressions of their autistic children.

In an update of their prior work, Sigman and Ungerer (1984) compared the sensorimotor skills, language development, and symbolic play behavior of autistic, mentally retarded, and normal children of equivalent mental age in order to identify deficits specific to autism. They found that the autistic children showed marked deficits both in play and in the capacity to imitate gestures and vocalizations, supporting their earlier work and confirming findings reported by Riguet et al. (1981). In all three groups, imitation and play were correlated significantly with receptive language. Recall that Piaget (1962) stressed that imitation, along with symbolic play and language, was part of children's emergent symbolic capacity. Interestingly, other sensorimotor skills thought to be indicative of representational abilities were associated with receptive language *only* for the normal and mentally retarded comparison groups. These findings indicate a striking *décalage* among sensorimotor skills involving representational thought in autistic children (see also Sigman & Ungerer, 1981) and suggest that autistic children have unique, specific deficits in imitation, symbolic play, and language that cannot be accounted for by level of cognitive development or degree of mental retardation alone.

Sigman and her colleagues (Sigman & Mundy, 1987; Sigman & Ungerer, 1984) posited that a defining characteristic of autism may be that autistic children are significantly *more* proficient in object permanence than in imitation and other symbolic activities. This finding has implications for theories of normal language development in that certain sensorimotor skills (e.g., object permanence) may not be as closely tied to language development as are other sensorimotor skills (e.g., imitation). Sigman and her collaborators hypothesize that object permanence may involve the capacity to recall information stored in memory necessary for problem solving rather than being specific to the emergence of symbolization.

To account for their results, this research team posited the existence of another related system that involves the ability to transform experience into play and linguistic symbols (Wolf & Grollman, 1982). In normally developing and mentally retarded children, these systems appeared to develop conjointly, since object permanence was significantly correlated with symbolic skills in these children. In autism, object permanence and symbolic capabilities do not appear to develop in tandem, suggesting that they are not interdependent systems.

Sigman and her colleagues proffer another related explanation for their results that is more consonant with that of prior investigators (Rutter, 1983). Specifically, they suggest that the symbolic impairment observed in autistic children may result from a striking social-cognitive deficit. This deficit appears to involve aberrations in specific aspects of representational abilities (e.g., imitation, joint attention, shared reference; Sigman & Mundy, 1987), as well as in the ability to process social experience. Because the acquisition of language, symbolic play, and imitation necessarily occurs in a social-communicative context, the ability to derive socially based information from social interaction and from observations of others is crucial for normal symbolic development (Mundy & Sigman, 1989). Autistic children's deficits in symbolic abilities may stem from their incapacity to utilize social-cognitive information. However, these deficits do not appear to derive from a solely motivational or socioemotional problem, since autistic children appear to have cognitive deficits in sequencing and abstraction that are not limited to symbolic domains (see Baron-Cohen et al., 1985; Cohen & Donellan, 1987; Dawson, 1989; Leslie, 1987; Rutter, 1983; and Sigman & Mundy, 1987, for reviews).

Language, Communication, and Social Knowledge in Children with Autism

As noted earlier, social-cognitive deficits are strikingly evident in autistic children's linguistic and communicative development. Autistic children have particular difficulty in comprehending and responding to "species-specific" social and communicative gestures, pragmatic uses of language and communication, pretend play, and so on (Curcio, 1978; Olley, 1985; Sigman, Mundy, Sherman, & Ungerer, 1986; Tinbergen & Tinbergen, 1972; Wing, 1981). Autistic children show deficits in the comprehension and use of each of these behaviors (Rutter & Garmezy, 1983). Lord (1985) has suggested that this broadly based difficulty with person-related knowledge interferes particularly with the acquisition of receptive language in autistic children. As Lord so cogently stated:

> For the [normal] infant, many of those interactions are with an adult, social and communicative meanings are constantly intertwined. . . . The child's early responses to language are appropriate, not because of "language" comprehension, but rather because of early developed abilities to use social and word knowledge in context and early established attention to speech and speakers. (p. 260)

That autistic children have trouble with symbolic processes, intertwined as they are with social and communicative meanings, is not surprising (see also Bretherton, 1984). Hermelin and O'Connor (1985) have termed this cognitive–affective problem a *logico-affective impairment*.

There is evidence that early *nonverbal* communication skills are associated with other representational capacities, such as language and symbolic play, in autistic children. Bruner (e.g., Bruner & Sherwood, 1983) has emphasized the importance of preverbal parent–child interaction for later language development. Mundy et al. (1986; see also Sigman & Mundy, 1987) assessed the relationship of nonverbal communication skills during social interaction to symbolic play and language in autistic children, mentally retarded children, and normal children of equivalent mental age. As reported in previous studies, marked individual differences in functioning were observed in the autistic children. Results indicated that both symbolic play and the capacity for establishing and maintaining joint attention during social interaction were significantly related to language and cognitive development in both autistic and cognitively comparable control children. However, partial correlational analysis indicated that symbolic play and joint attention had *partially independent* paths of association with language (see also Bates et al., 1979, for similar findings in normally developing children).

Symbolic play reflects representational abilities manifested in interactions with objects, whereas joint attention reflects representational processes inherent in social interaction. Both behaviors share the use of nonverbal signals serving communication in that both involve reference to objects and events. Werner and Kaplan (1963) posited that a child's understanding of reference and representational ability emerge conjointly in preverbal social interaction.

Since both symbolic play and joint attention were related to individual differences in language in autistic children, Mundy et al. (1986) suggested that assessment of symbolic play and nonverbal communication skills may provide a means of predicting the likelihood of language acquisition in autistic children. Both are also potentially useful targets for language intervention (see Schopler & Mesibov, 1985, for examples).

Social Understanding as Reflected in the Language of Autistic Children

In a series of studies, Tager-Flusberg (1989, 1992) compared children with autism and children with DS on several language and communication tasks designed to tap children's emergent "theory of mind." The two groups of children were matched on MLU (all could produce some language). Significant differences in the content, function, and form of language were observed between these groups, which Tager-Flusberg attributed to deficits in autistic children's social-cognitive understanding of self and other.

In one study, autistic children used strikingly fewer words referring to internal states, particularly mental or cognitive states such as thinking, knowing, and believing, than did children with DS. These results were interpreted as evidence for difficulties in explicitly referring to internal states. In a second study, Tager-Flusberg compared these groups on their ability to use language functionally within a conversation. Autistic children were significantly less likely to use language to exchange information during conversations with their mothers, revealing their lack of understanding that people can be sources of information. In a third study, Tager-Flusberg reported unique errors in the form of both questions and personal pronouns for children with autism, suggesting that these children lack understanding of speaker/listener roles and social perspective-taking during conversation (see also Baron-Cohen et al., 1985; Leslie, 1987).

In a similar series of studies, Loveland and her colleagues (Loveland, McEvoy, Tunali, & Kelley, 1990; Loveland, Tunali, Kelley, & McEvoy, 1989) reported that high-functioning children with autism performed significantly worse on both a referential communication task and a narrative storytelling task than did verbally matched children with DS. In the referential communication task, autistic children had poorer response adequacy and inappropriate use of gestures. In the storytelling task, autistic children had more difficulty grasping the story as a representation of meaningful events and were less aware of the listener's needs than were the children with DS.

Sigman and Mundy (1987) argue that this cognitive deficit in self–other understanding is basic to the social-cognitive deficit of children with autism commonly described in the literature. They posit that the development of social understanding is related fundamentally to social-affective development or, more precisely, affective relatedness. That is, aspects of social-cognitive understanding require some capacity to respond affectively, to be aware of the affective signals of self and other, and to see parallels between affective experiences of self and other. In children with autism, both social-cognitive and affective domains appear to be disordered (Baron-Cohen, 1989; Hobson, 1989; Leslie & Happe, 1989; Mundy & Sigman, 1989).

Social Development and Symbolic Processes in Children with Autism

It is well known that autistic children display abnormal social behavior (Kanner, 1943; Rutter, 1978; Wing, 1981). In his classic paper based on the observation of 11 autistic children, Kanner (1943) delineated extreme isolation and inability to relate to people ("autistic aloneness") as an essential criterion necessary for the diagnosis of autism.

Although there has been a great deal of clinical evidence and discussion in the literature about the social disturbances associated with autism, there has been little systematic study of the social *development* of these children (Rutter & Garmezy, 1983; Volkmar, 1987). This paucity of research may be due to the fact that many investigators have attributed the social impairments of autistic children to a more central cognitive deficit (Cox, Rutter, Newman, & Bartak, 1975; Hermelin & O'Connor, 1970; Wing, 1969). However, a recent renewal of interest in the study of social development in autistic children has been generated by the findings of the follow-up studies conducted on these children. A striking result of these longitudinal investigations is that the cognitive, linguistic, and social development of autistic children do not advance conjointly (Dawson & Lewy, 1989; Rutter & Garmezy, 1983). There is no central deficit that can account for all of the deviations associated with autism (Cantwell, Baker, & Rutter, 1978; Cohen & Donellan, 1987; Dawson, 1989; Frith, 1989; Mundy & Sigman, 1989; Rutter, 1978). Additionally, research has revealed that although autistic children deviate significantly from normal children, the severity of functioning varies greatly for each child (Lotter, 1978; Wing, 1978). Hence, several investigators have adopted a developmental model for studying the functioning of children with autism (see Baron-Cohen et al., 1985; Mundy & Sigman, 1989; Rutter & Garmezy, 1983, for a review). This approach has brought about a clearer understanding of the nature of each child's deviations and how the pattern of development is different from that of normal children.

The few studies that have investigated the early social development of autistic children directly have yielded results that run counter to earlier clinical portrayals of these children. For example, Ferrari and Matthews (1983) found evidence contrary to the notion that autistic children have an undifferentiated sense of self. In a study of the development of self-awareness in 15 autistic children, they found that over one-half of their sample evidenced clear self-directed behavior in a mirror-and-rouge self-recognition task (Amsterdam, 1972; Lewis & Brooks-Gunn, 1979). Moreover, it was found that those children who evinced visual self-recognition had significantly higher mental ages than those who did not recognize themselves. Thus, Ferrari and Matthews (1983) suggested that an undifferentiated sense of self seems to be a reflection of an overall developmental lag rather than a clinical characteristic of autism.

Similarly, the development of the capacity for visual self-recognition has been found to be associated with language development in autistic children. In their study of 52 autistic children (mean chronological age = 7.7 years), Spiker and Ricks (1984) found that 36 (69%) children showed mirror self-recognition. Those 16 without self-recognition were much more likely to be mute or to be lacking in communicative speech than those who could recognize themselves. Although this relation between this aspect of self-development and language was statistically significant, there was not a perfect correspondence between these two domains. Specifically, some children who recognized themselves had no language, whereas some who did not possessed communicative abilities. Consequently, though language may be important, it is not necessary and/or sufficient to explain the development of self-recognition.

Dawson and her colleagues (Dawson & Adams, 1984; Dawson & Galpert, 1986) provided evidence to suggest that autistic children's failure to imitate others, one of the earliest forms of communication, plus their deficits in the processing of verbal information, contribute significantly to their lack of social relatedness. In addition, the results of the development of visual self-recognition in autistic children reveal interesting information about the affective concomitants of their early self-aware-ness. Spiker and Ricks (1984) found that, unlike normal children (Lewis & Brooks-Gunn, 1979) or children with DS (Mans et al., 1978), 75% of the autistic children who recognized themselves exhibited accompanying neutral or negative as opposed to positive affect. Similarly, Schneider-Rosen and Cicchetti (1984) found that approximately three-fourths of maltreated youngsters showed neutral or negative affective reactions to their rouge-marked mirror self-images. While the meaning of these results, as well as their underlying developmental organization, are most cer-tainly different for autistic and maltreated children (e.g., the communicative devel-opment of maltreated children, though impaired, is far more advanced and normal than in autistic children; Gersten, Coster, Schneider-Rosen, Carlson, & Cicchetti, 1986), it is almost certain that the relationship between affect and cognition is impaired in both of these groups of atypical children (Cicchetti & Schneider-Rosen, 1984).

Other deficits in social-related understanding are also characteristic of autistic children. In a series of studies, Hobson (1983, 1984, 1986) reported evidence that autistic children showed marked impairments in recognizing and integrating attri-butes that are characteristic of people (e.g., differentiation of man, woman, boy, girl) and emotions (differentiation of happy, sad, angry, etc.). The same autistic children had far less difficulty in relating different characteristics of objects to each other. Following Kanner (1943), Hobson (1986) suggested that this deficit may be partially due to autistic children's difficulties in establishing reciprocity and bonding with others in early development. In normal children, he claims, such "person knowl-edge" is thought to arise from reciprocal social interaction and resulting feelings of "personal relatedness" with others. As a consequence of this deficit, autistic children are thought to acquire only a partial and distorted knowledge of person (Hermelin & O'Connor, 1985; Hobson, 1984, 1986). Rutter and Garmezy (1983) suggest that these findings are indicative of a cognitive deficit in the processing of stimuli relevant to affect and socialization, although the nature of the deficit remains obscure.

In their recent review, Dawson and Lewy (1989) proposed that autistic chil-dren's socioemotional impairments are closely linked to deficiencies in both arousal modulation and attention to social and nonsocial stimuli. They argue that deficiencies in arousal modulation directly influence autistic children's attention to, and processing of, social and nonsocial information as well as affective expression.

Sigman and Ungerer (1984) observed a group of 14 autistic children and a group of 14 normal children of equivalent mental age (mean mental age = 24.1 months) during free play and "strange-situation" (Ainsworth, Blehar, Waters, & Wall, 1978) contexts. Again, contrary to past clinical and observational evidence, it was found that autistic children were capable of differentiating between mother and strangers, and they exhibited some attachment behaviors similar to those of normal children. The results of this study also suggest that the capacity for attachment relationships was related to representational abilities. In normal children, it is generally found that the milestone of object permanence is a prerequisite for the demonstration of attachment behaviors. However, although all autistic children in this study evidenced object permanence, not all of them showed attachment behaviors. This finding implies that autistic children may require higher levels of symbolic maturity than normal children before they can demonstrate attachment behaviors.

Pointing to the bidirectional nature of parent–child relations, Dawson and Galpert (1988) examined autistic children's emotional displays and eye contact during social interaction with their mothers. Although autistic children produced rates of eye contact and emotional displays similar to those of developmentally matched controls, the autistic children had more difficulty combining emotion and eye contact in a way that conveys communicative intent. Dawson and Galpert suggested that this failure to use sustained eye contact in combination with social smiling may be interpreted by the mother as a signal that the child is not interested in social interaction with her. This interpretation might tend to curtail or terminate social interaction and reduce the frequency of the mother's positive emotional displays, thus contributing to difficulties in the establishment of parent–child attachment.

Conclusions and Future Perspectives

Throughout this chapter, we have contended that the study of atypical populations can enhance our understanding of the ontogenesis of normal symbolic processes. Specifically, the slower rate of development of children with DS and with autism allows us to explore in greater detail convergences and discontinuities among developmental domains. Because ample evidence is accumulating that the various domains of psychological development (e.g., social, emotional, cognitive, personality, language) are separate yet interacting systems (Hesse & Cicchetti, 1982; Izard, 1977), the study of the structure of these systems in atypical children can augment our knowledge concerning the nature of their interrelations in normal populations (Cicchetti & Schneider-Rosen, 1984). Moreover, we have stated that a developmental framework can enhance our understanding of the disorganization inherent in pathological development. Along similar lines, Cicchetti and Schneider-Rosen (1984, 1986) noted that atypical developmental patterns are best conceptualized as resulting from the lack of integration, organization, and differentiation of cognitive, linguistic, social, emotional, and biological development when considered in terms of the psychologically relevant competencies that are expected to emerge in the different domains and the salient developmental tasks that need to be accomplished (Greenspan, 1981; Sroufe, 1979).

An examination of the symbolic functioning of children with DS revealed that they were more delayed in expressive language than they were in nonlinguistic symbolic domains such as symbolic play (see also McConkey & Martin, 1985). Nonetheless, though delayed and somewhat atypically developing, the representational system of youngsters with DS was relatively intact. These results of studies of representational abilities extended earlier work that found striking similarity between the organization of development in infants with DS and mental-age–matched, nonhandicapped infants (Cicchetti & Mans-Wagener, 1987; Cicchetti & Serafica, 1981; Cicchetti & Sroufe, 1976, 1978; Mans et al., 1978; Thompson, Cicchetti, Lamb, & Malkin, 1985). The continued coherent nature of development beyond the sensorimotor period found in youngsters with DS extends and elaborates our earlier claims that their development is adaptive, organized, and meaningful (Cicchetti & Pogge-Hesse, 1982). Whereas most other groups of organically retarded children manifest vast differences and incoherence in their developmental organization from mental-age–matched normal children, youngsters with DS clearly show many striking similarities to their normal counterparts. These results suggest that the assumption that all organically mentally retarded children manifest abnormal development across all domains is incorrect. Just as it is necessary to keep etiological subgroups of mental retardation pure (e.g., cultural-familial vs. organic comparisons), it is equally critical to keep separate the various types of etiologies subsumed under the organic rubric (e.g., children with DS and hydrocephalic children should be analyzed independently).

In children with DS, where the basic social-communicative system is intact, a coherent, albeit slowed, pattern of development emerges. In autistic children, however, in whom the social-communicative system is disordered, disorganization is present. Moreover, object permanence and imitation, two abilities long presumed to require the same sorts of skills, do not cohere in autistic children.

When exploring the symbolic play of children with DS and autism, some noteworthy differences emerged. In our laboratory, we found that the symbolic play of children with DS reflected their social knowledge. With development, children with DS showed increasingly differentiated concepts of self and other in their enactive play schemes (Weiss, Beeghly, & Cicchetti, 1985). In addition, parallel advances were found in their ability to utilize language as a communicative social tool (Beeghly et al., 1990; Cicchetti & Beeghly, 1990a). Likewise, the self-language of children with DS (e.g., talking about their ongoing activities, using personal pronouns, giving adult directives, talking about their internal states) was highly related to advances in symbolic and cognitive development (Beeghly et al., 1990; Cicchetti, Beeghly, Carlson, & Toth, 1990). Interestingly, internal state language occurred significantly more often during symbolic play than during other kinds of play both in children with DS and in their nonhandicapped mental-age counterparts. These results are consistent with Kaplan's (1966) conceptualization that in normal development the process of symbolization becomes increasingly autonomous and that the self becomes more cognizant of its symbolic activities.

In autism, however, we do not observe this relative state of coherence. An *incoherence* in the development of autists emerges that is much akin to fractures in a crystal. This process appears to be much closer to Kaplan's (1966) descriptions of the primitive and syncretically fused symbolization that accompanies psychopathology. As Rutter (1983) has argued persuasively, there is strong support for the existence of a basic cognitive defect in autism. Despite the fact that Kanner (1943) labeled autism a disorder of affective contact, until recently the social-emotional abnormalities of autistic children have been the least investigated features of the syndrome. The results of the studies that have been conducted within the past decade converge and support the thesis that stimuli that are emotionally or socially laden pose the most difficulty for autistics. Apart from what this may reveal about how their autonomic and central nervous systems work, it is clear that there are abnormal processes preventing the normal integration of developing systems in autism and that some of these deviations may be socioemotional in nature. Thus, despite evidence revealing strong cognitive and social-cognitive components in autism (Baron-Cohen et al., 1985; Leslie, 1987), it is important to consider the socioemotional aspects of the disorder concomitantly (Hobson, 1990; Mundy & Sigman, 1989). Therefore, we believe that more research must be directed toward exploring the interrelations among the neurobiological, cognitive, affective, and symbolic domains in autism.

Implications for Other Atypical Populations

It is likely that the study of the role that the social communicative system plays in the emergence of language and play will illuminate the course of symbolization in other atypical populations. For example, we believe that the symbolic system of maltreated children (i.e., children who have been abused and/or neglected) should be investigated in great detail. Maltreated youngsters tend to form insecure attachment relationships (Carlson, Cicchetti, Barnett, & Braunwald, 1989; Crittenden, 1988; Schneider-Rosen, Braunwald, Carlson, & Cicchetti, 1985). Those who are insecurely attached show increasingly poor communicative development between the second and third years of life (Beeghly & Cicchetti, 1987b; Cicchetti, 1990b; Cicchetti & Beeghly, 1987; Cicchetti et al., 1990; Coster et al., 1989; Gersten et al., 1986). Important are the relative deficits and rapid decline in self-related language maltreated children manifest during this time period (Beeghly et al., 1989; Cicchetti, 1990c). It will be important to ascertain how these social-communicative difficulties affect symbolic development in later ontogeny. Similarly, the study of symbolic development in children of unipolar and bipolar depressed parents should reveal interesting information about symbolic processes (Cicchetti & Aber, 1986). For example, Egeland and Sroufe (1981) found that the offspring of ''psychologically unavailable'' caregivers manifested great decrements in cognitive functioning between 9 and 24 months. Perhaps psychological unavailability is one of the common features shared by some maltreating parents and most depressed parents that affects the security of the attachment relationship between parent and child (Cummings & Cicchetti, 1990). The episodic nature of the affective disorders makes it highly likely that there will be impairments in social-communicative functioning during the unremitted periods of the parent's illness. It may also prove to be the case that some of the sequelae remain during the remission phases (Field, 1989).

For theoretical as well as for empirical reasons, Cicchetti and Aber (1986) have argued that the toddlerhood period will prove to be a highly difficult one for the children of depressed parents. One reason is that the toddler's developing competencies and characteristic behavioral styles during this stage of development may prove to be particularly taxing to a depressed parent. Another factor could be that during late infancy/early toddlerhood, many of the social, emotional, and cognitive competencies implicated in later depression are at crucial stages of development (e.g., the development of an autonomous self, the ontogenesis of the affect of shame, and the construction of an internal working model or representation of the availability of attachment figures).

In addition to the toddler's possible contribution to the problematic social communicative system between a depressed mother and her infant, at least two features of the depressed mother's caretaking attitudes and behaviors could distort this system as well. The mother's psychological unavailability deprives her infant of a feeling of security and of the establishment of a secure base. Even when the mother is available, the depressed mother gives her child virtually no encouragement to be open to new experiences (Cicchetti, 1990b; Field, 1989). Moreover, the mother's overprotectiveness discourages her infant's exploration (Davenport, Zahn-Waxler, Adland, & Mayfield, 1984; Levy, 1944). Given the depressed mother's seemingly paradoxical combination of unavailability and overprotectiveness, the new representational and motoric capacities that burgeon during the first half of the second year of life will most likely be experienced by the mother as difficult, taxing, and challenging. This confluence of child and maternal "risk" and "challenger" factors (Cicchetti & Aber, 1986) could affect these toddlers' symbolic development.

It remains to be seen how similar to or different from normal the underlying processes of symbolization are in maltreated children and in children of depressed caregivers. We are confident that the results of such investigations will enhance our understanding of the normal and abnormal processes of symbolization in ways similar to those uncovered in research with other atypical groups of children. Once syndrome-specific impairments are discovered, the next step will be to identify and implement developmentally appropriate interventions that are targeted at ameliorating these difficulties (see Cicchetti, 1990b; Cicchetti, Toth, & Bush, 1988, for an elaboration).

ACKNOWLEDGMENTS

Support for portions of the research on symbolic development in children with Down syndrome presented in this chapter was provided by Grant No. 12-127 from the March of Dimes Birth Defects Foundation, by a grant from the Spencer Foundation, and by a grant from the John D. and Catherine T. MacArthur Network on the Transition from Infancy to Early Childhood. Partial support for preparation of this manuscript was provided by a postdoctoral fellowship to author Beeghly from the John D. and Catherine T. MacArthur Network on the Transition from Infancy to Early Childhood. We thank Donna Bowman for typing this manuscript and express our appreciation to both editors for their thoughtful assistance with the preparation of this chapter. We also thank Laraine Cicchetti, Sheree Toth, and Jennifer White for their constructive comments on a prior version of this manuscript. Correspondence should be addressed to Dante Cicchetti, Director, Mt. Hope Family Center, University of Rochester, 187 Edinburgh Street, Rochester, NY 14608.

REFERENCES

Ainsworth, M. D. S., Blehar, M., Waters, E., & Wall, S. (1978). *Patterns of attachment: A psychological study of the strange situation.* Hillsdale, NJ: Erlbaum.

Amsterdam, B. (1972). Mirror self-image reactions before age two. *Developmental Psychobiology, 5,* 297–305.

Baron-Cohen, S. (1989). The autistic child's theory of mind: A case of specific developmental delay? *Journal of Child Psychology and Psychiatry, 30,* 285–297.

Baron-Cohen, S., Leslie, A., & Frith, U. (1985). Does the autistic child have a theory of mind? *Cognition, 21,* 37–46.

Bates, E., Benigni, L., Bretherton, I., Camaioni, L., & Volterra, V. (1979). *The emergence of symbols: Cognitions and communication in infancy.* New York: Academic Press.

Bates, E., Bretherton, I., & Snyder, L. (1988). *From first words to grammar.* New York: Cambridge University Press.

Bates, E., O'Connell, B., & Shore, C. (1987). Language and communication in infancy. In J. Osofsky (Ed.), *Handbook of infant development* (pp. 149–203). New York: Wiley.

Bates, E., Thal, D., Whitesell, K., Fenson, L., & Oakes, L. (1989). Integrating language and gesture in infancy. *Developmental Psychology, 25,* 1004–1019.

Beeghly, M., Bretherton, I., & Mervis, C. (1986). Mothers' internal state language to toddlers. *British Journal of Development Psychlogy, 4,* 247–261.

Beeghly, M., Carlson, V., & Cicchetti, D. (1989). Child maltreatment, language, and the self system: Emergence of an internal state lexicon in maltreated 31-month-olds. Unpublished manuscript. Children's Hospital, Boston.

Beeghly, M., & Cicchetti, D. (1987a). An organizational approach to symbolic development in children with Down syndrome. *New Directions for Child Development, 36,* 5–29.

Beeghly, M., & Cicchetti, D. (1987b, April). Child maltreatment, attachment and the self: The emergence of internal state language in low SES children. Presented at the biennial meetings of the Society for Research in Child Development, Baltimore, MD.

Beeghly, M., Weiss-Perry, B., & Cicchetti, D. (1989). Structural and affective dimensions of free play behavior in children with Down syndrome. *International Journal of Behavioral Development, 12,* 257–277.

Beeghly, M., Weiss-Perry, B., & Cicchetti, D. (1990). Beyond sensorimotor functioning: Early communicative and play development of children with Down syndrome. In D. Cicchetti & M. Beeghly (Eds.), *Children with Down syndrome: A developmental perspective* (pp. 329–368). New York: Cambridge University Press.

Bell, R. Q. (1968). A reinterpretation of studies on the direction of effects in studies of socialization. *Psychological Review, 75,* 81–95.

Bell, R. Q., & Harper, L. (1977). *Child effects on adults.* Hillsdale, NJ: Erlbaum.

Belsky, J., & Most, R. (1981). From exploration to play: A cross-sectional study of infant free play behavior. *Developmental Psychology, 17,* 630–639.

Berger, J. (1990). Interactions between parents and their infants with Down syndrome. In D. Cicchetti & M. Beeghly (Eds.), *Children with Down syndrome: A developmental perspective* (pp. 101–146). New York: Cambridge University Press.

Berger, J., & Cunningham, C. (1981). The development of eye contact between mothers of normal versus Down syndrome infants. *Developmental Psychology, 17,* 678–689.

Bischof, N. (1975). A systems approach toward the functional connections of attachment and fear. *Child Development, 46,* 801–817.

Black, M., Freeman, B., & Montgomery, J. (1975). Systematic observation of play in autistic children. *Journal of Autism and Childhood Schizophrenia, 5,* 363–371.

Bretherton, I. (1984). Representing the social world in symbolic play: Reality and fantasy. In I. Bretherton (Ed.), *Symbolic play* (pp. 1–41). New York: Academic Press.

Bretherton, I., & Beeghly, M. (1982). Talking about internal states: The acquisition of an explicit theory of mind. *Developmental Psychology, 18*, 906–921.

Brown, R. (1973). *A first language*. Cambridge, MA: Harvard University Press.

Bruner, J., & Sherwood (1983). Thought–language interaction in infancy. In J. D. Call, E. Gallenson, & R. L. Tyson (Eds.), *Frontiers of infant psychiatry* (pp. 38–51). New York: Basic Books.

Cantwell, D., Baker, L., & Rutter, M. (1978). A comparative study of infantile autism and specific developmental receptive language disorder. IV. Analysis of syntax and language function. *Journal of Child Psychology and Psychiatry, 19*, 351–362.

Cardoso-Martins, C. (1984). *Early vocabulary acquisition by Down syndrome children: The roles of cognitive development and maternal language input*. Doctoral dissertation, University of Illinois at Champaign-Urbana.

Cardoso-Martins, C., & Mervis, C. B. (1985). The transition from sensorimotor Stage 5 to Stage 6 by Down syndrome children: A response to Gibson. *American Journal of Mental Deficiency, 90*, 177–184.

Carlson, V., Cicchetti, D., Barnett, D., & Braunwald, K. (1989). Disorganized/disoriented attachment relationships in maltreated infants. *Developmental Psychology, 25*, 525–531.

Cicchetti, D. (1984). The emergence of developmental psychopathology. *Child Development, 55*, 1–7.

Cicchetti, D. (1990a). An historical perspective on the discipline of developmental psychopathology. In J. Rolf, A. Masten, D. Cicchetti, K. Neuchterlein, and S. Weintraub (Eds.), *Risk and protective factors in the development of psychopathology* (pp. 2–28). New York: Cambridge University Press.

Cicchetti, D. (1990b). Developmental psychopathology and the prevention of serious mental disorders: Overdue détente and illustrations through the affective disorders. In P. Muehrer (Ed.), *Conceptual research models for prevention of mental disorders* (pp. 215–254). Rockville, MD: National Institutes of Mental Health.

Cicchetti, D. (1990c). The organization and coherence of socioemotional, cognitive, and representational development: Illustrations through a developmental psychopathology perspective on Down syndrome and child maltreatment. In R. Thompson (Ed.), *Nebraska symposium on motivation:* Vol. 36, *Socioemotional development* (pp. 275–382). Lincoln: University of Nebraska Press.

Cicchetti, D., & Aber, J. L. (1986). Early precursors of later depression. In L. Lipsitt and C. Rovee-Collier (Eds.), *Advances in infancy research* (Vol. 4, pp. 87–137). Norwood, NJ: Ablex.

Cicchetti, D., & Beeghly, M. (1987). Symbolic development in maltreated youngsters: An organizational perspective. *New Directions for Child Development, 36*, 47–68.

Cicchetti, D., & Beeghly, M. (Eds.). (1990a). *Children with Down syndrome: A developmental perspective*. New York: Cambridge University Press.

Cicchetti, D., & Beeghly, M. (1990b). An organizational approach to the study of Down syndrome: Contributions to an integrative theory of development. In D. Cicchetti & M. Beeghly (Eds.), *Children with Down syndrome: A developmental perspective* (pp. 29–62). New York: Cambridge University Press.

Cicchetti, D., Beeghly, M., Carlson, V., & Toth, S. (1990). The emergence of the self in atypical populations. In D. Cicchetti & M. Beeghly (Eds.), *The self in transition: Infancy to childhood* (pp. 309–344). Chicago: Chicago University Press.

Cicchetti, D., Ganiban, J., & Barnett, D. (1991). Contributions from the study of high risk populations to understanding the development of emotion regulation. In K. Dodge & J. Garber (Eds.), *The development of emotion regulation* (pp. 15–48). New York: Cambridge University Press.

Cicchetti, D., & Hesse, P. (1983). Affect and intellect: Piaget's contributions to the study of infant emotional development. In R. Plutchik & H. Kellerman (Eds.), *Emotion: Theory and research* (Vol. 2, pp. 115–169). New York: Academic Press.

Cicchetti, D., & Mans-Wagener L. (1987). Stages, sequences, and structures in the organization of cognitive development in Down syndrome infants. In I. Uzgiris & J. M. Hunt (Eds.), *Research with scales of psychological development in infancy* (pp. 281–310). Urbana: University of Illinois Press.

Cicchetti, D., & Pogge-Hesse, P. (1982). Possible contributions of the study of organic mentally retarded children to developmental theory. In E. Zigler & D. Balla (Eds.), *Mental retardation: The developmental difference controversy* (pp. 277–318). New York: Erlbaum.

Cicchetti, D., & Rizley, R. (1981). Developmental perspectives on the etiology, intergenerational transmission and sequelae of child maltreatment. *New Directions for Child Development, 11*, 32–59.

Cicchetti, D., & Schneider-Rosen, K. (1984). Theoretical and empirical considerations in the investigation of the relationship between affect and cognition in atypical populations of infants: Contributions to the formulation of an integrative theory of development. In C. Izard, J. Kagan, & R. Zajonc (Eds.), *Emotions, cognition, and behavior* (pp. 366–406). New York: Cambridge University Press.

Cicchetti, D., & Schneider-Rosen, K. (1986). An organizational approach to childhood depression. In M. Rutter, C. Izard, & P. Read (Eds.), *Depression in young people: Clinical and developmental perspectives* (pp. 71–134). New York: Guilford Press.

Cicchetti, D., & Serafica, F. (1981). The interplay among behavioral systems: Illustrations from the study of attachment, affiliation, and wariness in young Down syndrome children. *Developmental Psychology, 17*, 36–49.

Cicchetti, D., & Sroufe, L. A. (1976). The relationship between affective and cognitive development in Down's syndrome infants. *Child Development, 47*, 920–929.

Cicchetti, D., & Sroufe, L.A. (1978). An organizational view of affect: Illustration from the study of Down's syndrome infants. In M. Lewis & L. Rosenblum (Eds.), *The development of affect* (pp. 309–350). New York: Plenum Press.

Cicchetti, D., Toth, S., & Bush, M. (1988). Developmental psychopathology and incompetence in childhood: Suggestions for intervention. In B. Lahey & A. Kazdin (Eds.), *Advances in clinical child psychology* (pp. 1–71). New York: Plenum Press.

Cicchetti, D., & Wagner, S. (1990). Alternative assessment strategies for the evaluation of infants and toddlers: An organizational perspective. In S. Meisels & J. Shonkoff (Eds.), *Handbook of early intervention* (pp. 246–277). New York: Cambridge University Press.

Cohen, D., & Donellan, A. (Eds.). (1987). *Handbook of autism and atypical development.* New York: Wiley.

Coster, W., Gersten, M., Beeghly, M., & Cicchetti, D. (1989). Communicative development in maltreated and nonmaltreated 31-month-olds. *Developmental Psychology, 25*, 1020–1029.

Cox, A., Rutter, M., Newman, S., & Bartak, L. (1975). A comparative study of infantile autism and specific developmental receptive language disorder. II. Parental characteristics. *British Journal of Psychiatry, 126*, 146–159.

Coyle, J., Oster-Granite, M., & Gearhart, J. (1986). The neurobiologic consequences of Down syndrome. *Brain Research Bulletin, 16*, 773–787.

Crawley, S., & Spiker, D. (1983). Mother–child interactions and mental development in two-year-olds with Down syndrome. *Child Development, 54,* 1312–1323.

Crittenden, P. (1988). Relationships at risk. In J. Belsky & T. Nezworski (Eds.), *Clinical implications of attachment* (pp. 136–174). Hillsdale, NJ: Elbaum.

Cross, T., Nienhuys, T., & Kirkman, M. (1985). Parent–child interaction with receptively disabled children: Some determinants of maternal speech style. In K. Nelson (Ed.), *Children's language* (Vol. 5, pp. 247–290). Hillsdale, NJ: Erlbaum.

Cummings, E. M., & Cicchetti, D. (1990). Attachment, depression, and the transmission of depression. In M. T. Greenberg, D. Cicchetti, and E. M. Cummings (Eds.), *Attachment during the preschool years* (pp. 339–372). Chicago: University of Chicago Press.

Cunningham, C., Reuben, E., Blackwell, J., & Deck, J. (1981). Behavioral and linguistic developments in the interactions of normal and retarded children with their mothers. *Child Development, 52,* 62–70.

Curcio, F. (1978). Sensorimotor functioning and communication in mute autistic children. *Journal of Autism and Childhood Schizophrenia, 8,* 281–291.

Davenport, Y., Zahn-Waxler, C., Adland, M., & Mayfield, A. (1984). Early childrearing practices in families with manic-depressive parents. *American Journal of Psychiatry, 14,* 230–235.

Dawson, G. (Ed.). (1989). *Autism.* New York: Guilford Press.

Dawson, G., & Adams, A. (1984). Imitation and social responsiveness in autistic children. *Journal of Abnormal Child Psychology, 12,* 209–225.

Dawson, G., & Galpert, L. (1986). A developmental model for facilitating the social behavior of autistic children. In E. Schopler & G. Mesibov (Eds.), *Social behavior in autism* (pp. 237–256). New York: Plenum Press.

Dawson, G., & Galpert, L. (1987, April). Mothers' use of imitative play for facilitating eye contact and toy play in autistic children. Presented at the biennial meetings of the Society for Research in Child Development, Baltimore, MD.

Dawson, G., & Galpert, L. (1988, April). Affective exchanges between young autistic children and their mothers. Presented at the International Conference on Infant Studies, Washington, DC.

Dawson, G., & Lewy, A. (1989). Arousal, attention, and the socioemotional impairments of individuals with autism. In G. Dawson (Ed.), *Autism: New perspectives on nature, diagnosis, and treatment* (pp. 49–74). New York: Guilford Press.

DeMyer, M. K., Alpern, G. D., Barton, S., DeMyer, W. E., Churchill, D. W., Hingten, J. N., Bryson, C. Q., Pontius, W., & Kimberlin, C. (1972). Imitation in autistic, early schizophrenic, and nonpsychotic subnormal children. *Journal of Autism and Childhood Schizophrenia, 2,* 264–287.

DeMyer, M. K., Hingten, J. N., & Jackson, R. K. (1981). Infantile autism reviewed: A decade of research. *Schizophrenia Bulletin, 7,* 388–451.

Egeland, B., & Sroufe, L. A. (1981). Developmental sequelae of maltreatment in infancy. In R. Rizley & D. Cicchetti (Eds.), *Developmental perspectives on child maltreatment* (pp. 77–92). San Francisco: Jossey-Bass.

Emde, R., & Brown, C. (1978). Adaptation to the birth of a Down's syndrome infant: Grieving and maternal attachment. *Journal of the American Academy of Child Psychiatry, 17,* 299–323.

Fein, G. (1979). Echoes from the nursery: Piaget, Vygotsky, and the relationship between language and play. *New Directions for Child Development, 6,* 1–14.

Fein, G., & Apfel, N. (1979). The development of play: Style, structure, and situation. *Genetic Psychology Monographs, 99,* 231–250.

Fenson, L. (1984). Developmental trends for action and speech in pretend play. In I. Bretherton (Ed.), *Symbolic play* (pp. 249–270). New York: Academic Press.

Ferrari, M., & Matthews, W. (1983). Self-recognition deficits in autism: Syndrome-specific or general developmental delay. *Journal of Autism and Developmental Disorders, 13*, 317–324.

Field, T. (1989). Maternal depression effects on infant interaction and attachment behavior. In D. Cicchetti (Ed.), *Rochester symposium on developmental psychopathology* (Vol. 1, pp. 139–163). Hillsdale, NJ: Elbaum.

Fowler, A. (1990). Language abilities in children with Down syndrome: Evidence for a specific syntactic delay. In D. Cicchetti & M. Beeghly (Eds.), *Children with Down syndrome: A developmental perspective* (pp. 302–328). New York: Cambridge University Press.

Frith, U. (1989). *Autism: Explaining the enigma.* Oxford: Blackwell.

Ganiban, J., Wagner, S., & Cicchetti, D. (1990). Temperament and Down syndrome. In D. Cicchetti & M. Beeghly (Eds.), *Children with Down syndrome: A developmental perspective* (pp. 63–100). New York: Cambridge University Press.

Gersten, M., Coster, W., Schneider-Rosen, K., Carlson, V., & Cicchetti, D. (1986). The socioemotional bases of communicative functioning. Quality of attachment, language development, and early maltreatment. In M. E. Lamb, A. L. Brown, & B. Rogoff (Eds.), *Advances in developmental psychology* (Vol. 4, pp. 105–151). Hillsdale, NJ: Erlbaum.

Gollin, E. S. (Ed.). (1984). *Malformations in development.* New York: Academic Press.

Gollin, E. S., Stahl, G., & Morgan, E. (1989). On the uses of the concept of normality in developmental biology and psychology. *Advances in Child Development and Behavior, 21*, 49–71.

Greenspan, S. I. (1981). *Psychopathology and adaptation in infancy and early childhood.* New York: International Universities Press.

Hermelin, B., & O'Connor, N. (1970). *Psychological experiments with autistic children.* Oxford: Pergamon Press.

Hermelin, B., & O'Connor, N. (1985). Logico-affective states and nonverbal language. In E. Schopler & G. B. Mesibov (Eds.), *Communication problems in autism* (pp. 283–310). New York: Plenum Press.

Hesse, P., & Cicchetti, D. (1982). Perspectives on an integrated theory of emotional development. In D. Cicchetti & P. Hesse (Eds.), *Emotional development* (pp. 3–48). San Francisco: Jossey-Bass.

Hill, P., & McCune-Nicolich, L. (1981). Pretend play and patterns of cognition in Down's syndrome children. *Child Development, 52*, 611–617.

Hobson, R. P. (1982). The question of egocentrism: The coordination of perspectives in relation to operational thinking. *Journal of Child Psychology and Psychiatry, 23*, 43–60.

Hobson, R. P. (1983). The autistic child's recognition of age-related features of people, animals, and things. *British Journal of Developmental Psychology, 1*, 343–352.

Hobson, R. P. (1984). Early childhood autism and the question of egocentrism. *Journal of Autism and Developmental Disorders, 14*, 85–104.

Hobson, R. P. (1986). The autistic child's appraisal of expressions of emotion: A further study. *Journal of Child Psychology and Psychiatry, 27*, 671–680.

Hobson, R. P. (1989). Beyond cognition: A theory of autism. In G. Dawson (Ed.), *Autism: New perspectives on diagnosis, nature, and treatment* (pp. 22–48). New York: Guilford Press.

Hobson, R. P. (1990). On acquiring knowledge about people and the capacity to pretend: Response to Leslie (1987). *Psychological Review, 97*, 114–121.

Hodapp, R., & Zigler, E. (1990). Applying the developmental perspective to individuals with

Down syndrome. In D. Cicchetti & M. Beeghly (Eds.), *Children with Down syndrome: A developmental perspective* (pp. 1–28). New York: Cambridge University Press.

Izard, C. (1977). *Human emotions.* New York: Plenum Press.

Jennings, K., Harmon, R., Morgan, G., Gaiter, J., & Yarrow, L. (1979). Exploratory play as an index of mastery motivation: Relationships to persistence, cognitive functioning, and environmental measures. *Developmental Psychology, 15,* 386–394.

Jones, O. M. (1980). Prelinguistic communication skills in Down syndrome infants. In T. Field, S. Goldberg, D. Stern, & A. Sostek (Eds.), *High risk infants and children.* New York: Academic Press.

Kagan, J. (1981). *The second year.* Cambridge, MA: Harvard University Press.

Kanner, L. (1943). Autistic disturbances of affective contact. *Nervous Child, 2,* 217–250.

Kaplan, B. (1966). The study of language in psychiatry: The comparative developmental approach and its application to symbolization and language in psychopathology. In S. Arieti (Ed.), *American handbook of psychiatry* (pp. 659–688). New York: Basic Books.

Kennedy, M., Sheridan, M., Radlinski, S., & Beeghly, M. (1991). Play–language relationships in young children with developmental delays: Implications for assessment. *Journal of Speech and Hearing Disorders, 34,* 112–122.

Kopp, C., Krakow, J., & Vaughn, V. (1983). Patterns of self-control in young handicapped children. In W. A. Collins (Ed.), *Minnesota Symposia on Child Psychology* (Vol. 16, pp. 93–125). Hillsdale, NJ: Erlbaum.

Landry, S., & Loveland, K. (1988). Communication behaviors in autism and developmental language delay. *Journal of Child Psychology and Psychiatry, 29,* 621–634.

Langdell, T. (1978). Recognition of faces: An approach to the study of autism. *Journal of Child Psychology and Psychiatry, 19,* 255–268.

Largo, J., & Howard, J. (1979). Developmental progression in play behavior of children between nine and thirty months, II: Spontaneous play and language development. *Developmental Medicine and Child Neurology, 21,* 492–503.

Lenneberg, E. (1967). *Biological foundations of language.* New York: Wiley.

Leslie, A. M. (1987). Pretense and representation: The origins of "theory of mind." *Psychological Review, 94,* 412–426.

Leslie, A. M., & Frith, U. (1990). Prospects for a cognitive neuropsychology of autism: Hobson's choice. *Psychological Review, 97,* 122–131.

Leslie, A. M., & Happe, F. (1989). Autism and ostensive communication: The relevance of metarepresentation. *Development and Psychopathology, 1,* 205–212.

Levy, D. (1944). *Maternal overprotection.* New York: Columbia University Press.

Lewis, M., & Brooks-Gunn, J. (1979). *Social cognition and the acquisitions of self.* New York: Plenum Press.

Lewis, M., & Rosenblum, L. (Eds.). (1974). *The effect of the infant on its caregiver.* New York: Wiley.

Lord, C. (1984). Language comprehension and cognitive disorder in autism. In L. Siegel & F. Morrison (Eds.), *Cognitive development in atypical children: Progress in cognitive development research* (pp. 67–82). New York: Springer-Verlag.

Lord, C. (1985). Autism and the comprehension of language. In E. Schopler & G. B. Mesibov (Eds.), *Communication problems in autism* (pp. 257–281). New York: Plenum Press.

Lotter, V. (1978). Follow-up studies. In M. Rutter & E. Schopler (Eds.), *Autism: A reappraisal of concepts and treatment* (pp. 475–496). New York: Plenum Press.

Loveland, K. (1987). Behavior of young children with Down syndrome before the mirror: Finding things reflected. *Child Development, 58,* 928–936.

Loveland, K. A., McEvoy, R., Tunali, B., & Kelley, M. (1990). Narrative story telling in autism and Down's syndrome. *British Journal of Developmental Psychology, 8*, 9–23.

Loveland, K. A., Tunali, B., Kelley, M., & McEvoy, R. (1989) Referential communication and response adequacy in autism and Down syndrome. *Applied Psycholinguistics, 10*, 401–413.

MacTurk, R., Hunter, R., McCarthy, M., Vietze, P., & McQuiston, S. (1985). Social mastery motivation in Down syndrome and nondelayed infants. *Topics in Early Childhood Special Education, 4*, 93–109.

Mans, L., Cicchetti, D., & Sroufe, L. A. (1978). Mirror reactions of Down syndrome infants and toddlers: Cognitive underpinnings of self-recognition. *Child Development, 49*, 1247–1250.

McConkey, R., & Martin, H. (1985). The development of object and pretend play in Down syndrome infants: Longitudinal study involving mothers. *Trisomy 21*.

McCune, L. (1986). Symbolic development in normal and atypical infants. In G. Fein & M. Rivkin (Eds.), *Reviews of research:* Vol. 4, *The young child at play* (pp. 45–61). Washington, DC: National Association for the Education of Young Children.

McCune-Nicolich, L., & Bruskin, C. (1982). Combinatorial competence in symbolic play and language. In D. J. Pepler & K. H. Rubin (Eds.), *The play of children* (pp. 30–45). New York: Karger.

McCune-Nicolich, L., & Fenson, L. (1984). Methodological issues in studying early pretend play. In T. Yawny & A. Pellegrini (Eds.), *Child's play: Developmental and applied* (pp. 81–103). Hillsdale, NJ: Erlbaum.

Mervis, C. B. (1990). Conceptual development of children with Down syndrome. In D. Cicchetti & M. Beeghly (Eds.), *Children with Down syndrome: A developmental perspective* (pp. 252–301). New York: Cambridge University Press.

Miller, J. F. (1981). *Assessing language production in children.* Austin, TX: Pro-ed.

Motti, F., Cicchetti, D., & Sroufe, L. A. (1983). From infant affect expression to symbolic play: The coherence of development in Down syndrome children. *Child Development, 54*, 1168–1175.

Mundy, P., & Sigman, M. (1989). The theoretical implications of joint-attention deficits in autism. *Development and Psychopathology, 1*, 173–184.

Mundy, P., Sigman, M., Kasari, C., & Yirmiya, N. (1988). Nonverbal communication skills in Down syndrome children. *Child Development, 54*, 1168–1175.

Mundy, P., Sigman, M., Ungerer, J., & Sherman, T. (1986). Defining the social deficits of autism: The contribution of nonverbal communication measures. *Journal of Child Psychology and Psychiatry, 27*, 657–669.

Nicolich, L. (1977). Beyond sensorimotor intelligence: Assessment of symbolic maturity through analysis of pretend play. *Merrill-Palmer Quarterly, 23*, 89–99.

O'Connell, B., & Bretherton, I. (1984). Toddlers' play alone and with mother: The role of maternal guidance. In I. Bretherton (Ed.), *Symbolic play* (pp. 337–368). New York: Academic Press.

Olley, J. (1985). Social aspects of communication in children with autism. In E. Schopler & G. B. Mesibov (Eds.), *Communication problems in autism* (pp. 311–325). New York: Plenum Press.

Piaget, J. (1962). *Play, dreams, and imitation in childhood.* New York: Norton.

Piaget, J. (1981). *Intelligence and affectivity: Their relationship during child development.* Palo Alto, CA: Annual Reviews.

Piaget, J., & Inhelder, B. (1969). *The psychology of the child.* (H. Weaver, Trans.) London: Routledge and Kegan Paul.

Prior, M. (1979). Cognitive abilities and disabilities in infantile autism: A review. *Journal of Abnormal Child Psychology, 7*, 357–380.

Quinn, J., & Rubin, K. (1984). The play of handicapped children. In T. A. Yawkey & A. Pellegrini (Eds.), *Child's play: Developmental and applied* (pp. 63–81). Hillsdale, NJ: Erlbaum.

Rice, M. (1983). Contemporary accounts of the cognition/language relationship: Implications for speech-language clinicians. *Journal of Speech and Hearing Disorders, 52*, 17–29.

Ricks, D., & Wing, L. (1976). Language, communication and the use of symbols. In L. Wing (Ed.), *Early childhood autism*. New York: Pergamon Press.

Riguet, C., Taylor, N., Benaroya, S., & Klein, L. (1981). Symbolic play in autistic, Downs, and normal children of equivalent mental age. *Journal of Autism and Developmental Disorders, 11*, 439–448.

Rosenberg, S. (1984). Disorders of first language development: Trends in research and theory. In E. S. Gollin (Ed.), *Malformations of development* (pp. 195–237). New York: Academic Press.

Rubin, K., Fein, G., & Vandenberg, B. (1983). Play. In P. Mussen (Ed.), *Handbook of child psychology:* Vol. 4, *Socialization, personality, and social development* (pp. 693–774). New York: Wiley.

Rutter, M. (1978). Diagnosis and definition of childhood autism. *Journal of Autism and Developmental Disorders, 8*, 139–161.

Rutter, M. (1983). Cognitive deficits in the pathogenesis of autism. *Journal of Child Psychology and Psychiatry, 24*, 513–532.

Rutter, M., & Garmezy, N. (1983). Developmental psychopathology. In P. Mussen (Ed.), *Handbook of child psychology* (pp. 775–911). New York: Wiley.

Rynders, J., Spiker, D., & Horrobin, J. M. (1978). Understanding the educability of Down's syndrome children: Examination of methodological problems in recent literature. *American Journal of Mental Deficiency, 82*, 440–448.

Sameroff, A. (1983). Developmental systems: Contexts and evolution. In P. Mussen (Ed.), *Handbook of child psychology* (Vol. 1, pp. 237–294). New York: Wiley.

Sameroff, A., & Chandler, M. (1975). Reproductive risk and the continuum of caretaking casualty. In F. Horowitz (Ed.), *Review of child development research* (Vol. 4, pp. 187–244). Chicago: University of Chicago Press.

Santostefano, S. (1978). *A biodevelopmental approach to clinical child psychology*. New York: Wiley.

Schaeffer, H. R. (Ed.), (1977). *Studies in mother–child interaction*. New York: Academic Press.

Schneider-Rosen, K., Braunwald, K., Carlson, V., & Cicchetti, D. (1985). Current perspectives in attachment theory: Illustration from the study of maltreated infants. In I. Bretherton & E. Waters (Eds.), Growing points in attachment theory and research. *Monographs of the Society for Research in Child Development*, No. 209, *50*, 194–210.

Schneider-Rosen, K., & Cicchetti, D. (1984). The relationship between affect and cognition in maltreated infants: Quality of attachment and the development of self-recognition. *Child Development, 55*, 648–658.

Schopler, E., & Mesibov, G. (Eds.). (1985). *Communication problems in autism*. New York: Plenum Press.

Serafica, F., & Cicchetti, D. (1976). Down's syndrome children in a strange situation: Attachment and exploratory behaviors. *Merrill-Palmer Quarterly, 22*, 137–150.

Share, J. B. (1974). Developmental progress in Down's syndrome. In R. Koch & F. F. de la Cruz (Eds.), *Down's syndrome (mongolism): Research, preventions, and management* (pp. 78–88). New York: Brunner/Mazel.

Shatz, M., Wellman, H., & Silber, S. (1983). The acquisition of mental verbs: A systematic investigation of the first reference to mental state. *Cognition, 14*, 301–321.

Shimada, S., Kai, Y., & Sano, R. (1981). *Development of symbolic play in late infancy.* RIEEC Research Bulletin RRB 17. Tokyo: Gakugi University.

Sigman, M., & Mundy, P. (1987). Symbolic processes in young autistic children. *New Directions for Child Development, 36,* 31–46.

Sigman, M., Mundy, P., Sherman, T., & Ungerer, J. (1986). Social interactions of autistic, mentally retarded, and normal children and their caregivers. *Journal of Child Psychology and Psychiatry, 27,* 647–656.

Sigman, M., & Ungerer, J. (1981). Sensorimotor skills and language comprehension in autistic children. *Journal of Abnormal Child Psychology, 9,* 149–165.

Sigman, M., & Ungerer, J. (1984). Cognitive and language skills in autistic, mentally retarded, and normal children. *Developmental Psychology, 20,* 293–302.

Sorce, J., & Emde, R. (1982). The meaning of infant emotional expressions: Regularities in caregiving responses in normal and Down's syndrome infants. *Journal of Child Psychology and Psychiatry, 23,* 145–158.

Sorce, J., Emde, R., & Frank, M. (1982). Maternal referencing in normal and Down syndrome infants: A longitudinal analysis. In R. Emde & R. Harmon (Eds.), *The development of attachments and affiliative systems* (pp. 281–294). New York: Plenum Press.

Spiker, D. (1979). *A descriptive study of mother–child teaching interaction with high- and low-functioning Down syndrome preschoolers.* Doctoral dissertation, University of Minnesota, Minneapolis.

Spiker, D., & Ricks, M. (1984). Visual self-recognition in autistic children: Developmental relationships. *Child Development, 55,* 214–225.

Sroufe, L. A. (1979). Socioemotional development. In J. Osofsky (Ed.), *Handbook of infant development* (pp. 462–516). New York: Wiley.

Sroufe, L. A. (1989). Pathways to adaptation and maladaption: Psychopathology as developmental deviation. In D. Cicchetti (Ed.), *Rochester symposium on developmental psychopathology:* Vol. 1, *The emergence of a discipline* (pp. 13–40). Hillsdale, NJ: Erlbaum.

Sroufe, L. A., & Rutter, M. (1984). The domain of developmental psychopathology. *Child Development, 55,* 17–29.

Tager-Flusberg, H. (1988). On the nature of a language acquisition disorder: The example of autism. In F. Kessell (Ed.), *The development of language and language researchers: Essays presented to Roger Brown* (pp. 249–267). Hillsdale, NJ: Erlbaum.

Tager-Flusberg, H. (1989, April). *An analysis of discourse ability and internal state lexicons in a longitudinal study of autistic children.* Presented at the biennial meeting of the Society for Research in Child Development, Kansas City, MO.

Tager-Flusberg, H. (1992). Autistic children's talk about psychological states: Deficits in the early acquisition of a theory of mind. *Child Development, 63,* 161–172.

Thompson, R., Cicchetti, D., Lamb, M., & Malkin, C. (1985). The emotional responses of Down syndrome and normal infants in the strange situation: The organization of affective behavior in infants. *Developmental Psychology, 21,* 828–841.

Tilton, J., & Ottinger, D. (1964). Comparison of the toy play behavior of autistic, retarded, and normal children. *Psychological Reports, 15,* 967–975.

Tinbergen, E., & Tinbergen, N. (1972). Early childhood autism: An ethological approach. *Advances in Ethology, Journal of Comparative Ethology,* Supplement No. 10. Berlin: Perry.

Ungerer, J., & Sigman, M. (1981). Symbolic play and language comprehension in autistic children. *Journal of Abnormal Child Psychology, 9,* 149–165.

Ungerer, J., Zelazo, R., Kearsley, R., & O'Leary, K. (1981). Developmental changes in the representation of objects in symbolic play from 18 to 34 months of age. *Child Development, 52,* 186–195.

Volkmar, F. R. (1987). Social development. In D. Cohen, R. Paul, & A. Donnelan (Eds.), *The handbook of autism and disorders of atypical development* (pp. 41–60). New York: Wiley.

Vygotsky, L. (1962). *Thought and language.* (E. Hanfmann & C. Vakar, Eds. and Trans.). Cambridge MA: MIT Press.

Weiss, B., Beeghly, M., & Cicchetti, D. (1985, April). Symbolic play development in children with Down syndrome and nonhandicapped children. Paper presented at the biennial meetings of the Society for Research in Child Development, Toronto.

Weiss, P. (1969). *Principles of development.* New York: Hafner.

Werner, H. (1948). *Comparative psychology of mental development.* New York: International Universities Press.

Werner, H., & Kaplan, B. (1963). *Symbol formation: An organismic developmental approach to language and the expression of thought.* New York: Wiley.

Wing, L. (1969). The handicaps of autistic children: A comparative study. *Journal of Child Psychology and Psychiatry, 10,* 1–40.

Wing, L. (1978). Social, behavioral, and cognitive characteristics: An epidemiological approach. In M. Rutter & E. Schopler (Eds.), *Autism: A reappraisal of concepts and treatment* (pp. 27–46). New York: Plenum Press.

Wing, L. (1981). Asperger's syndrome: A clinical account. *Psychological Medicine, 11,* 115–129.

Wing, L., Gould, J., Yeates, S. R., & Brierley, L. M. (1977). Symbolic play in severely mentally retarded and in autistic children. *Journal of Child Psychology and Psychiatry, 18,* 167–178.

Wolf, D., & Grollman, S. (1982). Ways of playing: Individual differences in imaginative play. In K. Rubin & D. Pepler (Eds.), *The play of children* (pp. 1–19). New York: Karger.

Zigler, E., & Balla, D. (1982). (Eds.). *Mental retardation: The developmental difference controversy.* Hillsdale, NJ: Erlbaum.

12

Development of Symbolic Play in Deaf Children Aged 1 to 3

ELSA J. BLUM
BARBARA C. FIELDS
HELEN SCHARFMAN
DIANA SILBER

Background

Over a number of years, we have had the opportunity to observe deaf infants and their hearing and deaf parents in a therapeutic nursery at the Lexington School for the Deaf in New York City. When the project began, we were generally interested in understanding the unfolding of developmental processes in deaf infants and in parent–child relationships that were doubly burdened by the child's congenital deafness and parents' responses to the diagnosis of deafness in their children. We wanted to understand more fully how parents adapted to and coped with the unique issues involved in rearing a deaf child and to help and support them in their efforts to foster their child's development (Fields, Blum, & Scharfman, in press). This study of the symbolic play of deaf children was undertaken as a means of exploring the formation of their symbolic capacities.

The emergence of symbolic capacities is generally viewed as the major cognitive attainment of early childhood, paving the way for a wide range of social and academic achievements. The emergence of symbolic play provided the opportunity to observe the development of nonlanguage symbolization in the face of delay in acquisition of linguistic symbolization or acquisition of sign language rather than oral language. Of particular interest to us was the central importance of the parent–child relationship in symbolic development. Werner and Kaplan (1963) described symbol formation as emerging within the mother–child matrix, with increasing differentiation of symbol and referent. Responding in part to the dearth of research regarding maternal influence in symbol formation, Slade (1987a, 1987b) documented the central role of the mother in facilitating the continuation and elaboration of the toddler's play.

Language, in particular, has been viewed as a uniquely human symbolic capacity, ultimately making possible communication and contributing to complex organization of thought and experience. Language development has been conceptualized as having both cognitive and affective foundations, emerging as the infant individuates and begins to represent self and object, differentiating and increasingly distancing symbol and referent. In deaf infants who do not learn sign language, the emergence of the symbolic function as manifest in language is almost invariably markedly delayed and altered. For children who are native users of sign language, the acquisition of language milestones corresponds fairly well to the acquisition of these milestones in hearing children, except for the earlier appearance of first signs as compared with first oral words (Newport & Meier, 1985). It is not yet known how the lack of audition or the use of sign language rather than oral language may influence other aspects of symbolic development.

In addition to the vulnerability of deaf children in the area of language development, parent–child relationships are at risk. Parents often respond to the diagnosis of deafness with a variety of intense feelings that may interfere with their developing relationship with their child. Beyond this, in the absence of audition, early reciprocity may be compromised and parents may not receive anticipated feedback from the infant. Deaf parents' reactions to their children's deficit may be somewhat different, more ambivalent and less intense than those of hearing parents, because for them the birth of a deaf child is neither a complete surprise nor totally undesired. In our sample, all of the deaf mothers were children of hearing mothers who were often unaccepting of their daughters' deafness. Without exception the deaf mothers had been enrolled in oral schools for the deaf. Thus sign language was devalued and indeed prohibited both by the educational system and by the parents, and our group of deaf parents and their hearing mothers had never experienced the intimacy of a shared "mother tongue." Parenting either a deaf or a hearing child was colored by their own early experience. While both hearing and deaf parents had many obstacles to surmount in the rearing of their deaf children, many often found adaptive ways of coping with extraordinary problems and fostering development.

Our study of emerging symbolic capacities in young deaf children by the investigation of their developing symbolic play was facilitated by the recent proliferation of studies of normal children. Research exploring the play of hearing children during this age range often addresses development of solitary play or play with a parent in which the use of language in the analysis of the data is minimized. This research provides a basis for comparison with the play of deaf children. These investigations have described the sequential development of play from simple exploration and manipulation of objects to their representational use, with increasing perceptual distancing of symbol and referent and increasing planful sequential activity (Nicolich, 1977; Piaget, 1962).

We entertained the notion that perhaps for some deaf youngsters with very limited language, play would precede language as a means of making meaning and expressing thought. We felt that play might be particularly important in terms of serving adaptive functions such as mastery of anxiety and conflict in these young-sters, for many of whom language was not yet generally available. In normal development, the interrelationship of various domains of symbolic function remains little understood; only now are some researchers attempting to delineate their complexities (Wolf & Gardner, 1981). Several investigators have begun to explore the relationship of symbolic play to language development and see early symbolic play as emerging in tandem with language (Corman & Escalona, 1980; McCune-Nicolich, 1981). McCune views the development of symbolic play as a measure of the child's developing facility with symbolic representation and as a measure of cognitive maturity.

There has been little study of the symbolic play of deaf children and only one study of the symbolic play of deaf children 3 years of age or below. Gregory and Mogford (1983) studied longitudinally the play of six deaf children from ages 1 to 3. These children clearly demonstrated the capacity to use objects symbolically. According to these authors, however, their play differed from that of hearing children of the same age in that the deaf youngsters did not enact sequences of similar length and complexity.

By ages 3 and 4, the symbolic play of young children is generally studied in a social situation. Language seems increasingly crucial to the highly interactive play that takes place among hearing children as they assign roles and set complex scenes, and it is generally agreed that by this age there are already dramatic differences between the play of deaf and hearing children. But it is by no means clear whether these differences are due to a lag in the development of symbolic capacities necessary for this kind of play or to the difficulty in communication.

In a study of the play of hearing-impaired 4- and 5-year-olds, Darbyshire (1977) noted that object substitution and make-believe play were common in normally hearing controls but not in children with auditory deficits. Casby and McCormack (1985) found a relationship between expressive language and symbolic play in deaf children from 38 to 69 months. Studying the play of deaf and hearing 4-year-olds, Scharfman (1977) found major differences in the quality and nature of the play in the two groups. Although both groups of children spent approximately the same percentage of time in play overall, the deaf children spent more of their time as onlookers and in solitary play than did their counterparts; they engaged in less parallel play and in markedly less cooperative and dramatic play. Although some brief attempts at associative play in groups were noted, suggesting that there was an intent to play together, these efforts were quickly dissipated. This study suggested that the deaf child tended to do the obvious with the materials, to be more rigid in his or her use of objects, and to start a theme but rarely to elaborate or sustain it. In contrast, the hearing children tended to be more creative with materials, carry forward an idea, and elaborate upon a theme. Gross (cited by Gregory & Mogford, 1983) found that even when deaf nursery school children appeared to be playing together, close analysis indicated that they were involved in parallel rather than cooperative play.

The issue of the ultimate achievement of symbolic capacities by the deaf has been an area of particular controversy, contributing to the importance of understanding early development in this area. The very poor academic attainment of most deaf adults, generally not beyond fifth grade in reading, is well documented (Rainer,

Altshuler, & Kallmann, 1969). Trybus and Karchmer (1977) found that half of the hearing-impaired students aged 20 years and younger tested, in a variety of settings using a special edition of the Stanford Achievement Test, read below the 4.5 grade level, and only 10% of 18-year-old hearing-impaired students read at or above 8th-grade level. Allen (1986) found a leveling off of reading comprehension at about third-grade level for deaf students, with higher achievement in mathematics computation. Tomlinson-Keasey and Kelly (1978) note that the language deficiency of deaf children has been considered the primary factor in their poor academic performance. They argue, however, that deaf children's academic accomplishment is undermined not only because of inadequately developing language, but also because, in the absence of auditory input, their cognitive structures develop differently. They see the young deaf child as having difficulty in transforming the physical world into a symbolic world. Some studies have reported a paucity of symbolic capacities in deaf adults, affecting both intellectual and social domains. Furth (1966) took a different position, arguing that deaf individuals do not lack the ability to use nonlanguage symbol systems. The very high intellectual achievement of some deaf adults indicates that there must be means by which they have been able to develop adequate symbolic capacities despite even a profound auditory deficit. We felt that an enhanced understanding of the issues related to variability in early symbolic development might shed light on the precursors of later symbolic capacities. Slade (1986) stated that the "unique relationship between object relations, ego development, and symbolization which evolves during the early years may well foreshadow the later use and function of a variety of cognitive processes, such as purposeful thought, language, fantasy, and dreams" (p. 561).

The Present Study

Context

This study took place in the Therapeutic Infant Nursery under the aegis of the Mental Health Department of the Lexington School for the Deaf, now the Lexington Center for Mental Health Services. Entry into the nursery took place as soon as possible following diagnosis, generally between 6 and 18 months, and nursery participation continued until age 3 years. Parents and children attended two 1½-hour sessions each week.

The nursery is a preventive intervention program designed to promote optimal development in deaf infants by addressing a variety of developmental issues. The central role and reciprocal nature of the mother–child relationship formed the basis of the theoretical and clinical perspective and suggested the utilization of the tripartite model of intervention based on Mahler's (1968) design and adapted for a nursery setting by Galenson (1984). In this model, mother and child are seen together in the treatment, the therapist becoming a bridge between them, enriching a parent–child relationship jeopardized by the circular impact of congenital deafness and parental response to the handicapped child. In the nursery setting, symbolic play is promoted and valued as facilitating interrelated aspects of development. A youngster's initiatives are extended and elaborated; symbolic play is encouraged and at times modeled. In addition, as part of the intervention, parents are helped to understand play as a vehicle for making and expressing meaning. The nursery context both enhanced our study and imposed limitations upon it. Our data, enriched by our extensive contact with our subjects and their families, are of necessity colored by the participation of the subjects in a clinical intervention, as well as by the particular characteristics of the setting.

The Lexington School for the Deaf advocates oral education. In addition to nursery attendance, each child in our sample was seen twice a week by an educator of the deaf to facilitate language development. The one child included in our study who did not attend the nursery was also receiving oral training at another center. The reasons for parents' choice of oral settings for their youngsters merits consideration. All had come with the hope that their children would acquire oral language. For most hearing parents, this meant that their child would not be exposed to sign language because of a fear that this might impede their acquisition of oral language. To some degree, this was feared by deaf parents as well. They, too, valued oral language, and in fact some had themselves acquired fairly functional oral language. Thus several deaf parents also had some reluctance about introducing sign language to their babies very early. In some instances, although it was the primary language for the family, parents often did not sign specifically to their infants.

As previously noted, the hearing parents of the deaf parents of our subjects had generally not only valued oral language but had devalued sign language. In some cases, deaf parents' attitudes reflected their own early experience; in others, it was the hearing grandparents who had chosen the same oral school for their grandchildren as they had for their children. Thus attitudes toward signed communication and modes of communication varied from family to family, and in a few deaf families the children were signed to very little for the first year or so. Ultimately all of the deaf families used sign language, generally American Sign Language (ASL), and in one case a mixture of ASL and signed English was used. A few hearing families were also using some signs as a bridge to oral language. Their usage was generally limited by their inability to use sign language fluently, as well as their ambivalence toward using nonoral language. Within the nursery itself, the therapists used whichever mode or modes of communication the family preferred. Sign language, however, was overtly valued by the nursery staff. We believed that it was extremely important for the deaf parents to begin to value their own language as a communicative mode to share with their children. This facilitated early parent–child communication on both an affective and a semantic level, promoting language and emotional development. Over time there were shifts toward more positive attitudes regarding signing in both deaf and hearing parents. This also meant that in some families, where the ambivalence about the use of sign language could be resolved, there was a real difference in the use of signing between first and subsequent children, so that siblings who were later nursery participants had a very different experience with their parents than did their older siblings. (In all of our families, either both parents were deaf or both were hearing.)

Subjects

Included in this study were 16 deaf children aged 1 to 3 years. These children were normal in every way, as far as was known, except for their deafness. Developmental evaluations were conducted at least once a year by the senior author, using the Yale Child Study Center Revised Developmental Schedules, and all children were of at least average cognitive ability in nonlanguage areas.[1] None of the children included in the study displayed symptoms of major psychopathology.

The sample included seven males, four from deaf families and three from hearing families, and nine females, six from deaf families and three from hearing families. Of the total of 65 videotaped observations, 27 were of males, 8 from deaf families and 19 from hearing families; 38 were of females, 29 from deaf families and 9 from hearing families (Table 12.1).

Several pairs of siblings were included in the study. All children were living with both parents. Three of the youngsters participated in the nursery only briefly and were available for only one videotaped session. In two instances, children were approaching age 3 when the project began and other youngsters had not yet reached 3 when the project terminated. Longitudinal data including at least two videotaped sessions were available for 13 children.

The sample encompassed a wide socioeconomic range and a wide ethnic range as well, and was very likely representative of the New York metropolitan area, which the school serves.

All the children were congenitally deaf, so far as could be ascertained. Audiological testing indicated that 11 of the children were profoundly deaf, 3 were severely deaf, and 2 were moderately deaf. (Profound = loss > 90 decibels [dB]; severe = loss of 70–85 dB; moderate = loss of 50–65 dB.) All of the children had bilateral ear-level hearing aids except for one child, who had body aids, but their responses varied. Audiological tests revealed that with hearing aids, 1 child was left with a severe loss; 11 of the subjects had at least a moderate hearing loss; the remaining 4 had mild loss. These numerical test results do not, however, imply that this is the level of hearing that the child has available and utilizes outside of the testing situation. Although it is impossible to know precisely what a deaf infant experiences with hearing aids, it is known that background as well as foreground sounds are amplified and that sound is somewhat distorted. It is important to understand that the use of aids does not bestow normal hearing, nor were aids consistently used by all of the children. None of the subjects, even when using hearing aids, had the degree of acuity required for normal acquisition of oral language.

In terms of the linguistic competence demonstrated by our subjects, there was considerable variation within each mode of communication. A number of patterns were evident among our signing youngsters. These patterns included relatively limited competence by age 3, excellent language development from the beginning, and limited early competence followed by excellent sign development by age 3. Our oral subjects varied from virtual lack of expressive language to good acquisition of oral language for a deaf child; this, however, was at best markedly below typical language development for either a hearing child or a signing deaf child. Overall only two signing children and none of the nonsigning children were able to communicate by

TABLE 12.1.   Characteristics of Subjects and Play Scores

Subj	Sex	Family Hearing	Hearing Loss	Age	Play Level	SPT ae	Score
1	M	Deaf	Moderate	32	4	31	19
				36	5	31	19
2	F	Hearing	Profound	26	4	23	13
				34	4	29	17
				36	5	35	22
3	F	Deaf	Profound	17	5	13	5
4	F	Deaf	Profound	23	5	13	5
				31	5	26	15
				35	5	29	17
5	M	Deaf	Profound	19	1	14	6
				26	4	22	12
				31	4	29	17
				34	5	30	18
				36	4	29	17
6	M	Hearing	Profound	27	5	26	15
				31	5	22	12
7	M	Deaf	Severe	26	5	21	11
8	F	Hearing	Profound	16	2	<12	3
9	F	Deaf	Profound	13	2	<12	1
				17	2	<12	3
				21	4	15	7
				24	5	23	13
				26	5	29	17
				31	4	34	21
				33	5	35	22
10	F	Deaf	Severe	15	—	<12	0
				19	3	<12	4
				22	—	17	8
				25	4	22	12
				28	4	27	16
				32	4	31	19
				35	5	32	20
11	F	Deaf	Moderate	12	—	<12	0
				16	3	<12	3
				20	4	13	5
				23	4	21	11
				26	4	26	15
				28	5	26	15
				32	3	23	13
				35	5	36	23
12	F	Hearing	Severe	22	5	21	11
				25	5	34	21
				28	5	23	13
				31	5	32	20
				35	5	30	18

Subj	Sex	Family Hearing	Hearing Loss	Age	Play Level	SPT ae	Score
13	M	Hearing	Profound	12	1	<12	4
				16	1	<12	2
				19	3	15	7
				23	3	19	10
				26	4	17	8
				29	4	29	17
				35	5	30	18
14	M	Hearing	Profound	18	3	13	5
				21	5	18	9
				25	4	23	13
				28	5	22	12
				32	5	23	13
15	M	Hearing	Profound	14	3	19	10
				17	4	22	12
				20	4	31	19
				24	4	32	20
				27	4	36	23
16	F	Deaf	Profound	13	3	13	5
				19	1	13	5
				22	5	25	14

age 3 at a level that would be within the normal range for a hearing child of similar age and normal cognitive ability.

Method

The data of this study are derived from two sources: the therapist's notes of nursery sessions and videotaped play sessions. Therapists' notes were recorded following each session, according to a protocol organized to provide information along various lines of development, including play, language, cognitive development, separation-individuation, object relations, and affect. These notes, written after each session, were replete with observations of parent–child relationships and observations of play and language development, as well as reports of external family stresses or events, behavioral issues at home, and so on. Data were reviewed and summarized every few months, and each child's development was discussed at regular intervals in staff meetings; annual and final summaries were also written. Our data regarding language development were amplified by data gathered by the educators of the deaf.

Special play sessions were videotaped at intervals over the year. Each videotaping session included administration of the Symbolic Play Test (SPT) (Lowe, 1975; Lowe & Costello, 1976) and an unstructured 20-minute play segment with a variety of toys selected to promote symbolic play. Videotaping was done through a one-way mirror in an observation room adjacent to the special playroom used only for this purpose and for developmental evaluations. A parent was always with the child.

During the SPT, the parent was requested not to interact with the child. During the free-play segment, the parent was instructed not to initiate play or show the child what to do with the toys, but to respond to the child's play initiatives.

The SPT was designed to evaluate the development of symbolic function through observation of play and was especially intended for use with nonverbal children. Scoring is based on observation of discrete, spontaneous play behaviors in relation to four sets of miniature toys representing everyday objects. The first set of objects consists of a doll, cup, saucer, spoon, brush, and comb. The second set consists of a doll, bed, pillow, and blanket. The third set includes a table, chair, doll, tablecloth, knife, fork, and plate. The fourth consists of a tractor, trailer, man, and logs. The scoring is entirely unrelated to verbal production, nor are verbal directions given. A child's score is based on the number of scorable behaviors observed out of a possible 24 items. The more advanced items require that the child make the transition from applying schemas to the self to acting upon a doll. The standardization sample consisted of English children in nursery schools and day-care centers and was drawn from all social classes. The SPT was recorded and scored at the time of administration and again by another scorer viewing the videotape. Differences were readily resolved by repeated viewing of the tape. Scoring reliability was documented in the test manual (Lowe & Costello, 1976).

The 20 minutes of unstructured play was scored according to the Piagetian-derived system developed by McCune (McCune-Nicolich, 1983). Symbolic play is scored at five levels as follows:

Level 1. Presymbolic schemes involving enactive schemas rather than mental representation; for example, a child picks up a comb and touches it to his or her hair; there is no pretend element.

Level 2. Autosymbolic schemes in which pretending differentiates this level from the previous category; for example, the child eats from an empty spoon, closes his or her eyes, and pretends to sleep.

Level 3. Single-scheme symbolic games in which the child now "extends symbolism beyond his or her actions" by either (a) including another, such as feeding the mother or doll, or (b) pretending at another's actions, such as reading a book or mopping a floor.

Level 4.1. Single scheme combinations in which one pretend scheme is related to more than one actor or receiver of action; for example, the childs feeds the self and then feeds a doll.

Level 4.2. Multischeme combinations in which two or more different schemes are combined in a sequence; for example, the child holds a phone to his or her ear and dials, then talks.

Levels 5.1 and 5.2. Planned symbolic acts and combinations in which scoring reflects evidence of planning; for example, the child announces object substitution or a plan of action (5.1) or gives behavioral evidence of planning by searching for needed objects (5.2).

The free-play segment was scored by two different observers; differences were resolved by repeated viewings of the tape until a consensus could be reached. The criterion for obtaining a score at a given level was a single occurrence of behavior that warranted a score at that level. No distinction was made between Levels 4.1

and 4.2 or between Levels 5.1 and 5.2. In McCune's studies of hearing children, Level 4.1 play generally emerged at the same time as Level 4.2 play; similarly, Levels 5.1 and 5.2 were first seen during the same observation session. In the present sample, because of the lack of language development, verbal or signed accompaniment to play announcing intention, as would be required for a score at Level 5.1, was rarely evident. Virtually all Level 5 scores were based on inferences drawn from behavior that could be interpreted as searching for needed objects; frequently it was difficult to distinguish between Level 4 and Level 5 play. Because of the lag in language development for most of our subjects, making the verbal expression of intentionality difficult, the lack of a Level 5 score could not be interpreted to indicate that the child was not capable of planned symbolic acts, the criterion for a score at this level.

Analysis of Results

Play Development

In the section that follows, we will report quantitative results based on administration of a standardized measure and will consider, as well, qualitative data regarding our subjects. Because of the very small number of children available for study within our time frame, and because of the heterogeneity of this sample, some of our discussion will focus on descriptions of individual subjects as well as group variation. Given the nature of our findings, this level of description seems particularly meaningful. Quantitative analysis of the data is limited due to the uneven number of observations for the different subjects, as well as the heterogeneity and size of the sample. Table 12.1 lists the quantitative data with respect to each subject, including the scores on successive presentations of the SPT and scores of the concurrent free-play sessions (McCune-Nicolich, 1983), as well as the hearing status of families and the sex of the child. Figure 12.1 displays the SPT scores of both the boys and the girls, plotted against age compared with the normative sample. Figure 12.2 displays

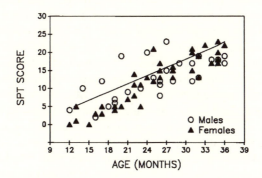

FIGURE 12.1 SPT scores by age and sex.

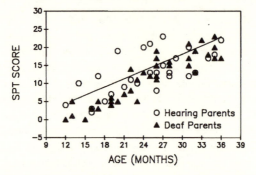

FIGURE 12.2 SPT scores by age and parental hearing status.

the SPT scores of subjects from deaf and hearing families compared with the normative sample. Figure 12.3 displays the longitudinal SPT scores for the subjects described individually.

A number of trends can be identified. In general, our subjects achieved age-equivalent scores on the SPT several months behind those of the hearing children in the standardization sample. Similarly, scores of their free play, according to McCune's system, lagged behind those of her subjects. Although the documented delay as measured by the SPT does not seem remarkable, we feel that qualitative differences in our subjects are more significant than the quantitative results imply. These will be addressed subsequently.

Although overall there was no difference between the average scores of boys and girls, there were some differences in age trends (Figure 12.1). Several of the girls seemed to be very slow starters, with low scores on the SPT at the younger ages. The observations of girls at the upper end of the age range, however, are little different from the norms. For the boys, the pattern is somewhat different. Several of the boys seemed to reach a plateau at a point considerably below the upper end of the scale, although one youngster followed a curve far above the norm for all of our observations.

Comparing the SPT scores of children of deaf families with those of children of hearing families yielded little difference, although a trend favoring the children of hearing families is evident. With regard to this trend, it can be argued that sign communication requires the use of the eyes and hands, and it would, of course, be nearly impossible to use the hands and eyes simultaneously for play and linguistic communication. Nevertheless, during the videotaped sessions themselves, there was relatively little use of sign communication during free-play segments and virtually none during the SPT, and it did not appear to interfere with play. It is also important to note that the free-play segment was scored only for the highest level of symbolic play achieved and not for its frequency or duration. It is possible, of course, that the use of hands and vision for communication may over time influence development of symbolic play, even though it did not seem to be an interference during the

SUBJECT 2 – ANNETTE

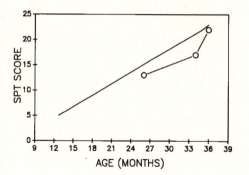

SUBJECT 6 – BARRY

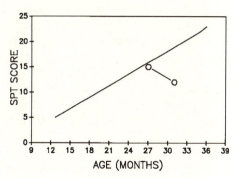

SUBJECT 9 – SARA

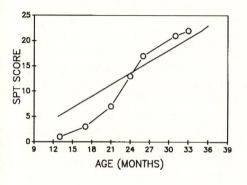

SUBJECT 10 – RONNIE

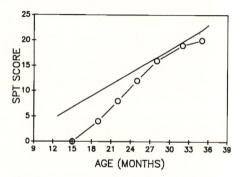

SUBJECT 12 – KATIE

SUBJECT 13 – TONY

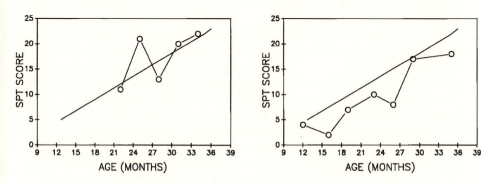

FIGURE 12.3 Trends in SPT scores in selected subjects.

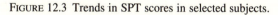

videotaping sessions. Even for nonsigning children, visual attention is critical for lip reading, as well as for interpretation of gesture and affect, and this may in some way adversely affect some aspects of play development.

Direct comparability of our scores on the free-play segments with McCune's results is difficult because our observations were less frequent, and there were fewer subjects at each age level. In addition, as described earlier, we could not distinguish between Levels 4 and 5. What is most comparable is the age at which Level 4 was achieved. More than 50% of McCune's subjects achieved Level 4 by 14 months of age, but not until 20 to 22 months did more than 50% of our subjects score at this level.

The variability among subjects and the different courses that play development took over time were important findings. In trying to understand our children's play development and its correspondence with language development and interpersonal relationships, we were confronted with a variety and complexity of patterns, rather than with clear-cut relationships, although, as noted earlier, some overall trends were apparent. Enriching our data but complicating their analysis was the heterogeneity of the small sample with respect to social, ethnic, and linguistic backgrounds. The parent–child relationship was of particular significance with respect to within-subject variability over time and between-subject differences within our sample. In no case did we see good play development in the context of a seriously compromised parent–child relationship. Consideration on a case-by-case basis of the subjects we were able to follow longitudinally suggested that there was no clear-cut relationship between the use of either oral versus sign language and the complexity or consistency of symbolic play. There was some relationship between language development and play complexity and elaboration, however, with numerous exceptions to the trend observed. The two children with the best sign acquisition and the two children with the best acquisition of oral language did seem to have the most elaborated play. Absence of language did not preclude symbolic play, however, nor was relatively good language acquisition always associated with consistent or well-elaborated symbolic play. We will present some descriptive data to amplify and enrich our quantitative results as well as to attempt to highlight some of the issues regarding the interrelationships among parent–child relations, affective development, language background, and symbolic play.

Subject 13[2]—Tony

Tony exemplifies youngsters whose play and affect varied in tandem with parental mood and availability. Play was vulnerable to ready regression as his affect reflected parental depression and withdrawal. He was the second deaf child born to hearing parents, who were completely opposed to the use of signing for their children. His oral language developed slowly; by age 2½ he used some two word utterances and occasionally a three-word utterance. By age 3 he did not yet use pronouns, refer to himself using a pronoun, encode plurals, or state his gender. He had begun to relate experience, using word and gesture. Tony's relationship with his mother was highly ambivalent. Her moods fluctuated widely. Often she was quite depressed and tended to withdraw; at other times she was relatively attuned to Tony's needs. His affective expression followed a variable course, reflecting the quality of his relationship with his mother at any given point in time. When she was depressed, he too appeared depressed and demonstrated limited investment in play. Tony was little able to make use of symbolic play for adaptive purposes at these times. The level of Tony's play on the SPT also fluctuated widely and was often delayed with respect to test norms. At 23 months he had not yet reached McCune's Level 4 in free play (combining play schemas). While his competence in symbolic play was demonstrated frequently, his performance was often very limited since play was vulnerable to rapid regression when depression interfered with his mother's capacity to be sensitively attuned to him.

Subject 12—Katie

Katie's development reflected an excellent endowment and a mutually rich and rewarding mother–child relationship. Also a child of hearing parents, she progressed unusually well in terms of her predominant affect, oral language, symbolic play, and object relations. It is important to note, however, that although her development of oral language was excellent compared to that of most deaf toddlers, it nevertheless lagged markedly behind what would be expected of a hearing child. By 2 years 3 months she began combining words, and by 2½ years she occasionally used three-word sentences. By age 3 she had begun to relate experiences verbally. Katie's generally excellent development proceeded despite a highly problematic marital situation with periodic parental separations and much conflict. Katie was an exceptionally attractive child whose play was unusually well elaborated. On her own initiative, but perhaps following the nursery model, Katie's mother engaged in joint symbolic play with her daughter on a daily basis. This shared activity was pleasurable for both. At 22 months, when she entered the nursery, Katie was able to use play for positive identification with her mother. She actually swallowed as she placed an empty spoon near the mouth of a doll. She held the doll gently in her arms or leaning over her shoulder so that it could burp. She put it to sleep, nicely covered, with a bottle near the mouth. She further demonstrated her identification with her mother by cleaning with a mop, reaching carefully into all the corners of the room, and washed dishes with fake water, using a sponge and drying the dishes with a towel. Within a few weeks of entry into the nursery, she was able to utilize symbolic play to help her master anxiety and integrate her experience regarding the fitting and use of her hearing aids by "aiding" dolls in her play.

Two major factors contributed to Katie's particularly good development. Her play and language were sparked and supported by a closely attuned and mutually satisfying mother–child relationship. This seemed to have overshadowed the highly problematic marital situation and fluctuating availability of her father. Her mother, with a great deal of help and support from her own mother, was generally able to maintain her positive and gratifying relationship with Katie, despite the distress that accompanied the marital tension and the diagnosis of her handicap. We wondered to what extent her unusual charm, prettiness, and intellectual responsiveness might have served to elicit positive affect and attention from her mother, and perhaps her grandmother, in a way that may have compensated for her deficit and mitigated their reactions to it. An additional factor was perhaps critical in the rapid pace of Katie's development. Her underlying superior intelligence was evident in all aspects of her functioning, on the various tasks of the Yale Scale of Developmental Tests, as well as in her spontaneous behaviors. This seemed to be of great significance in her capacity to utilize information optimally, to derive meaning and integrate perceptions with minimal cues—for example, in lip reading.[3]

Subject 6—Barry

The introduction of some signed vocabulary did not necessarily guarantee excellent development of either language or play. The critical issue in Barry's development was the effect of parental anxiety and its expression in an overly didactic mode of relating. Barry was the second deaf child born to hearing parents. Because his older sibling was deaf, Barry was evaluated by 2½ months of age, and he was fitted with hearing aids at 4 months. Isolated signs were introduced early as a bridge and supplement to the oral language Billy's parents hoped he would develop. While Barry's family knew some individual signs, they didn't really know the language, so signing was not used in a natural way for interpersonal communication. The teaching of signs as well as oral language involved unusual dedication and determination. This resulted in intensive attempts to teach and elicit language, to the exclusion of more normal playfulness and pleasure in other aspects of Barry's burgeoning autonomous functioning. Despite his mother's valiant but excessive efforts to teach him, he did not acquire signs especially rapidly. Oral language developed at what was probably an average pace for a deaf youngster. An overly didactic mother–son relationship prevailed, and the teaching of language served as another modality through which this relationship was enacted. Play, as measured both by the SPT and by observation during the nursery sessions, was often stilted and repetitious, rarely joyful. It was often controlled by the parent, utilized, from the parent's perspective, almost exclusively as a vehicle to elicit and teach language. During the course of nursery participation Barry's mother's intrusiveness was considerably reduced, most likely as she became reassured by Barry's beginning language acquisition and his growing communicativeness and spontaneity. Barry ultimately used language communicatively, but his achievement was not beyond that of most orally trained deaf youngsters. Symbolic play, never especially rich, took a secondary position and functioned only minimally as an expressive modality for him.

Subject 9—Sara

Just as there was marked variability among the children of hearing parents described previously, Sara and Ronnie (Subject 10, discussed next) highlight the vivid contrasts among the children of deaf parents. Sara was an adorable child, the first girl in a deaf family whose primary means of communication was signing. In contrast to Barry's (Subject 6) experience, signing was utilized as a rich and complete communicative system and, exposed to it from early infancy, Sara quickly became a fluent signer. She was a happy, enthusiastic youngster, and her symbolic play developed well. Although her symbolic play was somewhat less complex than Katie's

(Subject 12), it also involved mothering activities, indicating that she was utilizing play as an expression of positive identification with parental ministrations. Sara's rapid acquisition of signing permitted her to communicate as well as hearing toddlers. Her relationship with her mother was close and only minimally ambivalent. Although she seemed very bright and engaging, Sara's scores on the Yale Scales were only average; it is highly likely that the puzzlelike tasks tapped areas of development in which Sara was least invested, whereas her language development was an area of strength, serving a communicative function in a charming and well-related youngster.

Subject 10—Ronnie

In sharp contrast to Sara, Ronnie, also the third child of deaf parents, was developing especially poorly when she entered the nursery at 15 months of age. Generally little attuned to Ronnie's needs, her mother was teasing, ambivalent, and at times withholding. These characteristics were reflected in Ronnie's reciprocal attitudes. Of average intelligence, Ronnie was relatively uncommunicative, using little signing or gesturing, and was affectively subdued. Although signing was the main language used at home, initially her mother rarely signed specifically to her. By 2 years 8 months, Ronnie was just beginning to combine signs, and her sign vocabulary was not comparable in size to the vocabulary of the average hearing youngster her age. Ronnie's symbolic play developed slowly, as observed in both the nursery and the videotaped play sessions. She did not achieve Level 4 in free play until she was 25 months of age. Her scores on the SPT climbed, however, from markedly below the mean to within the average range during her second year in the nursery. Within the nursery, during the course of intervention, her symbolic play advanced, but it never achieved the degree of elaboration of Katie's or Sara's, for example. At 35 months she signed "sleep," putting a doll on a blanket with a handkerchief by its side; she then wrapped the handkerchief around the doll and signed "pooh." She wrapped the doll in a towel and began to clean the room with a mop, carrying the doll as she worked. Her play tended to be solitary unless interaction was initiated by her mother or the therapist. Her relationship with her mother had become less ambivalent and her affect somewhat brighter. While her competence in ASL increased and she often related past experiences to the therapist, by age 3 she typically strung no more than three signs together.

Subject 2—Annette

Annette illustrates nicely the possibility of well-developed symbolic play in the context of extremely limited language. She was the youngest member of a hearing family with a multilingual background. English was not spoken at home, and her parents were emphatically opposed to her learning sign language. Despite having at least average intelligence, she was markedly unsuccessful in acquistion of any oral language, compared with other deaf youngsters her age with the same degree of hearing loss. Our observations were corroborated by the educator of the deaf who worked with her. For example, at 2 years of age her language skills were placed at

1 year. By 3 years she used jargon, had a few gestures, and had acquired two or three signs despite parental disapproval, but she produced only a few poorly artic- ulated words. Her receptive language was also limited and context bound, requiring strong gestural and pantomimed support. By age 3 virtually no language was observed, but the reasons were not entirely evident. Annette wore her hearing aids consistently. Her strong intent to communicate was clear, and she did use gestures. On one level, despite the lack of language communication, she enjoyed a warm, close relationship with her father, who was her primary caregiver and playmate. But he was also provocative and teasing, often disrespectful of her dependency needs and autonomous strivings. Nevertheless, there was a richly playful quality that suf- fused his relationship with Annette. He was dramatic and enjoyed enacting scenarios for her. This may have influenced her ability to use play to make and convey mean- ing. Annette's relationship with her mother fluctuated according to variations in maternal mood and responsiveness. Affectively, Annette was at times vivacious and active, like her father; at other times she tended to withdraw, as did her mother. She reportedly recalled and enacted complex behavioral sequences at home and was frequently able to meet her own needs by taking direct action.

Her play was somewhat variable in the videotaped sessions, but at 36 months she was very much on target in terms of the score on the SPT. Although test scores and an occasional brief episode within the nursery indicated the capacity for appro- priately elaborated symbolic play for a youngster her age, qualitative nursery obser- vations revealed marked fluctuation and general limitations of her play. It is remark- able that her unusually limited language by no means precluded symbolic play, which far exceeded her language capacities, both in terms of developmental expec- tations and in terms of what could be expressed. It seems highly significant that at times she was able to use play for the purpose of expression, making meaning, and organizing thoughts and experiences. Of particular importance was the use, albeit limited, that she was able to make of play in the mastery of conflict and anxiety regarding separation, facilitated by the therapist in the nursery. Such play was also utilized to help Annette's parents understand and address her concerns about sepa- ration. This was especially significant for her development, since she was not able to use language for this purpose. Her capacity for symbolization through play by far surpassed her symbolic attainments in any other medium.

Discussion

While there were differences among our subjects with respect to their symbolic play, there were also notable commonalities. In general, the deaf children we studied demonstrated the capacity for symbolic play. On the average, this capacity developed at a slightly slower rate than in hearing children in terms of their scores on the SPT. Unlike ours, the subjects studied by Gregory and Mogford (1983) surpassed the performance of hearing children by age 30 months, while the present sample remained, on the whole, somewhat behind. The question arises of whether the per- formance of Gregory and Mogford's sample might have been facilitated by their being evaluated at home; on the other hand, the SPT norms are based on data collected outside the home, in nursery or day-care settings. Gregory and Mogford's subjects were learning oral English only.

The deaf children we studied, aged 1 to 3, seem to be competent in their acquisition of the prerequisites for symbolic play. As described by Fields (1979), they are capable of mental representation, as evidenced by a capacity for deferred imitation, as well as sustained and purposeful activity based on forethought. They are able to use toy replicas to represent real objects and are able to engage in simple pretend activities that replicate their own experience. Nevertheless, these capacities emerge somewhat later and their use is less consistent than in hearing children. In terms of qualitative issues, we essentially agree with Gregory and Mogford (1983), who view the children's functioning on the SPT as indicating that they have learned appropriate use of the objects but who nevertheless see their deaf subjects' symbolic play as quite different from that of their hearing control group. In contrast to the hearing subjects, they found the symbolic play of deaf infants to be sparse, inconsistent, somewhat repetitive, and lacking in age-appropriate complexity and structure. For most of our subjects, our observations were consistent with Gregory and Mogford's; the fluctuating quality of play in these subjects was evident in the free-play portion of our data, as well as in their SPT scores. Spontaneous play during observations made within the nursery, a more familiar setting than the room used for videotaping, tended to be much like the children's play in the videotaped sessions.

A number of factors seem to be related to the development and use of symbolic play in our subjects in terms of the variability among them, as well as the inconsistency and limitations seen in the play of many of them. One critical factor in the development of their symbolic play appears to be the quality of the parent–child relationship and the investment of the parent in the child's play. In two important studies, Slade (1987a, 1987b) pointed out that early symbolic play is affected both by the mother's facilitating interventions and by the quality of the mother–child bond. O'Connell and Bretherton (1984) also demonstrated that developmentally appropriate parent–child collaborative play alters the kinds of play behaviors children manifest. They noted variability in the capacities of mothers to attune their play interventions to the child's level. In our youngsters, both the quality of the parent–child relationship and the parent's attitudes toward play, particularly in the context of the child's handicap, affected play development. Not surprisingly, we found that parent–child relationships varied markedly along many other dimensions as well as play.

In no case did we find qualitatively adequate play development in the context of a seriously compromised parent–child relationship. In some cases, play fluctuated in tandem with the parental mood; in other cases, it was subverted by ongoing difficulties in the relationship. Some parents demonstrated a relatively good capacity to isolate their own distress in regard to the child's handicap, as well as other situational tensions, from their relationship with the child, at least most of the time, whereas others could not. Our subjects' reactions to shifts in parental mood were evident in their play, as well as in other aspects of their behavior. Parental depression, for example, was at times manifest in a tendency toward withdrawal from the child. This was reflected in the child's object relations, affect, and play.

In addition to the general influence of parental functioning and mood, there were a number of more specific ways in which play was affected by the quality of the parent–child interactions. With deaf children the facilitation of reciprocity in play is often burdened by didactic concerns on the part of the parents. While Barry's mother was a rather extreme example, she was by no means exceptional in her attitude. Both hearing and deaf parents tend to feel that if their deaf child is playing, he or she is not learning, and they frequently view play as wasting precious time that could be used in teaching language. Paradoxically, the parents' anxious and often intrusive demands for speech or sign language not only create tension between parent and child but also effectively end a play episode, adversely affecting the construction of symbols by pulling the child away from activity that builds meaning (Fields, Blum, & Scharfman, in press). Beyond the issue of being overly didactic with respect to teaching language, some parents tended to be unusually controlling, rarely respecting the child's autonomous strivings, often because lack of audition prevented the child from hearing parental admonitions, safety concerns, and so on. On the other hand, in several cases, parents were intuitively well attuned to their children's play initiatives and were facilitating. In other instances, participation in the nursery and work with the therapist helped the parent to value and understand the child's play.

One such example, observed in a youngster during a home visit, is most revealing. Benjamin, 19 months old, was born to deaf Orthodox Jewish parents. The therapist noticed that he was wrapping the string of a pull toy around his arm in an unusual way. When she realized that he was imitating his father putting on philacteries for prayer, she shared this observation with his mother. His mother agreed with great delight that this must be what he was doing and communicated by a prayer gesture her understanding to the child. He then extended his play by putting around his shoulders a small blanket that he often played with; he rocked back and forth, pretending that the blanket was a prayer shawl and that he was praying. He then gave both parent and therapist little blankets, which he indicated should be put around their shoulders, and laughed in delight as they imitated his praying (Fields, 1979). Both parent and child expressed enormous pleasure in their playful communicative interaction. The parental understanding of the play seemed to spark its further elaboration. This exemplifies how intervention helped shift the child's egocentric and solitary activity to one of shared communication and symbolic meaning. Yet, as we observed for many of the other children, this was a rare instance of symbolic play and required the intervention of an adult for its elaboration. Even at 31 months, Benjamin's play was still described as generally restricted and impoverished.

It is important to note that parenting a deaf child is fraught with serious challenges. That some parents adapted so well is perhaps more surprising than the degree of difficulty others encountered. Beyond the need to come to terms with their own grief, there are realistic anxieties and burdens. Special programs must be sought and attended, audiological evalutions and hearing aids must be fitted, and critical decisions must be made. Concerns about the youngster's ultimate functioning color early development. It is understandable that many parents, like Barry's, for example, because of their overriding anxiety about language acquisition, disregard many important areas of their child's development.

Just as parenting a deaf child requires numerous adaptations, growing up with a major sensory deficit requires adaptation and compensation. We can speculate on how the auditory deficit and compensatory mechanisms might be related to the quality of play we observed in our subjects. The distinction between competence and performance can be made with respect to their play; functioning at their optimal level is relatively rare for many of them. As noted earlier, these youngsters are especially dependent upon visual scanning for information about their environment with respect to changes and shifts that might seem threatening or, in any case, demanding of attention. It may be more difficult to focus visually on play materials for extended periods, and perhaps only in situations that are perceived as especially safe and stable is this possible. Communication, too, for both signing and nonsigning youngsters requires visual attention. Perhaps the effort involved in sustaining symbolic play is especially great in view of the multiple requirements for visual and manual function. Possibly play regresses readily when the effort required becomes too great and the gratification too limited.

In view of these issues, the play of the young deaf child seems particularly dependent upon adult involvement. While parental influence seems to be a significant factor in the development of symbolic play in normal youngsters, it is very likely even more crucial in the development of a child with a sensory deficit. Thus parents have the exceptionally difficult task not only of dealing with but also surmounting intense feelings of their own if they are to achieve the especially fine attunement required to understand what their deaf children are grasping and trying to express. Extra effort may be required of the parent to elicit a response from a young, nonverbal child, sometimes a rather passive partner who may readily tune out. The mediation of a parent or therapist may be required as an external organizer of experience, compensating for lack of internal language as an organizer, particularly for those youngsters most delayed in language. Adults focus the child's attention, facilitating return to an activity, just as language might function for hearing children, often observed talking as they play.

It appears that the lack of readily available language to aid in remembering, planning, and organizing experience, as well as communicating in conjunction with play, impinged on play development, affecting its consistency and elaboration for at least some of our subjects. It is important to emphasize that the deaf children we studied differed from each other not only in parental hearing status but, more importantly, in that they were learning different languages, including oral English, ASL, and signed English. They were acquiring language at variable rates, achieving by age 3 very different levels of language competence. Annette's development of symbolic play suggests that an almost complete lack of language does not entirely preclude the development of this capacity. Nursery therapists were aware, however, of the enormous difficulty entailed in helping children like Annette, almost totally lacking in language, to extend and elaborate their play, whereas with other children, even a few words or signs could be utilized to bridge isolated play schemas. On the other hand, although Barry's communication developed relatively well, it did not seem to facilitate play, not valued by his mother except as an accompaniment to language instruction. In many other children, however, whose language was better developed, play seemed to be more elaborated. Our two youngsters who were most adept with sign language demonstrated relatively complex play, essentially like that of their hearing peers, by age 3. Two of our nonsigning youngsters were exceptional in both their play and language development; for these children play was also equal to that of their hearing peers, although their relatively good language was not. Both of these children demonstrated superior intelligence on developmental tests, and both had generally positive and supportive relationships with their parents. One could postulate that the factors of intelligence and parent–child relationships provided the underpinnings for their excellent development of symbolic capacities in both spheres.

Of primary significance is the fact that our deaf subjects indeed have the cognitive and representational capacities that are prerequisite for symbolic play, despite the delay in language acquisition for most of them. Beyond this basic level, language appears to have an important role in complex, rich play sequences and later in permitting social play. While mental representation seems a necessary but not sufficient condition for language, language seems an essential component in the development of symbolic processes as these children shift from mental representation to increasingly complex symbolic activity. Gregory and Mogford (1983) describe the deaf children they studied as ''stuck in the appropriate use of objects,'' able to represent routine daily sequences but less able to use imaginative capacities. Wolf and Gardner (1981) differentiate between representation and symbolic expression. While we did see what would be considered symbolic expression, it was not frequent and was often dependent upon facilitation by the therapist. The question can be raised of how the relationship of play and language may shift during the different stages of development. While a severe delay in language acquisition did not preclude the development of competence in symbolic play in our subjects, language may be more critical in the development of more complex, imaginative play and of social play, particularly as the youngsters become preschoolers. We wonder whether early symbolic play may be more influenced by the quality of developing object relations and later, more highly elaborated play, might be increasingly influenced by language.

Despite the paucity and lack of elaboration of symbolic play in many of our subjects, within the nursery context play could be facilitated so that it was available to serve a variety of developmental and psychological functions. In some cases, parents' growing understanding both of the significance of play and of the meanings their youngsters were making through play enabled them to participate in mutually pleasurable, shared experience. The children felt understood, and both affective and semantic communication were promoted. Among many other functions, symbolic play served to strengthen identifications and to aid in body schematization. In the nursery, therapists also actively utilized play to help the youngsters deal with trauma and conflict, particularly with respect to the process of being fitted for hearing aids and becoming accustomed to using them, as well as to help the mastery of issues around separation and other developmental conflicts and trauma (Fields et al., in press).

It is important to note that our findings may not be representative of deaf infants in general. For this sample, even in instances where deaf parents were teaching their baby some form of sign language, the very fact that the parents chose a school advocating an oral rather than a sign approach may reflect an underlying bias. Future research should include the study of deaf children for whom sign language is the major communicative mode and who, as a result, may be developing more rapidly. Nevertheless, the present subjects share with the large population of deaf infants an auditory loss that from birth is interwoven with developing affective and cognitive processes. Even under optimal circumstances, perceptions of the human and non-human worlds must be organized and mentally represented somewhat differently in hearing-deprived children, affecting their most basic experience of self, other, and surround.

NOTES

1. The Yale Developmental Schedules are a composite of a number of items from well-standardized tests including the Gesell, Viennese Infant Scale, Merrill–Palmer, Bayley Scales, and the Stanford Binet. This composite has allowed for developmental evaluation of any child from birth to 6 years. It was developed by Dr. Sally Provence at the Yale Child Study Center and has been in use for over 25 years.

2. Subject numbers correspond to those in Table 12.1.

3. The issue of superior intelligence was also of major significance in the precocious play development of subject 15, the one subject who did not participate in the nursery. By 27 months his score on the SPT was equivalent to that of a 36-month-old, according to the test norms. This advanced development was reflected, as well, in his score on the Yale Scales and was undoubtedly a factor in his rapid acquisition of oral language.

REFERENCES

Allen, T. E. (1986). Patterns of academic achievement among hearing impaired students. In A. N. Schildroth & M. A. Karchmer (Eds.), *Deaf Children in America* (pp. 161–206). San Diego: College Hill Press.

Casby, M. W., & McCormack, S. M. (1985). Symbolic play and early communication development in hearing-impaired children. *Journal of Communication Disorders, 18*, 67–78.

Corman, H., & Escalona, S. K. (1980). Cognition, symbolic action and language learning. Unpublished manuscript. Albert Einstein College of Medicine, Bronx, NY.

Darbyshire, O. (1977). Play patterns in young children with impaired hearing. *Volta Review, 79*, 19–26.

Fields, B. (1979). A theoretical consideration of libidinal object constancy and object permanence: Issues related to normal development and hearing impairment. Unpublished master's essay, Sarah Lawrence College, Bronxville, NY.

Fields, B., Blum, E., Scharfman H. (1993). Intervention with very young children and their parents: A model based on the infant deaf. In E. Fenichel & S. Provence (Eds.), *Development in jeopardy: Clinical responses to infants and parents.* New York: International Universities Press.

Furth, H. G. (1966). *Thinking without language.* London: Collier-Macmillan.

Galenson, E. (1984). Psychoanalytic approach to psychotic disturbances in very young children. *Hillside Journal of Psychiatry, 6*, 21–240.

Gregory, S., & Mogford, K. (1983). The development of symbolic play in young deaf children. In D. R. Rogers & J. A. Sloboda (Eds.), *The acquisition of symbolic skills* (pp. 221–232). New York: Plenum Press.

Lowe, M. (1975). Trends in the development of representational play in infants from one to three years: An observational study. *Journal of Child Psychiatry, 16*, 33–47

Lowe, M., & Costello, A. (1976). *Manual for the Symbolic Play Test.* London: NFER–Nelson.

Mahler, M. S. (1968). *On human symbiosis and the vicissitudes of individuation* New York: International Universities Press.

McCune, L. (1985). Sequences in play. Unpublished manuscript. Rutgers University, New Brunswick, NJ.

McCune-Nicolich, L. (1983). A manual for analyzing free play. Revised. Unpublished manuscript. Rutgers University, New Brunswick, NJ.

McCune-Nicolich, L. (1981). Toward symbolic functioning: Structure of early pretend games and potential parallels with language. *Child Development, 52*, 785–797.

Newport, E. L., & Meier, R. P. (1985). The acquisition of American sign language. In D. Slobin (Ed.), *The Cross-linguistic study of language acquisition:* Vol. 1, *The Data* (pp. 881–938). Hillsdale, NJ: Erlbaum.

Nicolich, L. (1977). Beyond sensorimotor intelligence: Assessment of symbolic maturity through analysis of pretend play. *Merrill-Palmer Quarterly, 23*, 89–99.

O'Connell, B., & Bretherton, I. (1984). Toddler's play, alone and with mother: The role of maternal guidance. In I. Bretherton (Ed.), *Symbolic Play* (pp. 337–368). New York: Academic Press.

Piaget, J. (1962). *Play, dreams, and imitation.* New York: Norton.

Rainer, J. D., Altshuler, K. Z., & Kallmann, F. J. (1969). *Family and mental health problems in a deaf population.* Springfield, IL: Charles C. Thomas.

Scharfman, H. (1977). The play of hearing and hearing impaired four year olds—a comparison. Unpublished manuscript. Lexington School for the Deaf, New York, NY.

Slade, A. (1986). Symbolic play and separation-individuation. *Bulletin of the Menninger Clinic, 50*, 541–563.

Slade, A. (1987a). A longitudinal study of maternal involvement and symbolic play during the toddler period. *Child Development, 52*(2), 367–375.

Slade, A. (1987b). The quality of attachment and early symbolic play. *Developmental Psychology, 23*(1), 78–85.

Stern, D. (1974). Mother and infant at play: The dyadic interaction involving facial, vocal and gaze behaviors. In M. Lewis & L. Rosenblum (Eds.), *The effect of the infant on its caretaker* (pp. 187–214). New York: Wiley.

Stern, D. (1977). *The first relationship.* Cambridge, MA: Harvard University Press.

Tomlinson-Keasey, C., & Kelly, R. R. (1978). The deaf child's symbolic world. *American Annals of the Deaf, 123*, 452–459.

Trybus, R., & Karchmer, M. (1977). School achievement scores of hearing impaired children: National data on achievement staus and growth patterns. *American Annals of the Deaf, 122*, 62–69.

Werner, H., & Kaplan, B. (1963). *Symbol formation.* New York: Wiley.

Wolf, D., & Gardner, H. (1981). On the structure of early symbolization. In R. L. Schiefelbusch & D. D. Bricker (Eds.), *Early language: Acquisition and intervention* (pp. 287–328). Baltimore: University Park Press.

13

Play and Narrative in Inhibited Children: A Longitudinal Case Study

LOU-MARIÉ KRUGER
DENNIE PALMER WOLF

In the history of psychology, the importance of the construct of temperament has fluctuated as different psychological approaches to personality development have gained prominence. The first and most important shift was a shift from stable categories of people to malleable psychological dimensions (Kagan, 1989b). With the advent of psychoanalytic psychology, motivation became the focal point of the study of personality rather than stable inborn temperamental characteristics. Cognitive and social psychology also questioned the notion of inborn stable characteristics, and when issues of personality were addressed, the focus shifted to self-concept and beliefs about the self (Kagan, 1989b). More recently, with renewed interest in the biology of behavior, psychology has witnessed a renewal of interest in the notion that children are born with biases that predispose them to acquire certain behaviors, as well as certain motives and beliefs. However, this new interest in temperament is often accompanied by the qualifying notion that these biases and predispositions cannot be seen as always determining behavior. Whether they will come into play, and the extent to which they come into play, depend a great deal on the environment to which a child is exposed. Thus, the conception of temperament has changed over the years from one of an enduring characteristic intrinsic to a person to one of a syndrome that some individuals realize or exhibit under *certain* conditions.

To a large extent, the study of the temperamental trait of inhibition reflects these newer and changing views of temperament. In a series of studies conducted with infants and young children in the 1980s, Kagan, Snidman, and their associates identified two ''distinctive temperamental groups,'' those who were inhibited to the unfamiliar and those who were uninhibited to the unfamiliar. This classification was made on the basis on a complex set of behavioral and physiological measurements

(Kagan & Snidman, 1991). What is novel is that Kagan and Snidman suggest that "some infants are born with a physiology that biases them to develop one rather than another behavioral surface, *given certain environments*" (1991, p. 856). In many cases, it is in those environments that behavioral and physiological temperaments will be maintained.

In this chapter we will be concerned with the "certain environments" or contexts within which a temperamental trait such as inhibition is maintained. In particular, we will focus upon the *transactional environment* or network of human relationships that the child constructs and is constructed by. We will use a detailed analysis of the play and dialogue between a 5-year-old girl and her mother as our window into a particular transactional environment. As will be described, this child manifested all the features of extreme inhibition, beginning in infancy. A close look at this dyad as they negotiate meaning, and as the child struggles to find her narrative voice, provides a particularly compelling and dynamic look at the nature of transactional processes as they shift over time.

In discussing issues of context and behavioral inhibition, Stevenson-Hinde (1989) suggests that the caretaking environment or early relationships might influence the development and expression of a trait. She is very careful, however, to note that "the direction of effect, whether the child's characteristic drove the relationship or whether the relationship influenced the characteristic, is an issue that requires a precise formulation, in terms of differences between the participants at one particular time or changes in the participants across time" (p. 133). Although we want to reiterate the importance of the caretaking environment in the maintenance of a temperamental trait such as inhibition, we also want to suggest a reformulation of the question of the direction of effect. Instead of thinking that a particular kind of relationship will lead some—but not all—children to exhibit a trait, we agree with Sameroff (1975), who suggests that neither the traits (behavioral and physiological manifestations) nor the caretaking environment are constant in development. The constants in development are the processes by which such traits or characteristics are maintained in the continuous transactions between an infant and the caretaking environment, with both organism and environment characterized by a certain plasticity (Sameroff, 1975). This is not to deny that infants do display particular sets of temperamental traits and physiological characteristics, and that such traits and characteristics are often maintained throughout development. It is rather to argue that the process through which a temperamental trait such as inhibition is maintained is an extremely complicated process. It is not simply a matter of a given child interacting with a given environment, but rather a continuous transaction between a child and her environment, in which both child and environment are constantly changing and effecting changes in each other. The process through which traits are maintained is then a transaction between the child and her caretaking environment. This transaction, in turn, will also be a function of larger sociocultural issues such as how acceptable it is for a child to be inhibited in this culture or how acceptable it is for a child of this gender to be inhibited in this culture (Radke-Yarrow, Richters, & Wilson, 1988).

In their new and very specific conception of a temperamental trait of inhibition, Kagan and Snidman (1991, 1992) suggest that temperamental traits may be contextualized in a second way: The behavioral manifestation of the trait becomes apparent only in specific contexts. In other words, behavioral inhibition (withdrawal, shyness, fearfulness, timidity, lack of spontaneous remarks) will be displayed only in contexts that are considered to be unfamiliar, as in the presence of a stranger. Asendorpf (1990) further contributed to this contextual notion of inhibition by showing that although children maintain certain levels of inhibition to the unfamiliar, other contextual factors such as the degree of unfamiliarity and social-evaluative concerns, will also contribute to individual differences in inhibition in childhood. We will further argue that as the long-term context or caretaking environment is not a constant variable, the immediate context of unfamiliarity is also not a given. In other words, it does not necessarily inhere in how scary a mask is, or how strange a visitor is, or how challenging a task is. Objects and experiences can be threatening for more complex reasons (for instance, they may be intrusive, or they may imply a temporary disruption in maintaining a particular kind of familiar relationship from the mother). Also, for different children, unfamiliarity may be threatening for different reasons. It is therefore crucial to understand how different children make different sense of a situation.

In this chapter we will look at inhibition in one child, with the purpose of adding to our understanding of the contextual bases of temperament. We will investigate the ways in which the child's characteristics can provoke distinctive responses in others and how these responses become characteristic of the significant, as well as the novel, relationships in the child's life. In this way, a continuous, self-organizing system can be created. We will also look at the possibility that a caretaker's characteristic way of interacting with a child can lead the child to respond in certain distinctive ways—also setting in motion a continuous system. Throughout our discussion, we will extend the new conception of temperament by arguing the limits of any view of temperament that ignores its relational or systemic aspects.

Method

We will look in detail at the play of a 5-year-old girl called Rachel. She was a subject in a longitudinal study conducted by Jerome Kagan, Nancy Snidman, and their associates; the study was aimed at determining the infant predictors of inhibited and uninhibited profiles in children. In this longitudinal study, 52 Caucasian middle-class child–mother pairs were involved in a series of experimental tasks and physiological testing at 14, 20, 60, 72, 84, and 96 months. We will focus primarily upon Rachel's 60-month experimental protocol, which along with the protocols for later visits consisted of a series of narrative and narrative play tasks. At age 5, these tasks included two picture descriptions tasks, a bathroom script, a co-construction task with her mother, the telling of a story from a book without words, and the creation of a make-believe jungle with characters and problems (*replica play jungle* [RPJ]).

We chose Rachel for intensive study because, as an infant of 14 months, she was classified as being severely inhibited to the unfamiliar. When compared with uninhibited children, Rachel had peripheral and physiological reactions (such as larger increases in heart rate, pupillary dilation, and skeletal muscle tension to cognitive stress; larger rises in diastolic blood pressure when her posture changed from sitting to standing) that implied lower thresholds in the limbic system to novel and challenging events (Kagan, Reznick, & Snidman, 1988b, Kagan & Snidman, 1991). At 14 months Rachel was also classified as displaying the distinct behavior of an inhibited child: she was fearful and timid in the unfamiliar situations to which she was exposed. Kagan, Snidman, and their associates found these characteristics to be typical of inhibited children. These elevated behavioral and physiological levels of inhibition led Kagan and Snidman to predict that a child like Rachel would display extraordinarily high levels of inhibition to the unfamiliar at school age.

We set out to establish whether there are any discernible patterns in the interaction and transaction between a child categorized as severely inhibited and her mother. The centerpiece for our study of Rachel is her performance in two storytelling tasks at age 5. The first task is one that invites Rachel to make up a story to accompany the actions of play figures, and the second is one that invites her to join with her mother in retelling a piece of personal history. The latter narrative is considered a co-construction because mother and child recount a past event together. We will also examine the 14-month and school-age visits, although in less detail. This phase of the analysis will allow us to explore the relational aspects of the maintenance of temperament in a longitudinal frame. The dynamic exchange between Rachel, her mother, and the experimenter as Rachel is asked to create a narrative and a make-believe world offers a particularly clear look at some of the relational aspects of temperament, and at the ways processes of interaction and transaction between mother and child inform the development and maintenance of personality traits.

Replica Play as a Context for the Study of Inhibition

Replica play is symbolic play with small figures of the kind common among American children 2 to 5 years old, in which they create a small world where actions or whole narratives can be dramatized. This specific replica play task, the jungle task (RPJ), begins with the experimenter taking out of a plastic bag a variety of plastic wild animals, some shrubs, trees, and a pond and asking the child to help her (the experimenter) set up the jungle. The child is asked to identify the animals and to tell the experimenter what each animal can do (Prompt one). The scene is then set with the prompt "There once was a jungle and lots of animals lived there, even a great big elephant. Can you tell me more about the place?" (Prompt two). After the child's response, the first crisis in the jungle is introduced: "One day the lion said to the elephant: 'Elephant, you're so big and purple, you look like a great big purple grape.' What happened next? Now you make them talk to each other" (Prompt three). After the child's response, a second crisis is introduced with the following prompt: "Boom boom boom boom. It was the dragon. Closer and closer he came. Boom boom boom boom. And he landed smack in the middle of the pond" (Prompt four).

Usually the activity of symbolic play (including replica play) is described in terms of its affective and cognitive achievement of representation (Nicolich, 1977; Piaget, 1926; Watson & Fischer, 1977; Wolf, 1984; Wolf & Grollman, 1982; Wolf, Rygh, & Altshuler, 1984) or its expressive properties (Singer & Singer, 1990). Much less explored are the relational aspects of symbolic play: What does it entail in terms of trust and familiarity? What is it in terms of establishing joint intersubjectivity? What might be challenging or frightening about making one's imagination public to others?

Viewed in this light, there are several reasons why it is important to look at Rachel's behavior during a task such as RPJ. First, make-believe narrative play, in the presence of mother and a home visitor, involves a complex and particular flickering back and forth of alignments (Goffman, 1981). Second, it involves leaving the predictable world of the here and now. Finally, joint symbolic play calls on Rachel to establish an intense intersubjectivity with a virtual stranger (the experimenter).

Flickering Alignments

In this task, Rachel has to juggle what are often called *stances* (Wolf & Hicks, 1989) or *footings* (Goffman, 1981). At one moment she will be the narrator of the make-believe story, and she has to speak in the voices of the characters who live in the make-believe jungle or story world. At other moments she has to step outside that fictional world and occupy the here-and-now world. In the here-and-now world, she has to bear in mind that she is part of an experiment and that she is still, in the context of this home visit in the here and now, the child-host to the stranger-adult *and* a daughter to her mother. In other words, Rachel is constantly moving between "the different circles in play" or the different spheres of interaction. But this is a profoundly triadic situation. Rachel, her mother, and a home visitor, Diane, all occupy a joint, intimate space around the array of small toys. Consequently, Rachel has to make constant relational choices. In the case of the immediate world of face-to-face interaction, it becomes interesting, given the standard questions: Who will Rachel ask questions of? To whom will she comment or ask for help setting up the toys? In the case of the make-believe world, who will be a spectator and who will be a participant?

Choices of Worlds

In addition, as indicated earlier, if Rachel is to engage in the replica play, she also has to choose worlds. She has to be willing to leave the familiar, pragmatic world in which her interactions with her co-participants and the uses of the props are relatively predictable and safe and enter a make-believe world in which anything can happen. In addition, given the structure of the home visit, she has to be willing to do this with a virtual stranger—Diane, the home visitor and experimenter. More specifically, the jungle task asks that Rachel move gradually from the immediate and pragmatic world deeper and deeper into fantasy with Diane.

Joint Intersubjectivity

Finally, then, if Rachel is going to participate fully, she, the child, has to construct a story world in which characters living there address a problem. The story world is a world in which there is conflict and resolution. Given the structure of the task, in which her mother is officially only an observer, this means that Rachel will have to improvise jointly a solution to a difficult situation with the home visitor as a partner. In essence, she has to be willing to undertake the literal difficulty of improvising her way to a resolution (which could involve fumbling, repairs, or discussions about what path to pursue) and the fictional difficulties of the story world (how the danger in the jungle will be resolved and whether a violent, mean, or unpleasant solution is acceptable) jointly with a stranger.

With a detailed or micro-analysis of a text from Rachel's jungle task, we will show that what makes Rachel's behavior during this task so different from those of other children is her reluctance to assume different stances, to jump back and forth between different worlds. While some would argue that this reluctance to enter different worlds is determined by relatively stable temperamental characteristics, we will attempt, through our analysis of the text, to show that this reluctance is rather due to how Rachel constructs the particular interaction or how she understands the entering of the story world, in this case the imaginary jungle. We will also argue that this construction or understanding is not arbitrary but can be construed as a function of a continuous transaction between Rachel and her mother or primary caretaker.

However, because we also want to investigate patterns in and the eventual adaptiveness of the transaction between the child and her caretaking environment, we will look at Rachel's play longitudinally. We will therefore start our analysis with a brief look at Rachel at play in the presence of her mother at 14 months and, after a detailed analysis of Rachel at play at age 5, will conclude with a glance at her play at 6, 7, and 8 years old.

Playing in the Lab at 14 Months

We looked at Rachel and her mother in the laboratory at 14 months with the aim of identifying distinctive patterns of interaction within the dyad. At 14 months Rachel is able to stand up by herself and walk a few steps. She sometimes responds to her mother's words and actions, and can even say one or two words herself. We know that the emergence of a new mobility and a verbal self (Stern, 1985) typically implies a new phase in the mother–child relationship, a phase in which the tie between mother and child becomes less dependent and less symbiotic (Bowlby, 1982; Mahler, Pine, & Bergman, 1975). The child's elation at the mastery and opportunity brought about by walking are evident in her "love affair with the world" (Greenacre, 1957); the child of this age will typically delight in exercising her newfound autonomy to the hilt (Mahler et al., 1975). Parental affirmation of the child's abilities is particularly important at this moment in development, and will help to establish the child's sense of herself as confident and able. In addition, the mother and child now have to incorporate the newly acquired linguistic abilities of the child. Paradoxically, while language does make it possible for the child to share experiences with others, the actual ability to express her own experiences also makes her more differentiated and separate. Language can thus both affirm what is shared *and* emphasize the uniqueness of experiences that are not sharable. It opens up new possibilities of relatedness while making old ways of relating impossible or superfluous. In Rachel and her mother's approach to the novel situation of the laboratory playroom, it becomes possible to see how Rachel's developing capacities for reference and for separateness—pointing, gesturing, simple labeling—are integrated into the interaction by both mother and child. What will the mother and child do with these new possibilities for connection and individuation?

In the first task at 14 months, the "warm-up task," the mother and child are left by themselves in a laboratory with toys. They are videotaped through a one-way mirror. This task is important for two reasons. Because it is the first in a whole series of tasks, it is possible to observe the dyad's adaptation to novelty. And because it is the most unstructured of all the tasks, mother and child are given the opportunity to make sense of their situation as an interactive dyad with a well-developed transactional system. In their interaction and through language, they are constructing this novel situation in very particular ways.

During the 5-minute warm-up period, Rachel's mother plays with her and talks to her continuously. In comparison with other mother–child pairs, the number of utterances by Rachel's mother in this given time frame is extraordinarily high.[1] The content is also exceptional. The mother frequently addresses Rachel directly by saying her name. She also refers to herself ("Mommy") often, or more often than any of the other mothers. Rachel is constantly attended to by her mother, with her every action noted. For instance, the interaction starts with the following series of utterances by the mother:

(Rachel looks at the door.)
What does Rachel see?
(Mother looks over to the door. Rachel points to the door.)
The door closed. (Mother looks at child.)
Yes. (Child turns and looks at toys.)
What does Rachel see? (Child vocalizes, points to rubber duck.)
Duck! (Mother picks up the rubber duck and gives it to child.)
Oh, look it makes noise. Booboo.
It makes noise! (Mother squeezes the duck. Rachel takes duck from mother, looks at it closely.)
Can Rachel do it? (Rachel blows into the duck, looks at it closely.)
Can Rachel make noise? (Mother watches Rachel, Rachel squeezes the duck.)
There! (Rachel looks around the room holding the duck.)
What else does Rachel see? (Mother looks around the room, child points to the ball.)
A ball. (Mother picks the ball up.)
Rachel sees a ball.

When the sequence begins, Rachel is looking at the door through which the experimenter had just disappeared. Her attention is focused on something outside the dyad, but by asking the question "What does Rachel see?" the mother incorporates this interest into the mother–child interaction. This interactive style persists throughout the remainder of the warm-up period. Everything that Rachel does is described, commented upon, or interpreted by her mother. The mother's constant questions tightly frame Rachel's actions. In a variety of ways, Rachel is repeatedly asked to pay attention to Mommy and to include her mother in her play. She is not left to play by herself in her own way. Rachel does not seem to find this aversive and does react to the questions, descriptions, comments, and interpretations in various ways, for example, by pointing, vocalizations, or other actions. She is not yet able to talk, but she is nevertheless quite communicative.

In this interaction the intensely dyadic nature of the talk is apparent. For instance, when Rachel and her mother play ball, the mother repeatedly uses vocatives, which serve to maintain the connection linguistically between them within this novel world of the laboratory:

> Throw it to Mommy?
> Throw the ball to Mommy.
> Mommy will throw the ball to Rachel.
> There! Rachel is gonna throw the ball to Mommy
> Rachel, throw the ball to Mommy?
> Oh, Rachel, threw it!

The mother adapts to the novelty and artificiality of the lab situation by focusing on the child and encouraging the child to focus on her. She creates an intimate and close world between them and seems to protect Rachel by paying constant attention to her. She not only interprets and explains the situation to Rachel, she also interprets Rachel's reactions within the situation. She does not leave Rachel to explore this new world by herself but serves as an interpreter, keeping Rachel cradled in the safe, dyadic mother–child interaction. Although it is impossible to establish conclusively whether the mother is responding to specific behavioral characteristics displayed by Rachel (i.e., fearfulness, timidity), it is definitely possible to assert that Rachel's mother already interacts with her in a very distinct way.

The Jungle Task at 5 Years Old

Based on Rachel's physiological and behavioral profile at 14 months, Kagan and Snidman (1992) and their colleagues (Kochanska, 1991) would predict that Rachel's encounter with an unfamiliar event would be characterized by withdrawal, inhibition, shyness, fearfulness, and wariness, as opposed to approach, exploration, and enjoyment of the novel stimulus. In addition, they would predict that she would have maintained distinctive peripheral, physiological characteristics that imply low thresholds in the limbic system to novel and challenging events. As a consequence, it would be expected that in narrative and narrative play tasks she would be hesitant to act as speaker or to assume spontaneously the role of speaker.

TABLE 13.1. Number of Clauses Uttered by Participants (Ratified and Nonratified): RPJ, Age 5

Participant	Number of Clauses	Percent of Total Clauses
Rachel	81	31
Diane	84	32
Mother	95	37
Total of all three participants	260	100

Rachel's performance in the jungle task was remarkable in two ways. It deviated in extreme ways from the performances of other children on this task, and it differed greatly from her own performance in other tasks during the same experimental protocol. Although Rachel generally spoke less often and less spontaneously than other children, she did not do so consistently across tasks. For instance, while she spoke much less often than other children during the RPJ, she spoke as much as and more than other children in some of the other tasks. She also spoke only as herself, unlike other children, who typically assume the voice of a narrator and the voices of the characters in the jungle. It is therefore clear that it is not sufficient to say simply that Rachel spoke less often and less spontaneously than other children. The behavior of Rachel's mother in comparison to other mothers is also significant; she differs in both the quantity and the quality of her speech. Clearly, the differences between Rachel and other children are complex. To begin to understand the complexity of these differences, it is necessary to examine the jungle task and to explore all the roles and stances that participants in this situation are supposed to assume. It is only when we have a clearer sense of where exactly the differences are located that we can begin to understand what the differences mean or signify.

Rachel and Diane, the child and the interviewer, are the official or ratified participants of the jungle task. Rachel's mother is not expected to be a participant of the interactions but is expected to be (in Goffman's terms) a *ratified overhearer*. The first interesting aspect of what happens during Rachel's jungle task is that Rachel's mother, unlike the mothers of the other children in the study, becomes an active participant in the interaction. And although she is not supposed to talk at all, she talks more than either of the other participants (Table 13.1). While the very active participation of the mother in this task already suggests that there might be some element of overinvolvement in the relationship between mother and child, there are also other strong indications that the relationship is an extraordinary one.

The jungle task is a particular play and narrative task because the stories that are told during this task are make-believe stories or stories of fantasy. Make-believe play and narrative are characterized by an implicit agreement between the participants to create an alternative reality (Bretherton, 1984), a reality that does not have to represent or be connected to anything real in the lives of the participants. This means that Rachel's mother is not only originally excluded from this task in the sense that she is not a ratified participant in the conversation, she is also excluded from the story world in the way that all the participants of the interaction are excluded:

Although all of them end up being participants of the interaction in the speech event of this experimental task, they (Rachel, Diane, the mother) can never be characters in the story world. Their reality, and the relationships that they have in this reality, are temporarily subsumed by the alternative reality of the story world and the relationships between the characters living in the story world.[2] We will see in the mother's remarks that it seems very important to her to keep the relationship between her and Rachel prominent and real, even at the cost of entering the story world.

At the beginning of RPJ, while Diane is trying to get Rachel involved in the story world by asking questions about what the animals could do, Rachel's mother continues to interact with Rachel *as her mother* in the context of the home visit. For instance, when Diane asks Rachel, "What do you think the lion could do?" her mother immediately interjects, "Rachel, are you more comfortable on the floor? Can you reach better?" Rachel has no room to respond to Diane. While Diane's remark is meant to help Rachel to cross the boundary into the story world of the jungle, the mother's question keeps Rachel anchored in the context of the parent–child relationship. Because her mother's question has to do with her comfort and needs, she is also reminded of the dependency that is characteristic of this relationship.

This same pattern is repeated when Diane asks, "What do you think the lioness could do?" and Rachel's mother says, "Rachel, do you know what a lioness is?" Once again Diane is trying to induce Rachel to change her footing, while the mother again reminds the child of her being "Rachel" in the sphere of the home visit, the Rachel who needs her mother's help to answer the question. Even more telling is the mother's response when Rachel then says, "What?" She says: "It's a girl lion. Perhaps a mommy lion." These two sentences bring the characters of a girl and a mommy into the story world. Interestingly, they are also brought into the story within a single character, suggesting a certain lack of differentiation between girl and mommy.

Despite these maternal interferences, Rachel does continue to answer Diane's specific questions about what the animals could do. However, compared to those of other children, her answers are brief and there are no additional spontaneous remarks. Also conspicuous is the fact that she readily imagines that the big animals will act in threatening ways (the lion could eat you, the elephant could spray water on you), while she insists that she does not know what the smaller/younger/more vulnerable animals (the duck and the baby lion) could do. If one thinks about make-believe play as "a powerful, perfectly designed, developmentally accessible system for thinking about deeply felt concerns and for sharing these concerns with others" (Fein, 1991, p. 156), Rachel could well be communicating her own feelings of helplessness and vulnerability.

The task continues with Diane asking Rachel to tell her more about the jungle (first prompt). Rachel says that she does not know. The following conversation follows the second prompt (the purple grape prompt):

Diane: now you make up some stories.
you make them talk with each other.

Rachel: I don't know.

Mother: what do you think the elephant said when he was called a grape?

Rachel: um # I don't know.

Mother: Rach are you tired?

Rachel: xxx. (she is leaning back against the couch and mumbling)

Mother: what do you mean you don't know?
do you want me to tickle you to wake you up?
you look real sleepy.
you're not quite here.

Rachel: xxx.

Diane: what do you think they said? (said in a whisper)

Rachel: I don't know.

Diane: what do you think xxx.
make the lions talk.

Rachel: I don't know.

Diane: oop. (tree falls off table)

Mother: what did they say when the tree fell off?

Rachel: O. (Rachel laughs)

Diane: pretty silly huh?

Mother: well what did they say about that?

Rachel: O. (Rachel is still laughing)
I don't know.

Mother: what would you say if a tree suddenly fell off?

Rachel: I don't know. (Rachel laughs)

Diane: well.

Mother: what's so funny?

Rachel: what what did they say when the tree fell off?

Mother: well it did.

Mother: what did they say?

Mother: did they giggle?

Rachel: I don't know. (still laughing)

In this section Rachel is not only asked to assume the stance of narrator, but also to speak as the animals of the make-believe jungle. We have seen that the introductory parts of this task have been dominated by a virtual tug-of-war between the mother and Diane, with the mother trying to keep Rachel in the realm of their close, dependent mother–child relationship and Diane trying to persuade Rachel to jump into the circle of make-believe jungle. Not surprisingly, Rachel responds to the grape prompt by saying that she does not know, a response she repeats even when Diane makes the question more specific.

Her mother's response ("Rach, are you tired? What do you mean you don't know?") follows the same pattern. Rachel is addressed by her first name, which again situates her in the particular relationship with her mother, and not as an animal in the make-believe jungle. The mother's questions also serve to interpret Rachel's "I don't know"s. Rachel herself does not say that she is tired. Her mother, not accepting that Rachel perhaps really does not know (either because of a lack of imagination or because of how confused she is at this stage about where she should be and what she should say), tells both Rachel and Diane what the "I don't know"s mean. She uses them to explain away Rachel's failure to do the task and to emphasize Rachel's needs for rest and sleep in the real world. She also suggests a way in which the problem of Rachel's not being "all there" can be solved: She can tickle Rachel to wake her up. It is a problem that she can solve because, as Rachel's mother, she can tickle her. It is also a problem whose solution requires further physical intimacy. At this stage Rachel has not yet made any effort to communicate her feelings to Diane; it is her mother who has talked about her comfort and her sleepiness.

After another of Diane's attempts to get Rachel to "make the lions talk," a model of a tree is accidentally knocked off the table. Rachel's and her mother's reactions to this event are remarkable. The mother's question ("What did they say when the tree fell off?") is in the same format as those of the experimenter. Rachel responds to this question with a burst of laughter; it is her first spontaneous reaction in this task. Why does Rachel laugh?

Rachel probably knows that her mother's question, even though following the pattern of Diane's question ("What did they say . . .") is breaking the rules of the world of pretend play or make-believe. The happenings in the real world are not allowed to spill over into the story world if they cannot be incorporated into it in a logical way. The model of the tree falling off the table is a problem that does not occur in the time and place of the story world; it happens during the experimental task in the context of the home visit. There are many ways in which the tree falling off the table could have been dealt with. One of the participants might have commented that the tree had fallen off the table and should be picked up. Diane's "Oops" falls into this class of responses. Or the fallen tree might have been incorporated in the story world by introducing a hurricane (as Diane later does with the words "There was a hurricane"). However, the question "What did they say when the tree fell off?" is one that collapses the boundary between the story world and the world of the home visit. It asks what the characters who exist only in the story world say about something that happens outside the realm of the story world created by Diane. By breaking the unspoken rules of pretend play, the mother has exposed the fragility of the story world. The imaginary world is fragile not only because trees can fall off (as they do not in the real world), and because it can so easily be consumed and destroyed by what happens in the real world (whether it is the model of the tree falling off or Rachel being tired), but also because such a simple question can shatter the world created by make-believe and pretense.

The mother's comments serve to ridicule the whole idea of the story world and makes it impossible for Rachel to enter that world. The mother has no legitimate role in either the interactive aspects of RPJ or the story world, and therefore also makes it impossible for Rachel to enter this world in any way. The mother's and daughter's shared enjoyment (shared laughter and shared gaze) of this episode seems to indicate a certain closeness and intimacy, but it might be exactly the closeness and power of this sharing that hinders Rachel's involvement or participation in other worlds. Any move, however temporary, into a context that falls outside of their relationship as mother and child seems to be threatening to the mother and subsequently also to Rachel.

The tree that falls off the world, because it signifies the fragility of the story world for the child, consequently becomes the dominant theme in the interaction around the jungle props. After this episode, there is absolutely minimal involvement of Rachel in the story world. Typically she refuses to speak, even in the relatively safe voice of the narrator. Her refusal is maintained despite her mother's later efforts to help Diane entice her into the story world. At the end of the task another tree falls off, again eliciting spontaneous laughter from the child. Another tree falls over, and Rachel laughs even more. She now purposefully pushes the table, perhaps in an attempt to finally destroy the world that she experiences as threatening. The experimenter, in a brave attempt to incorporate this event of the real world into the story world, waves her arms and says, "There was a hurricane." This gets no response from Rachel. Her mother's subsequent questions, "What are the animals thinking about all that? What are they saying?" simply lead to more laughter and more rocking of the table. Her mother finally says "Rachel . . . no" and the experimenter ends the task.

We see then that although it is indeed true that Rachel talks very little during this task and never does so spontaneously, a micro-analysis of what happens during the task is necessary to illuminate why she does talk so little. Instead of saying simply that she talks less than other children, we can say that she has problems with even entering a circle in which she must temporarily give up the relationship with her mother, a relationship within which she is interpreted and protected. It is this reluctance to enter these specific circles that makes her quiet and reserved and eventually results in her being characterized as an inhibited child. We also suggest that the reluctance is not due only to certain inherent temperamental characteristics, but that it can be specifically linked to the relationship between mother and child. To explore this suggestion further, we will turn to a task in which Rachel talks as much as children who are classified as not inhibited and more than other children who are classified as inhibited.

The Narrative Task with Co-construction

The co-construction task is an experimental task in which mother and child are asked to jointly tell the experimenter about an interesting or exciting experience the two of them shared. The mother and child must share the telling of an episode in their shared history. This entails explicit or implicit negotiations about what constitutes an appropriate topic and about how the position of teller will be shared. Both mother and child are expected to be tellers during this task, creating one sequential structure rather than two parallel stories. Whether a primary teller emerges or not, the speaker holding the floor can expect her co-teller to confirm the story, to make simple additions, to elaborate, to repair, or to take over the floor. Any of these interruptions can be accepted or rejected by the speaker who has the floor.

TABLE 13.2.   Number of Clauses Uttered by Participants (Ratified): Coconstruction Task with Mother, Age 5

Participant	Number of Clauses	Percent of Total Clauses
Rachel	103	59
Diane	38	22
Mother	34	19
Total of all three participants	175	100

Rachel and her mother provide such an episode in the middle of the first experimental task. It is a picture description task in which she initially refuses to participate. The personal anecdote emerges from a rather spontaneous interaction between mother, child, and the experimenter; as a consequence, the experimenter does not insist on another co-construction elicited in the usual way at the usual place in the protocol. This telling event is transcribed as their co-construction task. Strictly speaking, we are therefore looking at a spontaneous conversation that is eventually labeled by the experimenter as a co-construction.

During the co-construction episode, Rachel's mother is constantly creating frames of interpretation for her and controlling the meaning of her experience. When speaking in the frame provided by her mother, Rachel is talkative and spontaneous, clearly enjoys herself, and is clearly the primary speaker (see Table 13.2).[3] However, as soon as she has to move into another sphere, that of the experimental task of picture description, where her mother cannot provide her with a framework, she becomes timid, wary, and unwilling to participate as a speaker. As the context of interaction changes from a task where the mother is a ratified participant to a task where she is not, Rachel quickly changes from not being inhibited to being inhibited. If, as Goffman (1981) suggests, it is the task of the "dexterous" speaker to jump back and forth, keeping different circles in play, we can say that Rachel is unwilling to leap into a circle where she has to be a speaker without her mother's framing, where she has the sole responsibility for constructing meaning.

Rachel and her mother's personal anecdote appears in the middle of a picture description task with the prompt "You can see the picture and I can't; tell me everything that you can see." Rachel does not even attempt to do the task by describing the picture. Despite Diane's repeated attempts to get Rachel's attention and interest, she remains uncooperative. Instead, Rachel looks constantly at her mother, who is sitting next to her on the couch and talks to her in a whisper. This shared gaze and shared volume, coupled with the physical closeness of mother and child on the couch, creates the impression of a very tight dyad. This impression is strengthened by the mother's response to Rachel's unwillingness to participate. Although she does repeat the instructions, she does so in a whisper. When Diane says, "Rachel, you're not looking at the picture," Rachel's mother says: "You're looking at your mommy. You're shy." This comment confirms the connection between mother and daughter and, interestingly enough, Rachel is described as shy by the mother! The mother thus describes Rachel's behavior, interprets it, but apparently does not try to change it. The involvement of the mother here is also significant because she is not expected to be a ratified participant during the picture description task; at the most, she is expected to be an overhearer.

Diane seems to be the outsider in the interaction, constantly trying to break through the circle of intimacy created by mother and child. Sitting on a chair facing the mother and child, she speaks loudly in an almost exaggerated tone of voice. In her attempt to draw the child into the task or to make her more comfortable, she focuses on the swings in the picture and temporarily becomes the teller as she tells Rachel how much she used to like to swing high so that she could touch trees. It is at this point that the conversation turns to Rachel's personal experience of swinging, with her mother saying to the experimenter: "Rachel goes so high on a swing that I get anxious. I cannot watch her." The co-construction episode follows this remark:

Mother: What have you learned to do on a swing recently?

Rachel: pump.

Diane: ah wow.

Rachel: and I can even start myself.

Diane: all by yourself?

Rachel: uhhum. (Rachel nods)

Diane: that's pretty neat
now you don't need anybody to push you.

Rachel: uhhum. (Rachel nods)

Mother: What have you done for Danny?

Rachel: I've taught him how to pump.
now he can start himself.

Rachel: and he's only three and a half.

Diane: Wow, he's a fast learner.

Rachel: uhhum. (Rachel nods)

Mother: are you a good teacher?

Rachel: uhhum. (Rachel nods)

Diane: oh I see.
it's not that he's a fast learner but that you're a good teacher.

Mother: what else are you trying to teach Danny?

Rachel: to skip.

Mother: uh hum. (Mother nods)

Diane: how's he doing?

Rachel: well once he really was skipping.

Diane: yeah.

Rachel: and other times he's been galloping.

Diane: Oh.
what's the difference between skipping and galloping?

Rachel: well skipping you change your feet
and galloping you just you don't change 'em

Diane: Oh I didn't know that. I'll have to try to gallop.
I guess I usually skip.

Rachel: uhhuh.

Mother: which one is easier?

Rachel: uh I guess galloping.

Rachel: if Danny is better at galloping.

Mother: that's true.

Diane: yeah yeah.

Mother: I don't know too many three and a half year olds who can skip.

Rachel: ah no.

Mother: can any one else in your class skip?

Rachel: I don't know.
because you see they've not really been skipping at school.

Mother: No?

Rachel: and neither and Danny hasn't been galloping at school.
he only gallops
and he well he doesn't skip most of the time any more.
but I think the time that he had learned to skip.
how old was he?
probably two.

Diane: yeah.

Mother: yeah.

Rachel: or maybe just plain three.
but certainly not three and a half.

Mother: he hasn't been three and a half for that long.

Rachel: right.
he hasn't skipped or galloped for as long as I've know him.
when he's three and a half.

The mother introduces a story but does not continue to tell it. Instead, she turns the story over to Rachel by asking a series of questions. By doing so, she is acknowledging Rachel's right to speak about her own experiences. However, a close investigation of her talk reveals that although her questions and comments are designed to hand the floor over to Rachel, they provide Rachel with a framework within which to understand and tell her experiences.

For instance, the first question, ''What have you learned to do on a swing recently?'', is a very specific question that does not allow too many possible answers: Rachel is to speak about a recent achievement on a swing. A more open question would have invited her to choose the content more freely; for instance, her mother might have asked what kind of fun she had in the park.[4] The mother uses her questions to interpret Rachel's experiences. In answering these questions Rachel speaks loudly, looks at Diane, and even offers a few spontaneous remarks; her speech and attitude have been transformed quite remarkably. Rachel's mother ends this particular series of questions with the remark and question: "I don't know too many three and a half year olds who can skip. Can anyone else in your class skip?" At this point Rachel launches into a mini-monologue and becomes the primary speaker, with only supporting interventions of her mother. Once her mother has framed and to a large extent interpreted her experiences for her, the once reluctant and timid speaker speaks confidently, loudly, and with conscious and exaggerated gestures.

The conversation moves on to other topics, and Rachel continues to be an enthusiastic and original participant. Particularly interesting is the following passage from this talk:

Mother: Tell Pam who you think might go to kindergarten with you next year.

Rachel: Mmm.

Mother: who am I thinking of? (points to dog)

Rachel: ah yeah.

Rachel: I thought you meant what kids.

Mother: no, because Pam wouldn't know the kids. But is there someone else who might go to kindergarten with you?

Rachel: ah yes!

Mother: can you tell Pam what problem we might gonna have?

Again the mother presents Rachel with very specific questions (probes and yes/no questions) rather than with more open-ended general questions (prompts). Moreover, this set of questions presupposes a certain symbiotic and exclusionary relationship. The first question is based on the assumption that the mother knows what the child thinks and that the child will know what the mother thinks the child thinks. When the child fails to answer, the mother changes the question to "Who am I thinking of?", suggesting again that the child should know what the mother is thinking. When she points to the dog, the child immediately knows what she means and says that she thought that her mother was referring to kids. This raises the question of why, if she did indeed think that her mother was referring to other kids, she did not name the kids initially. It is possible that she was afraid that this might have been the wrong answer—but how can you be wrong about your own thoughts? If initially she really did not know the answer to her mother's question, it is remarkable that she did not say that she did not know. The reasons for her reluctance to give an "I don't know" answer might be, first, that such an answer would have belied the symbiotic relationship between mother and child and, second, that it might have challenged the mother's very recent representation of Rachel as a competent and achieving child. The mother's collapsing of the thoughts of the child and herself into one, switching so easily between "who you think" and "who am I thinking of" also strongly supports the notion of an almost symbiotic relationship.

Rachel continues to relate the problem of the dog going to school in a very elaborate way. The following is an extract from the conversation that follows, and it provides a good example of the kind of talk Rachel is able to produce:

Diane: You said you were a good teacher.
do you think you could teach your teacher how to like dogs?

Mother: hum.

Rachel: (long pause) well but (long pause) Danny knows
I think before I taught him to skip
I think he knew how to gallop.

Diane: Uhhuh.

Rachel: and that is pretty close to skipping.
and what is pretty close to dogs that Mrs Eble might like?

Mother: so start with something that's close that she does like?

Rachel: yeah. (Rachel nods.)

Diane: you are a good teacher.

Rachel: yeah.

Mother: that's actually a very good idea Rachel.

Rachel: yeah and that's.

Mother: we know she likes guinea pigs right
because there's a guinea pig in the kindergarten classroom.

Rachel: right but is that close to dogs?.

Mother: umm.

Diane: It's an animal. It's got fur.

Rachel: But any way but runn-ing.
Danny knows how to run perfectly well.
and that's like skipp-ing
and guin and guinea pigs right?
Well running is close is sort of far away uh from skipping
and and guinea pigs is sort of far away from um dogsh
so I don't think it would work like an animals.

Diane: oh okay.

Mother: guinea pig isn't close enough to dogs?

Rachel: uhuh.

Mother: um. I don't know what's going to work.

Rachel: neither do I.

The remarkable change in Rachel as speaker is reversed as soon as the experimenter returns to the experimental task of picture description. Although her eventual description of the picture is more comprehensive than those of many other children, Rachel is again constantly looking at her mother and asking her mother's help in a subdued voice. With the second picture description task, which follows immediately after the first one, she again does not even attempt to describe the picture, explaining to her mother: "This one's tricky ... It's too tricky ... It's hard ... But mama ... I'm not used to this ... at all ... so I'm not very good at it." Although Rachel obviously has the skills to do the task, she does not have the confidence. Only when her mother carefully guides her is she able to participate. Without her mother's interpretations, she once again becomes cautious and timid.

During this episode, we see that Rachel will speak in the presence of a stranger and will engage in spontaneous talk. We also see that Rachel and her mother move into the task easily, with the mother maintaining control through her constant but subtle interpretation of Rachel's experience. These patterns are similar to those seen during the jungle task. Rachel does not resist her mother's interpretations, nor does she seem to mind the absence of any negotiation about turn taking. This relationship is remarkable for its extreme and unchallenged connectedness; it is a relationship that is both close and closed. Rachel's identification with her mother appears to be necessary to her functioning and to their functioning as a dyad. When this highly dependent relationship is not threatened from without, Rachel does not look like an inhibited child. When not asked to jump back and forth between different worlds during the make-believe jungle play, Rachel is more spontaneous and sociable.

Rachel in Later Years

It would be very simple to describe 5-year-old Rachel and her mother as overly identified with each other, overly involved, and excessively enmeshed. However, our longitudinal data suggest that we cannot be satisfied with this unidimensional and pathological characterization. When we see Rachel again at 6, 7, and 8 years old, we see her gradually moving out of the protective, interpretive spheres created by her mother, using her individual strengths and her connectedness to venture toward further individuation and separation.

When Rachel was 5 years old, she and her mother talked a lot about Rachel's individual and independent achievements (e.g., swinging high, being a good teacher, going to school). When seen again at age 6, Rachel had entered school and had thus passed an important milestone in her development. When visited by the experimenter, she was able to complete the whole protocol of experimental tasks without her mother being present. However, at both the 6- and 7-year visits, Rachel still spoke more and more spontaneously during the co-construction task with her mother than in other tasks.

At 6 years of age, Rachel's mother still plays the role of interpreter and explicator. The co-construction task is still the only task in which Rachel talks as much as or more than other children. However, whereas the process of arriving at shared meaning was marked by smoothness and acceptance at age 5, at age 6 Rachel is willing to challenge her mother on issues of fact and interpretation. The following mother–child exchange about a friend's sleep-over is different from previous exchanges and is therefore significant (Nina is the experimenter):

Nina: what did you do with her?

Rachel: & um . . .

Mother: & stayed up late and talked.

Rachel: No, Mom.
you only let us stay up until eleven.

Mother: right.
and she thought that wasn't late enough.

Nina: that's pretty late.
I think that's pretty late.

Rachel: and—the other day—and the first day she was over for a sleep-over wasn't really a sleep-over.
cause we were going to the alpine slide the next day.

Nina: oh.

Mother: so I wouldn't let them stay up any later than what?
ten ten thirty?

Rachel: no Mom.
nine, nine thirty.

Mother: was it that early?

Rachel: yeah mom it was that early.

Mother: oh.
I was mean.

In this excerpt we see that it is not only Rachel who has changed; her mother seems less concerned with interpreting her stories and now has few problems with Rachel challenging her. In an interesting twist, she even accepts Rachel's interpretation of *her* behavior, that is, that she was mean. Once again the content of the talk is revealing. In these episodes, Rachel and her mother continue to talk about Rachel's achievements; the mother always emphasizes Rachel's moves away from her mother. At age 5 they talked about Rachel swinging too high for her mother (see earlier). At age 6 they are talking about an alpine slide, with Rachel explaining in extraordinary detail how it works. Her mother comments: "Every summer Rachel has wanted to go faster down the alpine slide. She's been on it every summer of her life. The first time when she was seven months old. Always with an adult. She hasn't gone by herself yet, but she seems to like going down it faster than . . . I don't think I go fast enough for her anymore." At age 7 the anecdote is about Rachel learning to swim, with Rachel's mother telling most of the story: "And you know I did water babies that the Y does when she was exactly one and it was in deep water and she wanted me to let go of her and I didn't want to let go of her and so she didn't like it. So we quit. But this is working better, isn't it?" She then continues to explain how Rachel learned to swim and to jump off the diving board. Once again, she emphasizes Rachel's increasing independence and her ability to do things by herself: "We built a raft . . . and we had been talking about having Rachel jump off with somebody to catch her . . . but now that she has jumped off the diving board without anybody to catch her she can do it by herself." Interestingly, themes of individual achievement are often raised alongside themes of parental protectiveness and separation, suggesting that—for the mother at least—separation and individuation are ongoing concerns.

Rachel's jungle stories at ages 6 and 7 are clear, but very short and to the point in comparison with those of other children. Both stories are coherent and logical, and are told without any negotiations or interaction with the experimenter. The themes raised by Rachel in her jungle stories at both age 6 and age 7 suggest a representational solution to the dilemmas acted out at earlier visits. At 6, the short story she tells in response to the purple grape prompt (Prompt three) is: "He [the hippo] didn't like it. So he ran after the baby who lived, who stood, very close to his father who turned around and said: 'Don't bother my babies. That's the end'." At age 7 her response to the same prompt is: "Well um the elephant kids didn't have a mother and so there was no one there to protect them so the hippo got pretty mad and then on. The tiger kids were pretty good friends of the elephant and so they had their father straighten it out and they were all happy then." In fantasy play, which is often a way of thinking about important things, Rachel chooses to talk about parental protection. Even though the mother is not physically present when the jungle task is administered, Rachel introduces parent–child (in this case father–child) relationships into the story.

At 8 years of age, Rachel participates in the RPJ with quiet enthusiasm and much originality, and this time her mother is not in the picture at all. She moves into the story world of the jungle with ease, speaking at first in the voice of the narrator but eventually also assuming the voices of the animals. Although Rachel's emphasis on pattern and logic persists at this age, she can now successfully employ this ability to serve narrative and playful ends. She introduces themes at the beginning of the story, elaborates on them, and manages to maintain them, thus producing an interesting and organized jungle story. For instance, after the hippo is teased for looking like a big fat purple grape, the giraffe is teased for looking like a long piece of string. When the dragon comes, he asks for food and is offered first a grape and then a piece of string, with the hippo and the giraffe indignantly protesting, "I am not a grape" and "I am not a piece of string." Other themes are explicated in similar ways, and Rachel's jungle story at age 8 was one of the longest jungle stories recorded in the study.

At age 5, Rachel seemed timid, overanxious, and overinvolved with her mother; however, by age 8, she had adapted to the point of being able to participate in all tasks competently and confidently. This is not to say that she is a completely changed person with a changed temperament. It is rather to assert that for Rachel, development was an adaptive process. It is clear that Rachel's mother played a crucial role in this process. We see Rachel getting involved in a close and intimate dyadic relationship with her mother as early as infancy; it is even then a relationship with high levels of involvement and interdependency. At age 5 the relationship between mother and child can be characterized as remarkable for its level of identification and connectedness. At age 6 we start to see how the transactional relationship between Rachel and her mother slowly evolves as both child and mother change: The relationship, still close and intimate, is becoming more open as Rachel becomes stronger and her mother becomes more willing to let her go. And, while her mother continues to express her own separation anxiety, she allows Rachel more independence and seems willing to relinquish some of her own need for control. Rachel's mother is not simply an overidentified and overinvolved caretaker; she is part of a complex, reciprocal transaction between Rachel and her entire caretaking environment. At age 8, Rachel is ready and is allowed to play in the jungle by herself.

Conclusion

We have used this detailed analysis of the play of one child in order to show that a temperamental trait such as inhibition is not a constant in development. Rather, it is one component in a complex transaction between child and caretaking environment in which the trait can simultaneously be independent variable and dependent variable. It is difficult to determine the direction of causality, as both child and environment are continuously changing in an ongoing transaction, constantly effecting changes in the other.

Our longitudinal case study further demonstrates that the transaction between Rachel and her caretaking environment was ultimately an adaptive one. In this instance, early problems (such as excessive fearfulness, timidity, and overidentification) self-corrected during the process of development. In his rather optimistic view of development, Sameroff (1975) asserts that there is a self-righting tendency in the organism that will usually ensure a positive developmental outcome. He suggests that the failure of this tendency will result when (1) there is a constitutional deficiency/problem in the child or when (2) environmental forces present throughout development prevent it from operating. He suggests that in an environment that is flexible, open, and adaptable, problems will disappear in the normal restructuring implicit in development as the child advances in her construction and organization of her cognitive and social worlds. Conversely, if a social environment engages in rigid, stereotypical, and concrete thought and behavior, this self-correction will not take place during the process of development. Rachel's mother, as one of the important factors in her caretaking environment (others might be Rachel's father, the school, and the psychological establishment), initially responded to her child in ways that seemed extreme. However, her responses changed as Rachel became more confident, and—in an adaptive fashion—she developed new ways of interacting with Rachel. Also, it may have been the case that only in the very protective, close relationship with her mother could Rachel develop the way she did. Of course, it is possible that she might not have displayed the characteristics of inhibition at all if her mother had not interacted with her in the way she did. However, it is also possible that her shyness and timidity might have developed into severe problems had her mother not been as sensitive and flexible as she was.

Lerner and Lerner (1987) propose a *goodness-of-fit* model between the developing characteristics of children and presses or demands for adaptation present in their contexts. They state: "Good fits (or matches) are predicted to be associated with adaptive development; poor fits are expected to be associated with maladaptive development" (p. 400). We suggest that in the case of Rachel and her mother, there was indeed a goodness of fit, whereby mother and child continuously changed their expectations of and demands on each other. It is because of this sensitivity and flexibility of the mother, and later of both the mother and the child, that Rachel at age 8 can be considered to be a well-adapted child.

The case of Rachel illustrates how important it is to continuously try to understand the transactions between the child and her environment to determine how these transactions facilitate or hinder adaptation as both the child and her surroundings change and evolve (Sameroff, 1975). Such transactions are always and inevitably situated in specific sociocultural contexts and are thus shaped by what the culture expects of parents and children. The richness of this detailed qualitative analysis of Rachel makes clear the importance of developing ways to look at the transactions between children and their caretaking environments using large samples of child–parent pairs. It is important to investigate the idea that transactions between children and caretaking environments are highly specific and individual, yet always a function of the sociocultural context. Although other case studies in our current research confirm the notion of complicated transactions between mothers and children, we need to develop methods by which we can reliably compare the many transactions taking place in various systems at various times. The very rich data on a single child suggest that this will be no easy task.

ACKNOWLEDGMENTS

We would like to thank Jerome Kagan and his staff at the Harvard Infant Laboratories. This chapter was produced as part of Projects in Language Development Grant #SNOWHD23388, as well as a grant from the John D. and Catherine T. MacArthur Foundation.

NOTES

1. Many mothers do not play with their children during this time, but rather watch them play. Other mothers do engage in play with their children, but rarely in such a high frequency of verbal utterances seen in such a limited time frame. Number of utterances by mothers in other mother–child pairs studied varied between one and 85 utterances.

2. Although it is true that fantasy can be seen as simply another level of representation of reality, this link is not as obvious and direct as it is, for instance, in autobiographical stories.

3. Even children who are categorized as being extraordinarily inhibited to the familiar seldom do more than 50% of the talking during this particular task.

4. Fivush et al. (1987) make the useful distinction between *prompts* and *probes*, with probes being more general, open-ended questions and prompts being questions that ask for a specific type of information. Yes/no questions are even more specific in that they give a child a piece of information and only give the child the option to deny or confirm the information. Most of the mother's questions during this task are very specific—either probes or yes/no questions.

REFERENCES

Asendorpf, J. B. (1990). Development of inhibition during childhood: Evidence for situational specificity and a two-factor model. *Developmental Psychology, 62,* 250–263.

Bowlby, J. (1982). *Attachment and loss:* Vol. 1, *Attachment.* New York: Basic Books.

Bretherton, I. (1984). Representing the social world in symbolic play: Reality and fantasy. In I. Bretherton (Ed.), *Symbolic play: The development of social understanding* (pp. 3–41). Orlando, FL: Academic Press.

Fein, G. G. (1991). Bloodsuckers, blisters, cooked babies, and other curiosities: Affective themes in pretense. In F. S. Kessel, M. H. Bornstein, & A. J. Sameroff (Eds.), *Contemporary constructions of the child* (pp. 143–158). Hillsdale, NJ: Erlbaum.

Fivush, R., Gray, J., & Fromhoff, F. (1987). Two-year-olds talk about the past. *Cognitive Development, 2*, 393–409.

Goffman, E. (1981). *Forms of talk.* Philadelphia: University of Pennsylvania Press.

Greenacre, P. (1957). The childhood of the artist: Libidinal phase development and giftedness. *Psychoanalytic Study of the Child, 12*, 27–72.

Kagan, J. (1981). *The second year: The emergence of self-awareness.* Cambridge, MA: Harvard University Press.

Kagan, J. (1989a). Temperamental contributions to social behavior. *American Psychologist, 44*, 668–674.

Kagan, J. (1989b). The concept of behavioral inhibition to the unfamiliar. In J. S. Reznick (Ed.), *Perspectives on behavioral inhibition* (pp. 125–138). Chicago: University of Chicago Press.

Kagan, J., & Moss, J. (1983). *Birth to maturity.* New Haven, CT: Yale University Press.

Kagan, J., Reznick, J. S., & Gibbons, J. (1989). Inhibited and uninhibited types of children. *Child Development, 60*, 838–845.

Kagan, J., Reznick, J. S., & Snidman, N. (1988a). Biological bases of childhood shyness. *Science, 240*, 167–171.

Kagan, J., Reznick, J. S., & Snidman, N. (1988b). The physiology and psychology of behavioral inhibitions in children. *Annual Progress in Child Psychiatry and Child Development, 1988*, 102–127.

Kagan, J., Reznick, J. S., Snidman, N., & Gibbons, J. (1988). Childhood derivatives of inhibition and lack of inhibition to the unfamiliar. *Child Development, 59*, 1580–1589.

Kagan, J., & Snidman, N. (1991). Temperamental factors in human development. *American Psychologist, 46*, 856–862.

Kochanska, N. (1991). Patterns of inhibition to the unfamiliar in children of normal and affectively ill mothers. *Child Development, 62*, 250–263.

Lerner, R. M., & Lerner, J. V. (1987) Children in their contexts: A goodness of fit model. In J. Lancaster, J. Altman, A. Rossi, & L. Sherrod (Eds.), *Parenting across the lifespan* (pp. 377–404). New York: Aldine De Gruyter.

Mahler, M., Pine, F., & Bergman, A. (1975). *The psychological birth of the human infant.* New York: Basic Books.

Nicolich, L. M. (1977). Beyond sensory-motor intelligence: Assessment of symbolic maturity through analysis of pretend play. *Merrill-Palmer Quarterly, 23*, 89–101.

Piaget, J. (1962). *Play, dreams and imitation.* London: Kegan Paul.

Radke-Yarrow, M., Richters, J., & Wilson, W. E. (1988). Child development in a network of relationships. In R. A. Hinde & J. Stevenson-Hinde (Eds.), *Relationships with families: Mutual influences* (pp. 48–67). Oxford: Clarendon Press.

Sameroff, A. J. (1975). Early influences on development: Fact or fancy? *Merrill-Palmer Quarterly, 21*, 267–294.

Singer, D. G., & Singer, J. L. (1990). *The house of make-believe. Children's play and the developing imagination.* Cambridge, MA: Harvard University Press.

Stern, D. (1985). *The interpersonal world of the infant. A view from psychoanalysis and developmental psychology.* New York: Basic Books.

Stevenson-Hinde, J. (1989). Behavioral inhibition: Issues of context. In J. S. Reznick (Ed.), *Perspectives on behavioral inhibition* (pp. 125–138). Chicago: University of Chicago Press.

Watson, M., & Fischer, K. (1977). A developmental sequence of agent use in late infancy. *Child Development, 48*, 828–836.

Wolf, D. (1982). Understanding others: A longitudinal case study of the concept of independent agency. In G. Forman (Ed.), *Action and thought: From sensorimotor schemes to symbolic operations* (pp. 297–328). New York: Academic Press.

Wolf, D. (1984). Repertoire, style and format: Notions worth borrowing from children's play. In P. Smith (Ed.), *Play in animals and humans* (pp. 175–193). Oxford: Basil Blackwell.

Wolf, D., & Grollman, S. (1982). Ways of playing: Individual differences in imaginative style. In K. Rubin & D. Pepler (Eds.), *The play of children: Current theory and research* (pp. 1–19). New York: Karger.

Wolf, D., & Hicks, D. (1989). The voices within narratives: The development of intertextuality in young children's stories. *Discourse Processes, 12*, 329–351.

Wolf, D., Rygh, J., & Altshuler, J. (1984). Agency and experience: Actions and states in play narratives. In I. Bretherton (Ed.), *Symbolic play: The development of social understanding* (pp. 195–217). Orlando, FL: Academic Press.

14

Symbolic Play in the Interactions of Young Children and Mothers with a History of Affective Illness: A Longitudinal Study

ELIZABETH C. TINGLEY

Symbolic play serves important affective, cognitive, and social functions in children's development. Traditionally, the affective function of symbolic play was viewed as the mastery of impulses and expression of inner conflicts (Freud, 1969). A more contemporary author has argued that symbolic play gives children the opportunity to share and "play with" emotional experiences (Fein, 1987). One perspective, among many, on the cognitive function of symbolic play is that when children play symbolically, they are practicing subjunctive thought or learning to think "as if" (Bretherton, 1984). In the social domain, children's symbolic play abilities have been linked to competence with peers (Connolly & Doyle, 1984) and sociometric status in the preschool years (Howes, 1987). When children's tendency to engage in symbolic play is undermined, these important developmental functions may not be served.

Some have argued that symbolic play development rests on the child's maturing cognitive abilities (e.g., Piaget, 1952) rather than on social experience. When symbolic play is social, it has been suggested that it occurs primarily among peers (Rubin, Fein, & Vandenberg 1983). However, other work indicates that adult–child social experience plays several important roles in children's symbolic play.

In naturally occurring mother–child interaction, the evidence indicates that mothers are involved in children's symbolic play. Nelson and Seidman (1984) reported that mothers provide a context that facilitates the child's play. Work by Dunn and colleagues (Dunn, 1986; Dunn & Dale, 1984; Dunn & Wooding, 1977) indicated that with toddlers, mothers in the home did support the symbolic activities of their children. They did so primarily in a spectator role or by maintaining joint attention to the play. Although most pretend play was initiated by the child, most of it was not completed without at least some acknowledgment from the mother. Also, naturally occurring symbolic play received more attention from mothers than did object play. In their study of mother–baby pretend play in the home, Miller and Garvey (1984) found that caregivers were actively involved in the child's naturally occurring doll play. At 2 years of age, a child's mother was most likely to give explicit instructions to the child about how to play. She was also likely to create a context that suggested the mother–baby theme. By the time the child was 2½ years old, the mother's role had changed to that of an approving spectator.

Specific maternal behaviors promote higher-level, or symbolic, play. O'Connell and Bretherton (1984) found that with active guidance of the mother, 28-month-old children increased their symbolic play. Kreye (1984) reported that verbal definitions of play themes by mothers resulted in more interconnected symbolic uses of toys. Slade (1987a) found that both active participation and suggestions by the mother to child about play resulted in higher-level and longer symbolic play episodes.

The general quality of the social context, specifically the quality of the mother–child relationship, has also been shown to affect the quality of children's symbolic play. Securely attached children at 26 and 28 months spent more time in the highest level of symbolic play. When mothers were involved in the play of secure children, the quality of play was enhanced. This was not true when the mothers of insecurely attached children were involved in the play (Slade, 1987b). Belsky, Garduque, and Hrncir (1984) found that securely attached children were more likely than insecurely attached children to exercise their executive capacity in play (i.e., play more often at the highest level at which they were capable). Slade (1986), using detailed case histories, suggested that the quality of a 2-year-old's play may reflect the degree to which the attachment relationship supports the autonomy and intimacy needs of the child.

Quality and type of maternal responsiveness during play in infancy have been related to level and coherency of children's fantasy play during the preschool years (Monk, Altman, Jones, Sosa, & Ward, 1992). Mueller and Tingley (1990) noted significant associations between maternal sensitivity at 20 months and positive family themes in replica play at 4 years. In addition, maternal sensitivity at 20 months was negatively related to fantasy failure at age 4 for girls. Finally, Hetherington, Cox, and Cox (1979) reported that the fantasy play of children in the period immediately following a divorce is limited and rigid in quality. There is, then, a role for caretakers in promoting high-quality play and, more generally, in providing social experiences that influence the ways children choose to engage in symbolic play.

Another important aspect of mothers' involvement in children's symbolic play is its interpersonal function. Mothers who participate in or support symbolic play are engaging with their children in a domain that is central and pleasurable to most children. This engagement could promote children's sense that their activities are valued and their experiences shared. Sullivan (1953) suggested that preschool children need their parents' attention to their fantasy play because when "circumstances do not permit very much of this audience behavior of the authority figures . . . the child is actually lonely'' (p. 223). There is empirical evidence indicating that at least some types of maternal participation in play have positive effects on children's social behavior. For example, responsive maternal play has been shown to induce a positive mood in children (Lay, Waters, & Parke, 1989). Responsive maternal play was also related to children's cooperation during compliance tasks (Parpal & Maccoby, 1985). Perhaps maternal participation in symbolic play can be viewed as one opportunity (among many) in mother–child interaction for children to acquire a sense of relationships as satisfying and of themselves as worthy.

Children with affectively ill mothers are at risk for a host of behavioral and developmental problems (Beardslee, Bemporad, Keller, & Klerman, 1983). Our understanding of the social processes that, in part, transmit this risk has grown tremendously from recent research (see the review by Downey & Coyne, 1990). Yet there has been no investigation of depressed mother–child play interactions and children's play development. As indicated earlier, significant developmental functions are served by children's symbolic play. When children with depressed mothers are unable or unmotivated to engage in symbolic play, their experiences in other social domains, like peer relations, may also be compromised. Likewise, children who do not choose to play symbolically may find the affective functions of play— to engage with others around emotionally significant themes—unfulfilled. This could be a significant loss for children of depressed mothers, who have greater needs for emotional exploration and sharing than other children. Also, depressed mothers' inability to support symbolic play or atypical patterns of maternal involvement in play may reflect less than optimal mother–child interaction. These experiences in the play domain, then, may also contribute to children's perceptions of themselves and others.

Many dimensions of depressed mother–child interaction have been depicted that suggest that maternal involvement in children's symbolic play may not be optimal. Depressed mothers engaged in less interaction with their children than did well mothers (Cox, Puckering, Pound, & Mills, 1987). Depressed mothers were more negative in their interactions with their children than well mothers (Hops, Sherman, & Biglan, 1990; Longfellow, Zelkowitz, & Saunders, 1983; Panaccione & Wahler, 1986; Stoneman, Brody, & Burke, 1989). They also exhibited less positive kinds of interaction (Whiffen & Gotlib, 1989), contingent responding (Field, Sandberg, Garcia, Vega-Lahr, Goldstein, & Guy, 1985) and positive affect (Livingood, Daen, & Smith, 1983) than well mothers. These findings suggest that depressed mothers' support for children's symbolic play, in both general and specific senses, is likely to differ from that of well mothers.

There may, however, be considerable individual differences in how effective depressed mothers are in providing a context to facilitate symbolic play. Not all aspects of mother–child interaction have been found to be related to maternal depression. Some studies have found no associations between maternal depression and observational measures of interaction (Goodman, Lynch, & Brogan, 1989; Rogers & Forehand, 1983). Webster-Stratton and Hammond (1988) found no relation between maternal depression and three of four maternal behaviors: amount of maternal praise, commands, and negative physical interaction. Amount of physical, facial, and verbal affection was not associated with mothers' scores on the Beck Depression Index (Panaccionne & Wahler, 1986).

When negative results such as these are found, they should be considered as possible sources of individual differences in outcomes for children. That is, a mother who is depressed yet manages to praise her child or be affectionate may buffer the effects of her depression on her child. It could be that the social experiences of children whose depressed mothers can engage in appropriate interactions serve as protective factors for these children. Specific to this research, we ask: Are early within-group differences in mother–child play behavior predictive of later play behavior outcomes?

Where individual differences in depressed mothers' behavior are found, prior work directs us to dimensions of affective illness other than diagnosis. Maternal behavior, although related to diagnosis, varies more directly with the severity, chronicity, and individual symptom constellation of parental affective illness (Fendrich, Warner, & Weissman, 1990; Goodman & Brumley, 1990; Hammen, Burge, & Stansbury, 1990; Richters, 1987). Certainly, severity and/or chronicity of maternal illness have been related to child outcomes in a number of studies (Baldwin, Cole, & Baldwin, 1982; Billings & Moos, 1985; Cohn & Campbell, 1992; Frankel, Harmon, & Maslin-Cole, 1991; Goodman & Brumley, 1990; Gordon, Burge, Adrian, Jaenick, & Hiroto, 1987; Keller, Beardslee, Dorer, Lavori, Samuelson, & Klerman, 1986; Richters, 1987; Seifer & Barocas, 1991). Study of individual differences in depressed-mother and child behavior requires consideration of these factors.

This research examined the effects of maternal depression on the amount of symbolic play exhibited by children with their mothers and the amount of maternal participation in symbolic play. It was a secondary analysis of data on maternal depression and mother–child interaction collected at the National Institutes of Mental Health (NIMH). This study grew from preliminary work with the NIMH data analyzing an 8-minute segment of semi-structured mother–toddler interaction.[1] Contrary to expectation, both the amount of symbolic play produced by children and the amount of maternal involvement in symbolic play were found not to differ by maternal diagnostic category (Wolf, Watson, & Tingley, 1989). While these null results could result from a Type II error ($n = 45$), these preliminary findings also suggested several directions for further inquiry—the work to be reported here.

Might the similarities between diagnostic groups in play level and mother–child involvement in symbolic play be related to the demands of the semistructured play context? Would there continue to be no differences if unstructured activity was observed? Here mothers must "self-generate" play and involvement in play. In the research to be presented, it was proposed that during unstructured activity, well mothers would exhibit more symbolic play participation and the level of children's play level would be higher in well dyads. This would be true when children were toddlers and again when they were 5 to 6 years of age.

In addition, during spontaneous play, would mothers' participation in symbolic play be related to higher-level play by children? If so, would the relationship differ between diagnostic groups? It was proposed that well mothers' participation would foster higher-level play; this would be less true in the unipolar and bipolar dyads. It was also proposed that play level and maternal participation would be more related at Time 1, when children were 3 years old, than at Time 2, when they were 5½ years old.

Next, could it be that diagnosis alone was not a good predictor of maternal play involvement and children's play performance? Could it be that severity, chronicity, and current level of depression would be more closely associated with play behavior? It was expected that these dimensions of maternal illness would be associated with play level and maternal participation in play.

Finally, are mothers' differing capacities *within* diagnostic groups to foster symbolic play in any way a protective factor for these children? That is, how would these capacities be related to children's symbolic play behavior over time? In this study, it is proposed that earlier, high-quality mother–child play behavior will be associated with later high-quality play behavior.

Method

This study was a secondary analysis of data on maternal depression and mother–child interaction collected at the NIMH. A longitudinal design was employed, examining the play interactions of mother–child dyads at two points 3 years apart.

Subjects

The Subjects were 45 mothers and their children. Children were between 2½ and 3½ years of age at Time 1 ($m = 34$ months). At Time 2, they were between 5 and 6 years of age ($m = 64$ months). Mothers were diagnosed as experiencing an episode of unipolar depression ($n = 14$), an episode of bipolar depression ($n = 16$), or no psychiatric illness in their child's lifetime ($n = 15$). Diagnoses were obtained by clinicians using the Schedule for Affective Disorders and Schizophrenia–Lifetime, Research Diagnostic Criteria (SADS-L, RDC) (Endicott & Spitzer, 1979). The mothers were not necessarily experiencing a depressive episode at the time of the initial observation. In addition, the affective illnesses of these mothers were somewhat heterogeneous in their course. The amount of depression during the child's lifetime varied between 2% and 100%, and severity ratings ranged from severe to mild impairment of functioning. Global Assessment of Symptoms and Impairment (GAS) scores were between 10 and 60.

These subjects were a subsample of the original NIMH sample of 103 dyads. Diagnostic groups were matched for socioeconomic status, maternal education (Hollingshead, 1975), and child age. As a check on the matching procedures, analysis of variance on these variables by diagnostic group indicated no significant differences. (All *F* ratios were nonsignificant.)

Procedure

Mothers and children were videotaped during naturalistic interaction in an informal homelike apartment at NIMH at both assessments. The first portion of the first day of each assessment period constituted the data for this study. The apartment was equipped with age-appropriate toys designed to foster both symbolic and nonsymbolic play. At Time 1, all free time interspersed between times directly structured by the experimenter was observed for play behaviors. This time (varying between 24 and 36 minutes) was considered spontaneous activity. At Time 2, mothers and children had approximately 35 minutes of unstructured time in the apartment at the beginning of the visit. The inconsistent amount of spontaneous activity was controlled by treating relevant dependent measures as proportions of time observed.

Symbolic Play Measures

Children's play level and amount of maternal participation at each play level were measured in all unstructured time. Each 30-second interval was coded for child play level: no play, nonsymbolic play, or symbolic play. These levels were coded according to the play-level codes defined by Watson.[2] Nonplay was coded during pragmatic or functional activities (like eating, toileting, or clean-up), during moments of no activity, or during conversations about past and/or future events. Play was coded during object (toy) manipulation when toys were used functionally, without any "as if" behaviors. Symbolic play was coded when any object or role transformation occurred. Where two or more activity levels co-occurred in one interval, the highest level of activity was used to rate that interval.

The average level of child activity was calculated by assigning a score of 1 to functional activity, 2 to nonsymbolic play, and 3 to symbolic play. The values for the intervals were summed and divided by the number of intervals observed. Level of maternal participation (i.e., symbolic, nonsymbolic, or functional) was also measured in each 30-second interval.

Two advanced undergraduate psychology majors blind to maternal diagnostic status coded the Time 1 videotapes for play level and play participants. Two different coders, also advanced undergraduate psychology majors, analyzed the Time 2 data. After initial training of 10 to 12 hours on identical videotapes, each set of coders independently rated nine Time 1 or Time 2 videotapes, or 20% of the data. Interrater agreement was calculated by computing kappas (Cohen, 1960). For Time 1 play level, the kappa was .89; for Time 2 play level, it was .93. For the level of maternal participation, the Time 1 and Time 2 kappas were .82 and .84, respectively.

At Time 2 another set of measures was utilized to capture the greater complexity of 5-year-old play. These measures were obtained from observation of 30 minutes of the same spontaneous activity. Play was coded using the event as the unit of analysis. These measures were adapted from the work of Giffin (1984) describing eight metacommunicative options during play. These varied in the degree to which play was "in frame" (within the script of the ongoing fantasy) or "out of frame" (outside the script). Giffin argued that competent symbolic play was indexed by children's ability to stay in frame.

Two categories from Giffin's coding scheme were modified for use in this study. *Enactment* of play was coded as occurring when the child or mother acted out play and play actions were completely within the script. Some examples of enactment were talking like any pretend character ("I'm going into space" or "I'm going to eat you up"), making replica figures act like real characters, or acting in a role such as a tea drinker or preparer. *Narration* was partly in frame and partly out of frame. It occurred when the child or mother described events in the fantasy world but without acting in character. Examples included statements like "Now the little man is going to sleep" and "The space ship is broken and the guy doesn't know how to fix it."

These episodes could be distinguished from play coded as symbolic, but not enactment or narration, primarily by the presence of a theme elaborated by the players. This is in contrast to instances of simple object transformation (e.g., "This block is a truck") or setting the stage activities ("We have to get this spaceship all ready so they can go into space").

Enactment or narration was coded as events lasting for at least 5 seconds. Pauses of more than 10 seconds were counted as terminating the event. Enactment and narration were coded as co-occurring if actions or statements of both kinds were linked together without gaps of 10 seconds or more. The duration of enactment/narration events was recorded, as well as the number of enactment/narration events in which mother and child both participated.

One coder blind to maternal diagnostic status coded all videotapes, with a second coder coding 20% of the data. For interobserver agreement on categorical variables, kappas were again computed. For the categorization of events as enactment, narration, or enactment and narration, the kappa was .82. For event participants, the kappa was .89. Interobserver agreement on the length of enactment and/or narration events was calculated using interclass correlation, a reliability coefficient derived from analysis of variance (Bertko & Carpenter, 1976). The interclass correlation coefficient for duration of events was .96, in the excellent range, according to published guidelines (Cicchetti & Sparrow, 1981).

Measures of Maternal Depression

Several measures of the severity and chronicity of maternal depression, as well as current symptoms, were made at NIMH. These were used to analyze the effects of different dimensions of maternal depression on play variables. These measures are shown in Table 14.1.

As indicated earlier, a maternal diagnosis made prior to Time 1 referred to a diagnosis of the mother's depression at *some* point in the child's lifetime by experienced clinicians, using SADS-L, RDC (Endicott & Spitzer, 1979). This diagnosis did *not* reflect the current status of maternal illness. Severity of depressive symptoms was measured by the GAS score taken from the SADS-L and referred to the worst episode of maternal depression in the child's lifetime prior to the Time 1 visit. Chronicity of depression referred to the percentage of the child's lifetime during which mothers were depressed at preceding the Time 1 visit.

No direct assessment was made of current symptoms at Time 1. One available approximation of this was the maternal report of energy level on the day of the visit to NIMH. This was taken from the Profile of Mood States (POMS) (McNair, Lorr, & Droppelman, 1981), which mothers completed during the visit.

TABLE 14.1.   All NIMH Measures of Maternal Depression

Dimension	Instrument
Diagnosis Maternal diagnosis for depressive episode at some time in the child's life	SADS-L, RDC
Chronicity Percentage of child's life during which mother has been depressed prior to Time 1 visit	SADS-L, RDC
Severity Most severe episode of depression in child's life	GAS score (global assessment of symptoms and impairment) from SADS-L, RDC
Current Functioning Time 2 symptom type (depressed, manic, none)	Clinical interview based on SADS-L, RDC
Mother self-report of energy level (Time 1)	POMS

The presence of depressive symptoms at the Time 2 visit was determined by clinical interviews, using the SADS-L format. These cannot be considered true, blind diagnoses of affective illness, as the clinicians conducting the interviews were familiar with the study families, but they are believed to have sufficient reliability to indicate the depressive symptoms existing at Time 2. Time 2 symptoms were categorized as no current symptoms, depressive symptoms, and other (manic, hypomanic and anxious) symptoms.

Current symptoms were related to but not identical to the original diagnosis. Sixty-four percent of the unipolar group continued to be depressed. Forty-seven percent of the bipolar group reported symptoms of depression at Time 2, and 27% of this group reported other (including manic) symptoms. Of the well mothers, 81% reported no symptoms at Time 2. Evaluation of the relation between diagnosis and symptom type indicated that the two were not independent ($\chi^2 = 19.58$, $df = 4$, $p < .001$). (For further information on the ways in which these measures were obtained, the reader is referred to Radke-Yarrow, Nottelmann, Martinez, Fox, & Belmont 1992.)

Results

Four sets of analyses were performed. The first evaluated the association between the two dependent measures of play level and participation. Correlations between the dependent measures were obtained for the sample as a whole and for each diagnostic group. Differences between the correlations were evaluated using Fisher's r' to z transformation. The second analysis considered the effects of maternal diagnosis on play level, maternal participation, enactment/narration event duration, and joint mother–child enactment/narration events during spontaneous activity using analysis

TABLE 14.2.   Time 1 and Time 2 Pearson r Correlation Coefficients for Maternal
Participation and Child Play Level

	Time 1 Maternal Participation and Child Play Level	Time 2 Maternal Participation and Child Play Level
Unipolar dyads	.92	.62
Bipolar dyads	.60	.79
Well dyads	.53	.69

of variance. The third analysis examined the effects of diagnosis in conjunction with current maternal functioning, severity, and chronicity of maternal depression on play level, duration, and participation variables in the depressed groups only through analysis of covariance. The last analysis focused on the effects of maternal diagnosis in conjunction with the effects of Time 1 play and participation variables on Time 2 play and participation variables, again utilizing analysis of covariance.

Relation of Child Play Level to Amount of Maternal Symbolic Play Participation During Spontaneous Activity

This analysis addressed the question of the interdependence of child play level and maternal participation. Pearson r correlation coefficients assessing the relation between child play-level variables and maternal symbolic play participation variables for each group within each assessment are shown in Table 14.2. These results indicate that for the sample as a whole and for the well, unipolar, and bipolar groups separately, amount of maternal play participation was positively associated with child play level at Time 1 and Time 2.

Examination of the correlation coefficients of the different diagnostic groups suggested that the strength of this association might differ by group, especially for the Time 1 participation and play measures. Fisher's r' to z transformation of the correlations of play level and maternal participation at Time 1 between the well and unipolar groups indicated a significant difference ($z = 2.33$, $p = .01$). In the well dyads, maternal participation and play rank were less strongly associated than in the unipolar dyads. No other significant differences in the strength of association of level and participation variables were found when comparing well and unipolar dyads and well and bipolar dyads at Time 1 or Time 2.

Examination of the correlations within each group across Time 1 and Time 2 suggested that the association between maternal participation and child play level was different at Time 2 than at Time 1. Even though the correlations of each group at Time 1 and Time 2 are not independent, the difference between them was analyzed again using the Fisher's r' to z transformation. This was justified using the expected logic: that the difference in correlations between two independent groups tends to be larger than the difference between similar measurements of the same group at two points in time. This makes the Fisher's r' to z transformation a conservative test, given its assumption of independence. There was a difference between Time 1 and Time 2 association of maternal participation and child play level in the unipolar group only ($z = 1.92, p. < .05$). The association declined in strength over time only for the unipolar dyads.

Thus, contrary to the initial hypothesis, the relationship between maternal participation in play and children's play complexity was stronger for the unipolar dyads. The play level of children with unipolar-depressed mothers is more dependent on their mothers' involvement than is the play of children with bipolar or well mothers when the children were between 2 and 3 years of age. There were no differences in the strength of the association between maternal involvement and child play level between the diagnostic groups at Time 2.

Effects of Maternal Diagnosis on Play in Spontaneous Activity

This analysis considered whether or not mothers with a history of unipolar or bipolar affective illness and their children differed in the quality of symbolic play exhibited in unstructured time. *F* ratios, degrees of freedom, and significance levels for all analyses of variance for the dependent measures are shown in Table 14.3. These results indicate that there are no differences between the well and depressed dyads in level of children's play, duration of complex symbolic play episodes, amount of maternal participation in symbolic play during spontaneous activity at Time 1 or Time 2, or number of joint mother–child enactment/narration events. Again, contrary to the initial hypothesis, maternal diagnosis alone does not distinguish children's play level or maternal involvement in play even during unstructured or spontaneous activity.

Dimensions of Maternal Depression and Play and Participation Variables

This analysis focused on the effects of dimensions of maternal affective illness on play level and duration and on mother–child participation in symbolic play in the depressed dyads *only* at Time 1 and Time 2. The analysis asked if aspects beyond

TABLE 14.3. Means, Standard Deviations, *F* Ratios, and Significance Levels for Time 1 and Time 2 Play and Participation Variables by Maternal Diagnosis

| | Means (SD) | | | | | |
Variable	Unipolar	Bipolar	Well	F	df	p
Play Level						
Time 1 interval rank	2.14 (.33)	2.13 (.39)	2.07 (.28)	.19	2,41	.83
Time 2 interval rank	2.31 (.36)	2.34 (.35)	2.26 (.36)	.21	2,41	.82
Time 2 seconds of enactment narration	245 (211)	255 (248)	359 (414)	.63	2,41	.54
Maternal Participation						
Time 1 mother symbolic	.24 (.20)	.19 (.17)	.22 (.13)	.52	2,41	.60
Time 2 mother symbolic	.18 (.21)	.30 (.30)	.25 (.25)	.87	2,41	.42
Joint Mother–Child Participation						
Enactment/narration events with mother and child	3.36 (2.1)	3.79 (4.0)	4.12 (4.0)	.46	2,41	.64

TABLE 14.4.   *F* Ratios and Significance Levels for the Analyses of Covariance of Play Level, Duration, and Participation Variables by Dimensions of Maternal Affective Illness (Depressed Groups Only)

	F Ratios					
Dependent Variables	Covariates Combined	Time 1 Energy	Illness Severity	Illness Chronicity	Diagnosis (U & B)*	Time 2 Symptoms
T1 play level	3.23[b]	6.59[b]	.07	.37	.01	—
T2 play level	3.66[b]	—	3.50[b]	.75	.14	1.52
T1 mother particip.	3.84[b]	8.56[c]	5.68[b]	3.67[a]	.21	—
T2 mother symbolic	1.55	—	1.06	2.73[a]	1.77	1.97
Enactment/narration event duration	1.08	—	1.74	.00	.08	.97
Joint mother–child enactment/narration	2.43	—	3.72[a]	.00	.19	4.29[b]

[a]$p < .10$.
[b]$p < .05$.
[c]$p < .01$.
*Unipolar and bipolar diagnostic categories only.

type of affective illness are related to child play level and maternal participation. *F* ratios, degrees of freedom, and significance levels for all analyses of covariance for the dependent measures are shown in Table 14.4. Level of play produced by the children at Time 1 was related to their mothers' report of the energy level, a very general measure of current maternal functioning. Time 1 play level was not related to the severity of chronicity of maternal depression. Play level at Time 2 was not related to current symptoms or chronicity of maternal symptoms, although the covariates together were related to play rank. Time 2 play rank also tended to be related to depression severity ($F = 3.50$, $p = .08$). The number of seconds of enactment and/or narration during symbolic play by children was not related to any dimension of maternal affective illness. Overall there were very few effects of dimensions of maternal depression on the level of play produced by children during spontaneous activity at Time 1 or Time 2.

The proportion of 30-second intervals that the unipolar and bipolar mothers participated in symbolic play at Time 1 was related to the maternal report of energy level. This was also related to the severity of maternal depression. In addition, there was a trend for Time 1 maternal participation in symbolic play to be related to the chronicity of maternal depression. At Time 2, this variable was not related to any dimension of maternal depression, although the combined main effects of diagnosis and current symptoms tended to be significant ($F = 2.73$, $p = .07$). The number of Time 2 events of enactment/narration with mother–child participation was related to current maternal symptoms. Mother–child enactment/narration events were also somewhat related to the severity of maternal depression.

Unlike the analysis of the effects of diagnostic category on play behavior, other dimensions of maternal affective illness were somewhat related to quality of chil-

TABLE 14.5. *F* Ratios and Significance Levels for the Analyses of Covariance of Time 2 Play Variables by Time 1 Play Variables and Maternal Diagnosis

	TIme 1 Level	*Diagnosis*	*D* × *L*
T2 play level	3.41[a]	.69	.77
T2 mother participation	7,38[c]	.38	.58
Enact./narration duration	1.88	.18	.10
Mother–child enact./narration events	4.62[b]	.33	.39
	T1 Mother Particip.	Diagnosis	MP × D
T2 child play level	.35	2.19	4.23[a]
T2 mother participation	5.45[b]	1.23	3.47[b]
Enact./narration duration	.04	3.05[a]	2.41
Mother–child enact./narration events	3.26[a]	.45	1.04

[a]$p \leq .10$.
[b]$p \leq .05$.
[c]$p \leq .01$.

dren's play and were more strongly related to patterns of maternal involvement in symbolic play. Current functioning, as well as severity and chronicity of maternal depression, were related to how mothers with both unipolar and bipolar illness engaged in play with their children.

Relation of Time 1 Play Variables to Time 2 Play Variables

The last set of analyses concerned the relation of Time 1 play level and maternal participation in symbolic play to Time 2 symbolic play and participation measures. Is the quality of earlier mother–child play related to the quality of later mother–child play? The effects of diagnosis, the Time 1 covariates, and the interactions of the covariates and diagnosis were analyzed. Analyses of covariance for the play level and participation are shown in Table 14.5. Time 2 play level, as measured by interval rank and by the number of seconds of enactment and narration, tended to be related to Time 1 play level. Time 2 maternal participation in symbolic play was significantly related to Time 1 play level. There was no significant interaction of diagnosis and Time 1 play level, indicating that the Time 1 play level was related to Time 2 play variables in a similar way across diagnostic groups.

Time 2 maternal participation was also related to Time 1 maternal participation in play. However, the significant effect of the interaction of diagnosis and Time 1 mother participation indicates that the effect of the covariate was not the same for each group. Separate regression analyses were performed for each diagnostic group testing the relation of Time 1 maternal participation to Time 2 maternal participation and child play level. Standardized regression coefficients were .40 for the unipolar group ($F^{change} = 2.25, p = .16$), .73 for the bipolar group ($F^{change} = 14.79, p = .002$), and $-.10$ for the well group ($F^{change} = .13, p = .72$). Differences between the standardized regression coefficients (equivalent to Pearson r correlation coefficients) for each group were tested using the Fisher's r' to z transformation. The association between Time 1 maternal participation and Time 2 maternal participation was not different between the unipolar and well groups ($z = 1.22$). There was a difference in the association of Time 1 and Time 2 maternal participation in the bipolar and well groups ($z = 2.51$), with the association being stronger in the bipolar dyads.

There was a significant interaction effect for maternal diagnosis and Time 1 maternal participation in relation to Time 2 child play level. Separate regression analyses were performed testing the association of Time 1 maternal participation to Time 2 child participation for each diagnostic group. Standardized regression coefficients obtained from these analyses were .43 for the unipolar group ($F = 2.67$, $p = .13$), .51 for the bipolar group ($F = 4.53$, $p = .05$), and $-.45$ for the well group ($F = 3.50$, $p = .08$). Differences between standardized regression coefficients (equivalent to Pearson r correlation coefficients) were tested using the Fisher's r' to z transformation. The regression weights of the unipolar and well groups were significantly different ($z = 2.19$), as were those of these bipolar and well groups ($z = 2.56$). In both depressed groups, then, there was a positive association between Time 1 maternal participation and Time 2 child play level. For the well group, a moderate negative association was observed.

Mother–child enactment events also tended to be related to Time 1 maternal participation in play. There was also a trend for the diagnosis to be related to the duration of enactment/narration events at Time 2 after controlling for the effects of the covariate, Time 1 mother play participation.

Thus, prior play behaviors of mothers and children predicted later play behaviors. However, Time 1 maternal play behavior was related to Time 2 maternal and child play behavior in different ways for each diagnostic category. The play participation of bipolar mothers with their toddlers predicted the Time 2 play participation of this diagnostic group. Time 1 maternal participation in play was positively related to Time 2 child play level for the two depressed groups only. The history of play interactions had different effects for children whose mothers were and were not depressed.

Discussion

These results provide compelling evidence that children's capacity for symbolic play survives under a range of social and situational conditions. Some children exhibited high-quality symbolic play in the face of a maternal affective illness that severely limited their mothers' ability to express interest or pleasure in play. In many other cases, perhaps because of the basic nature of play, mothers continued to acknowledge and participate in children's symbolic play in spite of their depression, past or present. This is not to say that no relations between affective illness and the quality of play, and between mothers and children, were uncovered here. Rather, the effects of maternal depression on the quality of children's play and on the quality of mother–child interaction through play were complex.

There were different patterns of involvement by well and depressed mothers in children's symbolic play and different effects of that involvement on the quality of play produced by children. The ways depressed mothers played with their children were qualitatively distinct. The early history of mother–child dyads (severity and chronicity of maternal affective illness, as well as quality of prior mother–child play interactions) accounted for later behavior in the play domain to a greater degree in the depressed dyads than in the well dyads. Action and interaction were more historically determined for children of depressed mothers than for children with well mothers. Put another way, the effects of maternal depression persisted in the ways mothers and children played together over the course of at least 3 years. There were also considerable individual differences in the play behavior of depressed mothers. Some affectively ill mothers were very involved in the imaginative play of their children, and others were not. Given the greater interdependence of the play behavior of mothers and children in the depressed dyads, the capacity to play of some depressed mothers may serve as a protective factor for children's development. Conversely, when depressed mothers' capacity for symbolic play is impaired, this may have a greater impact on children's development than when participation in symbolic play is not a part of a well mother's repertoire.

Turning to specific findings, at Time 1 the relation between maternal participation in symbolic play and child play level was strongest in the unipolar dyads during spontaneous activity. This was contrary to expectation. It may be that children whose mothers have a history of unipolar depression have learned to follow or adjust their own actions to the behavior of their mothers, at least in the play domain. An alternative explanation, given that the correlational analysis does not tell us about the direction of effects, is that unipolar-depressed mothers do not initiate play at the symbolic level but rather join activity initiated by their children. What these data do tell us is that in the toddler period, mother–child play behavior is more interdependent in dyads with mothers who suffer from unipolar affective illness than is the play behavior of well or bipolar mothers and their children.

As in the preliminary study, no differences during unstructured activity were found between the diagnostic groups in the level of play produced by children or the amount of maternal participation in symbolic play at either Time 1 or Time 2. There were also no differences in the duration of the most complex symbolic play episodes (enactment/narration events) or the number of these episodes that mothers and children participated in. Considering the diagnosis, then, play level and participation varied as much within the unipolar, bipolar, and well groups as it did between these groups, even in unstructured activity. That is, some mothers with a history of affective illness and their children were as likely to exhibit high-level play as some mothers with a history of no psychiatric illness and their children even during unstructured activity.

However, variation in play behaviors within the depressed groups was related to dimensions of maternal affective illness other than diagnosis. Mothers' current functioning, measured at Time 1 as self-report of energy level, was significantly related to the level of children's play and to the amount of maternal play participation at a symbolic level. Current maternal symptoms at Time 2 were related to the number of joint mother–child narration/enactment events. This indicates that at both ages studied, play produced by children and the way mothers participate in play are vulnerable to mothers' current emotional state.

In addition, historical dimensions of maternal affective illness were related to play level and participation. At Time 1, only the extent of maternal participation was related to the severity and chronicity of depression. There was no relationship between these factors and the level of play produced by children. Interestingly, at Time 2, 3 years after measurement of these dimensions of depression, modest relationships were observed between them and play level and participation. Ratings of the most severe episode of maternal depression during the child's first 2½ years tended to be related to the level of play produced by children when they were between 5 and 6 years of age and to mutual mother–child high-level symbolic play (as indexed by the number of joint narration/enactment events). In addition, the percentage of the child's life during which mothers were depressed, as measured at Time 1, was somewhat related to the amount of maternal participation in symbolic play at Time 2. Thus, earlier severe, chronic maternal depression continues to be evident in the play interactions and behavior of mothers and children 3 years later.

There is evidence here supporting the notion that early high-quality play behavior of depressed mothers and their children leads to later high-quality play behavior, although overall the relation of Time 1 and Time 2 behaviors was found to be complex in these data. One of the most interesting findings in this regard is the trend indicating that the duration of enactment/narration differed between the diagnostic groups after controlling for the effects of Time 1 maternal participation. The duration variable reflects the amount of time the child was engaged in in-frame symbolic play or the most complex level of play assessed in this study. That is, children of depressed mothers do tend to produce less sustained, complex fantasy play when the individual differences in the ways their mothers involved themselves in symbolic play in the toddler period are controlled. This suggests that maternal involvement in play in the toddler period may, in fact, mitigate the association between maternal depression and suboptimal play interaction and behavior at later ages.

Early and later play behaviors were associated in other ways as well. Time 1 maternal participation in play was related to the Time 2 child play level differently for the well and depressed groups. For both depressed groups, Time 1 maternal participation was positively related to Time 2 child play level. Here earlier maternal involvement in symbolic play was associated with the later level of play produced by children. However, for the well dyads, there was an inverse relationship between earlier maternal participation and later child play level. This finding is difficult to interpret. Perhaps this inverse relation could be taken as evidence that, in general, the symbolic play of the children of well mothers is more determined by the history of their play interactions than is the play of children of depressed mothers. (The Time 1 maternal participation − Time 2 child play level in the well dyads only tended to be significant: $p = .08$.) The clearest finding regarding the relation of Time 1 maternal participation and Time 2 child play level was that the patterns of association were quite different in dyads with and without affective illness.

Time 1 maternal participation was also more strongly related to Time 2 maternal participation for the depressed dyads than for the well dyads. The association was strongest for the bipolar dyads. There was virtually no association between Time 1 and Time 2 maternal participation for the well dyads. Here again, the history of dyadic interactions seemed more influential for later behavior in the depressed dyads than in the well dyads.

These associations between Time 1 maternal behavior and Time 2 child and mother behavior need to be seen in light of the association of severity, chronicity, and current functioning to the Time 1 maternal participation variable. The continuing relation of Time 1 maternal participation to Time 2 play behavior should be seen, in part, as an indication of the enduring effects of dimensions of maternal affective illness, mediated through maternal behavior, on dyadic behavior. Here the point must also be made, though, that variability in maternal participation was only partially explained by dimensions of maternal affective illness. Thus, the relation of earlier maternal participation to later play behavior should also be seen as evidence for the notion that depressed mothers who can and do engage in symbolic play with their toddlers may support more optimal development than those who do not or cannot.

Time 1 child play behaviors also showed significant relations with Time 2 mother and child play behaviors. Level of play produced by children at Time 1 was positively related to level of play at Time 2 and to the number of mother–child enactment/ narration events in all three diagnostic groups. Children of well and depressed mothers who produced high-level play when they were toddlers were likely to continue to do so at ages 5 to 6 years. Child play level at Time 1 was also positively related to maternal participation at Time 2, but this effect was stronger for the depressed dyads (especially the bipolar group) than for the well dyads. Again, it seems that bipolar depressed mothers' tendency to involve themselves in symbolic play with their 5- and 6-year-old children may depend on a history of high-level play produced by the children.

These data do not suggest that symbolic play development or children's capacity for symbolic play is compromised when children have depressed mothers. All children in all diagnostic groups were able to produce high-level symbolic play. However, the relations noted here between maternal depression and children's symbolic play tell us that the likelihood that children will engage in high-level symbolic play with their mothers is somewhat reduced. In addition, these data show that there are qualitatively distinct patterns of maternal involvement in symbolic play in well and depressed groups, especially when considering the effects of current maternal functioning and the history of maternal affective illness. As a part of this picture, what are seen here are differing patterns of the relationship of early and later play behavior between mothers and children in well and depressed dyads.

We do not know if there are consequences of these patterns for children's development in domains other than mother–children play interaction. Maternal participation in play may be one interpersonal experience that contributes to children's sense that others are responsive to and value their activities. We can speculate, then, that children of depressed mothers, particularly those with mothers whose depression has been severe, chronic, and ongoing, would internalize different, perhaps less than optimal, views of self and others when their mothers do not involve themselves in symbolic play.

Two examples may help to illustrate what children are learning about themselves and others in the kinds of play interactions previously analyzed. One child, age 5, is dressing a doll. She hands one doll to her mother, asking her to put another outfit on the doll ''to get her ready for church.'' Her mother does not look up from her newspaper but takes the doll. The mother holds the doll in the air. She says ''Okay'' but does nothing. She continues to read. The girl looks up and looks hard at her mother, saying nothing for a minute or two. Then she says, "Do it. Why don't you do it?" somewhat angrily. There is another pause, again with no response. The girl returns to her own play and says, "It's fun to do it." The mother eventually begins to dress the doll but without making any verbal response.

This interaction can be compared to the interaction of another 5-year-old girl and her mother. The mother sees the chalkboard in the room and turns to the girl. She says enthusiastically, "Let's play school." The two take turns adopting the teacher and student roles, the "pupil" mother allowing herself to be chastised for not paying attention. As the teacher, she praises the girl's knowledge repeatedly. When the game is over, the mother sits back on the sofa, looks at the child, and says, smiling, "I got a big kick out of that." The girl smiles back.

The differing patterns of relationship portrayed here seem quite likely to communicate very different messages about the worth of the child's activity and self. We know that relationships are important, salient features of the young child's world and serve as constructive elements of the child's self and understanding of others.

There are also important individual differences among depressed mothers with regard to their ability to engage in symbolic play activities with their children. We need to consider that children's development may be protected, or even enhanced, by the behavior of those mothers who have a history of depression yet manage high-quality interactions with their children.

The fact that some depressed mothers do manage to invest in their children's symbolic play is both a hopeful finding and one with potential intervention implications. Perhaps work with the mother–child dyad could focus on promotion of symbolic play interactions. Alternatively, intervention with children of depressed mothers could focus on providing other opportunities for them to experience adult participation in and appreciation for their symbolic worlds. The finding of individual differences also tells future researchers that it is necessary to look at the behavioral variability within as well as between diagnostic groups when exploring the risk and protective factors for children's development associated with maternal depression.

ACKNOWLEDGMENTS

The author would like to thank Marian Radke-Yarrow for her generosity in making the NIMH data available and Catherine Snow for making the resources of her laboratory available to conduct the research. The author would also like to thank Deborah Belle, J. Michael Coleman, Jean Berko Gleason, Marian Radke-Yarrow, Louisa B. Tarullo, and Dennie P. Wolf for their helpful comments on earlier versions of this chapter.

NOTES

1. A more complete description of study subjects is found in the Methods section of this chapter.

2. Prior systems of analysis used with another portion of these data included a presymbolic level of play (Wolf, Watson, & Tingley, 1989). However, this level was rarely coded in the initial analyses because, by the age of the children in the study, most had progressed to

symbolic play and because this level is difficult to distinguish from symbolic play (Watson, personal communication, September, 1989). Thus, the presymbolic level was omitted here.

REFERENCES

Baldwin, A. L., Cole, R. E., & Baldwin, C. P. (1982). Parental pathology, family interaction, and the competence of the child in the school. *Monographs of the Society for Research in Child Development, 47*(5, Serial No. 197).

Beardslee, W. R., Bemporad, J., Keller, M. B., & Klerman, G. L. (1983). Children of parents with major affective disorder: A review. *American Journal of Psychiatry, 140*, 825–832.

Belsky, J., Garduque, L., & Hrncir, E. (1984). Assessing performance, competence, and executive capacity in infant play: Relations to home environment and security. *Developmental Psychology, 20*, 406–417.

Bertko, J. J., & Carpenter, W. T. (1976). On the methods and theory of reliability. *Journal of Nervous and Mental Disease, 163*, 307–218.

Billings, A. G., & Moos, R. H. (1985). Children of parents with unipolar depression: A controlled 1-year follow-up. *Journal of Abnormal Child Psychology, 14*, 149–166.

Bretherton, I. (1984). Representing the social world in symbolic play: Reality and fantasy. In I. Bretherton (Ed.), *Symbolic play: The development of social understanding* (pp. 1–44). New York: Academic Press.

Cicchetti, D. V., & Sparrow, S. S. (1981). Developing criteria for establishing interrater reliability of specific items: Applications to assessment of adaptive behavior. *American Journal of Mental Deficiency, 86*, 127–137.

Cohen, J. (1960). A coefficient of agreement for nominal scales. *Educational and Psychological Measurement, 20*, 37–46.

Cohn, J., & Campbell, S. B. (1992). Influences of maternal depression on infant affect regulation. In D. Cicchetti & S. Toth (Eds.), *Rochester Symposium on Developmental Psychopathology: Vol. 4, Developmental Perspectives on Depression* (pp. 103–130). Rochester, NY: Rochester University Press.

Connolly, J. A., & Doyle, A. (1984). Relation of social fantasy play to social competence in preschoolers. *Developmental Psychology, 20*, 797–806.

Cox, A. D., Puckering, C., Pound, A., & Mills, M. (1987). The impact of maternal depression in young children. *Journal of Child Psychology and Psychiatry, 28*, 917–928.

Downey, G., & Coyne, J. C. (1990). Children of depressed parents: An integrative review. *Psychological Bulletin, 108*, 50–76.

Dunn, J. (1986). Pretend play in the family. In A. W. Gottfried & C. C. Brown, (Eds.), *Play interactions: The contributions of play materials and parental involvement to children's development* (pp. 149–161). Lexington, MA: Lexington Books.

Dunn, J., & Dale, N. (1984). I a daddy: 2 year olds' collaboration in joint pretend with sibling and with mother. In I. Bretherton (Ed.), *Symbolic play: The development of social understanding* (pp. 131–158). New York: Academic Press.

Dunn, J., & Wooding, C. (1977). Play in the home and its implications for learning. In B. Tizard & D. Harvey (Eds.), *Biology of play* (pp. 45–58). Philadelphia: Lippincott.

Endicott, J., & Spitzer, R. L. (1979). Use of Research Diagnostic Criteria and the Schedule for Affective Disorders and Schizophrenia to study affective disorders. *American Journal of Psychiatry, 136*, 52–56.

Fein, G. (1987). The affective psychology of play. In A. W. Gottfried & C. C. Brown (Eds.),

Play interactions: The contributions of play materials and parental involvement to children's development (pp. 31–50). Lexington, MA: Lexington Books.

Fendrich, M., Warner, V., & Wiessman, M. M. (1990). Family risk factors, parental depression and psychopathology in offspring. *Developmental Psychology, 26,* 40–50.

Field, T. M., Sandberg, D., Garcia, R., Vega-Lahr, N., Goldstein, S., & Guy, L. (1985). Pregnancy problems, postpartum depression, and early mother–infant interactions. *Developmental Psychology, 21,* 1152–1156.

Frankel, K. A., Harmon, R. J., & Maslin-Cole, K. (1991, April). Depressed mothers of pre-schoolers: They don't always look as bad as they feel. Poster presented at the Biennial Meetings of the Society for Research in Child Development, Seattle, WA.

Freud, A. (1969). *Normality and pathology in childhood.* New York: International Universities Press.

Giffin, H. (1984). The coordination of meaning in the creation of a shared make-believe reality. In I. Bretherton (Ed.), *Symbolic play* (pp. 73–100). New York: Academic Press.

Goodman, S. H., & Brumley, H. E. (1990). Schizophrenic mothers and depressed mothers: Relational deficits in parenting. *Developmental Psychology, 26,* 283–291.

Goodman, S. H., Lynch, M. E., & Brogan, D. R. (1989, April). *Effects of maternal depression on child development: Toward a broad conceptualization of risk and outcome.* Paper presented at the Biennial Meetings of the Society for Research in Child Development. Kansas City, MO.

Hammen, C., Burge, D., & Stansbury, K. (1990). Relationship of mother and child variables to child outcomes in a high-risk sample: A causal modeling analysis. *Developmental Psychology, 26,* 24–30.

Hammen, C., Gordon, D., Burge, D., Adrian, C., Jaenick, C., & Hiroto, D. (1987). Communication patterns of mothers with affective disorders and their relationship to children's status and social functioning. In K. Hahlweg & M. J. Goldstein (Eds.), *Understanding major mental disorder: The contribution of family interaction research* (pp. 103–119). New York: Family Process Press.

Hetherington, E. M., Cox, M., & Cox, R. (1979). Play and social interaction in children following divorce. *Journal of Social Issues, 35,* 26–49.

Hollingshead, A. B. (1975). Four factor index of social status. Working paper. Department of Psychology, Yale University, New Haven, CT.

Hops, H., Sherman, L., & Biglan, A. (1990). Maternal depression and marital discord in children's behaviors: A developmental perspective. In G. R. Patterson (Ed.), *Depression and aggression in family interaction* (pp. 185–208). Hillsdale, NJ: Erlbaum.

Howes, C. (1987). Social competence with peers in young children: Developmental sequences. *Developmental Review, 7,* 252–272.

Keller, M. B., Beardslee, W. R., Dorer, D. J., Lavori, P. W., Samuelson, H., & Klerman, G. R. (1986). Impact of severity and chronicity of parental affective illness on adaptive functioning and psychopathology in children. *Archives of General Psychiatry, 43,* 930–937.

Kreye, M. (1984). Conceptual organization in the play of preschool children: Effects of meaning, context, and mother child interaction. In I. Bretherton (Ed.), *Symbolic play: The development of social understanding* (pp. 299–335). New York: Academic Press.

Lay, K., Waters, E., & Park, K. A. (1989). Maternal responsiveness and child compliance: The role of mood as mediator. *Child Development, 60,* 1405–1411.

Livingood, A. B., Daen, P., & Smith, B. D. (1983). The depressed mother as source of stimulation for her infant. *Journal of Clinical Psychology, 39,* 369–375.

Longfellow, C., Zelkowitz, P., & Saunders, E. (1983). The quality of mother–child relationships. In D. Belle (Ed.), *Lives in stress* (pp. 163–178). Beverly Hills, CA: Sage.

Lyons-Ruth, K., Zoll, D., Connell, D., & Grunebaum, H. U. (1986). The depressed mother and her one year old infant: Environment, interaction, attachment and infant development. *New Directions for Child Development, 34*, 61–82.

McNair, D. M., Lorr, M., & Droppleman, L. F. (1981). *EITS manual for the Profile of Mood States.* San Diego: Educational and Industrial Testing Service.

Miller, P., & Garvey, K. (1984). Mother–baby role play: Its origins in social support. In I. Bretherton (Ed.), *Symbolic play: The development of social understanding* (pp. 101–130). New York: Academic Press.

Monk, C., Altman, S. C., Jones, P., Sosa, L., & Ward, M. J. (1992, May). Early mother–infant interaction and its relation to preschoolers' pretense play. Poster presented at the Eighth Annual Conference on Infant Studies, Miami, FL.

Mueller, E. C., & Tingley, E. C. (1990, Summer). The bear's picnic: Children's representations of themselves and their families. In I. Bretherton & M. Watson (Eds.), *Children's perspectives on the family, new directions for child development* (Vol. 48, pp. 47–66). San Francisco: Jossey-Bass.

Nelson, K., & Seidman, S. (1984). Playing with scripts. In I. Bretherton (Ed.), *Symbolic play: The development of social understanding* (pp. 45–71). New York: Academic Press.

O'Connell, B., & Bretherton, I. (1984). Toddlers' play alone and with mother: The role of maternal guidance. In I. Bretherton (Ed.), *Symbolic play: The development of social understanding* (pp. 337–367). New York: Academic Press.

Panaccione, V. F., & Wahler, R. G. (1986). Child behavior, maternal depression and social coercion as factors in the quality of child care. *Journal of Abnormal Child Psychology, 14*, 263–278.

Parpal, M., & Maccoby, E. E. (1985). Maternal responsiveness and subsequent child compliance. *Child Development, 56*, 1326–1334.

Piaget, J. (1952). *The origins of intelligence in children.* New York: International Press.

Radke-Yarrow, M., Nottelmann, E., Martinez, P., Fox, M., & Belmont, M. (1992). Young children of affectively ill parents: A longitudinal study of psychosocial development. *Journal of the American Academy of Child and Adolescent Psychiatry, 31*, 68–77.

Richters, J. (1987). Chronic versus episodic patient-related interactions of depressed women. *Journal of Consulting and Clinical Psychology, 55*, 341–436.

Richters, J. (1987). Chronic versus episodic patient-related stress and the adjustment of high-risk offspring. In K. Halweg & M. J. Goldstein (Eds.), *Understanding major mental disorder: The contribution of family interaction research* (pp. 74–90). New York: Family Process Press.

Rogers, T. R., & Forehand, R. (1983). The role of parent depression in interactions between mothers and their clinic referred children. *Cognitive Therapy and Research, 7*, 315–324.

Rubin, K., Fein, G., & Vandenberg, B. (1983). Play. In E. M. Hetherington (Ed.), *Handbook of child psychology:* Vol. 4, *Socialization, personality and social development* (pp. 693–773). New York: Wiley.

Seifer, R., & Barocas, R. (April, 1991). A comparison of maternal diagnosis, severity of illness and symptom dimensions as predictors of 4-year child status. Poster presented at the Biennial Meetings of the Society for Research in Child Development, Seattle, WA.

Slade, A. (1986). Symbolic play and separation-individuation. *Bulletin of the Menninger Clinic, 50*, 541–563.

Slade, A. (1987a). A longitudinal study of maternal involvement and symbolic play during the toddler period. *Child Development, 58*, 367–375.

Slade, A. (1987b). Quality of attachment and symbolic play. *Developmental Psychology, 23*, 78–85.

Stoneman, Z., Brody, G. H., & Burke, M. (1989). Marital quality, depression and inconsistent parenting. *American Journal of Orthopsychiatry, 59,* 105–117.

Sullivan, H. S. (1953). *The interpersonal theory of psychiatry.* New York: Wiley.

Webster-Stratton, C., & Hammond, M. (1988). Maternal depression and its relationship to life stress, perceptions of child behavior problems, parenting behaviors, and child conduct problems. *Journal of Abnormal Child Psychology, 16,* 299–315.

Whiffen, V. E., & Gotlib, I. H. (1989, April). *Infants of postpartum depressed mothers: Temperament, cognitive status and mother–infant interaction.* Paper presented at the Biennial Meetings of the Society for Research in Child Development. Kansas City, MO.

Wolf, D. P., Watson, M. W., & Tingley, E. C. (1989, April). Individual differences in the behavioral repertoires of depressed mothers. Poster presented at the Biennial Meetings of the Society for Research in Child Development, Kansas City, MO.

Index

Aber, J. L., 226
Abuse, 226
    sexual, 46
Academic attainment, deafness and, 240–41
Action play. *See* Self–other action play
Adams, A., 218
Adamson, L., 150
Adler, L., 152–55
Affection, bond of, 59
Affective disorders, maternal, 184, 226, 286–302
    analysis of influence of, 293–98
    measures of, 292–93
Affective experience
    consolidation of, 94–95
    of deaf children, 259
    in Down syndrome, 210, 212–14
    in dramatic play, 117, 123, 188–204
    language and, 170, 175
    preoedipal, 82
    representation of, 7, 9, 12–13, 22
    symbolization and, 51–52, 66, 71
Aggression
    in dramatic play, 117
    gender and, 173, 183–84
    in self–other action play, 142–44
    social class and, 174
Ainsworth, M. D. S., 96
Allen, T. E., 241
Ambivalence, capacity for, 115
Amen, E., 38
American Sign Language (ASL), 242, 257
Anal phase, 144
Anderson, A. R., 189
Anxiety
    about giving and receiving, 129, 131

over loss of identity, 126
play invoked by, 33–46
play themes reflecting, 74, 75
pretense and, 190
repression and, 50
separation, 203
in separation–individuation process, 137
Arousal modulation, 223
Asendorpf, J. B., 263
Associative play, 196
Attachment, 134
    in autism, 224
    in Down syndrome, 210
    insecure, 96, 203, 226, 287
    secure, 97, 203, 287
Attention
    coordination of, 150
    joint, 151, 220, 287
Autism, 206–10, 217–27
    language development in, 209, 210, 215, 217–21
    social–cognitive deficits in, 217, 219–24
    symbolic play in, 218–19
Axline, V., 63

Bakeman, R., 150
Barnett, L. A., 40, 41
Bates, J. E., 151, 160, 163
Bayles, K., 160, 163
Bayley scale, 151, 159, 213
Beck Depression Index, 289
Belsky, J., 97, 287
Bernstein, B., 174
Best, H., 39
Blehar, M., 96

Bond of affection, 59
Borderline personality, 13, 19
Borker, R. A., 172, 176
Boundaries, self–other. *See* Self–other boundaries
Bowlby, J., 96
Boyatzis, C. J., 150
Bretherton, I., 134, 255, 287
Bruner, J. S., 114, 106
"Bus driver" game, 144

Casby, M. W., 240
Cassidy, J., 104, 134
Catharsis, play as, 34
Challenger disaster, 67–68
Chase and reunion games, 140
Checklist procedures, 152
Chodorow, N., 171, 172
Cicchetti, D., 22
Clarke-Stewart, K. A., 150, 151
Clinical theme, 57–59
Co-construction task, 273–79
Cognitive deficits, 209
Cognitive development
    of deaf children, 258, 259
    dramatic play and, 127–28
    in Down syndrome, 210, 212–14
    mother–child interaction and, 151
    symbolization and, 148, 286
Cognitive psychology, 3, 261
Coherence, 96
Communicative play, 45–46
    dramatic, 116, 129
    secondary symbols in, 57
Cooperative play, 196, 240
Coping, symbolization and, 65–72
"Cops and robbers" game, 144
Countertransference, 105
Cox, M., 287
Cox, R., 287
Crawley, S., 214, 215
Cross-identification, 114–15, 122, 123, 126–27,
    131–32
Crying motif in role play, 121–22, 142
Cummings, E. M., 179

Darbyshire, O., 240
Dawson, G., 218, 223, 224
Deaf children, 238–59
    case examples of, 250–54
Death of parent
    coping with, 69–71
    fantasies of, 75, 76
Decentration, 211, 217
Decontextualization, 211, 212, 216, 217

Demos, V., 96
Denial, 89–90
Depression. *See* Affective disorders, maternal
Depressive position, 115
Desensitization, 35, 36
Developmental psychology
    language in, 170
    play in, 64
Developmental psychopathology, 206–10
Developmental structuralist approach, 4–6
Differentiation subphase, 135, 136, 145
Diffuseness, 208
Disguise theory, 82
Disintegration, 208
Disorganized families, 83–85
    language in, 90–91
Divorce
    coping with, 67–68
    fantasy play after, 287
    response to, 73, 77, 78
    "sleeper effect" of, 184
Doctor play, 143
Down syndrome, 163, 206–17, 224–27
    aberrant social development in, 214–5
    cognition and affect in, 212–14
    language development in, 215–17
    social understanding in, 216–17
    symbolic play in, 211–12
Dramatic play, 111–31. *See also* Role play
    affective organization of, 188–204
    cognitive basis of, 127–28
    cross-identification in, 114–15, 126–27
    self–other boundaries in, 126–27
Dreams, symbols in, 86, 87
Drives
    ego function and, 72
    unconscious wishes and, 87
Drucker, J., 92, 98, 103
Dunn, J., 286
Dyadic relationship patterns, 17
Dyadic role play, 112, 115, 123, 126

Eakins, S. L., 39
Egeland, B., 226
Ego function
    delay of gratification and, 65
    drives and, 72
    play and regression in, 203
    symbolization and, 79
    verbalization and, 76
Ego psychology, 54, 55
Eichenbaum, L., 171–72
"Elevator operator" game, 144
Emotional re-fueling, 139

Emotions. *See* Affective experience
Empathy, 114
 failures of, 102
 gender differences in, 173
Enactment, 75, 103–4
 language and, 89, 91, 94
 measures of, 291–92
 of memories, 78
 in transference, 101
Environment
 holding, 97
 temperament and, 262, 282, 283
Erikson, E., 5, 63, 183, 190
Exclusions, game of, 113

False self, 95
Fantasy
 adaptive function of, 51–52
 as clinical theme, 57–59
 coping through, 68–69
 differentiation of reality and, 35, 85, 126
 mother–child interaction and, 287–88
 narratives of, 269
 shared, 55–56
 structural development of, 53–55
 symbolization in, 53, 75–77, 86
 unconscious and, 49
 as wish fulfillment, 36
Fears, play themes reflecting, 74
Ferrari, M., 222
Footings, 265
Fort/da game, 114
Free association, 20–21
Freud, A., viii, 20–21, 49–50, 52, 54, 63, 86
Freud, S., viii–ix, 34, 62–65, 86–89, 95, 104, 112
Furth, H. G., 241

Galenson, E., 241
Galpert, L., 224
Galumphing, 193, 199
Gardner, H., 190
Garduque, L., 97, 287
Garmezy, N., 223
Garvey, C., 55, 135
Garvey, K., 287
Gender
 dramatic play and, 128
 narratives and, 169–85
 role play and, 144
 temperament and, 262
Generalized episodes, 134
Giffin, H., 304
Gilligan, C., 171, 179, 184

Gilmore, J. B., 38–39
Global Assessment of Symptoms and Impairment
 (GAS), 290
Goffman, E., 269, 274
Goldfield, E. C., 150
Goodness-of-fitmadel, 282
Goodwin, M. H., 172
Gratification, delay of, 65
Greenspan-Lieberman Observational Scale, 4, 6,
 29–30
Gregory, S., 240, 254, 258
Gruendel, J., 134

Hammond, M., 288
Harris, P. L., 91
Hermelin, B., 220
Herzog, J., 127
Hetherington, E. M., 287
Hide-and-seek, 120–21, 123
 in treatment, 129
Hobson, R. P., 223
Hodapp, R. M., 150
Holding environment, 97
Hrncir, E., 97, 287

Identification. *See also* Cross-identification
 in dramatic play, 117
 masculine and feminine, 144
 with parents, 71, 72
 in role play, 142
 with therapist, 79
Imitation, 218–19, 223, 225
Impulse control, 67, 75
 and inhibition of play, 203, 204
Inability to play, 81, 128
 case of examples of, 82–86
Inanimate objects, play with, 135–36
Indicator behaviors, 20
Individual differences, 148
 in autistic children, 220
 in depressed mothers, 289
 in dyadic interaction, 163–64
 in narratives, 171
Inhibited children, 261–85
 coconstruction task with, 273–79
 replica play of, 268–73
Integration, 211, 217
Interactive mode of representation, 8
Interfused-subordinated dimension, 208
Intermediate area, 136, 143
Interpretation
 of content of play, 48–51, 56–59
 of dramatic play, 130

Interpretation (*continued*)
  meaning in, 86–91
  meaningful to child, 82
  of metaphoric constructions, 72
  unsuccessful, 84, 101–3
Intersubjectivity, 266
Interventions
  with deaf children, 241, 256
  to encourage dramatic play, 197–204
  studies of, 190–91
Introjection, 114, 115, 131
  pathological, 129
IQ
  anxiety-invoked play and, 39–40
  maternal behaviors correlated with, 151

Joint attention, 151, 287
  autism and, 220

Kagan, J., 261–64, 268
Kanner, L., 221, 223, 225–226
Kaplan, B., 66, 95, 96, 207, 208, 225, 238
Kaplan, N., 104, 134
Kelly, R. R., 241
Kennedy, M., 216
Klein, M., viii, 50, 63, 86, 114
Kohut, H., 95, 96
Kreye, M., 287

Labeling, 92
Lability, 208
Labov, 171
Language, 62, 65. *See also* Verbalization
  in autism, 209, 210, 215, 217–21
  deafness and, 238–43, 256–58
  in Down syndrome, 209, 210, 215–17
  enactment and, 89, 91, 94
  gender differences in, 172, 173
  of inhibited child, 267, 269
  interpretation via, 90–91
  in maltreated children, 226
  mother–child interaction and, 151, 163
  narrative, 170, 171
  object constancy and, 93
  as representational tool, measures of, 23
  social class and, 174
  symbolic play and, 148, 149
Leaving Game, 111–31
  gender and, 128
  hide-and-seek as background element of, 120–21
  meaning of, 122–23
  origins of motif of, 119–20
  proto-drama in, 117–118
  reversal of activity in, 116–17

reversed roles in, 118–19
  role play and, 123–28
  "you cry" motif in, 121–22
Lerner, J. V., 282
Lerner, R. M., 282
Lever, J., 172
Levin, H., 37
Lewy, A., 223
Lexington School for the Deaf, 238, 241, 242
Limits, testing, 75
Logico-affective impairment, 220
Lord, C., 220
"Love affair with the world," 266
Loveland, K. A., 221
Lowe, M., 4
Lyons, M. P., 171

McClure, J., 138, 140
McCormack, S. M., 240
McCune, L., 4, 21, 246, 248, 250
McDevitt, J., 137
Mahler, M., 93, 135, 139, 241
"Mail carrier" game, 143
Main, M., 104, 134
Maltreated children, 226
Maltz, D. N., 172, 176
Mastery, 34
  in deaf children, 240
  by desensitization, 35
  in Down syndrome, 212
  by dramatic play, 117
  pretense to facilitate, 204
  in rapprochement subphase, 141
  in self–other action play, 136, 142
  by symbolization, 71, 74
Matthews, W., 222
Meaning, 81–105
  in dramatic play, 122–23
  in interpretation, 86–91
  of narratives, 92–94, 171
  sharing, 95–97
Memories
  acting out, 78
  in infancy, 134
  of mother–child interaction, 139
  object permanence and, 219
  play as expression of, 171
Metaphoric constructions. *See* Symbolization
Microanalytic technique, 152
Miller, A., 96
Miller, P., 287
Miller, S., 193
Mirroring, 121, 127
  gender and, 128
  in rapprochement subphase, 141

Mogford, K., 240, 254, 258
Moments, 137
Mood, 12
Moore, O. K., 189
Morality, gender and, 171, 184
Mother–child interaction
    and ability to express emotions, 96
    affective illness and, 286–302
    deafness and, 238, 239, 241, 255–57
    in Down syndrome, 214–15
    dramatic play in, 112
    games in. *See* Self–other action play
    inhibition and, 262, 263, 266–83
    mutual regulation in, 148–64
    in peekaboo game, 114
    quantitative profile of, 4, 21, 22
Moves, 152–53
Mueller, E. C., 287
Multiple reversed roles, 113
Mundy, P., 220
Mutual regulation, 148–64
    intervention in, 163–64
    and qualities of dyadic interaction, 150–52
    study of, 152–64
    symbolization and, 149–50
    techniques for observing, 152–54

Narcissism, 96
Narratives
    development of, 92–94
    disturbances in reality testing in, 85
    gender differences in, 169–85
    inability to construct, 81, 84
    of inhibited children, 261–85
    meaning in, 91
    measures of, 292
    in therapeutic relationship, 95, 97
Narrative truth, 79
National Institute of Mental Health (NIMH), 289, 290, 292
Need achievement, anxiety-invoked play and, 39–40
Neglected children, 226
Nelson, K., 95–96, 134, 286

Object constancy, 11, 114–15, 122, 142–46
    consolidation of, 13
    emotional, 115
    representational development and, 88
    symbolization and, 93
Objective self, 127, 142
Object relations, 95–97
    preoedipal, 82
Object permanence, 219, 225
Object representations, 133

O'Connell, B., 255, 287
O'Connor, N., 220
Oedipal phase, play of, 113
Olson, S., 160, 163
On the way to self and object constancy subphase, 142–46
Oral phase, 144
Orbach, S., 171–72
Organizational approach, 206–10

Palmar Sweat Index, 40, 41
Parallel play of deaf children, 240
Parten, M. B., 196
Peekaboo game, 114, 136, 137, 140, 144
Peller, L., 5
Personality disorders, 13
Pettit, G. S., 151
Phallic-oedipal phase, 14
Piaget, J., 3, 11, 20, 21, 52–53, 64, 88, 93, 172, 212, 218
Picture description task, 273–79
Pine, F., 90, 137
Play
    action. *See* Self–other action play
    anxiety-invoked, 33–46
    and child treatment, 63–65
    and clinical process, 86–91
    developmental perspective on, 53–56
    dramatic. *See* Dramatic play
    functions of, 91–98
    in inhibited children, 261–85
    measures of, 21–23
    with older children 98–101
    psychoanalytic perspective on, 49–53
    role. *See* Role play
    solitary, 119
    structural analysis of, 53–55
    symbolic. *See* Symbolization
    therapist's failure to, 101–3
Pollak, S., 179, 185
"Police" game, 144
Practicing subphase, 139–40, 145
Prenarrative envelopes, 134
Preoedipal phases, 72, 82, 88
Preoperational period, 88
    Down syndrome children during, 212
Pretend play. *See* Dramatic play
Primary process thinking, 9, 11, 203
Primordial sharing situation, 97
Projection, 114, 115, 129, 131
    pathological, 129–30
Projective identification, 114
Psychoanalysis, 48–60
    agent of therapeutic change in, 86
    consolidation of sense of self in, 115

Psychoanalysis (*continued*)
  inability to play in, 128
  narrative truth in, 79
  play in, 34, 36, 63, 64, 203
  temperament in, 261
Psychoanalytic developmental psychology, 3

Rapprochement subphase, 140–41, 145–46
Reality testing, disturbances in, 85
Reflection, emergence of, 97–98
Regression in dramatic play, 203
Relationships
  gender differences in, 171–73, 184–85
  mother–child. *See* Mother–child interaction
  narratives of, 175–83
  preoedipal, 82
Renison, N., 38
Repetition compulsion, 34, 36, 37, 40, 42, 46
Replica play, 264–65, 268–73, 281
  family themes in, 287
Representation, Freud's theory of, 87
Representational development, 3–30, 88
  in autism, 219, 220, 224
  case examples of, 23–29
  compromised, 81–83
  deafness and, 255, 258
  differentiation and consolidation in, 11–20
  drama in. *See* Dramatic play
  emergence of representational capacity, 6–11
  in self–other action play, 133–46
  structuralist approach to, 5–6
  systematic clinical assessment of, 20–23
Representations of interactions that have been
    generalized (RIGs), 134
Repression, 50, 52–53, 86, 88
  disguise theory of, 82
Repressors, 40
Reversed roles, 112, 116–20, 123, 126, 128
Reversibility of roles, 112–13, 119, 128, 130
Ricks, M., 223
Ricoeur, P., 86
Rigidity, 208
Riguet, C., 218
Rocissano, L., 151, 163
Role play. *See also* Dramatic play
  self–other action play and, 133, 141–45
Rutter, M., 223, 225

Sameroff, A. J., 262, 282
Santostefano, S., 103
Scarlett, W. G., 103
Schafer, R., 106–7
Schedule for Affective Disorders and
    Schizophrenia-Lifetime, Research
    Diagnostic Criteria (SADS-L, RDC), 290

Schneider-Rosen, K., 223, 224
Scripts, 134
Seidman, S., 286
Self, sense of
  in autism, 222
  bad, 130
  cross-identification and, 114–15
  in dramatic play, 120, 126–28, 131
  inability to develop, 96
  and representational capacity, 6, 12
  in self–other action play, 133
  symbolic play and, 64
Self–other action play
  away from mother, 139–40
  fluidity of representations in, 140
  with inanimate objects, 135
  role play and, 133, 141–45
  separation and reunion in, 136–37
  of sharing, 140–41
  transitional phenomena in, 138
Self–other boundaries, 126–27
Sensitizors, 40
Sensorimotor period, 4
  in autism, 219
  in Down syndrome, 210, 212
Separation, dramatic role play of. *See* Leaving
    Game
Separation anxiety, 203
Separation-individuation, 148
  dramatic play and, 118, 120, 122, 124, 126
  inhibition and, 280
  self–other action play and, 134–46
  symbolization and, 96
Sexual abuse, communicative play about, 46
Shared fantasy, 55–56
  therapeutic use of, 59
Share states of engagement, 150
Sharing games, 140–41
Sigman, M., 215, 218, 219, 221, 223
Sign language, 238, 239, 242, 243, 257, 258
Slade, A., 54, 134, 163, 239, 241, 255, 287
Smilansky, S., 190, 191
Snidman, N., 261–64, 268
Social class, narratives and, 170, 171, 174
Social-cognitive deficits, 209
  in autism, 217, 219–24
  in Down syndrome, 216–17
Social psychology, 261
Solitary play, 119
Spearman Rank correlations, 159
Spence, D., 79, 105
Spiker, D., 214, 215, 223
Sroufe, L. A., 134, 226
Stances, 265
Stanford Achievement Test, 241

State sharing, 137
Stern, D. N., 51, 93, 114, 134, 138
Stevenson-Hinde, J., 262
Storm, B., 40
Strange situation paradigm, 223
Structural analysis of play. *See* Play: Structural
    analysis of
Subjective self, 127
Sullivan, H. S., 287–88
Superego formation, 144
"Superhero and villian" game, 144
Symbolic Play Test (SPT), 245–48, 252–55
Symbolization, 4–5, 62–80, 148–49
    in autism, 206–10, 217–27
    case examples of, 67–79
    cognitive basis of, 127, 128
    coping and, 65–72
    in deaf children, 238–59
    disguise theory of, 82
    in Down syndrome, 206–17, 224–27
    in dramatic play, 115, 123, 126
    in fantasy play, 53
    inhibition and, 264–65
    meaning and, 86–91
    measures of, 291–92
    mother–child interactions and, 96–97
    mutuality of, 149
    in narratives, 94
    object constancy and, 93
    object relations and, 95–97
    parental affective illness and, 286–302
    in rapprochement subphase, 141–42
    self–other action play and, 134, 136, 138
Symbols, primary versus secondary, 50–51, 57
Synchronous dyads, 151
Syncresis, 208

Tager-Flusberg, H., 221
Temperament, 261–63, 282
Thematic Apperception Test (TAT), 179
Therapeutic relationship, 89
    development of, 95–97
Tomlinson-Keasey, C., 241
Transactional environment, 262, 282, 283
Transference, 60
    consolidating, 59

enactment in, 101
    playing in, 128
Transitional phenomena, 138
Trauma
    and inability to play, 64
    and repetition compulsion, 34
Truth, narrative, 79
Tukey's Honestly Significant Difference (HSD)
    test, 157

Unconscious
    made conscious through interpretation,
        86
    play as window to, 49–51
    symbolization and, 86–89
Ungerer, J., 215, 218, 223

Verbalization, 65, 77–79
    in dramatic play, 117–19, 123
    metaphoric, 74
    in play, 75–76
Vygotsky, L., 51–52, 59, 71

Waelder, R., 5, 34, 92
Wall, S., 96
Wallerstein, J. S., 184
Wardell, E., 37
Waters, E., 96
Watson, M. W., 291
Webster-Stratton, C., 288
Werner, H., 66, 95, 96, 207, 208, 238
Whitman, R. D., 40
Wing, L., 215
Winnicott, C., 60
Winnicott, D. W., 49–51, 56–60, 82, 87, 92, 95,
        96, 98–99, 102, 103, 113, 114, 122, 123,
        126, 131–32, 136, 143
Wishes, interpretation of, repressed, 86, 88
Wish fulfillment, 36, 37, 40, 42, 43, 46
Wolf, D. P., 54, 55, 97, 190,
Wolff, P., 3

Yale Child Study Center Revised Developmental
    Schedules, 243
Yatchmink, Y., 151, 163